*The Clinical Use of*
# Hypnosis in
# Cognitive Behavior Therapy

*A Practitioner's Casebook*

**Robin A. Chapman, PsyD, ABPP,** is a clinical psychologist at McLean Hospital, Belmont, MA, and North Shore Counseling Center, Beverly, MA, and maintains a private practice. He is currently an instructor in psychology in the Department of Psychiatry, Harvard Medical School.

Dr. Chapman earned his doctorate from the Illinois School of Professional Psychology in 1990 and earned a certificate in Cognitive Behavioral Therapy from the Adler School of Professional Psychology in 1994. He is board certified in cognitive and behavioral psychology by the American Board of Professional Psychology. Additionally, he is an approved consultant in clinical hypnosis granted by the American Society of Clinical Hypnosis. His teaching experience includes graduate classes at the Illinois School of Professional Psychology and the Chicago School of Professional Psychology. He has taught undergraduate psychology classes at Elmhurst College.

*The Clinical Use of*
# Hypnosis in Cognitive Behavior Therapy

*A Practitioner's Casebook*

**Robin A. Chapman,** PsyD, ABPP, Editor

 *Springer Publishing Company*

Springer Publishing Company, Inc.
11 West 42nd Street
New York, NY 10036

*Acquisitions Editors: Sheri W. Sussman and Lauren Dockett*
*Production Editor: Sara Yoo*
*Cover design by Joanne Honigman*
*Cover background image by Richard A. Chapman*
*Cover foreground image by Noah Chasek*

06 07 08 09 10/5 4 3 2 1

---

**Library of Congress Cataloging-in-Publication Data**

The clinical use of hypnosis in cognitive behavior therapy /
  [edited by] Robin A. Chapman.
      p. cm.
   Includes bibliographical references and index.
   ISBN 0-8261-2884-X
   1. Hypnotism—Therapeutic use. 2. Cognitive therapy.
   3. Hypnotism—Therapeutic use—Case studies. 4. Cognitive
   therapy—Case studies. I. Chapman, Robin A.
RC497.C576 2006
616.89'162—dc22                                    2005017673

---

Printed in the United States of America by Sheridan Books, Inc.

*This book is dedicated to Gladys & Albert Kroon and William Chapman.*

# Contents

# Contributors

**Assen Alladin, PhD, CPsych,** is a clinical psychologist at Foothills Medical Centre and Adjunct Assistant Professor in the Department of Psychology and Psychiatry, University of Calgary, Canada. He is the president of the Canadian Society of Clinical Hypnosis, Alberta Division. He is a member of the Canadian Psychological Association, the American Society of Clinical Hypnosis, and the International Society of Hypnosis. Dr. Alladin was trained as a psychiatric nurse and a social worker before entering psychology and clinical psychology. He received his bachelor of science in psychology from the University of London, master of science in psychopathology from the University of Leicester, diploma in clinical psychology from the British Psychological Society, and doctorate from Manchester University. Dr. Alladin has been teaching and practicing clinical hypnosis for 25 years. He is interested in the empirical validation of hypnotherapy, and integrating hypnosis with cognitive behavior therapy. He has published several papers on cognitive hypnotherapy for depression and has conducted workshops in this area nationally and internationally. He is an associate fellow of the British Psychological Society and a fellow of the Royal Society of Medicine.

**E. Thomas Dowd, PhD, ABPP,** is professor of psychology at Kent State University. He is a fellow of the American Psychological Association, a member of the Association for the Advancement of Behavior Therapy, and holds two board certifications through the American Board of Professional Psychology. He is past president of the American Board of Cognitive and Behavioral Psychology. His scholarly interests are cognitive behavior therapy and hypnotherapy.

**Gary R. Elkins, PhD, ABPP, ABPH,** is a professor in the Department of Psychiatry and Behavioral Sciences at Texas A&M University College of Medicine. He is the director of the Mind-Body Cancer Research Program at Scott and White Clinic and Hospital in Temple, Texas.

**Carol Ginandes, PhD,** is a clinical health psychologist who holds staff appointments at Harvard Medical School and McLean Hospital, where she offers consultation and training in behavioral medicine, psychotherapy and hypnosis. In her clinical practice in Watertown, Massachusetts, she specializes in an integrative approach to hypnosis and psychotherapy to address a wide range of mind/body issues. She has coconducted seminal pilot trials of hypnotic interventions designed to accelerate bone fracture, and, more recently, postsurgical wound healing. She lectures and teaches widely and is often cited in radio, television, and national publications.

**William L. Golden, PhD,** is a licensed psychologist specializing in cognitive-behavior therapy and hypnotherapy. He has a private practice in New York City and Briarcliff Manor in West Chester County, New York. He is assistant professor at Cornell Medical College and is on the faculty of the Albert Ellis Institute. He has published articles and contributed to books on stress management, cancer, hypnosis, cognitive behavior therapy, and sports psychology. He is the author of three volumes, *Hypnotherapy: A Modern Approach, Psychological Treatment of Cancer Patients*, and *Mind Over Malignancy: Living with Cancer.*

**Gina M. Graci, PhD,** is an assistant professor of medicine and of psychiatry and behavioral sciences at Northwestern University Feinberg School of Medicine, and director of the Psychosocial Oncology Program at The Robert H. Lurie Comprehensive Cancer Center of Northwestern University. Dr. Graci is also a licensed clinical psychologist and accredited behavioral sleep medicine specialist at The Robert H. Lurie Outpatient Clinical Cancer Center at the Northwestern Medical Faculty Foundation.

As director of Psychosocial Oncology, Dr. Graci oversees assisting patients and family members with the emotional and social aspects of cancer and treatment, including proper nutrition and management of such symptoms as fatigue, sleep disturbances and depression.

Dr. Graci received a doctorate degree in clinical psychology from the University of North Texas. She is actively involved in the City of Hope's DELEtCC (Disseminating End of Life Education to Cancer Centers) Project, and in Gilda's Club Chicago. She is the recipient of numerous research grants, and is currently an investigator on three cancer research projects at the Feinberg School. Dr. Graci also has presented and published widely and is frequently interviewed by national and local print and broadcast media.

**Peter Kane, PhD,** is an instructor in clinical psychology at Northwestern University. He received his doctorate from Vanderbilt University. His research centers on parent-child conflict and the development of psychopathology during childhood and adolescence.

**Joel D. Marcus, PsyD,** is a senior staff psychologist at Scott and White Clinic and Hospital where he completed a post-doctoral fellowship in Clinical Health Psychology and Mind-Body Cancer Research. He directs the Psychosocial Clinical Services in the Department of Oncology at Scott and White Clinic in Temple, Texas.

**Marc I. Oster, PsyD, ABPH,** is the associate director of clinical training and associate professor of psychology at the Illinois School of Professional Psychology at Argosy University-Schaumburg (IL). Dr. Oster received his doctorate in clinical psychology from Forest Institute of Professional Psychology in 1986 and a certificate in cognitive-behavioral therapy from the Adler School of Professional Psychology in 1995. He has achieved diplomate status with the American Board of Psychological Hypnosis and the American Board of Forensic Examiners, and is a fellow of the American Psychological Association and the American College of Forensic Examiners. In addition, Dr. Oster is a fellow and past president (2003–2004) of the American Society of Clinical Hypnosis. He currently serves as a board member of the American Board of Psychological Hypnosis and is a trustee of the American Society of Clinical Hypnosis Education and Research Foundation.

**Mark A. Reinecke, PhD, ABPP, ACT,** is professor of psychiatry and behavioral sciences and chief of the Division of Psychology at Northwestern University. He received his doctorate from Purdue University. Dr. Reinecke is a distinguished fellow and former president of the Academy of Cognitive Therapy. He is a fellow of the American Psychological Association and a diplomate of the American Board of Professional Psychology in Clinical Psychology and Clinical Child and Adolescent Psychology. Dr. Reinecke's research and clinical interests include childhood depression and suicide, cognitive and social vulnerability for depression, and cognitive mediation of adjustment to chronic illness.

**Kathy Sexton-Radek, PhD,** is a Professor of Psychology at Elmhurst College and Director of Psychological Services for Suburban Pulmonary and Sleep Associates. Dr. Sexton-Radek received her Doctorate from Illinois Institute of Technology and completed postdoctorate training in Clinical Psychopharmacology and Sleep Medicine. Dr. Sexton-Radek has several peer reviewed publications in the area of Behavioral Medicine.

# Foreword

It is a source of great personal pride and satisfaction to have been able to witness the exponential growth of cognitive behavioral therapy. Only a few years ago—or so it seems—the reader likely would not have understood what CBT meant or stood for. Prior to the mid 1970s, one could not find any literature on this topic with descriptors such as "cognitive therapy" or "cognitive behavior therapy." The view at that time was that this "new therapy" was so dreadfully simple or simplistic that it could not have much of an impact on the established psychodynamic world. In the late 1970s and early 1980s, CBT practitioners were the barbarians at the gates of traditional (i.e., psychodynamic) psychotherapy.

In those early days, I spent much of my teaching time presenting the basics of CBT. I had to articulate in a new way what others had said years earlier, that thinking has a profound effect on how we feel and how we act. This concept had been expressed by Freud, Adler, Frankl, and many others. We were also echoing the stance of the Stoic philosophers that when we are troubled, it is more our view of events than the events per se that are the source of our difficulty. However, the contemporary presentation of these ideas was the work of pioneers like Beck, Ellis, Lazarus, Meichenbaum, and others. Even so, we were careful, in those days, not to make too many promises about what we could treat with CBT. At the Center for Cognitive Therapy (also known as the Mood Clinic) at the University of Pennsylvania, we treated depression. The director, Aaron T. Beck, always the scientist, demanded empirical support for all that we did. Patients who were primarily diagnosed with anxiety were referred to other clinicians. We were the depression mavens. We later added cognitive therapy for anxiety to our treatment, and even later treated patients with substance abuse and others with personality disorders. Now that we have entered the twenty-first century, CBT is the standard by which empirically based treatment is measured. For the "barbarians at the gates," the gates have opened, and CBT is living comfortably within established methods of clinical practice. What has brought about this change in attitude towards CBT has been its expansion to include new patient groups, the utilization of new clinical contexts, and the expansion of treatment to include new areas of psychopathology.

An interesting note on the development of CBT is that in the "early" days we tried to keep it pure. We tried to avoid the use of terms or even techniques that evoked the misconceptions of the "old days." We wanted to establish ourselves as a new and effective treatment. This was difficult to do in that practitioners like Beck and Ellis were classically trained in psychoanalysis. In retrospect, their early psychodynamic training influenced their CBT formulations. In reviewing the most recent CBT literature, we see terms such as resistance, transference, countertransference, therapeutic alliance, and mindfulness. All of these are now used unabashedly. CBT has matured to the point of being inclusive rather than parochial. CBT has expanded into disciplines such as nursing, psychiatry, and social work, from its early development in psychology. Like Beck, Ellis, Wolpe, and others, my early training was in a psychodynamic model, a model that I practiced for several years before my epiphany and conversion to CBT. As part of my education and training in a New York psychodynamic style, my reading of the history of the development of the psychodynamic model included a familiarity with its early history, including Freud's experience with Charcot. We were not taught to practice hypnotic work. This was viewed, in those days, as a mere transit point for Freud in his search for and attainment of his goal of an effective treatment model. The hypnotic method, however, had its own proponents, notably Milton Erickson and his followers. In various forms, general hypnotic work has been used with great success for many years. There has, in fact, been a parallel movement of hypnotic work that has developed over the years. It is only more recently, however, that these two movements have touched, merged, and shared skills and techniques. In the words of Walt Kelly's Pogo, "We have met the enemy, and he is us." It is now far more difficult to differentiate between "us" and "them."

What Chapman has compiled in this volume is the "A" list of practitioners of hypnosis, which is part of their work in CBT. Having had the good fortune in my career to have been in the right place at the right time, I have had the privilege of having studied and worked with such notables as Aaron T. Beck, Albert Ellis, Kurt Adler, Alexandra Adler, and many others. Over the years I have also had the good fortune of having worked with many of the contributors to this volume. Some have been collaborators and others have been personal friends, and some are familiar to me because of their scholarship. All are talented and skilled clinicians.

The entire project, from its beginning to this superb publication has been a confluence of talent. My initial contact with Dr. Robin Chapman was when he was part of a yearlong cognitive behavioral training program that I led in Chicago. Even then I was impressed with his clinical insights and high level of scholarship. At that time, Robin and I discussed his skill in using hypnosis as a CBT technique. I encouraged him to share his skills, interests, and training with others. When Robin first contacted me about developing this volume, I tried to be as encouraging as possible. The idea was a good one, the book was needed, and Robin was the right person to do it. He then contacted international and well-published experts in the field, the likes of Marc Oster, Tom Dowd, Bill Golden, Mark Reinecke, and the others who gave their valuable time to write chapters. Robin's goal was to edit a casebook rather than the more traditional "how-to" book in hypnosis. The contributors cover the broad range of clinical problems from depression, anxiety, and sleep disorders to posttraumatic stress disorder and anger. Thus far, Robin had made several excellent moves. He had an idea, he acted on his idea, he called me, he contacted the best people in the field, he decided to write for the frontline troops (practicing clinicians), and then he contacted one of the premier clinical publishers in this area, Springer Publishers in New York. He had the opportunity to work with Springer's editor-in-chief Sheri Sussman. Many of the contributors to this volume have been published by Springer. Together, the synergy would have made Wertheimer happy. However, the whole of this book is certainly greater than the sum of its parts. The reader should be cautioned, however; these chapters are not written for casual reading. They need to be read slowly and to be carefully digested. They need to be studied and reread. For the clinician familiar with CBT and trained in hypnosis, this volume is a gem.

My fear that CBT would grow complacent and stop developing has, to this point, been assuaged. We have seen new authors with new ideas, experienced authors with new ideas, and new applications of old treatments, all with a view toward providing empirical support for CBT. This volume is an example of CBT's vigor and forward-looking focus. One of the great strengths of this volume is that Robin requested that each of the contributors offer their conceptualizations of CBT and hypnosis to the reader. This is, perhaps, the greatest value. The "how-to" can be easily mastered. To have an expert clinician share their conceptualization and the conceptual process is of inestimable value. The key to effective therapy, whether it is CBT or another model, is the ability to form a conceptualization and then use it to craft a treatment protocol. I am pleased to be part of this volume, if only to write the foreword. What a wonderful experience this has been!

Arthur Freeman, EdD
ABPP Diplomates in Clinical, Behavioral, and Family Psychology
University of St. Francis, Fort Wayne, Indiana

# Preface

About 10 years ago , I was asked by Marc Oster to teach a class on the use of hypnosis with cognitive behavior therapy. Marc knew of my interest in both hypnosis and cognitive behavior therapy. In my clinical work, I had often used hypnosis in the treatment of phobias and anxiety disorders. However, when asked to teach a class on the topic I found few references for the class. Only a handful of books addressed the use of hypnosis and cognitive behavior therapy at that time. *The Clinical Use of Hypnosis in Cognitive Behavior Therapy* is the book that I was looking for to illustrate the use of hypnosis with cognitive behavior therapy.

Today the practitioner has more choices. However, previous books addressing this subject have stressed the research and theory of cognitive behavior hypnosis. Less attention has been given to the actual process of integrating these approaches in treatment situations. Previous case studies provided minimal clinical rationale and process for determining when to use a hypnotic strategy. Cognitive behavior therapy relies on case conceptualization to guide the use of various cognitive and behavioral strategies. This book contends that the use of hypnotic interventions can be guided by case conceptualization and used with other cognitive behavior techniques. This model of integration relies on neither a new cognitive model nor eclecticism, but rather on a comprehensive case conceptualization model that integrates theory and therapy. The practitioner will find detailed case studies that provide both a theoretical base and practical guidance for applying this integrated approach to clinical work.

This edited book is organized into two parts—the first part provides a theoretical and research base for understanding the combination of hypnosis and cognitive behavior therapy, while the second half illustrates this combination through clinical cases, which are presented by practitioners with expertise in their particular fields addressing problems such as anxiety, depression, pain management with cancer patients, mind/body conditions, PTSD, sleep disorders and anger problems. The final chapter provides a blueprint to becoming a practitioner who uses hypnosis with cognitive behavior therapy.

*The Clinical Use of Hypnosis in Cognitive Behavior Therapy* is intended for practicing clinicians, such as psychologists, social workers, psychiatric nurses, psychiatrists, and mental health counselors, who are interested in learning about the use of hypnosis with cognitive behavior therapy. Practitioners trained in both cognitive behavior therapy and clinical hypnosis will find this book helpful in their clinical work with clients. Practitioners trained in either cognitive behavior therapy or hypnosis will find this book helpful if they are considering adding to their clinical approach. This book is not intended as a substitute for clinical training in either cognitive behavior therapy or hypnosis. Many good books and seminars already exist for training in both these clinical skills. However, training in using hypnosis with cognitive behavior therapy has been largely left to the individual practitioner. *The Clinical Use of Hypnosis in Cognitive Behavior Therapy* is also intended for graduate students interested in learning about the use of hypnosis and cognitive behavior therapy.

# Acknowledgments

This volume is truly the effort of many contributors, including authors and other participants for whom I am grateful. This volume would not be possible without the inspiration of Arthur Freeman who provided postdoctoral training and case consultation in cognitive behavioral therapy. Another key influence was Marc Oster who provided training and consultation in hypnosis and encouraged the exploration of hypnosis and cognitive behavioral therapy. I am indebted to Rita Koba for her careful proofreading and grammatical knowledge. I am also grateful to Sam Migdole who provided early editing of the first chapter. Sheri Sussman and Lauren Dockett of Springer Publishing provided support, direction and encouragement throughout this project. Last but not least, this project would have ended prematurely without the constant support and encouragement of my wife, Rita.

# Part I

# Background

Chapter 1

# Introduction to Cognitive Behavior Therapy and Hypnosis

Robin A. Chapman

Clients and their respective clinical practitioners often have misperceptions about hypnosis. These misperceptions have been shaped through years of interesting but inaccurate portrayals of hypnosis in movies, plays, and books. The hypnotist is often depicted as an individual with seemingly magical powers, manipulating the unsuspecting innocent, with penetrating eyes and authoritative voice commands. Vampires, space aliens, witch doctors, and evil scientists have all been portrayed as using hypnosis to achieve their dubious ends.

Many others are introduced to hypnosis as a form of entertainment at comedy clubs or on television talk shows. With the hypnotist's simple commands for sleep and snaps of the fingers, volunteers from the audience are clucking like chickens or acting out fantasies, making the audience laugh. These hypnotized individuals appear to behave in ways that may be considered out of character or contrary to their normal behavior. Some clinical practitioners themselves have further exacerbated this pejorative image of hypnosis. Controversial hypnosis treatments of individuals with multiple personality disorders, victims of UFO abductions, and victims of satanic cults have resulted in sensational and problematic news accounts that cast doubt on the acceptable use of hypnosis and perpetuate stereotypes of it.

Clearly, clinical hypnosis is in need of a "makeover" by an image consultant. The sensational, entertaining, and fictionalized accounts of hypnosis have confused the clinical practitioner and client alike. Cognitive behavior therapists may not have considered treating clients with hypnosis, given its history and public perception. Cognitive behavior therapists are more likely to rely on techniques derived from experimental research supported by outcome studies and may be unaware that hypnosis has a positive history in research. Even so, sociocognitive theorists have recently attempted to correct the derogatory image of hypnosis, by promoting and documenting its effectiveness, especially to convince the scientific community of the value of hypnosis (Lynn & Sherman, 2000).

## BACKGROUND ON THE PROPOSED INTEGRATION OF CBT AND HYPNOSIS

This book emphasizes the integration of cognitive behavior therapy (CBT) and hypnosis from both theoretical and psychotherapy perspectives. It is the position of this book that integration of hypnosis from a cognitive behavior perspective will enhance and increase the potential efficacy of therapeutic treatment. Similarities and differences in both are explored to provide the context for this integrationist perspective.

The purpose of this book is to provide a clinical case approach for the practitioner. It provides a framework with which to clinically integrate cognitive behavior therapy and hypnosis strategies. Multiple approaches to case conceptualization and treatment provide methods for integration of theory and therapy. It is hoped that this approach will provide an understanding that will guide the cognitive behavior therapist in the use of hypnosis as well as enhance the treatment offered to clients when hypnosis is utilized as an adjunct treatment.

A review of the early research reveals little or no integration of behavior therapy and hypnosis (Clarke & Jackson, 1983). What it does show is that cognitive behavior practitioners are more likely to consider relaxation training and imagery procedures rather than hypnosis, to achieve similar therapeutic goals. Training programs for cognitive behavior therapy are not likely to emphasize the role of hypnosis in treatment. On the other hand, practitioners from other theoretical models may routinely use hypnosis while not considering cognitive behavior strategies. The techniques used by many of these therapists are similar to those employed by cognitive behavior therapists, however (Golden, 1994).

Several barriers can be identified that may impede the integration of cognitive behavior treatment and hypnosis. They include the role of working with the unconscious in hypnosis, and lack of agreement on the definitions of hypnosis and cognitive behavior treatment. An additional barrier is the limited theoretical understanding that hypnosis is an adjunct treatment to cognitive behavior treatment.

## Differing Views of the Unconscious

The role of the unconscious plays a large part in this division between CBT and hypnosis. Behavior therapy has traditionally rejected the role of the unconscious, while other therapies, such as psychodynamic therapy, have embraced the unconscious. The role of the unconscious is not the only perceived barrier to integration of CBT and hypnosis. The definition of hypnosis and associated concepts of induction and trance are also problematic from the CBT perspective. An integral part of this perspective is its reliance on operational definitions and empirical research. Practitioners of other models that use hypnosis may view the CBT perspective as setting a limitation and a minimization on their skill and flexibility. Eclectic psychotherapy approaches, on the other hand, can incorporate both CBT and hypnosis, with less debate and controversy. Technical eclecticism (Lazarus, 1981) allows the therapist to borrow freely from diverse therapy approaches without accepting the theoretical understanding of any particular therapy approach.

A precedent can be found for the integration of psychotherapy and hypnosis in psychoanalysis. Freud originally embraced hypnosis as a productive approach within his psychoanalytic framework. Hypnosis is considered a method for directly accessing the unconscious, allowing the therapist more direct communication with the unconscious, and thus facilitating more effective treatment. Freud eventually turned to free association when hypnosis seemed too unreliable. Jung followed suit, initially using and eventually abandoning the practice of hypnosis. Jung harbored many reservations about the use of hypnosis due to the paucity of knowledge concerning its nature and the apparent control of the client by the therapist (Hannah, 1997). Currently, hypnosis is used as an adjunct treatment in eclectic, existential, psychodynamic, and cognitive behavior therapies.

## Hypnosis as an Adjunct Treatment

Cognitive behavior approaches have already used hypnosis as an adjunct treatment. As early as 1949, Salter explained hypnosis in terms of a classical conditioning model of learning, that is, the therapist's words are considered to be classically conditioned stimuli that elicit the conditioned response of hypnosis. Joseph Wolpe's systematic desensitization, a therapeutic technique for treating anxiety and fear, is based on classical conditioning. This counter-conditioning model consists of inducing a relaxed state and then, through a hierarchy of small steps, introducing feared stimuli, ranging from the least to the most anxiety provoking. The relaxed state can be achieved through a variety of techniques, including hypnosis. Practitioners employing desensitization often use hypnosis to enhance the relaxed state of their clients. Wolpe (1990) further stressed the importance of counter conditioning in hypnosis: "If standard hypnotherapy has not had impressive long-term results, it is because it has not usually brought the suggested response into effective opposition with the one to be eliminated" (p. 5).

## Definitions of Hypnosis

Many diverse theories and definitions of hypnosis have been postulated. In 2003 the Society for Psychological Hypnosis, Division 30 of the American Psychological Association, offered a revision of the definition and description of hypnosis. A committee representing a broad range of theoretical orientations developed this definition.

This definition describes hypnosis as a procedure that can be used to facilitate therapy by using suggestion and induction procedures.

The current definition prepared by the Executive Committee of the American Psychological Association, Division 30, Society of Psychological Hypnosis (www.apa.org) reads as follows:[1]

> Hypnosis typically involves an introduction to the procedure during which the subject is told that suggestions for imaginative experiences will be presented. The hypnotic induction is an extended initial suggestion for using one's imagination, and may contain further elaborations of the introduction. A hypnotic procedure is used to encourage and evaluate responses to suggestions. When using hypnosis, one person (the subject) is guided by another (the hypnotist) to respond to suggestions for changes in subjective experience, alterations in perception, sensation, emotion, thought or behavior. Persons can also learn self-hypnosis, which is the act of administering hypnotic procedures on one's own. If the subject responds to hypnotic suggestions, it is generally inferred that hypnosis has been induced. Many believe that hypnotic responses and experiences are characteristic of a hypnotic state. While some think that it is not necessary to use the word "hypnosis" as part of the hypnotic induction, others view it as essential.
>
> Details of hypnotic procedures and suggestions will differ depending on the goals of the practitioner and the purposes of the clinical or research endeavor. Procedures traditionally involve suggestions to relax, though relaxation is not necessary for hypnosis and a wide variety of suggestions can be used including those to become more alert. Suggestions that permit the extent of hypnosis to be assessed by comparing responses to standardized scales can be used in both clinical and research settings. While the majority of individuals are responsive to at least some suggestions, scores on standardized scales range from high to negligible. Traditionally, scores are grouped into low, medium, and high categories. As is the case with other positively-scaled measures of psychological constructs such as attention and awareness, the salience of evidence for having achieved hypnosis increases with the individual's score.

While the consensus across different theories has produced this potentially useful definition of hypnosis, it may compromise a more comprehensive understanding of it from specific theoretical

---

[1]Permission to reproduce this document is freely granted.

perspectives. Nevertheless, this revised definition of hypnosis can be considered a starting point in the understanding of hypnosis from a cognitive behavior perspective, as it encompasses many of the commonalities that are identified in the current expanded range of cognitive behavior theory.

## Cognitive Behavior Therapy

A concise definition of cognitive behavior therapy has become elusive in recent years. Distinct perspectives ranging from applied behavior analysis to constructivism can be found in the behavior and cognitive literature. In fact, 20 distinguishable forms of cognitive behavior therapies have been identified, although analysis of these models yields important commonalities such as an emphasis on learning theory and research (Craighead, Craighead, Kazdin, & Mahoney, 1994). With this consideration, three major groups have emerged, including behavioral, cognitive, and cognitive behavior therapy models. A brief review of the definitions of the behavioral and the cognitive models may provide an understanding of how the current definition of cognitive behavior therapy has evolved.

Early definitions of behavior therapy highlighted the role of operant and classical conditioning. Emphasis was placed on observable events and not on internal states or constructs. Current practitioners of applied behavior analysis continue to emphasize these elements in describing the applied behavior analysis model. The following definition emphasizes learning principles and the experimental approach:

> Applied behavior analysis is the science in which procedures derived from the principles of behavior are systematically applied to improve socially significant behavior to a meaningful degree and to demonstrate experimentally that the procedures employed were responsible for the improvement in behavior. (Cooper, Heron, & Heward, 1987)

In 1960, Eysenck offered a highly accepted definition of behavior therapy as the application of modern learning theory to alter human behavior and emotions (Goldfried & Davison, 1994). But behavior therapists and researchers have considered the previously mentioned definitions as too narrow to accurately represent the scope of current behavior therapy. These narrow definitions have been broadened to encompass current approaches to behavior treatment and research. The behavioral model continues to emphasize the role of the experimental approach, while emphasizing the identification of specific antecedents, organismic and consequent variables (Goldfried & Davison, 1994). One of the significant changes offered by this broadened definition was the inclusion of the organismic variable, which included internal states such as the person's cognitions and physiological status. This perspective allowed the integration and further consideration of cognitive variables.

The cognitive therapy model emphasized internal constructs such as automatic thoughts, images, and schemas. Cognitions were considered central to the development of psychopathology and its treatment. However, behavior theory and techniques were not eschewed but incorporated into cognitive theory and treatment.

Aaron Beck (1976) described cognitive therapy as an active, directive, time-limited, structured approach used to treat a variety of psychiatric disorders. This therapy is based on the underlying theoretical rationale that an individual's affect and behavior are largely determined by the way in which he or she structures the world.

Many aspects of the behavior and cognitive models are integrated into current conceptualizations of the cognitive behavior model. Craighead et al. (1994) offer a definition of the cognitive-behavior model that assumes a reciprocal determinism between the environment and the person. The person variables include the biological, behavioral, cognitive, and emotional characteristics of the client. The major tenet of this model posits that all domains of human functioning and their interactions are important in assessing, describing, and treating human problems in living. Overall, this model provides an integrative and interactional approach that encompasses many of the important aspects of behavior and cognitive therapies that were described above.

## Clinical Hypnosis Theories

Researchers and practitioners have offered many theories of hypnosis. These theories diverged in the 1960s, into the dichotomy of state and nonstate. The state theory explained that trance was an altered state of consciousness, while the nonstate theory rejected this premise, explaining that hypnotic behaviors were complex social behaviors.

This debate continued with the conceptualization, in the 1980s, of the state and nonstate as special process and social psychological models. This development resulted in new theories that outdate the earlier dichotomous thinking of the state and nonstate theories of consciousness. These new positions can more accurately be described as points on a continuum rather than as a dichotomy (Kirsch & Lynn, 1995).

Kirsch and Lynn (1995) have contributed important research and theoretical perspectives to the scientific understanding of hypnosis. They argue that the dichotomous thinking of state versus nonstate theories of hypnosis is inaccurate. They have described three current theories of hypnosis, including the neo-dissociative model, the socio-cognitive model, and the dissociated control model for elaboration of this perspective.

The neo-dissociative model proposes that a communication barrier exists within the ego that separates awareness, producing a perception of involuntary responding to hypnotic procedures. This division of consciousness that allows behavior without awareness is defined as dissociation. The socio-cognitive model posits that all suggestions are processed through executive functions (a cognitive structure that performs planning and monitoring functions) without a division of consciousness. The individual's beliefs, expectations, and interpretation of suggestions are hypothesized to produce this behavior. Individuals may be unaware introspectively of the cognitive processes involved in responding to a hypnotic suggestion. This model does not require concepts such as altered state or dissociation to explain the theory. The dissociated control model proposes that central control, which is an executive cognitive structure that is responsible for planning and monitoring functions, and subsystem control structures that are relatively autonomous subordinate cognitive behavioral systems that are arranged hierarchically exist. Hypnotic induction modifies the executive control structure, allowing a weakening of central control over the subsystem control. It is important to note that this process is not explained as a division of consciousness, but rather as a direct activation of the subsystem component. The hypnotic response is considered to be due to the hypnotherapist's suggestion and is not cognitively mediated.

Kirsch and Lynn (1995) concluded that the understanding of hypnosis as a state or nonstate model is inaccurate and does not represent the current perspective of diverse researchers and practitioners. Areas of agreement among these different perspectives have moved the understanding of hypnosis—originally thought of as two discrete positions—to a continuum of positions on the issues of altered state and trait. These three new models represent this more complex approach to understanding hypnosis.

Consideration of various theoretical perspectives of hypnosis continue to spark controversy and the interest of researchers and practitioners. The *American Journal of Clinical Hypnosis* devoted an entire issue to exploring current theories of hypnosis (see vol. 42, 2000).

Specifically, Rossi (2000) offers a comprehensive psychobiological model of hypnosis. The cellular-genetic-protein level of mind-body communication and healing is described according to 10 different hypotheses. Additionally, this proposed model is offered as a method that may resolve many of the current theoretical debates.

Barber's (2000) research has indicated that three major types of highly or very good responsive hypnotic subjects can be identified. These include the fantasy prone, amnesia prone, and the positively set. When identified, the subject type can then be paired effectively with a matching hypnosis technique, which enhances effectiveness. This, in part, provides an explanation for differences in responding to different hypnotic techniques.

## Cognitive Behavior Hypnosis

Aaron Beck was the founder of cognitive therapy and a seminal contributor to the theory and practice of cognitive behavior therapy. Alford and Beck (1997) describe cognitive therapy as a "theory of theories" (p. 11). This meta-theory articulates the role of cognitive schemas in the process of therapy and in the operation of other psychological systems. "*Cognition provides a theoretical bridge to link the contemporary behavioral, psychodynamic, humanistic and biopsychosocial perspectives of psychopathology and effective psychotherapy*" (italics added) (Alford & Beck, p. 44). This cognitive bridge may provide a model not only for cognitive behavior clinicians but also for clinicians practicing from other perspectives to integrate elements of cognitive behavior and hypnotic strategies from a case conceptualization approach.

## QUESTIONS TO CLARIFY THE PROPOSED INTEGRATION OF CBT AND HYPNOSIS

The practitioner is faced with many complexities and issues surrounding the scientific, the theoretical, and the clinical perspectives regarding the integration of cognitive behavior therapy and hypnosis. In order to better understand this integration, the following questions are posed and discussed.

### What if Any Commonalities Exist Between Cognitive Behavior Therapy and Hypnosis?

Cognitive behavior therapy and hypnosis share many similar techniques and theoretical positions. Cognitive behavior therapy is comprised of both cognitive and behavioral interventions. Cognitive interventions may include the downward arrow technique, idiosyncratic meaning, labeling of distortions, decatastrophizing, advantages and disadvantages, and replacement imagery. Behavioral interventions may include assertiveness training, behavioral rehearsal, social skills training, relaxation training, graded task assignments, and homework. This is only a partial list of the possible interventions utilized in a cognitive behavior therapy approach.

Hypnosis usually includes an induction procedure, which may be direct or indirect, formal or informal, and may use hetero-hypnosis or self-hypnosis. Relaxation is usually the necessary first step in most induction procedures. Often included in the induction procedure is the repetition of monotonous, rhythmical, sensory stimuli for the fixation of the client's attention. A close relationship also exists between hypnosis and imagery. Many induction procedures use visual, auditory, and kinesthetic images.

The use of relaxation and imagery procedures is common to cognitive behavior therapy and hypnosis. Cognitive behavior practitioners often use progressive relaxation as the standard for relaxation training. This involves systematically tightening and relaxing 16 muscle groups while focusing on differences in physical sensation

(Bernstein & Borkovec, 1973). Hypnosis often employs relaxation techniques that appear to be quite similar to the progressive relaxation protocol.

Investigators have also described similar cognitive strategies between cognitive behavior therapy and Milton Erickson's model of therapy. Both provide the client with a productive strategy. One of the most common cognitive strategies is reframing, which involves the interpretation of the client's behavior as consistent with treatment objectives, even when the behavior initially appears to be inconsistent.

The behavioral model of successive approximation has been identified in the Ericksonian pacing and leading technique. Both cognitive behavior therapy and the Ericksonian models reinforce the client for stepwise progress and encourage further improvements. Verbal positive reinforcement is given after each small step is accomplished (Golden, Dowd, & Friedberg, 1987). Techniques associated with operant conditioning can also be found in the use of hypnotic interventions such as successive approximation and positive reinforcement. Relaxation inductions usually begin with small steps such as attending to breathing, muscle relaxation, and, finally, imagery. At each step the subject receives positive verbal reinforcement.

## Do Clinical Models Exist for This Integration?

Researchers and practitioners have described several models of cognitive behavior hypnosis. These models are associated with the multiple cognitive behavior models that currently exist, and are described as follows:

*Cognitive Skills Model:* The cognitive skills model (Diamond, 1989) focuses on the cognitive process that can be considered both voluntary and involuntary. Individuals can be taught hypnotic skills just as they can be taught any other cognitive skill. This model draws from a wide range of psychotherapy approaches, which include cognitive behavior, phenomenological, psychoanalytic, humanistic-existential, and strategic therapies. This model does not reject the constructs of trance and/or altered states of consciousness. Hypnotizability is considered a skill that can be learned and is not an unmodifiable trait. Cognitive behavior techniques such as self-instructional training, thought stopping, and shaping are often used to teach and enhance the individual's hypnotic skills (Golden et al., 1987).

*Cognitive Developmental Model:* The cognitive developmental model (Dowd, 1993) is derived from developmental and constructivist movements within cognitive behavior therapy. This model considers two types of knowing, tacit and explicit knowledge. Tacit knowledge is developed prior to the development of formal language, while explicit knowledge is acquired through the development of language. Explicit knowledge can then be modified through verbal processes that are associated with cognitive therapy. Tacit knowledge, on the other hand, is considered more amenable to change through therapeutic interventions that focus on images and feelings. This understanding leads to two types of cognitive restructuring using hypnosis, the restructuring of cognitive events (automatic thoughts) and the restructuring of core cognitive structures (schemas). Hypnosis can be useful as it allows modification of tacit cognitive schema and reduces resistance to change.

*Cognitive Behavior Hypnosis Model:* The cognitive behavior hypnosis model (Kirsch, 1993) considers hypnosis an adjunct intervention to cognitive behavior interventions. Common cognitive behavior interventions, such as relaxation, imagery, behavioral practice, successive approximation, and cognitive restructuring, are integrated with the use of hypnotic interventions. This approach rejects the construct of the altered state, while embracing a nonstate position. The nonstate position defines hypnosis as a suggestion of change in the person's experience and behavior within a social interaction between client and therapist (Kihlstrom, 1985). The emphasis is clearly on the social interactions, including expectations and beliefs, and not on a distinct state of consciousness. This model further posits that cognitive behavior interventions such as relaxation and imagery are so similar to hypnotic approaches as to be indistinguishable. This approach suggests, "For the cognitive behavior therapist, hypnosis is merely a new label for what is already being practiced" (Kirsch, p. 168). The models just described offer different perspectives for the clinical integration of cognitive behavior therapy and hypnosis.

## Does the Use of Hypnosis Require Consideration of the Construct of the Unconscious?

The construct of the unconscious is a significant point of contention between the psychodynamic and behavioral perspectives. Psychodynamic theory and therapy are well grounded in the unconscious, while the behavioral approach rejects the unconscious along with other internal processes. However, the addition of the cognitive perspective with behavioral therapy has reopened this topic for investigation and therapeutic consideration.

Psychotherapy has generally thought that the unconscious is accessed by inducing or producing an altered state of conscious, for example through hypnosis. Historically, hypnosis has been closely linked to the concept of inducing altered states of consciousness. Since its inception, hypnosis has been associated with a sleeplike state. In fact, James Braid, a physician who practiced during the mid-nineteenth century, derived the term "hypnosis," from the Greek root "hypnos" meaning sleep. Indeed, hypnosis has been represented in theatre and movies mainly as a sleeplike state.

As mentioned before, Freud embraced the use of hypnosis with his patients early in his career as a psychiatrist. He described the unconscious as the major source of psychopathology and hypnosis as a method to access the unconscious, but he eventually rejected hypnosis in favor of his techniques of free association and dream interpretation.

Milton Erickson, psychiatrist and noted hypnotherapist, began in 1950's to expand on the favorable aspects of the unconscious. He pioneered the use of indirect approaches to hypnotic suggestion. An indirect approach allowed the freeing of unconscious potential from the limitations of consciousness. "You build your technique around instructions that allow their conscious mind to withdraw from the task, and leave it all up to the unconscious" (Erickson et al., 1976, p. 18).

The concept of an altered state of conscious has been a powerful tool for psychotherapists in explaining and conducting hypnosis with clients. The altered state model proposes that the root of a problem and its solution may reside in the unconscious, which can be accessed through hypnosis.

Psychotherapists utilizing an eclectic approach have a range of perspectives for describing the role of the unconscious within a therapeutic encounter. The cognitive behavior therapist, however, has limited options for reconciling the construct of the unconscious within the cognitive behavior framework.

Dollard and Miller (1950) offered an early reinforcement theory of the unconscious, translating traditional psychoanalytic thought into learning theory. They mainly described the unconscious as the product of reinforcement. The person was thought to have no consciousness of the impact of reinforcement on their behavior due to the lack of intervening labels or symbols. Unconscious behavior patterns were then considered the result of conditioning during infancy before the development of language. An additional aspect of the unconscious includes repression, which Dollard and Miller described as "the automatic tendency to stop thinking and avoid remembering" (p. 220). Later behavioral theorists and therapists abandoned this combination of learning theory and psychoanalysis to focus on the essential aspects of learning theory.

Cognitive behavior therapists may have been reintroduced to the concept of unconscious processing by psychiatrist Aaron Beck in the mid-1970s. Beck (1976) described cognitive events that were latent or unobserved as automatic thoughts, which he defined as discreet, specific, unquestioned, and idiosyncratic ideas that occur outside of awareness. Mahoney (1980) proposed that the introduction of the cognitive perspective into the behavioral model made the consideration of unconscious events inevitable. Meichenbaum and Gilmore (1984) suggested that cognitive theory and therapy have many links to unconscious processes as understood in psychodynamic theory and therapy. A cognitive reconceptualization of the unconscious may provide a forum for rapprochement between the cognitive behavioral and psychodynamic perspectives. Cognitive theory and therapy are comprised of cognitive events, cognitive processes, and cognitive structures, and are delineated below. They are all related to the unconscious.

*Cognitive events* are marked by automatic thoughts, which are described as a form of unconscious processing. These thoughts allow a person to drive a car automatically or unconsciously after learning to drive. Other examples of unconscious processing can be seen in covert trial and error judgments, and recall of memories.

*Cognitive processes* refer to those processes that shape mental representations such as search and storage mechanisms, inferential processes, and retrieval processes. These are also described as metacognitive activities that usually occur automatically. These activities are considered to be well rehearsed. Metacognitive activities are often thought to function in an automatic, unconscious manner.

*Cognitive structures* can best be understood as cognitive schemas. A schema is a relatively enduring structure that functions like a template. The schema can be thought of as being implicit or operating at an unconscious level. The therapist and the client are often unaware of the influence of the schema guiding and influencing their perceptions of the world and their behavior. According to Meichenbaum and Gilmore (1984),

> Rather than view unconscious processes as the repository of unverbalized needs that have grown out of arrested psychosexual development and that have been subjected to repression, one can instead view unconscious processes in terms of information-processing mechanisms (i.e., cognitive processes and structures) that may be subject to independent cross-validations. (p. 289)

## Is There Any Research to Support the Use of Hypnosis as an Adjunct to Cognitive Behavior Therapy?

This question was investigated by a meta-analysis of 18 studies, which included the following problem areas: obesity, pain, insomnia, anxiety, phobia, performance, ulcer, and public speaking (Kirsch, Montgomery, & Sapirstein, 1995). These studies included the following cognitive behavior techniques: relaxation, covert modeling, imagery, coping suggestions, self-monitoring, self-reinforcement, systematic desensitization, stimulus control, and cognitive restructuring.

The study was based on a nonstate perspective, which hypothesizes that hypnosis can augment a therapy outcome through its effects on the client's beliefs and expectations. A fairly substantial effect was discovered when hypnosis was added as an adjunct to cognitive behavior therapy. For example, " . . . the average client receiving cognitive behavior hypnotherapy showed greater improvement than at least 70% of the clients receiving nonhypnotic treatment" (Kirsch et al., 1995). Clients benefited from hypnosis added to cognitive behavior therapy across the broad list of problems identified by the meta-analysis study. The addition of hypnosis to the treatment of obesity was found to be particularly effective: " . . . the current data suggest that training in hypnosis should be included routinely as a part of training in cognitive behavioral treatments" (Kirsch et al., p. 219).

## Can the Cognitive Behavior Clinician Accomplish the Same Goals Without the Use of Hypnosis?

The cognitive behavior clinician begins with the understanding that hypnosis is not a type of psychotherapy. It is considered a technique that facilitates the process of psychotherapy. It is clear that many of the techniques associated with hypnosis may overlap and appear similar to techniques found in the practice of cognitive behavior therapy. Relaxation training and imagery are common cognitive behavior therapy techniques. Relaxation training is prevalent in the cognitive behavior approach to stress, anxieties, and phobias. Imagery techniques allow the person to mentally visualize fearful or helpful situations. Systematic desensitization, an early and effective behavioral technique, employs both relaxation and imagery. These similarities allow the cognitive behavior therapist to accomplish many of the same goals and outcomes with or without the formal use of clinical hypnosis. The clinician can then decide whether to use a cognitive behavior intervention such as imagery or relaxation, with or without hypnosis. Self-regulation therapy offers a cognitive behavior model using suggestion without hypnosis (Kirsch, Capafons, Cardena-Buelna, & Amigo, 1999). Case conceptualization provides a guide to the most effective cognitive behavioral interventions for an individual. Therefore, case conceptualization can be used to determine whether the use of hypnosis would be effective in the treatment of an individual.

## How Would the Cognitive Behavior Clinician Decide to Use Hypnosis?

This proposed integrative model of cognitive behavior hypnosis relies on the case conceptualization model (Freeman, Pretzer, Fleming, & Simon, 2004; Persons, 1989). The initial assessment has two main goals: first to obtain a problem list, and second, to develop an initial case formulation. The case conceptualization allows the therapist to target specific interventions, which address overt and underlying mechanisms. This reduces the trial and error method of trying intervention after intervention to see which one works with a given client. The client may also suggest or inquire about the use of certain cognitive, behavioral, and/or hypnotic techniques. If the client's interest in a particular technique, such as hypnosis, is a good fit with the therapist's case conceptualization, then hypnosis may be an important intervention to consider. The preferred technique may fit the client's conceptualization of his/her problem and thus reduce potential obstacles to treatment. Increased compliance with treatment interventions and homework assignments may be observed.

The case conceptualization also helps the therapist navigate the therapeutic relationship and anticipate and plan for further obstacles in treatment. Assessment and treatment are considered to occur simultaneously, each one informing the other, and leading to revision when necessary. Persons (1989) considers the therapist's hypothesis about the underlying mechanisms to be one of most important features of the case formulation, which plays a central role in guiding the therapist's choice of interventions. The therapist's understanding of the client's overt behaviors, cognitions, and affect, along with the hypothesis about the underlying mechanisms, including both biological factors and schemas, guides the choice of interventions.

Several cognitive and behavioral interventions have been identified and used with clients having a variety of psychological problems (Freeman et al., 2004). Common cognitive interventions may include the downward arrow technique (a specific automatic thought is identified and implications of considering it true are explored); idiosyncratic meaning (the therapist asks questions to understand the client's terminology); labeling of distortions (particular cognitions are identified and labeled); de-catastrophizing (the therapist asks questions concerning the worst case scenario); advantages and disadvantages (the explicit pros and cons of maintaining a particular behavior are listed), and replacement imagery (adaptive alternative images are generated to replace dysfunctional images).

Common behavioral interventions may include assertiveness training (the person is taught assertive skills to use in place of aggressive or passive approaches); behavioral rehearsal (provides the opportunity for the client to develop or polish desired skills); social skills training (this training addresses the skills not mastered during the client's development); relaxation training (specific training for relaxation may include progressive muscle relaxation, imagery, or hypnosis); graded task assignments (complex tasks are broken into manageable smaller tasks using a shaping strategy), and homework (the client is asked to complete therapeutic tasks outside the session). This is not an exhaustive list of possible cognitive and behavioral interventions. For example, a hypnotic intervention is usually marked by a trance induction, which may contain many of the behavioral elements of relaxation training and include a cognitive element that resembles the use of imagery.

## SUMMARY

Cognitive behavior therapy and hypnosis have many shared elements that increase the ease and the effectiveness of clinical integration. The cognitive behavior model can also be a framework for the integration of cognitive behavior therapy and hypnosis. Cognitive therapy and theory offer an "effective and coherent approach" and provide "a unifying or integrative paradigm for psychopathology and psychotherapy" that also may be applied to the integration of hypnosis (Alford & Beck, 1997).

This book is divided into two sections. The first section presents the foundation for the integration of cognitive behavior therapy and hypnosis; the second section presents clinical applications using this integrative approach. Clearly, a number of cognitive behavior and hypnotic approaches exist today. The various authors of the case chapters in this volume reflect this range of theoretical and treatment approaches within the cognitive behavior model.

In the first chapter, commonalties in techniques, research supporting the effectiveness of combined strategies, existing clinical models, shared treatment goals and an understanding of the unconscious are identified and discussed. Chapter 2 presents a brief history of hypnosis, its definition, and clinical cases to illustrate the use of common hypnotic strategies. Chapter 3 describes the assumptions and tenets of cognitive behavior therapy and hypnosis. The efficacy and effectiveness of these techniques are also reviewed. Chapter 4 presents a case conceptualization model for the integration of clinical behavior therapy and hypnosis. A comprehensive case presentation of a woman with panic disorder without agoraphobia is described. This chapter allows the reader to walk through the case using a cognitive behavior case conceptualization that leads to the inclusion of hypnosis. The use of various cognitive behavior techniques and hypnotic techniques are described within this case as well.

The second section of the book presents clinical applications illustrating the use of cognitive behavior therapy with hypnosis. Chapter 5 presents the treatment of anxiety, phobias and psycho-physiological conditions. The SORC model is described for assessment, which includes stimulus, organism variables, response, and consequences. Chapter 5 presents case studies of clients with panic disorder, phobic disorder, and irritable bowel syndrome (IBS). These are frequent diagnoses that are treated successfully with cognitive behavior therapy and hypnosis. This chapter describes the use of the role of negative self-hypnosis, and the use of two-column thought records and systematic desensitization.

Chapter 6 presents the treatment of depression using cognitive behavior therapy and hypnosis and offers a cognitive dissociative model of depression, which is based on the negative self-hypnosis model. A review of other treatment approaches and a description of the disorder are also offered. The author of chapter 6 also provides a detailed description of a first-aid technique to energize clients who have depression. Cognitive restructuring using hypnosis is described in the case presentation. Additionally, a brief report of a study of this model is included.

Chapter 7 addresses the treatment of anger, using cognitive behavior therapy and hypnosis. As anger is not currently a DSM IV diagnosis, the author describes the importance of treatment for this condition. Models from a cognitive behavior and a Buddhist perspective are described, as the underlying techniques are similar. A detailed case study is presented, which includes the use of progressive muscle relaxation, deepening hypnotic technique, identification and modification of maladaptive schemas, and paradoxical suggestion.

Chapter 8 presents the treatment of posttraumatic stress disorder using cognitive behavior therapy and hypnosis. The use of a constructive narrative perspective (CNP) is described for assessment and treatment. Several assessments of hypnotizability are described in the comprehensive case presentation. This case describes a complex diagnostic picture and previous treatment failures.

Chapter 9 addresses mind/body conditions using cognitive behavior therapy and hypnosis. The author presents an eclectic model, the extended strategic treatment model, which uses cognitive behavior techniques, hypnotic techniques, and psychodynamic techniques. Various conditions are described and treated, including smoking cessation, swollen tongue, fibroids, prostatitis, hyperemesis, abdominal surgery, genital warts, and multiple sclerosis ambulation problems. The author briefly reports on two controlled research studies that indicate that this model accelerates the healing of nondisplaced ankle fractures and early post surgical wound resolution.

Chapter 10 addresses pain and distress management in cancer patients, using cognitive behavior therapy and hypnosis. Background information concerning the diagnoses of cancer is provided. A bio-psychosocial assessment and a crisis matrix model are described. The role of self-hypnosis and problem solving are also addressed.

Chapter 11 addresses sleep disorders as treated with cognitive behavior therapy and hypnosis. Background information such as stages of sleep, assessment, and disorders of sleep is reviewed. Case studies are presented, using standard cognitive behavior and hypnotic techniques.

The final chapter addresses the process of becoming a practitioner who uses cognitive behavior therapy and hypnosis. A plan is proposed and described for the practitioner interested in adopting this integrated process.

## REFERENCES

Alford, B. A., & Beck, A. T. (1997). *The integrative power of cognitive therapy.* New York: Guilford.

American Psychological Association, Society of Psychological Hypnosis, Division 30. *The Division 30 Definition and Description of Hypnosis.* Retrieved March 29, 2005, from http://www.apa.org/divisions/div30/hypnosis.html

Barber, T. H. (2000). A deeper understanding of hypnosis: Its secrets, its nature, its essence. *American Journal of Clinical Hypnosis, 42,* 208–272.

Beck, A. T. (1976). *Cognitive therapy and the emotional disorders.* Guilford, CT: International Universities Press.

Berstein, D. A., & Borkovec, T. D. (1973). *Progressive muscle relaxation training: A manual for the helping professions.* Champaign, IL: Research Press.

Clarke, J. C., & Jackson, J. A. (1983). *Hypnosis and behavior therapy: The treatment of anxiety and phobias.* New York: Springer.

Cooper, J. O., Heron, T. E., & Heward, W. L. (1987). *Applied behavioral analysis.* Upper Saddle Creek, NJ: Prentice Hall.
Craighead, L. W., Craighead, W. E., Kazdin, A. E., & Mahoney, M. J. (1994). *Cognitive and behavioral interventions: An empirical approach to mental health problems.* Boston: Allyn & Bacon.
Diamond, M. J. (1989). The cognitive skills model: An emerging paradigm for investigating hypnotic phenomena. In N. P. Spanos & J. F. Chaves (Eds.), *Hypnosis: The cognitive behavioral perspective* (pp. 380–399). Buffalo, NY: Prometheus Books.
Dollard, J., & Miller, N. E. (1950). *Personality and psychotherapy: An analysis in terms of learning, thinking, and culture.* New York: McGraw-Hill.
Dowd, E. T. (1993). Cognitive developmental hypnotherapy. In J. W. Rhue, S. J. Lynn, & I. Kirsch (Eds.), *Handbook of clinical hypnosis* (pp. 215–231). Washington, DC: American Psychological Association.
Erickson, M. H., Rossi, E. L., & Rossi, S. I. (1976). *Hypnotic realities. The induction of clinical hypnosis and forms of indirect suggestion.* New York: John Wiley & Sons.
Freeman, A., Pretzer, J., Fleming, B., & Simon, K. M. (2004). *Clinical applications of cognitive therapy* (2nd ed.). New York: Plenum.
Golden, W. L. (1994). Cognitive-behavioral hypnotherapy for anxiety disorders. *Journal of Cognitive Psychotherapy: An International Quarterly, 8,* 265–274.
Golden, W. L., Dowd, E. T., & Friedberg, F. (1987). *Hypnotherapy: A modern approach.* New York: Pergamon.
Goldfried, M. R., & Davison, G. C. (1994). *Clinical behavior therapy.* New York: John Wiley.
Hannah, B. (1997). *Jung: His life and work.* Wilmette, IL: Chiron.
Kihlstrom, J. F. (1985). Hypnosis. *Annual Review of Psychology, 36,* 385–418.
Kirsch, I. (1993). Cognitive-behavioral hypnotherapy. In J. W. Rhue, S. J. Lynn, & I. Kirsch (Eds.), *Handbook of clinical hypnosis* (pp. 151–171). Washington, DC: American Psychological Association.
Kirsch, I., Capafons, A., Cardena-Buelna, E., & Amigo, S. (1999). *Clinical hypnosis and self-regulation: Cognitive-behavioral perspectives.* Washington, DC: American Psychological Association.
Kirsch, I., & Lynn, S. J. (1995). The altered state of hypnosis. *American Psychologist, 50,* 846–858.
Kirsch, I., Montgomery, G., & Sapirstein, G. (1995). Hypnosis as an adjunct to cognitive-behavioral psychotherapy: A meta-analysis. *Journal of Consulting and Clinical Psychology, 63,* 214–220.
Lazarus, A. A. (1981). *The practice of multi-modal therapy.* New York: McGraw-Hill.
Lynn, S. J., & Sherman, S. J. (2000). The clinical importance of sociocognitive models of hypnosis: Response set theory and Milton Erickson's strategic interventions. *American Journal of Clinical Hypnosis, 42,* 294–315.
Mahoney, M. J. (1980). Psychotherapy and the structure of personal relationships. In M. J. Mahoney (Ed.), *Psychotherapy process: Current issues and future directions.* New York: Plenum.
Meichenbaum, D., & Gilmore, J. B. (1984). The nature of unconscious processes: A cognitive-behavioral perspective. In D. Meichenbaum & K. S. Bowers (Eds.), *The unconscious reconsidered* (pp. 273–298). New York: John Wiley.

Persons, J. B. (1989). *Cognitive therapy in practice: A case formulation approach.* New York: W. W. Norton.

Rossi, E. L. (2000). In search of a deep psychobiology of hypnosis: Visionary hypotheses of a new millennium. *American Journal of Clinical Hypnosis, 42,* 178–207.

Salter, A. (1949). *Conditioned reflex therapy.* New York: Capricorn.

Wolpe, J. (1990). *The practice of behavior therapy* (4th ed.). New York: Pergamon.

Chapter 2

# Hypnosis: History, Definitions, Theory, and Application[*]

Marc I. Oster

The history of hypnosis has been detailed many times and by numerous sources (e.g., Wester, 1984; Wester & Smith, 1987; Gravitz, 1984; Crasilneck & Hall, 1985; Kroger, 1977). While the name for what we today call hypnosis has changed over time, the use of suggestive therapies probably dates back to Egypt some 4000 years ago and to Greece and Rome about 2000 years ago (Gravitz, 1984). What follows is a brief summary of some of the major developments and people involved in the history of hypnosis.

## THE MODERN DEVELOPMENT OF HYPNOSIS

The terms "mesmerism" and "mesmerized," which are used synonymously with the terms "hypnotism" or "hypnotized," are commonly recognized. Mesmerism[1] is derived from the name of the eighteenth century, German-born physician Franz Anton Mesmer, who received

---

[*]Copyright ©2006 by Marc Oster.
[1]Mesmerism is defined in the *Merriam-Webster Collegiate Dictionary* (2003), 11th edition, as "hypnotic induction held to involve animal magnetism: *broadly*: HYPNOTISM."

his medical degree at the University of Vienna in 1766. He had a significant role in the development of hypnosis, and is universally considered the "father" of modern hypnosis. Mesmer believed that the body responded to various planetary gravitational forces, which he termed "animal magnetism," although he thought that any magnetic force could be used for healing. Mesmer also believed that a fluidlike substance in nature that transported this gravity. He believed that manipulating these magnetic forces would restore a person to harmony and balance, and thus good health (Melite, n.d., www.findarticles.com).

Mesmer's practice using magnetic techniques flourished for many years, especially after he moved to Paris to avoid legal proceedings against him for its use. He and his followers drew so much attention that the King Louis XVI of France established a royal commission to study mesmerism, how and why it seemed to work (Melite, n.d.). After much study by well-respected scientists, including Benjamin Franklin, the commission's conclusion was that although Mesmer's patients did improve nothing in what Mesmer did could account for such improvements. What we now understand probably contributed to the improvements was not so much Mesmer's techniques as it was the therapeutic relationship he had with his patients.

## How Hypnosis Was Named and Its Early Practitioners

The term "hypnosis" was first used by the physician James Braid in 1841 (Crasilneck, 1985). The term is derived from the Greek "hypnos" meaning sleep. Braid saw the patient's experience as being much like an induced sleep, thus his derivation of the term. When we observe a hypnotized subject, Braid's term makes sense. The contemporary understanding of hypnosis is that the patient is in hypnosis and not under hypnosis. The person in hypnosis appears to the observer to be sleeping. The hypnotized person is motionless, quiet; their breathing is slow and shallow, their heart rate has dropped as has their blood pressure, and their eyes are closed. This looks like sleep, but isn't. If a person is observed sleeping they show all of these signs and more. They might snore, breath heavily at times, and move around a lot, but the most common difference is that sleepers don't usually wake up when they are softly asked to, whereas the hypnotized person almost always responds to the instruction to wake up.

But how do we know the hypnotized person isn't asleep? Besides the behavioral observations described above, the EEG patterns of someone sleeping, relaxing, meditating, or in hypnosis show that all of these are different states. The hypnotized brain is not just like the sleeping brain. In fact, even though the hypnotized person looks as though they are sleeping, their thought process is very active. The patient's attention is so focused, like a laser beam, on an idea or theme that their body systems slow or quiet down, making them look asleep. Like many clinicians who use hypnosis, I admit to using the words "asleep" and "wake up" even though I know that the patient is not sleeping. So, if the hypnotized subject is not sleeping or waking up specifically, why do I use these words? It's simply because everyone understands what they mean and how to physically and mentally recreate the experience. These are common terms that save us time and make our work as therapists more efficient. Braid's other contribution was that he rejected the magnetism theories of Mesmer and emphasized the importance of suggestion as the prime treatment modality.

In other early uses of hypnosis, James Esdaile, a Scottish physician and surgeon, performed a number of operations in India using hypnosis as the sole anesthesia. Kroger (1977) reported the first recorded use of hypnoanesthesia in 1821, to perform surgery. Esdaile's and Braid's work moved hypnosis towards scientific acceptance. Neurologist Jean Martin Charcot, practicing in the later 1800s, believed that hypnosis was similar to hysteria and that both were the products of a diseased nervous system, which further contributed to the accepted use of hypnosis.

Braid's ideas were advanced in the late 1800s and early 1900s by Liebeault, a physician, and Bernheim, a neurologist, who stressed the role of suggestibility in hypnosis. This approach became more widely accepted than the pathological perspective of Charcot.

Freud studied with Charcot in 1885, and in 1895, with Breuer coauthored *Studies on Hysteria*, which emphasized the use of hypnosis to recover early memories in order to release stored-up emotions from the unconscious. Freud eventually rejected hypnosis in favor of his psychoanalytic technique of free association. It was thought that his rejection of hypnosis was due, in part, to his limited skill at using it and to his dislike of having more personal contact with patients that using hypnosis required, compared to free association, which required less personal contact. However, late in his life Freud began to reconsider the value of hypnosis and encouraged his followers to explore it as a useful psychiatric tool.

At about the same time, in the early 1900s, psychiatrist Morton Prince became known for using hypnosis in the treatment of multiple personality disorder. Also, in the early 1900s, Alfred Binet, who was most noted for developing the first modern IQ test in 1904 and for publishing a book on animal magnetism, showed an interest in hypnosis. Pierre Janet, a French physician continued the investigation of hypnosis in spite of its lack of popularity due to Freud's initial rejection of it.

The scientific acceptance of hypnosis began anew with Clark Hull's book *Hypnosis and Suggestibility: An Experimental Approach*, published in the mid-1900s, in which he described controlled experiments covering a wide range of hypnotic phenomena. A contemporary of Hull's, Ernest Hilgard was also a leader in hypnosis research, most notably his work at Stanford University's Laboratory of Hypnotic Research, which became a training ground for many contemporary researchers and clinicians using hypnosis.

In the late 1920s, Hull mentored a young medical and psychology student, Milton Erickson, who would be most instrumental in changing the use of contemporary hypnosis, with theories and techniques that enabled him to successfully treat those who were previously thought to be untreatable. Erickson's hypnotherapy is characterized by indirect induction, brief number of sessions, utilization of the person's attributes, and use of metaphors. Many of Erickson's ideas have been incorporated not only into the modern language of hypnosis but also into the field of psychotherapy in general.

## Professional Recognition of Hypnosis

Professional organizations began to emerge with the establishment of the International Society for Clinical and Experimental Hypnosis (ISCEH) in 1949. ISCEH was expanded into the International Society of Hypnosis (ISH) in 1959, with the Society for Clinical and Experimental Hypnosis (SCEH) becoming a North American chapter. The *International Journal of Clinical and Experimental Hypnosis* was the official

SCEH journal and adopted as the official ISH journal. As is often the case, there were political and philosophical differences among the founders of SCEH during the early 1950s. While the core SCEH group favored the research or academic perspective, a growing group of clinical or practice-oriented members were emerging under the leadership of psychiatrist Milton Erickson. While grounded in and appreciative of the science of hypnosis, Erickson spent his career largely as a practicing psychiatrist. In 1957, several like-minded clinicians under Erickson's leadership founded the American Society of Clinical Hypnosis (ASCH), with membership restricted, like SCEH, to professionals in medicine, psychology, and dentistry. Both ASCH and SCEH have since opened their membership to social workers, master's degreed nurses, family therapists, podiatrists, chiropractors, mental health counselors, and speech pathologists. Erickson was the founding editor of the *American Journal of Clinical Hypnosis*.

In 1955, the British Medical Association reported its approval of hypnosis as a viable medical treatment modality. The American Medical Association followed suit in 1958, not only recognizing hypnosis as a legitimate treatment method but also recommending that hypnosis training be included in the curriculum of all medical schools. Psychologists followed shortly thereafter by recognizing hypnosis as both a useful psychological treatment tool and a subject of academic inquiry, and by establishing the American Psychological Association's Division 30 for Psychological Hypnosis (now called the Society for Psychological Hypnosis) in the early 1960s. At about the same time, the American Board of Clinical Hypnosis was incorporated to oversee board certification in clinical hypnosis. This organization oversaw diplomate examinations by its member boards, the American Board of Medical Hypnosis, the American Board of Hypnosis in Dentistry, and the American Board of Psychological Hypnosis (offering certification in clinical and experimental hypnosis). In recent years, a fourth board, the American Hypnosis Board of Clinical Social Work, was established to recognize advanced competency in hypnosis for use by social workers.

## RECENT DEFINITIONS OF HYPNOSIS

Defining hypnosis can, at times, bring to a halt any further discussion of the topic, because writers often cannot agree on what defines it.

The range of definitions includes hypnosis being whatever the writer says it is, to all aspects of treatment as being hypnosis, to using complex neurophysiological explanations. For the purposes of this chapter, I present three definitions of hypnosis: a very simple one, the revised definition of the Society for Psychological Hypnosis (APA), and my own combination of the two.

The first definition is elegant in its simplicity. Spiegel and Spiegel (2004) indicate that hypnosis involves three elements: focus of attention, dissociation, and suggestibility. They claim that without the presence of all three elements, it is not hypnosis. Further, the Spiegels do not see the need for a formal procedure for hypnosis to occur.

The second definition is one prepared by the Executive Committee of the American Psychological Association, Division 30, Society of Psychological Hypnosis (www.apa.org). This definition describes hypnosis as usually employing an induction procedure, providing suggestions for relaxation, and acknowledges that persons vary in their responsiveness to suggestions. It goes on to state, as noted in Chapter 1, that the induction procedure results in the subject or patient's experiencing alterations in perception, sensation, learning, and behaviors.

Finally, I prefer a blending of the two latter definitions. When I present hypnosis to my patients, I explain that it is the result of a collaborative interpersonal interaction or relationship between the patient and myself. Hypnosis can be defined as a highly focused, heightened awareness that "purifies" the treatment field—the mind, enabling the client or patient to be more receptive to alternative ideas and experiences. As a result of this collaborative relationship, the client or patient can experience alterations in sensation, perception, thoughts, or behaviors.

# THEORIES OF HYPNOSIS

What theoretical approach should a practitioner take? The theory of hypnosis is often explained in terms of psychoanalytic, Ericksonian, social learning, or social psychological approaches, to name a few. (Chapter 1 of this volume includes descriptions of clinical hypnosis, including Hilgard's neo-dissociative model, Kirsch and Lynn's socio-cognitive model, the psychobiological model, as well as Erickson's model of therapy.) In addition to the variety of psychological theories of hypnosis, there are several general theoretical styles to consider. For example, one might consider a style of hypnosis that is symptom focused. Within this style, the hypnotic suggestions can be directive in nature. About 20% of the population is thought to respond well to directive suggestion (Brown & Fromm, 1987). Generally these people are highly hypnotizable, somewhat dependent in personality style, and at least average in intelligence. The second style is dynamic. By this approach, the therapist might use hypnosis as a vehicle for the exploration of coping and mastery of a psychological conflict, or for uncovering a conflict and acquiring insight. One's theoretical style of hypnosis can be supportive in nature, such as in ego strengthening. Some follow a developmental or structural psychoanalytic approach, which creates a structure for the patient to experience more stability and integration.

The kinds of hypnotic suggestion used are also a consideration within one's theoretical style. Suggestions can be delivered in a directive manner in which the therapist is an authorative source relying on persuasion and the patient's uncritical acceptance. Or suggestions can be permissive in which the hypnosis relies on the patient's ability to respond. Hypnosis is something that therapist and patient do together. The therapist establishes the right condition for the patient's self-discovery and their acquisition of insight. Suggestions can take the form of an active problem-solving session. The indirect delivery of suggestions can be less confrontive than directive approaches but can also be confusing to patients.

## APPLICATION: WHAT HYPNOSIS IS GOOD FOR

When teaching beginning workshops or courses, or when speaking to the public, or even professional groups, I'm often asked, "Is hypnosis good for (a certain malady)?" For many years my reply would include the various conditions—psychological, medical, and dental—for which hypnosis is helpful. Sometimes my replies were met with hopeful surprise and sometimes with disappointment.

Is hypnosis good for pain management, preparation for childbirth, resolving psychological problems, depression, skin disorders, intestinal problems, cancer, anxiety, traumatic stress reactions, stress management, performance enhancement, fear of flying, and so on? Yes, it's good for all these things and more. But, in more recent years my answer to the question of what hypnosis is good for has taken on a somewhat different response. Now I reply—especially when addressing a clinical professional audience, "That depends. What is it you're looking to accomplish?"

Hypnosis might be useful in any of several areas. It might be used to reduce or eliminate symptoms. Hypnosis might be used to explore or understand one's history or dynamics. It might be used as a tool to teach self-control or self-regulation. Along that line, hypnosis might be used to enhance or strengthen one's sense of confidence. I sometimes explain hypnosis in this instance as being like the glue that holds together the various interventions used in the nonhypnotic part of the therapy session. Finally, with any given patient, hypnosis might be used for any one or all of the above-mentioned purposes.

More specific examples concerning the effectiveness of hypnosis mediated therapy were reported by Lynn, Kirsch, Barabasz, Cardena, and Patterson (2000). Lynn et al. summarized the research to date and reported that hypnosis has shown considerable efficacy for induced analgesia, presurgical preparation, irritable bowel syndrome, asthma, smoking cessation, reducing nausea related to chemotherapy, and for enhancing the effectiveness of cognitive behavior therapy, as well as for treating trauma. Hammond (1994) summarized the literature to date and found additionally that hypnosis is effective with anxiety and stress-related disorders, sexual dysfunction, and eating and sleep disorders.

## Determining Hypnotizability

Hammond (1998), in discussing hypnotic talent and ability, indicates that one's ability to experience hypnosis and its various phenomena is not an all-or-nothing attribute, but follows a continuum from light trance to very deep (plenary) trance. Light trance is characterized by relaxation, while plenary trance is characterized by stuporous feelings and the loss of awareness of external world. Historically, there has been debate as to whether or not hypnosis is a state into which one enters or an ability one already possesses. Both sides have presented ample support for their position. Strong support for hypnosis being a relatively stable ability that one possesses is the finding based on subjects' performance on formal scales of hypnotizability correlates .82 after 15 years' time and .71 after 25 years' time (Piccione, Hilgard, & Zimbardo, 1989). Support for the position that hypnotizability is modifiable is found in the work of Gfeller (1993). This researcher developed procedures by which the subject's experience of hypnosis could be enhanced or trained so that they had a greater experience than their measured capacity might have suggested possible.

A number of formal measures of hypnotizability have been developed and are summarized in detail by Hammond (1998). Among the more commonly used, individually administered scales are the Stanford Hypnotic Susceptibility Scale (SHSC), Form C; the Stanford Hypnotic Clinical Scale (SHCS; Hilgard & Hilgard, 1983); and the Hypnotic Induction Profile (HIP; Spiegel & Spiegel, 1987). For group administration, the Harvard Group Scale of Hypnotic Susceptibility (HGSHS), Form A, is used (Shor & Orne, 1962).

Hypnosis is a valuable tool to add to, or to enhance one's ability to provide treatment in their chosen modality. There are many ways it can be integrated into one's current practice. The therapist can conduct a formal assessment of a patient's hypnotic ability which can produce far more useful information than a standardized score or rating of low, medium, or high hypnotizability. An introduction to hypnosis itself will provide the patient with a taste of the hypnotic experience without the demand of immediately resolving their problem, enabling the learning of hypnosis to be less threatening or anxiety provoking for the patient. Introducing the patient to hypnosis also provides the clinician with a description of how the patient experiences it and what hypnotic phenomena will be useful to integrate into the interventions.

## Sample Applications of Hypnosis

My first example of using hypnosis as adjunct treatment demonstrates a permissive, indirect hypnotic induction, utilizing age regression. Age regression consists of the patient reliving past experiences. With this approach, I made use of the patient's images, language, and kinesthetic memory and experience. The imagery enabled her to access positive memories and activate positive thoughts in the present.

## Case 1: Sue

This example involves Sue, a woman in her late 30s, who was suffering from a profound depression of many years. In spite of her suicidal and homicidal ideation, Sue was able to function outside of a hospital, although barely. Her psychologist and psychiatrist wanted me to use hypnosis to help control some of her ruminations. By the time we met, the patient's needs had changed. Sue had been informed she would need maintenance electroconvulsive therapy (ECT), twice weekly, for an as-yet-to-be-determined period of time. Having had this kind of treatment previously, she suffered anticipatory anxiety that was overwhelming and complained of pain in her arms and body as the anesthetic for ECT entered her veins.

In taking Sue's history, I learned that in her youth she had been an Olympic-caliber speed skater. Since she could identify almost nothing in her life that brought her pleasure, I used the experience of her racing as both my hypnotic induction and my intervention. And so my hypnotic induction began: "As you get comfortable in the chair and let your eyes close, I'd like you to remember when you are much younger. Remember back when you used to race. Allow your mind to experience yourself standing on the starting line just before a race. As you stand at the starting line, you feel comfortable in your racing suit, covered from head to toe in the tight clothing that racers wear. You are positioned with the toe of one skate blade on the ice and the other skate blade facing forward. You are bent at the waist with one arm cocked behind you and one arm cocked in front of you, waiting for the starter's signal."

At this point I described for her in detail the image of two racers skating around the rink. Within that description, I spoke to Sue about her capacity to control pain. This was something that she has had within her for many years. I spoke about how as the race starts and her body gets in tune with the experience, she begins to lose awareness of any discomfort in her body. She is only aware of her body making racing movements that seem unconscious. All the while, her body releases its natural painkillers, enabling her to complete a very intense physical experience without feeling any discomfort.

I then described for her the experience of the race coming to its conclusion. I began by saying to Sue, "And as the race comes to its finish, you do what all racers do when the race comes to its finish. As you cross the finish line you stand upright; with one skate blade pointing forward and one skate blade slightly off to the side; with one hand you effortlessly slide the hood off of your head; then you place your hands on your hips as you glide around the rink gradually slowing down." This was followed with some additional description of how her body could benefit from the long-term effects of those natural painkillers that were released during the race. I then provided some instruction for terminating her hypnotic experience and reorienting herself to the room.

As Sue opened her eyes and stretched, she looked at me and smiled, asking, "When did you race?" When I replied that I had never raced, she asked how I knew exactly what racing felt like. I explained to her that when Olympic speed skating was very popular, I used to watch it on television and paid close attention to what I was watching. She had commented in our discussion that she used to train and race against some local Chicago speed-skating celebrities. As I was writing her actual name on the receipt at the end of our session, it appeared familiar to me. After pondering it for a moment, I looked up at her and asked if I had watched her race on television as well. She smiled and said, "Yes, you did." I felt honored to be in her presence and showed it. When she came back for a second session, she smiled as she asked me if I knew what she had done during the past week. She indicated that, for the first time in 20 years, she had gone ice-skating. She said it felt to her as if she had never stopped skating; it felt just as it had 20 years before.

## Case 2: Joseph

This second example makes use of a very naturalistic application of hypnosis. I induced no formal hypnosis. Formal hypnosis usually employs a ritual for induction and deepening while informal hypnosis relies on informal naturally occurring hypnotic phenomena. Capitalizing on the comfort of our relationship, Joseph began telling his story. In doing so, the experience itself was hypnotic. My task was to observe and listen, watching for the right time and listening for the meaning Joseph was seeking in his telling of his story. This intervention makes use of a narrative approach, both Joseph's and mine. Joe was telling his story and I was using his story to pace and lead him towards my intervention, the restructuring of his experience, the creating of a new ending for the old story. Later, with a new patient, Mary, I applied Joseph's successful resolution of his experience to her similar experience.

In December 1988, I was finishing the second year of my postdoctoral residency. The setting was the department of psychiatry in a general medical hospital. Joseph was employed at the same hospital. He worked in the maintenance department and was specifically assigned to the psychiatric units. All of our staff knew Joseph and were very comfortable with his presence on our units. He was very comfortable working around psychiatric patients, both adults and adolescents. While we were comfortable with Joseph and thought we knew him pretty well, we were to find out that we didn't know him as well as we thought.

Joseph apparently had some medical problems. His neurologist had recommended a spinal examination procedure. Joseph was to refrain from any alcohol use 24 hours prior to the procedure. Upon admission, Joseph was asked about alcohol use in the past 24 hours, which he denied. No blood tests were administered. Joseph was given Valium prior to the procedure. Within the hour, Joseph was near psychotic and running around the hospital grounds. Joseph was restrained and brought to the adult psychiatric unit for examination and follow up, as needed.

Joseph did not lie about *abstaining* from alcohol for the previous 24 hours. In fact, he had had no alcohol for the previous 48 hours. One fact we didn't know about Joseph was that he was a chronic alcoholic. We had little opportunity to have observed his alcoholism because his most severe alcohol use was during the holidays in December, each December for the past 20 years.

I had an especially good relationship with Joseph, so when I was assigned to treat him I was a bit uncomfortable with the circumstances. It was difficult to see someone known to me in such distress. What follows is a description of a single session intervention with Joseph. However, before he and I could get to our single session, he required about a week to sober up.

It did, in fact, take about a week for Joseph's body to clear the alcohol. It also took time for Joseph to realize what had happened and where he was—in his own hospital on the very psychiatric unit in which he worked. Joseph also knew he was in serious trouble with his employer. Apparently, the hospital had witnessed more than one annual binge. Much of my work with Joseph during that first week was simply reassuring him. Once the alcohol cleared his system and he overcame his embarrassment, he was ready to talk about his problem. The session, the details of which are summarized below, lasted about 90 minutes.

Unknown to most of us, Joseph's annual binge was but one of his symptoms of what was diagnosed as posttraumatic stress disorder. He clearly met all the DSM-III-R criteria. Joseph's story begins, for our purposes, when he was in his early 20's. In 1968, Joseph was in the army and was stationed in Vietnam.

Joseph described his Vietnam experience as pretty typical of most soldiers at that time. It was the end of the second week of December. As part of a small convoy, Joseph was driving a truck with his best friend Mike seated next to him when the convoy was ambushed. The truck was hit and overturned into a ditch by the road.

While the others were occupied with the attack, Joseph heard Mike calling him. He located Mike in another part of the ditch. As Joseph came upon him, he saw Mike had a serious, gaping abdominal wound. In fact there was little of Mike's abdomen left. Joseph crawled to Mike and took him in his arms. With a look of shock and terror, Mike said to Joseph, "Please don't let me die." Joseph assured Mike he wouldn't let him die. Unfortunately, that was not within Joseph's control. It was about 10 days before Christmas 1968 when Mike died in Joseph's arms.

Although Joseph used alcohol to excess throughout the year, every December, for the past 20 years, Joseph had increased his drinking starting at the beginning of the month, so that by mid-December he was numb to the world around him. By January 1st of each year his job was at risk and his marriage was again on the verge of collapse.

I could see that in telling his story, as I observed, Joseph was already hypnotized, entranced, numbed, or focused, depending on how one views the storytelling process. Joseph wiped the tears from his eyes as he looked up at me, as if offering me an opening. I found myself returning his gaze and nodding my head "yes" as I slid my chair closer to his, sitting almost knee-to-knee. The remainder of this session is paraphrased as follows:

| | |
|---|---|
| Doctor: | . . . and Mike says, "Joseph, please don't let me die." |
| Joseph: | Yes. |
| Doctor: | . . . and Mike died. |
| Joseph: | Yes. |
| Doctor: | . . . and each year approaching the anniversary of Mike's death you begin drinking more and more. |
| Joseph: | Yes. |
| Doctor: | . . . doing anything you can to not feel the pain of Mike's death. . . . |
| Joseph: | Yes. |
| Doctor: | . . . and of your loss. |
| Joseph: | Yes. |
| Doctor: | . . . and of the sadness and guilt you feel for not keeping your word to Mike . . . |
| Joseph: | Yes. |
| Doctor: | . . . and soon, based on the past 20 years, you too will be dead, just like Mike . . . |
| Joseph: | Maybe. Yes. |
| Doctor: | Then your promise to him will be over. |
| Joseph: | Yeah, I guess so. |
| Doctor: | . . . then you will have let Mike die! |
| Joseph: | (There was no response followed by a long pause.) |
| Doctor: | So, Mike was a pretty special guy. |
| Joseph: | (Sitting up) Yes. |
| Doctor: | He must have meant a lot to you. |
| Joseph: | Yes, he did. |
| Doctor: | You must miss him terribly! |
| Joseph: | (Tears coming down his cheek) Yes . . . |
| Doctor: | I bet you've talked about Mike when you went to your group at the Vet Center. |
| Joseph: | Yeah, a lot. |
| Doctor: | . . . and I bet you've talked a lot about how Mike died. |
| Joseph: | Yeah, I did. |
| Doctor: | I wonder what made Mike so special. |
| Joseph: | (Joseph elaborated on Mike's qualities; and a smile begins to appear on his face.) |
| Doctor: | Yeah. . . . Your daughter, Tracy, is pretty special too, isn't she? (She was then 17 years old and had been deaf since early childhood.) |

| | |
|---|---|
| Joseph: | Yeah, she sure is! |
| Doctor: | I wonder if Tracy knows about Mike and what he meant to you. |
| Joseph: | (Pause) No. She doesn't. |
| Doctor: | . . . and I wonder if Kelly (Joseph's other daughter) or if Julie (Joseph's wife) knows about Mike and what he meant to you? |
| Joseph: | (Pause) No, they really don't. |
| Doctor: | . . . you probably have a few pictures of Mike, and Mike and you together. |
| Joseph: | (Smiling and again sitting upright) Oh sure, lots of pictures. |
| Doctor: | Joseph, you really didn't mean to let Mike die, did you? |
| Joseph: | No! |
| Doctor: | . . . and you'd like him here with you right now, wouldn't you? |
| Joseph: | Yeah, I would. |
| Doctor: | . . . and if you're dead, then Mike will surely be gone forever, won't he? |
| Joseph: | Yes. |
| Doctor: | Mike asked you not to let him die. But each year for the past 20 years you've been letting Mike down. (pause) But now . . . , you can change all that. Mike can live through you, but only if you are here and alive! For the past 20 years Mike's memory has been a terribly painful one for you and your family, although they really didn't even know him. Twenty years ago you didn't know how to keep your promise to Mike; and the pain of that was too great to face. But now you can begin keeping that promise. You can start now by talking with Tracy and Kelly and Julie and your friends at the Vet Center about how Mike lived and why he was so important to you. You can include, on your wall along with your family pictures, a picture of Mike. You can include him on your Christmas card list and gift list. |
| Joseph: | (Looks confused) |
| Doctor: | Yes, you can get a gift for Mike each mid-December and pass it along to someone else who could benefit from Mike's goodness. |

Joseph:     (Joseph was looking deeply engrossed/entranced in this
            conversation)
Doctor:     Joseph, December no longer need bring painful memories
            of how Mike died and the pain that caused you, but it
            can he a memory of who Mike was, and how he lived,
            and the meaning his life holds for you.

At this point the atmosphere had become pretty emotional, so I
suggested we end the session for the day. While Joseph's "cure"
may have been facilitated in this one session, his "healing" continues.
While seeing a patient at the same hospital 1 year later, I saw Joseph
again. At that time Joseph hadn't had a drink since before his hospitalization. He was still employed at the hospital and his supervisor
reported he was doing very well.

Unfortunately Julie's divorce from Joseph became final around
the 1-year anniversary of Joseph's hospitalization. Although now
divorced, both Julie and Joseph report getting along quite well. I
ran into Joseph again at the same hospital 2 years after our previous
encounter, or 3 years post hospitalization. Joseph continues to be
a nondrinker. He remains active in AA. He is also active at the Vet
Center helping others to remember their "Mike" in a different way.

## Case 3: Mary

Three years after working with Joseph, I met Mary who was 29 at
the time. Each August for the past 10 years she had become depressed. Each August, Mary's mother would begin mourning the
death of Mary's older brother. This mourning would increase in
intensity until October, the anniversary of Jim's auto accident, and
Mary would become severely depressed.

It was many months before Mary would even mention her
brother by name. Then one day she was finally talking to me about
Jim, not even knowing she had said his name out loud. During the
long pause after she realized she had stated his name, I began telling
her about Joseph and Mike. As with Joseph's treatment, I had not,
at that time, used any formal hypnosis with Mary.

Three and a half years later Mary had not suffered a recurrence
of her depression. Twenty three years after Mike's death, Joseph is
helping others rewrite their memories of loved ones lost.

The case of Mary involved the use of hypnotic exploration and age regression to identify her source of extreme fear and anxiety. Using the information I learned from that initial hypnotic exploration with Mary, I used it to help her cope and decrease her anticipatory anxiety about her mother's mourning of her brother. Sue's case which I described above involved a restructuring of her original experience as a successful speed skater and then the application of her new understanding of it to her present experience of failing to find any pleasure in life. In the final case, using Kimberly's own interests, her desire to make use of the Pac-Man video game imagery, this imagery was introduced as a tool that she could use for practicing self-efficacy and mastery both in preparation for the forthcoming gynecological procedure and in the future.

## Case 4: Kimberly

Kimberly was a young woman in her late 20s. She sought hypnosis to help her manage her anxiety about an upcoming gynecological procedure. Although relatively routine, the anticipation of the procedure was causing her a great deal of anxiety. She reported that her fear had little to do with the procedure per se, but more to do with her never having needed medical care beyond her regular gynecological and dental exams. Her level of fear still seemed out of proportion. I commented to her that she recently required stitches to close a cut in her eyebrow from a minor accident and managed that without any problem. She denied it as being that simple, stating she needed sedation to quiet her in order to have the suturing done.

When we were to begin the hypnosis work, I first chose to explore her reported and observed disproportionate anxiety. After an induction and deepening of her hypnosis, I began the exploration in hopes of shedding some light on her fears. During the exploration procedure, I asked for an ideomotor response to the query of whether she had ever felt a similar kind of anxiety. Ideomotor responses consist of individuals during hypnosis to respond to questions with involuntary movements of fingers to simple questions. Her response was affirmative. I then asked her to go back to a time when she felt that similar kind of anxiety and signal when she had found that time. She did, and I asked her to tell me about the details, such as her age, the situation, who was present, and so forth.

Kimberly began to describe an incident that occurred when she was a little girl, perhaps 5 or 6 years old. She had fallen and cut her head. The wound was sufficient that it required a trip to the hospital emergency room and stitches. She described lying in the back seat of the family car with her head on her grandmother's lap while her mother drove her to the hospital. Kimberly reported not feeling anxious until she looked at her grandmother's face and saw her expression of fear and concern. Upon seeing her grandmother's concern, Kimberly became similarly fearful and anxious. It is interesting to note that the event that seemed to have ignited her present day fear was her recent trip to the emergency room for stitches following a fall and injury to her head, much like the event of 20 years earlier that she had forgotten.

While in hypnosis, as Kimberly was reporting the event from her childhood and becoming anxious in her reporting, I asked her what she would have wanted her grandmother to do or say that could have eased Kimberly's fears. She replied that she would have wanted her grandmother to say to her, "Everything will be all right."

We continued with our use of hypnosis to address her upcoming gynecological procedure. The hypnotic preparation was essentially a rehearsal of the upcoming gynecological procedure. In describing the anticipated event, I concluded the description by saying that when the doctor has completed the procedure, the attending nurse will look at you and say, "The doctor is finished, and everything will be all right."

A couple of weeks later, following gynecological the procedure, Kimberly returned to my office to update me on how it went. As expected, it went well and the results of the test were negative. Seemingly more important to Kimberly than the test results was her experience with the nurse. She reported that of course there was a nurse assisting the doctor, and when the procedure was finished, the nurse had come to the head of the table, taken Kimberly's head in her hands and looking down at her, said that the procedure was finished and that "everything will be all right." Kimberly added that the nurse just happened to be an older, grandmotherly woman!

Although this would be a good place to end this story, there is more. Kimberly's gynecological procedure had to do with a concern about abnormal cells on her cervix. At a three-month follow-up her results were negative as they were at 6 months. However, she had a positive test result at her nine-month follow-up. This necessitated a different, more complicated and painful procedure. Understandably, this led to a renewal of her anxiety and fear, but for more obvious reasons—the implications of the positive test results.

This time when I saw Kimberly her anxiety was significant. She walked into my office and began pacing back and forth from her chair to the door. I watched from my chair as if watching a tennis match and the ball going back and forth across the court. I followed her movement, pacing her as she paced for a few minutes. Then rather abruptly I said to her, "Sit down here," pointing to her chair. Without hesitation or interruption, she immediately sat down and I began the hypnotic induction. In order to help her remain focused during the procedure, I made a tape recording of the hypnotic induction. She was to practice with the tape prior to the procedure and to bring the tape with her to listen to during the procedure.

At her request, I included in this session imagery pertaining to her body, especially taking the necessary actions to destroy the abnormal cells on her cervix. The imagery, again at her request, was her playing the old Pac-Man video game in which she would visualize Pac-Men traveling throughout her body searching for and destroying the abnormal cells.

This time, however, the procedure didn't go as before. When the doctor visually examined her cervix, he was taken aback and made a comment conveying some surprise. Kimberly had to be interrupted as she was listening to her tape. She saw a look of surprise on the doctor's face and questioned him. He reported to her that upon visual examination, he had found no abnormal cells. He was surprised, in part, because not only did the lab results suggest abnormal cells, he personally saw such cells on the previous examination. The doctor canceled the additional procedure. As of this writing, some 15 years later, Kimberly has had no abnormal pap-test results or related gynecological problems.

## REFERENCES

American Psychological Association, Society of Psychological Hypnosis, Division 30. (2005) *The Division 30 Definition and Description of Hypnosis.* Retrieved March 29, 2005, from http://www.apa.org/divisions/div30/hypnosis.html

Brown, D. P., & Fromm, E. (1987). *Hypnosis and behavioral medicine.* Hillsdale, NJ: Lawrence Erlbaum Associates Publishers.

Crasilneck, H. B., & Hall, J. A. (1985). *Clinical hypnosis: Principles and applications* (2nd ed.). New York: Grune & Stratton.

Gfeller, J. (1993). Enhancing hypnotizability and treatment responsiveness. In J. Rhue, S. J. Lynn, & I. Kirsch (Eds.), *Handbook of clinical hypnosis.* Washington, DC: APA Books.

Gravitz, M. A. (1984). Hypnosis in the historical development of psychoanalytic psychotherapy. In W. C. Wester & A. H. Smith (Eds.), *Clinical hypnosis: A multidisciplinary approach.* Philadelphia: J. B. Lippincott.

Hammond, D. C. (1994). *Medical and psychological hypnosis: How it benefits patients.* Des Plaines, IL: American Society of Clinical Hypnosis.

Hammond, D. C. (1998). *Hypnotic induction and suggestion: An introductory manual.* Bloomingdale, IL: American Society of Clinical Hypnosis.

Hilgard, E. R., & Hilgard, J. R. (1983). *Hypnosis in the relief of pain* (Rev. ed.). Los Altos, CA: William Kaufman.

Kroger, W. S. (1977). *Clinical and experimental hypnosis* (2nd ed.). Philadelphia: J. B. Lippincott.

Lynn, S. J., Kirsch, I., Barabasz, A., Cardena, E., & Patterson, D. (2000). Hypnosis as an empirically supported clinical intervention: The state of the evidence and a look to the future. *International Journal of Clinical and Experimental Hypnosis, 48*(2), 239–259.

Milite, G. A. (n.d.). *Gale encyclopedia of psychology.* Retrieved February 1, 2005, www.findarticles.com/p/articles/mi_g2699/is_005/ai2699000549

Piccione, C., Hilgard, E. R., & Zimbardo, P. G. (1989). On the degree of stability of measured hypnotizability over a 25-year period. *Journal of Personality and Social Psychology, 56,* 269–295.

Shor, R. E., & Orne, E. C. (1962). *Harvard Group Scale of Hypnotic Susceptibility, Form A.* Palo Alto, CA: Consulting Psychologists.

Spiegel, H., & Spiegel, D. (2004). *Trance and treatment: Clinical uses of hypnosis* (2nd ed.). Washington, DC: American Psychiatric Association.

Wester, II, W. C. (1987). *Clinical hypnosis: A case management approach.* Cincinnati, OH: Behavioral Science Center.

Wester, II, W. C., & Smith, A. H. (1984). *Clinical hypnosis: A multidisciplinary approach.* Philadelphia: J. B. Lippincott.

Chapter 3

# Cognitive Behavior Therapy and the Utility of Hypnosis as an Adjunct to Treatment

Peter Kane and Mark A. Reinecke

Although many seminal works in cognitive behavior therapy were written nearly half of a century ago, the field has undergone particularly rapid development over the past 25 years. Efficient, empirically supported treatments for a range of major disorders have been developed during this time, based on these models (Chambless et al., 1996; Kazdin & Weisz, 2003). During this same period, there have been simultaneous efforts to integrate other treatment approaches, including hypnosis, into cognitive behavior therapies to treat a number of problems. As a result, a body of literature on hypnosis as an adjunct to cognitive therapy has emerged. However, questions remain about the empirical status of cognitive behavior hypnotherapy. Given the explicit empirical nature of the field, the goals of this chapter are to (a) review central tenets and empirical evidence supporting cognitive behavior therapy, (b) review the literature on the role of hypnosis in cognitive behavior therapy, (c) discuss possible mediators and moderators of hypnosis as a component of cognitive behavior therapy, and (d) discuss the status of cognitive behavior hypnotherapy as an empirically supported treatment.

## ASSUMPTIONS AND TENETS OF COGNITIVE BEHAVIOR THERAPY

Like psychodynamic models of psychotherapy, cognitive behavior models might best be described as a "school of thought" rather than as a unified theory (Reinecke & Freeman, 2003). As alternative models vary both conceptually and in practice, it can be difficult to define the scope of cognitive behavior therapy. Cognitive models might usefully be characterized along a continuum ranging from radical constructivism to behaviorally oriented rationalism. Despite conceptual distinctions among these approaches, they share a number of fundamental assumptions (Dobson & Dozois, 2001; Reinecke & Freeman, 2003).

First, the way individuals interpret events and situations mediates how they subsequently behave and feel. Beliefs are proposed to interact in a transactional manner with affect and behavior, with their resulting effects on events in the individual's environment. Thus, human experience and behavior are the products of an ongoing interaction between specific, related "person variables" (beliefs and cognitive processes, emotions, and behavior) and environmental variables. These variables influence one another in a reciprocal manner over the course of time. Thus, there is no primary cause. Rather, each is seen as both an initiator and a product inherent to a transactional process.

Second, the assignment of meaning of events and situations is an active and ongoing process. The construing of events allows individuals to derive or abstract a sense of meaning from their experiences and permits them to understand events with the goal of establishing their "personal environment" and of responding to events. As a result, behavioral and emotional functioning are seen as goal-directed and adaptive. From this perspective, humans are seen as active users and seekers of information.

Third, individuals develop idiosyncratic belief systems that guide their behavior. Beliefs and assumptions influence an individual's perceptions and memories, and lead the memories to be activated by specific stimuli or events. The individual is rendered sensitive to specific "stressors," including both external events and internal emotional experiences. Beliefs and assumptions contribute to a proclivity to attend selectively to and recall information that confirms the content of the belief system, and to fail to notice information that is inconsistent with those beliefs.

Fourth, stressors contribute to the impairment of an individual's cognitive processing and activate maladaptive coping responses. A system is established in which the activation of maladaptive coping behaviors contributes to the maintenance of aversive environmental events and the consolidation of the belief system. The person who believes, for example, that "others are unhelpful and do not care about me" might withdraw from interacting with others or alienate him/herself from family and friends, thus strengthening their belief in the unsupportive nature of others and the importance of reducing time spent in social behaviors.

Fifth, the cognitive model proposes specificity of cognitions to types of problems (e.g., the cognitive specificity hypothesis). Clinical syndromes and affective states can be distinguished by the specific content of the belief system and the cognitive processes that are activated. For example, depressed individuals tend to view themselves as incompetent and defective, whereas anxious individuals are inclined to see themselves as vulnerable to danger and unable to cope effectively with these potential threats.

Additionally, other theorists have attempted to identify the fundamental characteristics of cognitive behavior therapies. As Dobson and Dozois (2001) note, each assumes that (a) cognitive activity affects behavior; (b) cognitive activity may be monitored and changed, and (c) that behavioral and emotional change may be effected through cognitive change. In addition, these models implicitly assume that (d) cognitive processes are ongoing, active, and adaptive; (e) affective, behavioral, and cognitive factors interact in a reciprocal manner over time, and (f) that there is a relationship between cognitive contents (i.e., what a person thinks), cognitive processes (i.e., how they use this information), and the occurrence of specific symptoms (Reinecke & Freeman, 2003). Although there are different classes or types of cognitive behavior therapy, all are based on a cognitive mediation paradigm, that is to say, they all assume that internal, covert cognitive processes mediate human adaptation, and that changes in cognition can lead to behavioral and emotional change.

## EFFICACY AND EFFECTIVENESS OF COGNITIVE BEHAVIOR THERAPY

The conditions described here indicate their response to the use of cognitive behavior therapy, as shown by empirical studies.

### Depression

The results of empirical outcome studies support the role of cognitive behavior therapy in successfully treating depression (Hollon & Shelton, 2001; Robinson, Berman, & Neimeyer, 1990). A number of randomized controlled trials that have been published in recent years support the utility of cognitive behavior therapy for treating depression among adults (for reviews see: DeRubeis & Crits-Christoph, 1998; Hollon, Thase, & Markowitz, 2002; Lambert & Davis, 2002) and youths (see Curry, 2001; Harrington, Whittaker, Shoe-bridge, & Campbell, 1998; Reinecke, Ryan, & DuBois, 1998). In fact, Dobson's (Dobson, 1989) meta-analysis of outcome studies indicated a greater degree of change for cognitive behavior therapy compared with a waiting-list or no-treatment control, pharmacotherapy, behavior therapy, or other types of psychotherapies. Additionally, initial findings indicated that relapse and recurrence rates were lower for patients who received cognitive behavior therapy than for those who had received medications. Thus, cognitive therapy appears to offer sustained benefits (Hollon, Shelton, & Loosen, 1991) for persons with depression.

### Anxiety Disorders

Cognitive behavior models and interventions have been proposed for a range of clinical disorders and conditions. These models have been put to empirical test, and treatments derived from them have received substantial empirical support. Generalized anxiety disorder (GAD), for example, can be understood as stemming from deficits in the regulation of affect in conjunction with a desire to avoid worry

(Mennin, Turk, Heimberg, & Carmin, 2003). Controlled outcome studies suggest that cognitive behavior therapy may be helpful in reducing anxiety among patients with GAD and that gains are maintained over time (Blowers, Cobb, & Mathews, 1987; Borkovec & Costello, 1993; White, Keenan, & Brooks, 1992).

Additionally, a number of protocols have been developed based on cognitive behavior models of panic disorder (Clark, Salkovskis, & Chalkley, 1985; Clark et al., 1994; Craske, Brown, & Barlow, 1991). These protocols typically consist of a psychoeducational explanation of panic attacks, the presentation of a cognitive rationale, cognitive restructuring, relaxation training, controlled breathing, exposure to anxiety-provoking cues, and panic induction (Hofmann, 2003; Hofmann & Spiegel, 1999). Controlled outcome studies indicate that these approaches are superior to wait-list, medication, pill placebo, and relaxation training controls (Beck, Sokol, Clark, Berchick, & Wright, 1992; Sokol, Beck, Greenberg, Berchick, & Wright, 1989). Given the strength of these findings, cognitive behavior therapy has been recognized as an efficacious treatment for panic disorder by both the American Psychiatric Association (1998) and the Division of Clinical Psychology of the American Psychological Association (Chambless et al., 1996).

Research on social anxiety, completed in recent years, has led to important advances in its conceptualization and treatment (Clark & Wells, 1995; Rapee, 1997). Cognitive factors associated with social anxiety include negative self-evaluations, magnified perceptions of criticism or negative evaluation by others, attentional and memory biases, heightened sensitivity to others' behavior, and the belief that one should be able to control others' reactions and impressions. Cognitive behavior interventions, including psychoeducation, relaxation training, identification of maladaptive thoughts and expectations, rational disputation, social skills training, and in-vivo exposure, have been developed during recent years (Butler & Wells, 1995; Chambless & Hope, 1996; Merluzzi, 1996).

Outcome studies indicate that these approaches are superior to wait-list and supportive therapies, and that gains tend to be maintained over time (Taylor, 1996; Wilson & Rapee, 2003).Wait-list controls refer to patients who receive no active treatment for a prescribed period of time (typically 2–8 weeks) before being randomly assigned to an active treatment arm. They may complete symptoms inventories or meet with clinicians to discuss their concerns during the wait-list period. Wait-list conditions, as such, may be viewed as an attempt to control for spontaneous improvement and expectation effects after an individual has been accepted into a treatment trial. Individuals receiving supportive therapy, like those in an active treatment condition, will meet with a therapist on a regular basis and will complete symptom inventories. Supportive therapy may be seen as an attempt to control for therapist attention, treatment expectancy effects, as well as the effects of "non-specific" therapeutic factors, such as therapeutic warmth and positive regard (Taylor, 1996; Wilson & Rapee, 2003).

## Bipolar Disorder

Although treatment protocols have been developed for cognitive therapy with bipolar patients (Basco & Rush, 1996; Otto & Reilly-Harrington, 2002), the best-supported and most widely accepted form of treatment for these disorders continues to be pharmacotherapy. Although useful, antidepressant and mood stabilizing medications often are not entirely effective (Gitlin, Swendsen, Heller, & Hammen, 1995). Relapse and recurrence rates for both depressive and manic episodes are unacceptably high, and poor medication compliance is a significant problem. With this in mind, clinical researchers have developed psychosocial treatments to assist with the management of these disorders.

Case studies and noncontrolled research suggests that cognitive-behavioral interventions may be useful in alleviating dysphoria, in improving medication compliance, and in enhancing general adjustment among patients with bipolar disorder (Bauer, McBride, Chase, Sachs, & Shea, 1998). The results of several randomized controlled trials also have been promising (Scott, 2001; Scott, Garland, & Moorhead, 2001; Lam, 2000; Perry, 1999; Zaretsky, 1999) and suggest that cognitive behavior therapy may be a useful adjunct to medications.

Cognitive behavior models and treatments have also been developed for such diverse problems as body dysmorphic disorder (Veale, Gournay, Dryden, &. Boocock, 1996; Veale & Riley, 2001), obsessive-compulsive disorder (Clark & Purdon, 2003), anger management (Dahlen & Deffenbacher, 2001), psychotic disorders (Chadwick, Birchwood, & Trower, 1996; Haddock & Slade, 1996; Tarrier et al., 1998), marital problems (Epstein & Schlesinger, 2003), and eating disorders (Fairburn, Shafran, & Cooper, 1998; Le Grange, 2003).

# HYPNOSIS IN TREATMENT

Hypnosis has a long history in the fields of psychology and psychiatry. How long depends, at least in part, on how clinical hypnosis is defined. A sensible argument can be made that it dates at least to the time of Jean Martin Charcot, who in 1873, described the treatment of a patient with hysterical paralysis by making a "suggestion in the waking state" (p. 316). Traditional approaches to hypnotherapy have typically involved the induction of a trance or hypnotic state in a client, during which the therapist makes suggestions for symptom reduction. During this state, the therapist makes suggestions for a patient to experience changes in sensation, perception, thinking, or behavior. A hypnotic induction is used to establish a hypnotic context that typically includes relaxation instructions. Hypnosis, from this perspective, may be seen as an independent modality of therapy comparable to psychodynamic, behavioral, or cognitive behavior approaches (Kirsch, Montgomery, & Sapirstein, 1995).

More recently, however, hypnosis has been used as an adjunct to other forms of psychotherapy (Kirsch et al., 1995; Rhue, Lynn, & Kirsch, 1993). Contemporary hypnotherapy differs both conceptually and in practice from traditional approaches. Rather than relying on hypnotic suggestion as the primary means of symptom relief, today's hypnotherapy consists of incorporating hypnosis into an established therapeutic modality. Thus, a range of therapeutic techniques is introduced after a hypnotic trance has been induced. Empirically supported interventions, such as those used in CBT, may be used in conjunction with hypnosis by incorporating suggestions for symptom relief once a hypnotic state has been induced. As Kirsch et al. (1995) suggest, the question to be answered is not whether hypnosis works better or worse than another therapeutic modality, but whether it enhances the effectiveness of another intervention.

Research on hypnosis was, for many years, limited to psychodynamic hypnotherapy. Since the early 1980's, however, empirical attention has been directed toward the use of hypnosis in conjunction with other forms of psychotherapy, including cognitive behavior interventions. As Kirsch et al. (1995) rightly note, distinctions between these modalities have not always been clear given the use of imagery and relaxation in many forms of behavioral and cognitive psychotherapy.

How might hypnosis enhance psychotherapy? Answers to this question vary depending on the conceptual view of hypnosis one adopts. Traditional hypnotherapists contend that an altered state of consciousness can be produced by hypnotic inductions in suggestible individuals. It is proposed that in this state individuals experience markedly increased suggestibility, greater clarity and intensity of imagery, increased tolerance for logical incongruities, and more primary process thinking. From this perspective, the benefits of the addition of hypnosis to an intervention stem from the induction of the hypnotic trance, which may be seen as a unique cognitive state.

Cognitive behavior theorists and researchers, however, have suggested that a different process may be at play. Rather than arguing for a unique, qualitatively distinct hypnotic state, these theorists suggest that the effects of hypnosis on therapy outcome occurs through individuals' expectations and beliefs (Barber, 1985; Coe, 1993; Kirsch, 1985, 1990). The hypnotic state is not seen as a distinct level of consciousness, but as a form of relaxed, reflective awareness. Although cognitive behavior and hypnotic state theorists may agree that hypnosis may affect treatment outcomes, they differ with regard to proposed mechanisms for this effect.

Controlled outcome research indicates that the effect sizes for hypnosis are modest. Clinical hypnosis is not recognized as an empirically supported treatment for any psychiatric disorder at this time. One might anticipate, then, that the additive benefit of supplementing cognitive behavior therapy with hypnotherapy would be small. Indeed, Kirsch et al. (1995) highlight several important reasons for expecting modest effect sizes. First is the role of hypnosis as an adjunct to treatment. Many of the procedures used in standard cognitive behavior therapy (such as guided imagery) are similar to those used in hypnosis. The effects of adding these components to a standard cognitive behavior treatment program may be small relative to the main effects of the treatment. Second, there are marked individual differences in hypnotizability. Whereas some individuals may be readily hypnotized, others may be unable to be hypnotized. Therefore, the addition of a hypnotic component to cognitive behavior therapy is likely to benefit only a subset of all treatment participants. As Levitt (1993) points out, only those who are sufficiently predisposed to hypnosis are likely to gain significantly from its use as an adjunct to psychotherapy. Third, not only do individuals differ in their ability to be hypnotized, but they also vary in their beliefs and expectancies about hypnosis itself. Thus, it might be expected that only those with positive attitudes and expectations regarding hypnosis would benefit from its addition to their therapy. Moreover, it is reasonable to anticipate that those with negative beliefs and expectations regarding hypnosis may show limited treatment success with it. Last, and perhaps most importantly, there are striking similarities between typical hypnotic inductions and standard relaxation training utilized in many cognitive behavior treatments. As Kirsch et al. (1995) note,

> . . . all that is needed to convert relaxation training into a hypnotic induction is the addition of the word hypnosis. Instead of saying "more and more deeply relaxed," the therapist says "more and more deeply hypnotized." Because relaxation training is a frequent component of behavior therapy, the addition of hypnosis to behavior therapy may consist of little more than the use of the word "hypnosis." (p. 215)

It is conceivable that the addition of a hypnotic condition so similar to a standard cognitive behavior intervention may in fact be superfluous.

## EMPIRICAL STATUS OF HYPNOSIS AS AN ADJUNCT TO COGNITIVE BEHAVIOR THERAPY

Hypnosis has been used as an adjunct to cognitive behavior therapy for a variety of problems. Combined hypnotic and cognitive behavior treatments have been employed to treat pain, anxiety disorders, obesity, smoking cessation, depression, and hypertension. The previously discussed limitations on effect sizes notwithstanding, some empirical evidence suggests that hypnosis may offer a statistically, and perhaps clinically, significant benefit when used as an adjunct to cognitive behavior psychotherapy.

The results of several meta-analyses suggest that hypnosis may significantly enhance cognitive behavior therapy. In their meta-analysis of 18 studies comparing cognitive behavior therapy in a hypnotic context to standard cognitive behavior therapy for a range of problems, Kirsch et al. (1995) found a significant mean effect size for hypnosis as an adjunct to treatment. Thus, the addition of hypnosis seemed to enhance treatment gains. Significant positive mean effect sizes for hypnosis as an adjunct were consistent across self-report and behavioral assessments of change. The authors concluded that clients receiving cognitive behavior hypnotherapy were more improved at the end of treatment than 70% of those clients who received only cognitive behavior treatment. Thus, hypnosis appeared to enhance treatments for a range of problems, and significant findings were not limited to one type of outcome measure.

Many of the studies reviewed by Kirsch et al. (1995) were methodologically flawed, however. As a consequence, it is difficult to have confidence in the results obtained. Several of the studies, for example, did not use standardized measures of clinical outcomes or blind, independent evaluators. Moreover, differences often existed in the length of treatment between hypnotic and nonhypnotic conditions. It is possible, as such, that the differences observed may have stemmed from variations in the intensity of the clinical intervention (a "dose effect") or increased levels of therapist attention. Finally, some studies included only clients who were determined to be highly hypnotizable. They did not employ an intent-to-treat design with random assignment. Since that time, a number of methodologically sound studies have been completed. Shortcomings in early studies, and the recent publication of several well-controlled outcome studies, indicate that a closer examination of the findings on cognitive behavior hypnotherapy may be warranted.

## Anxiety Disorders

The use of cognitive behavior techniques, such as systematic desensitization, cognitive restructuring, exposure, and relaxation, for treatment of anxiety disorders is not new (for reviews see Lyddon & Jones, 2001; O'Donohue, Fisher, & Hayes, 2003; Reinecke & Clark, 2003). Hypnotherapists have argued that these techniques can readily be used in conjunction with hypnosis and provide more benefits to clients than if cognitive behavior therapies are applied alone.

The results of several recent studies lend some support to this claim. For example, hypnosis was found to enhance the effects of cognitive behavior therapy for public speaking anxiety (Schoenberger, Kirsch, Gearan, Montgomery, & Pastyrnak, 1997). Both interventions included in-vivo exposure and cognitive restructuring, whereas the hypnotic condition also included hypnotic induction and suggestions in place of relaxation training. Although both treatment conditions (e.g., hypnotic adjunct to cognitive behavior therapy and nonhypnotic cognitive behavior therapy) were found to reduce anxiety on self-report measures relative to a control group receiving no intervention, only those in the hypnotic treatment differed significantly from the control group behavioral and subjective indices of anxiety during an extemporaneous speech. Additionally, clients treated in the hypnotic condition showed faster declines in anxiety than those treated in cognitive behavior therapy alone. However, in their study of panic disorder with agoraphobia, Van Dyck and Spinhoven (1997) did not find that hypnosis enhanced effects of cognitive behavior therapy. Clients in the exposure group did not differ from those in the exposure-plus-hypnosis group. Findings regarding the efficacy of hypnotherapy as an adjunctive treatment for anxiety disorders, then, are mixed. Additional controlled outcome studies are warranted.

## Smoking Cessation

Several studies have investigated the role of hypnosis as an adjunct to cognitive behavior therapy for smoking cessation. In a controlled study of group psychotherapy, Jeffrey, Jeffrey, Greuling, and Gentry (1985) found that a combined hypnotic and cognitive behavior therapy for smoking cessation treatment was superior to a wait-list control condition. Thirty-one percent of the subjects in the treatment condition abstained from smoking after 3 months compared to none of the wait-list subjects. These results were replicated in a subsequent study comparing the same conditions with larger sample sizes (Jeffrey & Jeffrey, 1988). Unfortunately, comparisons were not made between cognitive behavior therapy with and cognitive behavior therapy without an adjunctive hypnosis component. It is not possible to conclude from these studies, then, whether hypnosis serves as a clinically useful adjunctive treatment for smoking.

This comparison was made, however, in two psychotherapy outcome studies. Schubert (1983), for example, evaluated the effects of hypnotic cognitive behavior therapy and a similar treatment without hypnosis. Both treatments employed a cognitive restructuring component and differed in their use of hypnosis versus relaxation. Schubert found lower smoking relapse rates between the two treatments compared to a wait-list control. Differences were not found, however, in the relative effectiveness of the two treatment conditions. The addition of hypnosis to CBT did not appear to enhance the effectiveness of psychotherapy.

More recently, Frank, Umlauf, Wonderlich, and Ashkanazi (1986) examined differences between a cognitive behavior treatment comprised of self-monitoring, problem solving, and self-reinforcement and a hypnosis and problem-solving treatment. At a 6-month follow-up, these authors found no differences between the two treatments in smoking abstinence rates. Once again, the addition of hypnosis did not appear to enhance the effectiveness of cognitive behavior therapy.

## Obesity

A number of studies in addition to those reviewed by Kirsch et al. (1995) have examined the role of hypnosis as an adjunct to cognitive behavior therapy for obesity. Bolocofsky, Spinler, and Coulthard-Morris (1985) compared the utility of two behavioral management programs, one with and one without hypnosis, for weight reduction. Subjects were randomly assigned to one of the two conditions. Each treatment consisted of a weight diary, stimulus control, relaxation, and reinforcement contingencies for utilizing the treatment program. The hypnotic condition included hypnotic induction, suggestions, and self-hypnosis employed outside of treatment sessions. At post-treatment the groups did not differ in the average reduction of weight among subjects. However, at 8-month and 2-year follow-ups, subjects in the hypnotic condition continued to lose weight. In contrast, subjects in the cognitive behavior group did not show continued weight loss. Additionally, at these follow-ups, those in the hypnotic condition reported greater compliance with the treatment regimen.

These findings suggest that a combination of CBT and clinical hypnosis may be more effective than CBT alone in facilitating weight reduction.

## Pain

Although a number of studies suggest that hypnosis may be effective for reducing pain associated with medical procedures (Haanen et al., 1991; Kuttner, Bowman, & Teasdale, 1988; Patterson, Everett, Burns, & Marvin, 1992) and headaches (ter Kuile et al., 1994), few studies have examined effects of cognitive behavior therapy, with or without hypnosis, for managing experimental pain. The results of several well-controlled early studies yielded contradictory findings (Miller & Bowers, 1986, 1993; Spanos, Ollerhead, & Gwynn, 1985/ 1986).

More recently, Milling, Kirsch, Meunier, and Levine (2002) compared the effects of hypnosis, stress inoculation training, stress inoculation training with hypnosis, and a no treatment control in the reduction of pain. Subjects were randomly assigned to one of the four conditions. The authors found that the three treatment conditions significantly reduced pain. No differences in pain reduction were observed, however, between the three active treatment conditions. The hypothesis that hypnosis would facilitate cognitive behavior pain management was not supported.

In a subsequent study, Milling, Levine, and Meunier (2003) randomly assigned subjects to one of six conditions: stress inoculation training, stress inoculation training with hypnosis, nonhypnotic suggestions, hypnotic suggestions, hypnotic induction, and a no-treatment control. As in their earlier study, these authors found that each of the active treatments reduced pain relative to the control condition. Once again, however, no differences were observed between the active treatments. As before, hypnosis did not enhance cognitive behavior pain management. Curiously, no enhancement effect was found under conditions optimized to find such an effect. In order to detect such an effect, this study explicitly employed a large sample of participants who were determined to be high in suggestibility.

Taken together, research on hypnotic enhancement of cognitive behavior treatment has yielded inconsistent results. Consistent with previous reviews (Kirsch et al., 1995), evidence indicates that hypno-therapy may be a useful adjunctive treatment for weight reduction. Nonetheless, hypnotherapy has not consistently been found to be an efficacious treatment for anxiety, smoking, or pain management. It is worth acknowledging, though, that there have been few well-controlled, randomized trials evaluating the effectiveness of hypno-sis as an adjunct to cognitive behavior therapy (Schoenberger, 2000). Although cognitive hypnotherapy has generally outperformed wait-list or no-treatment control conditions in reduction of clinical symp-toms, findings comparing hypnotic enhancement treatments to cog-nitive behavior treatment have been equivocal (Schoenberger).

## MEDIATION OF CHANGE IN HYPNOSIS

As we have seen, hypnosis *may* enhance treatment gains in cognitive behavior therapies for some patients under some conditions. As is so often the case in psychotherapy research, the more central question then arises—"Which treatment is most effective for which patient under which conditions?" Our focus shifts from asking the question "Does the treatment work?" to identifying predictors of treatment response and to understanding mechanisms of therapeutic improve-ment. Unfortunately, moderators and mediators of change in hypno-sis and combined cognitive behavior hypnotherapy have received little study. Our understanding of the mechanism of therapeutic change in hypnosis is, at best, rudimentary. We do not have an answer to the simple, basic question, "How does hypnosis work?"

Baron and Kenny (1986) defined a mediator as a "generative mechanism through which a focal independent variable is able to influence the dependent variable of interest" (p. 1173). It is a variable that changes in response to treatment, is associated with improve-ment, and can plausibly serve as a mechanism of change. Traditional state theorists in the hypnosis literature have suggested that there are distinct properties of the hypnotic trance that may be the mecha-nisms through which hypnosis affects clinical outcomes. Alterna-tively, cognitive behavior theorists have proposed that individual beliefs and expectancies about the treatment process mediate treat-ment gains. These response expectancies have been defined as ex-pectations regarding an individual's nonvolitional reactions to situational cues. Evidence indicates that response expectancies may be associated with treatment effectiveness. It appears, for example, that expectancies of treatment effectiveness may produce pain relief due to the generation of a cognitive set (Milling, Kirsch, Allen, & Reutenauer, 2002; Milling & Breen, 2003; Montgomery, Weltz, Seltz, & Bovbjerg, 2002). Expectancy effects may be more pronounced in treatments employing hypnosis than in other modalities of psycho-therapy, and may act as partial mediators of outcome for patients receiving a combination of cognitive behavior therapy and hypnosis. The possibility exists, as such, that a cognitive variable—treatment expectancy—may serve as a mediator of clinical improvement in pain management.

## MODERATORS OF CHANGE

Baron and Kenny (1986) define a moderator as a variable that "parti-tions a focal independent variable into subgroups that establish its domains of maximal effectiveness in regard to a given dependent variable" (p. 1173). Put another way, moderators are variables that, although not influenced by the treatment itself, can influence the treatment response. These are baseline, prerandomization charac-teristics of individuals that influence the treatment effect size. Mod-erators of hypnosis have been found. Hypnotic suggestibility, for example, appears to moderate the effects of hypnotic treatments for pain reduction (Milling & Breen, 2003; Montgomery et al., 2002). However, investigations of moderators in combined cognitive behav-ior and hypnotic treatments have received less attention in the literature and the results are less clear.

Patients' expectancies of treatment outcome may also serve as moderators of treatment gains in hypnotherapy for anxiety. Schoen-berger, Kirsch, Gearan, Montgomery, and Pastyrnak (1997), for exam-ple, found that labeling relaxation training as "hypnotic" appeared to enhance treatment effectiveness for social phobia. They observed that the "hypnotic" treatment was associated with greater expectan-cies for change among subjects than was the nonhypnotic treatment, and that these expectancies were associated with improved treat-ment results.

Some hypnotherapists have argued that only clients who are highly susceptible to hypnosis should be expected to benefit from hypnotic components of interventions. Hypnosis should, quite reasonably, be most effective for highly hypnotizable clients (Schoenberger, 2000). However, empirical evidence for differential treatment outcomes in cognitive hypnotherapy that depends on hypnotizability is mixed. Whereas Van Dyck and Spinhoven (1997) found a significant relationship between hypnotizability and clinical improvement for subjects in a hypnotic treatment group, Schoenberger et al. (1997) did not. Additional research on obesity and smoking cessation have also produced mixed findings (Levitt, 1993).

A number of variables have been found to moderate the effectiveness of cognitive psychotherapy. These include gender, ethnicity, SES, diagnosis, comorbidity, duration, and severity of illness, intellectual level, and social support. Unfortunately, relationships between these variables and treatment outcome have received little attention in the hypnotherapy literature. In their meta-analysis, Kirsch et al. (1995) did not observe that the type of problem being treated was associated with variations in effect sizes. More recently, Milling and Breen (2003) and Milling Kirsch, Allen, and Reutenauer (2002) found that hypnotic suggestibility did not moderate combined hypnotic and cognitive behavior treatments. The lack of evidence for moderators in this study, particularly for hypnosis variables such as suggestibility, is unexpected given the accumulated evidence showing moderation of treatment gains by suggestibility in purely hypnotic treatment studies (Montgomery et al., 2002). To date, no significant moderators of the effectiveness of cognitive hypnotherapy have been identified.

Moderator and mediator analyses can be methodologically challenging (Kraemer, Wilson, Fairburn, & Agras, 2002; Schatzberg & Kraemer, 2000). As they are secondary analyses, moderator analyses have lower power than the primary comparisons. They consequently are at risk for type II error (false negative results). Studies must be designed with these power considerations in mind. Moreover, measurement difficulties can complicate research in this area. As Schoenberger (2000) notes, several scales used to assess hypnotizability may be measuring suggestibility. In order to assess hypnotizability, it may be necessary to administer these measures twice, once without the hypnotic induction and once with the induction (Schoenberger). The difference between the two scores would provide an assessment of responsiveness to hypnosis rather than to the suggestions (Schoenberger). The timing of these hypnotizability assessments, however, can also be problematic. The administration of measures of hypnotizability prior to treatment can influence expectations regarding the usefulness of hypnosis; that is to say, patients who perceive that they have done poorly on a measure of hypnotizability may come to expect that the treatment they will receive will be ineffective. Although assessment of hypnotizability at the posttreatment phase may be preferred, this method is also not without potential problems. When measured after treatment, participants' experiences during treatment may impact their responsiveness to subsequent hypnotic inductions (Schoenberger). These assessments assume, as well, that hypnotizability is, in fact, an individual trait phenomenon, and that it does not vary over time or in response to changes in mood.

Overall, empirical evidence supports cognitive behavior theories regarding potential mediators of change, whereas little consistent evidence has been found for treatment moderators. That said, it should be acknowledged that research on mediators and moderators of change in hypnosis has been limited. The majority of studies supporting the mediating role of expectancies have focused on pain management. Mediators of change with hypnosis and CBT with adjunctive hypnosis need to be examined in studies of other problems. In a similar manner, few studies have examined moderators of change in hypnosis, and none have been adequately powered to detect differences.

# EMPIRICALLY SUPPORTED TREATMENTS

Efforts in the past decade have been made to develop criteria for empirically supported psychotherapies. A task force of the Division of Clinical Psychology (Division 12) of the American Psychological Association developed guidelines defining these therapies (Chambless & Hollon, 1998). Based on these guidelines, three categories of empirically supported psychotherapies have been derived. Treatments may be seen as efficacious if at least two independent studies have demonstrated that the treatment is better than no treatment. Efficacious and specific treatments are those that have two or more independent studies showing that the therapy is superior to another treatment or a placebo. Finally, possibly efficacious therapies are those for which there is one study that has not been replicated.

Specific methodological criteria have been proposed for psychotherapy outcome research for a treatment to be considered an empirically supported therapy. Minimum sample sizes are necessary in order to generate reliable and valid estimates. Chambless and Hollon (1998) recommend 25 to 30 subjects for each treatment group. Participants must be randomly assigned to treatment conditions, with evaluations of clinical improvement completed by independent raters who are blind to the treatment received by the patient. It has been recommended that a range of reliable, objective outcome measures be administered.

Chambless and Hollon (1998) also discussed necessary treatment characteristics. Treatments should be adequate in duration to impact the problem of interest in the treatment groups. Therapists need to be adequately trained and monitored during the period of intervention to assure treatment fidelity. Follow-up evaluations and assessments are recommended to determine whether treatment gains are maintained, and to identify factors associated with relapse and recurrence.

Based on these criteria, hypnosis and adjunctive hypnotherapy do not meet the criteria for an empirically supported therapy. Accordingly, Bolocofsky et al.'s (1985) study was methodologically strong, and suggests that hypnosis may be designated a "possibly efficacious" adjunct to behavioral weight management. Replication of these findings is needed given negative findings within this literature. Additional research is needed for cognitive behavior hypnotherapy to be considered an empirically supported psychotherapy. Schoenberger (2000) recommends that research attention might first be directed to problems for which hypnotic interventions have demonstrated some efficacy, such as anxiety disorders and obesity. We would concur. For hypnosis to be established as an empirically supported adjunctive treatment, however, significant methodological and conceptual difficulties must be overcome.

# CONCLUSION

Cognitive models of psychotherapy have received substantial empirical support during recent years, and treatments based on these approaches have been applied to a wide range of important clinical problems. At the same time, clinicians and investigators have begun to explore the ways in which hypnosis may supplement or facilitate gains achieved with cognitive psychotherapy. Although findings to date have been mixed, they suggest, thus far, that hypnosis may be a useful adjunctive treatment for obesity and anxiety. Our confidence in this conclusion is limited, however, as few well-controlled outcome studies have been completed, and therefore, our understanding of moderators and mediators of change in hypnosis is quite limited.

With these considerations in mind, clinicians and scholars might attempt to develop more refined models for understanding processes of change during hypnosis, and articulate how these proposed processes may or may not be similar to processes of change in cognitive behavior psychotherapy (Dimidjian & Dobson, 2003). It is not sufficient to simply propose that the induction of a hypnotic trance is, by definition, therapeutic, and that hypnotizability is a moderator of therapeutic improvement. Rather, models of therapeutic change must be developed that are congruent with findings from the experimental cognitive psychology literature.

Additional, well-controlled outcome studies will be needed to establish whether hypnosis is an efficacious treatment in its own right, and whether it is a clinically useful adjunct for other forms of psychotherapy, such as CBT. The effectiveness of hypnosis alone, and in conjunction with cognitive behavior psychotherapy, may vary from disorder to disorder. Moreover, one should not anticipate that hypnosis would be an effective intervention for all problems or for all individuals. Our attention, as clinicians and investigators, should be directed to identifying predictors and moderators of therapeutic change. Relations between age, gender, ethnicity, symptom severity, comorbidity, intellectual level, SES, diagnosis, and treatment outcome are worthy of exploration.

Although findings regarding the efficacy of hypnosis in the acute treatment of various disorders have largely been negative, the possibility exists that hypnosis may facilitate relapse prevention, at least for some conditions. Long-term, carefully controlled follow-up studies are needed to address this issue. If the efficacy of hypnosis as a treatment for a specific disorder can be demonstrated, or if it can consistently be shown to facilitate or magnify the effectiveness of an empirically supported treatment, such as CBT, then a more careful exploration of mediators of change will be warranted.

In conclusion, initial findings regarding the efficacy of hypnosis, while mixed, are provocative. We are left, then, with an interesting question—might one of the oldest forms of clinical intervention augment the effectiveness of one of the newest? A good deal of conceptual, clinical, and empirical innovation will be required to answer this question.

# REFERENCES

American Psychiatric Association. (1998). Practice guidelines for the treatment of patients with panic disorder. *American Journal of Psychiatry, 155*, 1–34.

Barber, T. X. (1985). Hypnosuggestive procedures as catalysts for psychotherapies. In S. J. Lynn & P. Garske (Eds.), *Contemporary psychotherapies: Models and methods* (pp. 333–375). Columbus, OH: Merrill.

Baron, R. M., & Kenny, D. A. (1986). The moderator-mediator variable distinction in social psychological research: Conceptual, strategic, and statistical considerations. *Journal of Personality and Social Psychology, 51*, 1173–1182.

Basco, M., & Rush, A. (1996). *Cognitive-behavioral therapy for bipolar disorder.* New York: Guilford.

Bauer, M., McBride, L., Chase, C., Sachs, G., & Shea, N. (1998). Manual-based group psychotherapy for bipolar disorder: A feasibility study. *Journal of Clinical Psychiatry, 59*, 449–455.

Beck, A. T., Sokol, L., Clark, D., Berchick, R., & Wright, F. (1992). A crossover study of focused cognitive therapy for panic disorder. *American Journal of Psychiatry, 149*, 778–783.

Blowers, C., Cobb, J., & Mathews, A. (1987). Generalised anxiety: A controlled treatment study. *Behaviour Research and Therapy, 25*, 493–502.

Bolocofsky, D. N., Spinler, D., & Coulthard-Morris, L. (1985). Effectiveness of hypnosis as an adjunct to behavioral weight management. *Journal of Clinical Psychology, 41*, 35–41.

Borkovec, T., & Costello, E. (1993). Efficacy of applied relaxation and cognitive-behavioral therapy in the treatment of generalized anxiety disorder. *Journal of Consulting and Clinical Psychology, 61*, 611–619.

Butler, G., & Wells, A. (1995). Cognitive-behavioral treatments: Clinical applications. In R. Heimberg, M. Liebowitz, D. Hope, & F. Schneier (Eds.), *Social phobia: Diagnosis, assessment, and treatment* (pp. 310–333). New York: Guilford.

Chadwick, P., Birchwood, M., & Trower, P. (1996). *Cognitive therapy for delusions, voices, and paranoia.* Chichester, UK: Wiley.

Chambless, D. L., & Hollon, S. D. (1998). Defining empirically supported therapies. *Journal of Consulting and Clinical Psychology, 66*, 7–18.

Chambless, D. L., & Hope, D. A. (1996). Cognitive approaches to the psychopathology and treatment of social phobia. In P. M. Salkovskis (Ed.), *Frontiers of
cognitive therapy* (pp. 345–382). New York: Guilford.
Chambless, D. L., Sanderson, W. C., Shoham, V., Johnson, S. B., Pope, K., S.,
Crits-Christoph, P., et al. (1996). An update on empirically validated therapies.
*The Clinical Psychologist, 49*, 5–18.
Charcot, J. (1873). Clinical lectures on certain diseases of the nervous system,
trans. E. P. Hurd (Detroit: G. S. Davis, 1888), lecture 8; original French, Lecons
sur les maladies du systeme nerveux. In W. Sahakian (1968), *History of psychol-
ogy* (p. 316). Itasca, IL: F. E. Peacock.
Clark, D. A., & Purdon, C. (2003). Cognitive theory and therapy of obsessions
and compulsions: A critical re-examination. In M. Reinecke &. D. Clark (Eds.),
*Cognitive therapy across the lifespan: Evidence and practice* (pp. 90–116). Cambridge, UK: Cambridge University Press.
Clark, D. M., Salkovskis, P. M., & Chalkley, A. J. (1985). Respiratory control as
a treatment for panic attacks. *Journal of Behavior Therapy and Experimental
Psychiatry, 16*, 23–30.
Clark, D. M., Salkovskis, P. M., Hackman, A., Middleton, H., Anastasiades, P., &
Gelder, M. (1994). A comparison of cognitive therapy, applied relaxation, and
imipramine in the treatment of panic disorder. *British Journal of Psychiatry,
164*, 759–769.
Clark, D. M., & Wells, A. (1995). A cognitive model of social phobia. In R. Heim-
berg, M. Liebowitz, D. Hope, & F. Schneier (Eds.), *Social phobia: Diagnosis,
assessment, and treatment* (pp. 69–93). New York: Guilford.
Coe, W. C. (1993). Expectations and hypnotherapy. In J. W. Rhue, S. J. Lynn, &
I. Kirsch (Eds.), *Handbook of clinical hypnosis*. Washington, DC: American
Psychological Association.
Craske, M. G., Brown, T. A., & Barlow, D. H. (1991). Behavioral treatment of
panic disorder: A two-year follow-up. *Behavior Therapy, 22*, 289–304.
Curry, J. (2001). Specific psychotherapies for childhood and adolescent depres-
sion. *Biological Psychiatry, 49*, 521–533.
Dahlen, E., & Deffenbacher, J. (2001). Anger management. In W. J. Lyddon & J.
V. Jones (Eds.), *Empirically supported cognitive therapies: Current and future
applications* (pp. 163–181). New York: Springer Publishing.
DeRubeis, R., & Crits-Christoph, P. (1998). Empirically supported individual
and group psychological treatments for adult mental disorders. *Journal of
Consulting and Clinical Psychology, 66*, 37–52.
Dimidjian, S., & Dobson, K. (2003). Processes of change in cognitive therapy.
In M. Reinecke & D. Clark (Eds.), *Cognitive therapy across the lifespan: Evidence
and practice* (pp. 477–506). Cambridge, UK: Cambridge University Press.
Dobson, K. S. (1989). A meta-analysis of the efficacy of cognitive therapy for
depression. *Journal of Consulting and Clinical Psychology, 57*, 414–419.
Dobson, K. S., & Dozois, D. (2001). Historical and philosophical bases of the
cognitive-behavioral therapies. In K. S. Dobson (Ed.), *Handbook of cognitive-
behavioral therapies* (Vol. 1, pp. 201–274). New York: Guilford.
Epstein, N., & Schlesinger, S. (2003). Treatment of family problems. In M. Reinecke, F. Dattilio, & A. Freeman (Eds.), *Cognitive therapy with children and
adolescents* (2nd ed., pp. 304–337). New York: Guilford.

Fairburn, C. G., Shafran, R., & Cooper, Z. (1998). A cognitive behavioural theory of anorexia nervosa. *Behaviour Research and Therapy, 37*, 1–13.

Frank, R. G., Umlauf, R. L., Wonderlich, S. A., & Ashkanazi, G. S. (1986). Hypnosis and behavioral treatment in a worksite smoking cessation program. *Addictive Behaviors, 11*, 59–62.

Gitlin, M., Swendsen, J., Heller, T., & Hammen, C. (1995) Relapse and impairment in bipolar disorder. *American Journal of Psychiatry, 152*(11), 1635–1640.

Haanen, H. C. M., Hoenderdos, H. T. W., van Romunde, L. K. J., Hop, W. C. J., Mallee, C., & Terwiel, P. (1991). Controlled trial of hypnotherapy in the treatment of refractory fibromyalgia. *Journal of Rheumatology, 18*, 72–75.

Haddock, G., & Slade, P. (1996). *Cognitive-behavioural interventions with psychotic disorders*. London: Routledge.

Harrington, R., Whittaker, J., Shoebridge, P., & Campbell, F. (1998). Systematic review of the efficacy of cognitive behaviour therapies in childhood and adolescent depressive disorder. *British Medical Journal, 316*, 1559–1563.

Hofmann, S. (2003). The cognitive model of panic revisited. In M. Reinecke & D. Clark (Eds.), *Cognitive therapy across the lifespan: Evidence and practice* (pp. 117–137). Cambridge, UK: Cambridge University Press.

Hofmann, S. G., & Spiegel, D. A. (1999). Panic control treatment and its applications. *Journal of Psychotherapy Practice and Research, 8*, 3–11.

Hollon, S., & Shelton, R. (2001). Treatment guidelines for major depressive disorder. *Behavior Therapy, 32*, 235–258.

Hollon, S., Shelton, R., & Loosen, P. (1991). Cognitive therapy and pharmacotherapy for depression. *Journal of Consulting and Clinical Psychology, 59*, 88–99.

Hollon, S., Thase, M., & Markowitz, J. (2002). Treatment and prevention of depression. *Psychological Science in the Public Interest, 3*, 39–77.

Jeffrey, T. B., & Jeffrey, L. K. (1988). Exclusion therapy in smoking cessation: A brief communication. *International Journal of Clinical and Experimental Hypnosis, 36*, 70–74.

Jeffrey, T. B., Jeffrey, L. K., Greuling, J. W., & Gentry, W. R. (1985). Evaluation of a brief group treatment package including hypnotic induction for maintenance of smoking cessation: A brief communication. *International Journal of Clinical and Experimental Hypnosis, 33*, 95–98.

Kazdin, A., & Weisz, J. (Eds.). (2003). *Evidence-based psychotherapies for children and adolescents*. New York: Guilford.

Kirsch, I. (1985). Response expectancy as a determinant of experience and behavior. *American Psychologist, 40*, 1189–1202.

Kirsch, I. (1990). *Changing expectations: A key to effective psychotherapy*. Pacific Grove, CA: Brooks-Cole.

Kirsch, I., Montgomery, G., & Sapirstein, G. (1995). Hypnosis as an adjunct to cognitive-behavioral psychotherapy: A meta-analysis. *Journal of Consulting and Clinical Psychology, 63*, 214–220.

Kraemer, H., Wilson, G., Fairburn, C., & Agras, W. (2002). Mediators and moderators of treatment effects in randomized clinical trials. *Archives of General Psychiatry, 59*, 877–883.

Kuttner, L., Bowman, M., & Teasdale, M. (1988). Psychological treatment of distress, pain, and anxiety for young children with cancer. *Developmental and Behavioral Pediatrics, 9*, 374–381.

Lam, D., Bright, J., Jones, S., Hayward, P., Schuck, N., Chisholm, D., et al. (2000). Cognitive therapy for bipolar disorders: A pilot study of relapse prevention. *Cognitive Therapy and Research, 24,* 503–520.

Lambert, M., & Davis, M. (2002). Treatment for depression: What the research says. In M. Reinecke & M. Davison (Eds.), *Comparative treatments of depression* (pp. 21–46). New York: Springer Publishing.

Le Grange, D. (2003). The cognitive model of bulimia nervosa. In M. Reinecke & D. Clark (Eds.), *Cognitive therapy across the lifespan: Evidence and practice* (pp. 293–314). Cambridge, UK: Cambridge University Press.

Levitt, E. E. (1993). Hypnosis in the treatment of obesity. In J. W. Rhue, S. J. Lynn, & I. Kirsch (Eds.), *Handbook of clinical hypnosis* (pp. 533–553). Washington, DC: American Psychological Association.

Lyddon, W., & Jones, J. (Eds.). (2001). *Empirically supported cognitive therapies: Current and future applications.* New York: Springer Publishing.

Mennin, D., Turk, C., Heimberg, R., & Carmin, C. (2003). Focusing on the regulation of emotion: A new direction for conceptualizing and treating generalized anxiety disorder. In M. Reinecke & D. Clark (Eds.), *Cognitive therapy across the lifespan: Evidence and practice* (pp. 60–89). Cambridge, UK: Cambridge University Press.

Merluzzi, T. (1996). Cognitive assessment and treatment of social phobia. In P. W. Corrigan & S. C. Yudofsky (Eds.), *Cognitive rehabilitation for neuropsychiatric disorders* (pp. 167–190). Washington, DC: American Psychiatric Press.

Miller, M. E., & Bowers, K. S. (1986). Hypnotic analgesia and stress innoculation in the reduction of pain. *Journal of Abnormal Psychology, 95,* 6–14.

Miller, M. E., & Bowers, K. S. (1993). Hypnotic analgesia: Dissociated experience or dissociated control. *Journal of Abnormal Psychology, 102,* 29–38.

Milling, L. S., & Breen, A. (2003). Mediation and moderation of hypnotic and cognitive-behavioural pain reduction. *Contemporary Hypnosis, 20,* 81–97.

Milling, L. S., Kirsch, I., Allen, G. J., & Reutenauer, E. L. (2002). *The effects of hypnotic and non-hypnotic suggestion on pain.* Paper presented at the 53rd annual meeting of the Society of Clinical and Experimental Hypnosis, Boston, MA.

Milling, L. S., Kirsch, I., Meunier, S. A., & Levine, M. R. (2002). Hypnotic analgesia and stress inoculation training: Individual and combined effects in analog treatment of experimental pain. *Cognitive Therapy and Research, 26,* 355–371.

Milling, L. S., Levine, M. R., & Meunier, S. A. (2003). Hypnotic enhancement of cognitive-behavioral interventions for pain: An analogue treatment study. *Health Psychology, 22,* 406–413.

Montgomery, G. H., Weltz, C. H., Seltz, M., & Bovbjerg, D. H. (2002). Brief presurgery hypnosis reduces distress and pain in excisional breast biopsy patients. *International Journal of Clinical and Experimental Hypnosis, 50,* 17–32.

O'Donohue, W., Fisher, J., & Hayes, S. (Eds.). (2003). *Cognitive behavior therapy: Applying empirically supported techniques in your practice.* Hoboken, NJ: John Wiley.

Otto, M., & Reilly-Harrington, N. (2002). Cognitive-behavioral therapy for the management of bipolar disorder. In S. Hofmann & M. Tompson (Eds.), *Treating chronic and severe mental disorders: A handbook of empirically-supported interventions* (pp. 116–130). New York: Guilford.

Patterson, D. R., Everett, J. J., Burns, G. L., & Marvin, J. A. (1992). Hypnosis for the treatment of burn pain. *Journal of Consulting and Clinical Psychology, 60*, 713–717.

Perry, A., Tarrier, N., Morriss, R., McCarthy, E., & Limb, K. (1999). Randomized control trial of efficacy of teaching patients with bipolar disorder to identify early symptoms of relapse and obtain treatment. *British Medical Journal, 318*, 149–153.

Rapee, R. M. (1997). Potential role of childrearing practices in the development of anxiety and depression. *Clinical Psychology Review, 17*, 47–67.

Reinecke, M., Ryan, N., & DuBois, D. (1998). Cognitive-behavioral therapy of depression and depressive symptoms during adolescence: A review and meta-analysis. *Journal of the American Academy of Child and Adolescent Psychiatry, 37*, 26–34.

Reinecke, M., & Clark, D. (Eds.). (2003). *Cognitive therapy across the lifespan: Evidence and practice.* Cambridge, UK: Cambridge University Press.

Reinecke, M., & Freeman, A. (2003). Cognitive therapy. In A. Gurman & S. Messer (Eds.), *Essential psychotherapies: Theory and practice* (2nd ed., pp. 224–271). New York: Guilford.

Rhue, J. W., Lynn, S. J., & Kirsch, I. (1993). *Handbook of clinical hypnosis.* Washington, DC: American Psychological Association.

Robinson, L., Berman, J., & Neimeyer, R. (1990). Psychotherapy for the treatment of depression: A comprehensive review of controlled outcome research. *Psychological Bulletin, 108*, 30–49.

Schatzberg, A., & Kraemer, H. (2000). Use of placebo control groups in evaluating efficacy of treatment of unipolar major depression. *Biological Psychiatry, 47*, 736–744.

Schoenberger, N. E. (2000). Research on hypnosis as an adjunct to cognitive-behavioral psychotherapy. *International Journal of Clinical and Experimental Hypnosis, 48*, 154–169.

Schoenberger, N. E., Kirsch, I., Gearan, P., Montgomery, P., & Pastyrnak, S. L. (1997). Hypnotic enhancement of a cognitive behavioral treatment for public speaking anxiety. *Behavior Therapy, 28*, 127–140.

Schubert, D. K. (1983). Comparison of hypnotherapy with systematic relaxation in the treatment of cigarette habituation. *Journal of Clinical Psychology, 39*, 198–202.

Scott, J. (2001). Cognitive therapy as an adjunct to medication in bipolar disorder. *British Journal of Psychiatry, 178*(Suppl. 41), 164–168.

Scott, J., Garland, A., & Moorhead, S. (2001). A pilot study of cognitive therapy in bipolar disorders. *Psychological Medicine, 31*(3), 459–467.

Sokol, L., Beck, A., Greenberg, R., Berchick, R., & Wright, F. (1989). Cognitive therapy of panic disorder: A non-pharmacological alternative. *Journal of Nervous and Mental Disease, 177*, 711–716.

Spanos, N., Ollerhead, V. G., & Gwynn, M. I. (1985/1986). The effects of three instructional treatments on pain magnitude and pain tolerance: Implications for theories of hypnotic analgesia. *Imagination, Cognition, and Personality, 5*, 321–337.

Tarrier, N., Yusupoff, L., Kinney, C., McCarthy, E., Gledhill, A., & Haddock, G. (1998). Randomised controlled trial of intensive cognitive behaviour therapy for patients with chronic schizophrenia. *British Medical Journal, 317*, 303–307.

Taylor, S. (1996). Meta-analysis of cognitive-behavioral treatments for social phobia. *Journal of Behavior Therapy and Experimental Psychiatry, 27*, 1–9.

ter Kuile, M., Spinhoven, P., Linssen, A. C. G., Zitman, F. G., Van Dyck, R., & Rooijmans, H. G. M. (1994). Autogenic training and cognitive self-hypnosis for the treatment of recurrent headaches in three different subject groups. *Pain, 58*, 331–340.

Van Dyck, R., & Spinhoven, P. (1997). Does preference for type of treatment matter? A study of exposure in vivo with or without hypnosis in the treatment of panic disorder with agoraphobia. *Behavior Modification, 21*, 172–186.

Veale, D., Gournay, K., Dryden, W., & Boocock, A. (1996). Body dysmorphic disorder: A cognitive-behavioural model and a pilot randomized controlled trial. *Behaviour Research and Therapy, 34*, 717–729.

Veale, D., & Riley, S. (2001). Mirror, mirror on the wall, who is the ugliest of them all? The psychopathology of mirror gazing in body dysmorphic disorder. *Behavior Research and Therapy, 39*, 1381–1393.

White, J., Keenan, M., & Brooks, N. (1992). Stress control: A controlled comparative investigation of large group therapy for generalized anxiety disorder. *Behavioural Psychotherapy, 20*, 97–113.

Wilson, J., & Rapee, R. (2003). Social phobia. In M. Reinecke & D. Clark (Eds.), *Cognitive therapy across the lifespan: Evidence and practice* (pp. 258–292). Cambridge, UK: Cambridge University Press.

Zaretsky, A., Segal, Z., & Gemar, M. (1999). Cognitive therapy for bipolar depression: A pilot study. *Canadian Journal of Psychiatry, 44*, 491–494.

Chapter 4

# Case Conceptualization Model for Integration of Cognitive Behavior Therapy and Hypnosis

Robin A. Chapman

Each clinical case presents the practitioner with several vital questions as to the best treatment. Some practitioners use a "trial-and-error" approach, applying several techniques until one seems to work, while others tend to adhere mechanically to "a one-fits-all" approach. The CBT practitioner must consider a number of possible treatment approaches such as imagery, cognitive restructuring, progressive relaxation training, systematic desensitization, behavioral rehearsal, social skills training, and exposure. This partial list illustrates the complexity of choosing the most appropriate treatment approach for a given client. The use of hypnosis as adjunctive treatment is likely to complicate this important clinical decision, because many therapeutic gains can be accomplished with or without hypnosis, and hypnosis can overlap more conventional behavioral approaches such as progressive muscle relaxation and imagery.

A review of current clinical theories and definitions has suggested several perspectives for the clinical integration of cognitive behavior treatment and hypnosis. These perspectives range from a relabeling of cognitive techniques as hypnosis, to attributing the hypnotic experience to an altered state. The objective of this chapter is to present an integrated clinical approach to the use of hypnosis as an adjunctive treatment to cognitive behavior therapy.

This chapter also explores the decision-making process in selecting hypnosis as treatment and outlines a method to determine when to use a hypnotic technique. The premise of the chapter is that a case conceptualization approach is the best and most efficient method for the integration of hypnosis and cognitive behavior therapy. This is consistent with the practice of cognitive behavior therapy. The practitioner can consider the use of clinical hypnosis using a case conceptualization model, as they would any other cognitive behavioral technique. A detailed case is presented in the chapter, employing both cognitive behavior and hypnotic strategies. This case exemplifies the use of a case conceptualization approach in the process of integrating these strategies. The assessment, case conceptualization, and descriptions of the therapeutic approaches are illustrated. This case follows one year of treatment, over 30 sessions, of a woman who experienced high levels of anxiety and panic attacks.

## CASE CONCEPTUALIZATION

Case conceptualization has been considered one of the critical components of cognitive behavior therapy (Beck, 1995; Freeman, 1992; Persons, 1993) and has been described as the "highest-order clinical skill" (Freeman, 1992, p. 14). The development of a case conceptualization is considered essential for disorders coded on both Axis I and Axis II of the DSM-IV. Case conceptualization is quite useful when cases are confusing or complex, which is likely to occur when the client meets the criteria for a personality disorder.

Case conceptualization has been defined as the therapist's hypothesis of the nature of the psychological mechanisms (schemas) underlying the patient's difficulties (Persons, 1989). Freeman (1992) further defines case conceptualization as a picture or model of the patient's problems. If this conceptualization is well developed, then the patient's thoughts and behaviors become more understandable and predictable. The compilation of a problem list and the development of a hypothesis about the patient's underlying psychological mechanisms (schemas) are considered key components in the cognitive behavior case conceptualization (Freeman, 1992; Persons, Mooney, & Padesky, 1995).

Cognitive behavior case conceptualization is represented by several approaches. Beck (1995), Freeman (1992), and Persons (1989) have developed slightly different approaches to case conceptualization. However, a great deal of uniformity is found when these approaches are compared. Freeman has suggested that an individual case conceptualization must meet several criteria: "(a) It must be useful, (b) simple, (c) theoretically coherent, (d) explain past behavior, (e) make sense of present behavior, and (f) be able to predict future behavior" (p. 16).

The importance of developing treatment conceptualizations has been emphasized by both scholars and practitioners representing a wide range of therapeutic approaches. "Therapy has been taught and practiced as a reactive experience, that is, the therapist responds to what the patient brings to therapy or the specific session. The conceptual model demands that the therapeutic encounter be far more proactive" (Freeman, 1992, p. 14).

Freeman (1992) has suggested the following steps in developing the case conceptualization:

1.  Careful evaluation of the patient's problems based on the relevant historical data typically collected in a structured interview.

2.  The development of hypotheses about why the patient responds in a particular manner, probable formative elements of style, the operative schemas, and the best possible points of entry into the case.

3.  Hypotheses may be shared with the patient for their reaction and redirection in the process.

4.  Finally, the therapist uses the conceptual framework to elicit specific thoughts, assumptions, images, meanings, or beliefs. This aids in the guided discovery process.

This case conceptualization model emphasizes the importance of understanding the patient's schemas. "The schemas are the organizing factors around which perception is built" (Freeman, 1992, p. 22). The schema is the lens through which one defines oneself as an individual and as part of a group. Schemas are usually developed early in the individual's life from experiences and identification with significant others. These experiences may result in schemas of gender, culture, and family.

Schemas can exist on two continua, active or inactive, and noncompelling or compelling. Active schemas govern everyday behavior, while inactive schemas are dormant and lie outside the person's awareness. These latter schemas are activated during times of stress and return to a dormant state once the perceived threat passes. Minimal energy and attention are focused on noncompelling schemas while compelling schemas may dominate the individual's actions. This distinction is important as therapists often address the compelling schemas early in treatment, which only results in the early termination of the client. The focus on noncompelling schema is considerably less anxiety provoking and threatening. This model suggests the use of the critical incident technique for treatment conceptualization. The patient or other significant individuals in the patient's life are asked to describe a situation or incident they perceive as indicative of the patient's problems.

This model also suggests that the working hypotheses can be shared with the patient using a Socratic dialogue. Reframing and the use of visual sketches of how the therapist sees the patient's problems are described. Freeman (personal communication, April 1996) described case conceptualization as beginning at the initial contact with the person. This may occur during the initial telephone contact or while noticing the behavior and appearance of the patient in the waiting room. The therapist begins to develop hypotheses before the formal assessment. This approach is contrary to the accepted idea of a formal assessment before the development of a conceptualization.

In summary, the case conceptualization approach allows the clinician to formulate hypotheses about the client's problems. This includes the identification of current problems and an understanding of the cognitive schemas underlying these current difficulties. Additionally, this allows the clinician to choose appropriate and hopefully helpful cognitive behavioral interventions as well as the utilization of hypnosis to help achieve the goals.

The case conceptualization model allows the practitioner to target specific interventions that will be most helpful to the client and minimize potential treatment obstacles. Clinical practitioners can use the case conceptualization model to guide their consideration of hypnosis as an adjunctive treatment.

The background information, case conceptualization, and summary of sessions that follow are presented to illustrate the clinical decision-making process to use hypnosis in this particular case. Detailed case material is provided to demonstrate the clinical considerations when using hypnosis. The interweaving of cognitive behavioral and hypnotic interventions is described throughout the sessions. However, key points are exemplified in the Treatment Plan section, session 4, and session 16.

## CASE PRESENTATION

Lisa S is a 34-year-old, white, female, single mother with two children, a son 12 years old and a daughter 15. Lisa has always lived in her parent's home, with her two children, throughout her life. Lisa had an associate degree in art and was employed as an operations engineer, adjusting electronic equipment. This client received workman's compensation due to injury sustained while riding in an elevator at work, which resulted in her anxiety and phobic reaction to elevators.

Lisa is the third of four children. She has two brothers, ages 32 and 37, and a sister 39. Lisa described her family as very supportive and loving. She had recently become engaged to a long-term boyfriend.

Lisa described her presenting problems as "anxiety and panic attacks, head pressure, confused thoughts, not sleeping, rapid heart beat, roller coaster sensation, pain in the back and left side from neck to ankle, all caused from being trapped in an elevator for six hours the first time and being trapped a second time for 35 minutes." These problems began one month after Lisa was trapped on an elevator at work. She was trapped alone on the elevator when it stopped between floors and would not respond to the controls. Lisa experienced a second incident in which the elevator doors did not open for 35 minutes. She identified the following as worsening her problems (possible antecedents): elevators, certain sounds like loud talking, the flicker of the television, being alone, traffic, crowds, and waiting.

Lisa had experienced few medical problems in her life. She had surgery for a tubal ligation the fall preceding this treatment. However, since the elevator incidents, she had visited several emergency rooms complaining of chest pains and heart palpitations. Physical examinations revealed no medical cause and diagnosed these complaints as a panic disorder. Lisa was referred to a psychiatrist who prescribed Zoloft 50 mg. bid and Xanax 3 mg. daily. She was treated for back pain and left-side pain due to an injury sustained during a fall in the elevator. She attempted to hoist herself up to the elevator hatch with her belt and fell in the process. Her primary care physician then treated her for bruised and strained muscles. No other medical problems were identified during a recent physical examination.

It is important to note that Lisa denied having prior anxiety or phobic reactions before the initial elevator incident. She reported that since the incident she had been thinking daily about being trapped on the elevator and attempting to extricate herself using the elevator controls and then hoisting herself to the hatch at the top of the compartment using her belt. She then imagined falling and hurting her back and left side.

## Assessment, Diagnosis, and Case Conceptualization (Sessions 1 & 2)

The initial evaluation of Lisa's case consisted of a structured clinical interview. Lisa avoided eye contact and nervously glanced around the office. She sat cross-legged, tapping her foot rapidly on the floor. She spoke quietly at a rapid pace, occasionally looking at me. Lisa indicated that she felt hopeless about the value of therapy, as she had recently completed one year of insight-oriented psychotherapy. She described feeling supported and understood during this course of treatment; however, her anxiety and avoidance had increased. Her therapist referred the case for cognitive behavior treatment for anxiety and the phobic avoidance of elevators.

*Formal Assessment Measures:* The Multimodal Life History Inventory, the Beck Depression Inventory (BDI-II), the Beck Anxiety Inventory (BAI), and the Minnesota Multiphasic Personality Inventory-2 (MMPI-2) were administered.

*Multimodal Life History Inventory* (Lazarus & Lazarus, 1991): This instrument provides a comprehensive, multidimensional collection of client data. Seven modalities are assessed: behavior, affect, sensation, imagery, cognition, interpersonal, and drugs/biology. The Multimodal Life History Inventory is a structured questionnaire that increases the likelihood of obtaining information that allows the development of effective treatment interventions. The inventory was mailed to Lisa for completion before the first session, allowing her adequate time to think about each of the questions and hopefully to increase its accuracy. Lisa reported an additional benefit, "I thought the questions helped me understand my problem more clearly." This inventory may provide the beginning of a reconceptualization of the client's problems. The client may begin to understand the transactional nature of stress and coping, and specific difficulties can be identified as addressable problems.

The following is the modality profile developed from Lisa's responses to the Multimodal Life History Inventory:

*Behavior:*      Loss of control, Outbursts of temper
                 Withdrawal
                 Concentration difficulties
                 Crying
                 Sleep disturbance, insomnia

*Affect:*        Panicky
                 Anxious
                 Fearful
                 Depressed
                 Sad
                 Tense

*Sensation:*     Tension
                 Unable to relax
                 Dizziness
                 Palpitations
                 Rapid Heart Rate
                 Chest pains
                 Excessive sweating
                 Tingling
                 Muscle spasms

| *Imagery:* | (–) | Being trapped in elevator |
| | | Losing control & not coping |
| | (+) | Being happy |
| | | Succeeding |

| *Cognitions:* | "I should be good at everything I do." |
| | "I am a victim of circumstances." |
| | "It is very important to please people." |
| | "Play it safe, don't take risks." |
| | "I should strive for perfection." |
| | "I should never be upset." |

| *Interpersonal:* | Resides with mother |

| *Drugs/Biology:* | Chest pain and palpitations |
| | Swelling in feet and lower leg (result of a fall while trapped in elevator) |
| | Sertraline (Zoloft) 50 mg (bid) & alprazolam (Xanax) 3 mg (daily) |

*BDI and BAI Scales:* Lisa scored 20 on the BDI-II, indicating moderate depression, and scored 36 on the BAI, indicating severe anxiety. These scores are consistent with symptoms of anxiety-related disorders. These scales are given before each session to obtain a measure of progress and to aid in the treatment process.

*MMPI-2:* The MMPI-2 was administered to Lisa for further exploration of the minimal progress in the preceding year of treatment and to clarify the diagnosis. She scored in the elevated range on scales 1 (hypochondrias), scale 3 (conversion hysteria), and scale 8 (schizophrenia). This pattern of scores suggests a diagnosis of depression, a somatoform disorder, and a personality disorder (histrionic and dependent characteristics). She may present her symptoms in a dramatic manner that may obscure the progress and treatment, or become overly dependent on the support of her therapist.

*DSM-IV Diagnosis:* Lisa met the criteria for the following diagnosis:

Axis I—Panic Disorder with Agoraphobia
    Generalized anxiety disorder
    Specific phobia, situational type (elevators)

Axis II—R/O personality disorder not otherwise specified (dependent and histrionic traits)

Axis III—Injury to back and left side, sustained during an escape attempt from the elevator

Axis IV—Psychosocial and environmental problems, unable to work due to phobia (severe) and financial difficulties (moderate)

Axis V—Moderate to serious impairment

The severity of the client's traumatic experience and symptom profile suggested a possible diagnosis of posttraumatic stress disorder. However, the client did not meet the required criteria for this diagnosis.

*Case Conceptualization:* The following case conceptualization was developed from the data given above. Case conceptualization has been considered one of the critical components of cognitive behavior therapy (Beck, 1995; Freeman, 1992; Persons, 1993). Case conceptualization has been defined as the therapist's hypothesis about the nature of the psychological mechanisms (schemas) underlying the client's difficulties (Persons). Freeman further describes case conceptualization as a picture or model of the client's problems. If this conceptualization is well developed, then the client's thoughts and behaviors become more understandable and predictable.

Persons' (1989, 1993) model of case conceptualization was chosen for Lisa's case as it provides a comprehensive approach. The objective of the case conceptualization is to improve the treatment outcome by guiding the therapist's choice of interventions. The client's problems occur at two levels, overt difficulties and underlying mechanisms. The overt difficulties level addresses the client's overt presenting problems while the underlying mechanisms level addresses the underlying psychological mechanisms that produce and maintain the overt difficulties. The process of developing a case conceptualization has seven sections: problem list, hypothesized underlying mechanisms, relation of mechanism to problems, current precipitants, origins of the mechanisms, treatment plan, and predicted obstacles to treatment.

The following is the initial case conceptualization using the material from the clinical interview of Lisa and other assessment instruments, based closely on Persons' (1989) model.

## A. Client's Problems

1. *Panic Attacks.* Lisa met the DSM-IV criteria for panic attacks. She experienced many of the symptoms, including palpitations and accelerated heart rate, sweating, trembling, shortness of breath, feeling of choking, chest pain, nausea, hot flushes, dizziness, feelings of unreality or being detached from oneself, tingling in the hands and feet, fear of dying, fear of going crazy, and fear of doing something uncontrolled. This client reported that she is incapacitated by these attacks. Her typical automatic thoughts include, "I can't control these feelings. Something terrible is going to happen. I might die or go crazy."

2. *Anxiety Symptoms.* Lisa's score on the BAI fell into the severe range. Her symptoms included restlessness, difficulty concentrating, irritability, muscle tension, and difficulty falling asleep. The client reported that her physical symptoms fell into the very severe range. Her specific worries included work, family, finances, and health.

3. *Avoidance.* Lisa appeared to have a phobic avoidance of riding in elevators. She also avoids traveling alone and prefers to be accompanied by a family member.

4. *Sleep Disturbance.* Lisa had difficulty going to sleep and had insomnia on a nightly basis. She often took an additional Alprazolam to help her sleep.

5. *Depressive Symptoms.* Lisa's score on the BDI-II fell into the moderate range. These symptoms appeared to be secondary to her anxiety and avoidance. The client appeared hopeless and felt helpless. She perceived her previous year of therapy as having been unhelpful in the control of her anxiety and fear. Her typical automatic thoughts included, "I think that I am beyond help. Maybe nobody can help me."

6. *Employment Problems.* Lisa is not going to work, as her current job requires travel in multi-story buildings. She cannot return to work due to her phobic avoidance of elevators. Lisa experiences a great deal of anxiety and excessive worry about losing her job and her growing financial difficulty. She

has requested another position that does not require the use of elevators.

The preceding list of problems was developed collaboratively with the client. Another possible problem may be the client's dependent personality style. This was not included on the problem list, as the client did not view her personality style as problematic. The initial focus of treatment was the panic attacks. This was agreed upon collaboratively, as the client identified the panic attacks as her "major problem" because they were "incapacitating."

## B. Hypothesized Underlying Mechanism(s)

These mechanisms (cognitive, behavioral, and biological variables) cause and maintain the client's current problems, usually in interaction with stressful life events.

The cognitive variables included underlying dysfunctional attributes about her self, others, and the world. Lisa's self-attributions may include, "I am helpless, weak, and incompetent." Lisa's attributions about others may include, "Others are competent and can provide support." Her attributions about the world may include, "The world is a lonely and dangerous place." Her possible unconditional statements or conditional statements may include, "If I am abandoned, then I will die. I can function only if I have access to somebody competent."

Her behavioral variables can be best understood from a traditional behavioral analysis perspective. This includes the identification of possible antecedents, behaviors, and consequences. Lisa's behavior may be described as avoidant. Her possible antecedents include worry, apprehension of the worst happening, and misinterpreted physical sensations. The consequences that maintain her behavior may be a reduction in her physical sensations and increased attention from family members.

Her biological variables include a possible physiological vulnerability. This might be determined, in part, by genetic transmission. First-degree relatives of panic disorder clients are more likely to have experienced a panic disorder (Barlow, 1993). This is a possible underlying mechanism for Lisa, although she reports no knowledge that others in her family have experienced anxiety or panic symptoms.

## C. How the Mechanism Produces the Problems

Lisa's panic attacks (Problem 1) may be the result of a misinterpretation of physical sensations and a physiological vulnerability. She is likely to believe that she is helpless and incompetent to cope with the catastrophic thoughts that emerge from this misinterpretation.

Lisa's anxiety symptoms (Problem 2) are the result of similar cognitive and biological variables that are related to her panic disorder. Her primary belief is that the world is a dangerous place.

Lisa's avoidance (Problem 3) is most likely due to her apprehension of additional panic attacks (Problem 1). She clearly avoids traveling without companions. This may be due to her belief that she can function only if she has access to someone competent. Lisa's sleep disturbance (Problem 4) is due to her overall increase in anxiety, which is probably maintained by her belief that the world is a dangerous place. Lisa's depressive symptoms (Problem 5) are due to her belief that she is helpless and incompetent. This belief may have been strengthened by what she perceived as a year of unproductive therapy. Her employment problems are due to the effects of her need to avoid elevators at her workplace (Problem 3). Her job opportunities with her current firm, which would meet this need, are limited given that her work requires travel in elevators, which is common in the Chicago metropolitan area where she lives.

## D. Current Precipitants of the Problem

The precipitant for Lisa's difficulties appears to be the incident where she was trapped alone on an elevator. Her central belief is that she is helpless and incompetent. Lisa believes that she can function only if she has access to somebody competent. When trapped in the elevator, she was cut off for 6 hours from obtaining help, or the support of others, which may have activated these central beliefs.

## E. Origins of the Mechanism

Lisa reported no incidence of turmoil, abuse, or separation while she was growing up. She reported that she always felt supported and encouraged by her parents. However, the cognitive and behavioral patterns that currently affect her life may have resulted from her parents encouraging dependence upon the family instead of providing opportunities for Lisa to develop needed coping, problem solving, and assertiveness skills. Somehow Lisa received the message that the world is a dangerous place and that she needs someone to help her. This is Lisa's central schema, which was dormant and did not govern her day-to-day behavior until the elevator incident. This schema is now quite compelling and produces many automatic thoughts and cognitive distortions for her. This hypothesized schema will be examined and modified as more clinical data is gathered throughout treatment.

## F. Treatment Plan

Lisa's treatment plan called for weekly individual cognitive behavioral therapy. The consideration of hypnosis as an adjunctive treatment strategy as part of treatment is described below.

The possible cognitive behavioral interventions are as follows:

- Provide a cognitive behavioral conceptualization of anxiety and panic.

- Introduce Lisa to the CBT treatment approach. Emphasize collaboration, structure, and problem solving, with eventual reliance on herself.

- Teach Lisa coping skills for anxiety such as relaxation training. These may include breath retraining, imagery, and progressive muscle relaxation components. During the relaxation training, the client should be carefully observed for a paradoxical anxiety reaction. Some individuals respond to relaxation training with an increase in anxiety instead of an experience of relaxation. The experience of additional anxiety may result in premature termination of therapy and increase Lisa's current thoughts of hopelessness about treatment. There will be a focus on the development of cognitive techniques for developing more rational responses and self-instructions for Lisa to cope with anxiety and panic.

- As Lisa develops coping skills for anxiety and panic, her exposure to feared situations can be introduced. Given her frustration and hopelessness with previous therapy, it is of primary importance that she develops a sense of self-efficacy. Lisa should develop confidence in her coping skills before moving onto exposure techniques. Systematic desensitization using imagery and a gradual shaping approach may also be helpful for her.

- As treatment continues, consider the use of hypnosis with Lisa as this may enhance the above-mentioned interventions. Hypnosis is a common technique used in systematic desensitization for relaxation and imagery. Many individuals respond favorably to a hypnotic relaxation intervention while experiencing discomfort when nonhypnotic relaxation procedures are utilized.

- Self-hypnosis may be the most useful approach as this may increase Lisa's sense of self-efficacy and reduce her dependency on the therapist and outside resources. Her hypothesized schemas include: (a) the world is a dangerous place, (b) you can't cope with the world on your own, and (c) you should have someone to help.

## G. Predicted Treatment Obstacles

Lisa might terminate therapy early if she is pushed too quickly into exposure strategies. The client described her previous year of insight-oriented psychotherapy as supportive, but she felt helpless and hopeless about therapy lessening her anxiety and fears. Therefore, a gradual shaping approach with appropriate positive reinforcement (verbal encouragement) may help reduce her negative feelings toward therapy.

Lisa's hypothesized dependent-histrionic personality style may be an obstacle to her treatment. She may have difficulty acknowledging her role in any therapy progress. She is likely to attribute decreased levels of anxiety to her parents, the therapist, or the medication. Thus, an emphasis on Lisa's role in lessening her anxiety would be necessary. Histrionic clients are often described as global and impressionistic in their thinking. Beck and Freeman (1990) describe this thinking style as an inability to focus on specifics. The basic elements of teaching Lisa to monitor and identify specific thoughts would be important. Overall, the independent practice of using coping skills and the development of personal approaches to the techniques would be encouraged and reinforced in Lisa. The collaborative approach would be emphasized. Clear limits and structure would be provided for each therapy session. It is hoped that this would help foster the development of the client's sense of self-efficacy.

The discontinuation of medication should be considered a goal for Lisa's therapy. She is likely to attribute a disproportionate amount of her coping to her medication. This may result in relapse if her medication is not carefully discontinued.

## H. Initial Treatment Sessions 1 & 2

I shared information regarding the cognitive behavior model of anxiety and panic with Lisa. An emphasis was placed on building therapist-client rapport and a working alliance with the client. A Subjective Units of Discomfort Scale (SUDS) was developed collaboratively with Lisa. I asked Lisa to close her eyes and imagine situations where she felt the most, moderate, and the least amount of anxiety. As she imagined each situation, she was asked to give it a number for future reference. The most anxious situation she labeled 100, the moderately anxious situation she labeled 50, and least anxious situation she labeled 0. The highest anxiety-provoking situation she identified was in being trapped in the elevator. Everyday hassles such as paying bills, disciplining her children, and traveling in the neighborhood were in the moderate range for her. She found watching television with her family, reading, and bathing as the most relaxing and the least anxiety-causing. I then asked Lisa to remember this scale for later use in her treatment.

During this session I introduced a two-column, situation and feelings thought record for Lisa's self-monitoring. An example follows:

| Situation | Feelings |
|---|---|
| Riding home from the doctor's office heavy traffic with my brother | Strong heart palpitations, head pressure, nervous 95% |

| Trying to sleep at night | Shaking, chest pains, heavy breathing, anxious 90% |

## Treatment Session 3

Lisa's scores on the BAI were 37 and the BDI-II, 27. These scores continue to reflect a severe level of anxiety and a moderate level of depression. I introduced Lisa to the structure of CBT sessions, agenda setting, homework, and feedback. She reported that this therapy "seemed a lot different than her previous therapy." The major focus of this session was in teaching her relaxation skills. Progressive muscle relaxation, meditation, and hypnosis were briefly described to her as possible approaches to relaxation training. Lisa reported no interest in learning meditation or hypnosis but was interested in learning progressive muscle relaxation. This technique identifies 16 major muscle groups that are tightened and then relaxed systematically. Cognitive behavior therapists commonly use this technique to teach clients relaxation skills. Specific cognitions that were identified in Lisa's case included, "I must be in control." I also introduced Lisa to the three-column dysfunctional thought record (DTR). Her homework included completing the (DTR) and daily practice of relaxation skills. Below is an example of one of Lisa's completed three-column DTRs:

| Situation | Thoughts | Feelings |
|---|---|---|
| At a shopping mall in a crowd | I'm closed in. I can't breathe. I can't see. | Anxious 85–90% |
| Driving to school | I need to map out directions. I can't be nervous. I might get a tire blow out. | Nervous 75% |
| Waiting in check-out line at the store | I can't wait. There's too many people. I've got to leave. I can't stay here. | Nervous & Anxious 70% |

# Treatment Session 4

BAI = 48, BDI = 28. These scores continue to reflect a severe level of anxiety and a moderate level of depression for Lisa. The client was very withdrawn and quiet throughout the first half of this session. She related that she had panic attacks "all week" and could not practice the relaxation skills. Lisa stated, "I've had over a year of therapy, I was looking for a miracle and it didn't happen," and "I think I should just stop the therapy." She may best be described as feeling helpless and hopeless. These thoughts and feelings were consistent with the hypothesis drawn from the case conceptualization. I offered support and empathy for her feelings and slowly focused her attention on her homework. Lisa had attempted the relaxation protocol at home, but found the practice too difficult as it increased her anxiety level.

I realized that Lisa might be experiencing a paradoxical anxiety reaction and might terminate therapy prematurely. I then considered the use of a hypnotic relaxation technique instead of continuing the relaxation training, and assessing for the presence of a paradoxical anxiety reaction. Lisa reconsidered hypnosis and agreed that it was "worth a try." I taught her a self-hypnotic technique using progressive relaxation, breath counting, and guided imagery.

Initially, I asked Lisa to fixate on her body and breathing during the hypnotic induction. This included resting comfortably in her chair, breathing in slowly and deeply through her nose and exhaling through her mouth. The emphasis was placed on noticing the sensations of her breath. This relaxation induction proceeded using several of the elements of progressive muscle relaxation that I taught her earlier. Each of the 16 major muscle groups was identified and the client was asked to relax each group without tensing them. I then used the staircase method to deepen the client's relaxation (Hammond, 1992). This technique consists of having the client imagine walking down a staircase and giving her suggestions for deeper relaxation as she does. The image of an elevator is sometimes used, but clearly this image would not be relaxing for this client. Finally, I asked Lisa to use visual imagery. This consisted of asking her to imagine a very pleasant and relaxed place using multi-sensory imagery.

Lisa responded favorably to this intervention, and she agreed to practice the technique at home. After I actively addressed her cognitive distortions concerning the therapy she agreed to continue treatment.

## Treatment Sessions 5 Through 11

In the previous sessions (1 through 10), Lisa responded favorably to the structure of cognitive therapy sessions and actively participated in both the sessions and the homework assignments. Progress in her ability to cope with anxiety and panic has been slow but steady. She reported that she experienced fewer and less severe panic attacks as these sessions progressed. Her total scores recorded on the BAI decreased from the severe to the moderate range, while the total scores on the BDI-II decreased from the moderate to the minimal range. This pattern of scores suggests that her depression may be related to her anxiety. As Lisa developed coping skills for anxiety, her level of depression markedly decreased. It is quite possible that her depressive symptoms remitted as she developed a sense of hope and felt less helpless. While the antidepressant medication could have contributed to this decrease, she had been on this medication for the preceding year without an appreciable change in depressive symptoms.

Lisa demonstrated positive gains in the development of her coping skills (per her self-report and observed session practice) and a decrease in overall anxiety with substantially fewer depressive symptoms. She continued to practice self-hypnosis. Additionally, Lisa had personalized her relaxation exercises with an audiotape of ocean sounds and developed her own imagery. Lisa's involvement in enhancing and personalizing these exercises was encouraged and reinforced. She continued to identify her automatic thoughts when anxious and increased her ability to develop alternatives and look for evidence to dispute the thoughts. This can be seen in her homework, which is the completion of her dysfunctional thought record. An example of this DTR follows:

| Situation | Thoughts | Feelings | Alternative Response |
| --- | --- | --- | --- |
| Driving to the store | I might have an accident | Nervous 85% | Deep breathing Self-instructions for relaxation |

| | | | |
|---|---|---|---|
| Walking to the El | I'm alone. I'm not getting better. Why can't I do what I used to do? | Nervous 90% | "Keep trying to make it." "I must keep walking, it will get better." Deep breathing |

Lisa had stated a desire to return to work as soon as possible. Her psychiatrist and health insurance company supported this goal. Given her improvement and desire to return to work, exposure procedures were initiated.

The initial exposure technique used was a traditional systematic desensitization approach to treat her phobic avoidance and fear of riding elevators. A hierarchy of anxious events on the elevator was developed collaboratively with Lisa during session seven. She assigned the SUDS levels to each step of the hierarchy. The original was written on 3 × 5 cards. They are presented as follows with number one as the least anxiety provoking.

*Hierarchy for Systematic Desensitization for Elevators:*

| Situation | SUDS Level |
|---|---|
| 1. Approaching the elevator | 35–40 |
| 2. Standing in front of the elevator door | 40 |
| 3. Elevator door opens | 42 |
| 4. Stepping onto the elevator | 55 |
| 5. Doors close | 55–60 |
| 6. Looking for the inspection label and phone | 60 |
| 7. Elevator begins to ascend | 70 |
| 8. Elevator stops at a floor and doors have not opened | 85–90 |
| 9. Doors open and step off | 90 down to 40 |

Lisa reported an increase in anxiety due to her thoughts and images while constructing the hierarchy during session eight. During session nine, she was exposed to the images that elicit the lowest levels of anxiety. She reported that she was highly uncomfortable with this procedure. She did not attend the next session, citing that the new office was too far to travel. During session 10, she revealed that her anxiety and panic were elevated throughout the week due to thoughts and images of the elevator. Due to Lisa's highly aversive reaction to the traditional form of systematic desensitization, a hypnotic desensitization approach was utilized.

In summary, the client's previous treatment sessions (1 through 10) have proceeded from the development of coping skills for anxiety and fear (increased self-efficacy) to specific coping skills for control of panic attacks to exposure to feared situations (systematic desensitization for phobic avoidance and fear of elevators).

## Treatment Sessions 12 Through 15

Lisa continued to respond favorably to the structure of cognitive therapy sessions in session 12 through 15. Her participation in both the therapy sessions and the homework assignments were noted. Total scores recorded on the BAI decreased from the moderate to the mild range, while the total scores on the BDI-II continued to fall into the minimal range. She reported no panic attacks during this time period; however, she did report episodes of high anxiety. Lisa coped with these episodes by using cognitive strategies and self-hypnosis for relaxation and distraction.

Systematic desensitization for treatment of Lisa's phobic avoidance and fear of riding in elevators was initiated during these sessions. As with the traditional use of this treatment technique, the steps of the hierarchy were addressed from the least to the most related anxiety. Lisa had reacted adversely to the traditional form of systematic desensitization. She canceled the session after the initial treatment, as her thinking about and imagining the first step resulted in a high level of anxiety. Therefore, a hypnotic desensitization approach was utilized (Golden, Dowd, & Friedberg, 1987). This procedure differs from traditional systematic desensitization as it uses a hypnotic induction to relax the client before the imaginal exposure. Lisa had responded favorably to self-hypnosis training for relaxation, and it was thought that she might have a similar response to progressing through the hierarchy while remaining in a relaxed state.

Another variation on the traditional use of this technique is the use of coping imagery (Golden, Dowd, & Friedberg, 1987; Freeman, Pretzer, Fleming, & Simon, 1990). Accordingly, Lisa was asked to imagine the fears and anxieties associated with the elevator and then to imagine tolerating the anxiety and coping with any difficulties that might arise. This approach allowed Lisa to experience limited anxiety as she imagined herself coping. There are some similarities to Goldfried and Davison's (1994) self-control variation of systematic desensitization, which suggests that the client can learn to relax when confronted with anxiety and fear in specific situations, such as in Lisa's exposure to elevators. Lisa progressed through the first half of the hierarchy during these sessions. Overall, the use of hypnosis and coping imagery may have increased Lisa's compliance with treatment and prevented her early termination of therapy.

Several behavioral experiments were developed collaboratively with Lisa during these sessions. She would engage in self-exposure activities such as walking to the elevated train station and using the elevator when visiting her psychiatrist. She was encouraged to take "small steps in a gradual manner and stop when her coping strategies were exhausted." Many examples of the power of shaping strategies are demonstrated in the literature (Bellack, Hersen, & Kazdin, 1985; Goldfried & Davison, 1994; Freeman, Pretzer, Fleming, & Simon, 1990). Shaping strategies allows a task to be less overwhelming and more manageable by helping the client break large tasks into smaller, more manageable tasks. This is especially important for Lisa given the severity of her anxiety and avoidance behavior. I provided support and encouragement for Lisa's self-exposure experiments. Each venture into situations of self-exposure was verbally reinforced. Goldfried and Davison indicate that the client regards approval from the therapist as a potential reinforcer.

The scores on the BAI and the BDI-II showed a sudden increase in anxiety and depression for Lisa in session 15, although this spike fell below scores obtained early in treatment. Lisa described several stressors that she associated with this increase in dysphoric feelings: her sudden decision to return to work immediately, her fiancée's mother having a stroke during the week, and pushing herself in the self-exposure experiments. Each of these stressors was explored and coping strategies were suggested.

## Treatment Session 16

Lisa's total scores on the BAI and the BDI-II returned to their previous respective mild and minimal levels before the stressors identified during session 15. She continued her homework. This included the completion of the DTR and development of alternative cognitive strategies and the daily practice of self-hypnosis for relaxation and self-exposure experiments, albeit at a much slower rate than before. Lisa reported that she not only "got on the elevator" at her psychiatrist's office, "but rode it to his second floor office." The use of the systematic desensitization hierarchy was continued without reaching the next step. She reported that she had recently noticed that when her arm and back hurt that her anxiety level increased. Lisa had injured herself while attempting to climb through the hatch in the roof of the elevator.

I introduced Lisa to the use of hypnosis for the relief and control of the pain. Hypnoanalgesia, a hypnotic technique that diminishes pain, was considered, given her favorable responses to self-hypnosis for relaxation and hypnotic desensitization. Hypnoanalgesia is considered more difficult than many other hypnotic phenomena such as relaxation, imagery, and muscle catalepsy (Eimer & Freeman, 1998). Therefore, this technique was used only after collaboration with Lisa and careful assessment of her response to hypnosis. It is also important to note that her fall in the elevator may have contributed to this pain. However, a recent physical examination failed to reveal a physiological cause for the pain.

I discussed this technique with Lisa and focused on the use of touch, with a demonstration not utilizing hypnosis. The progressive relaxation induction that was previously taught to the client for self-hypnosis and systematic desensitization was utilized. After the client felt relaxed, the following directions were introduced to produce hypnoanalgesia: "I would like you to focus your attention on your left hand. I'd like you to allow this area (using my index finger to draw very light circles in a continuous circle on the top of the client's hand between her wrist and knuckles) here to become numb (M. Oster, personal communication, 1998). All sensation within this area will fade, this absence of feeling, the dullness, the numbness will feel as if you had an injection of Novocain, as in the dentist's office." I then asked Lisa to direct the flow of this pleasant numbness to her wrist and then up her forearm and bicep to her shoulder.

I gave suggestions for diminished pain, allowing Lisa to feel pain that might signal a need for medical attention. She reported that she enjoyed the technique and would practice it at home with her progressive relaxation induction. The instructions for homework were modified to just include imagining the circle drawn on the back of her hand.

## Treatment Sessions 17 Through 25

Lisa's anxiety level as measured by the BAI increased from the mild to the moderate range during session 17. Lisa reported experiencing a severe panic attack, which resulted in a trip to the emergency room. She experienced a pain in her left arm and thought that it was an early sign of an impending heart attack. The hospital discharged her with a diagnosis of panic disorder. Lisa's depression level as measured by the BDI-II continued in the minimal range. Her anxiety level fell back into the mild range during sessions 18 through 25.

I thought that Lisa might not have had enough time to practice the hypnoanalgesia technique as it was only introduced the week before. The technique was again conducted during session 17 with emphasis on home practice.

Lisa has continued the self-exposure behavioral experiments. These included walking further distances alone, driving further distances alone, and riding for longer periods of time on elevators. Her coping skills, the completion of daily thought records with alternatives, and practicing self-hypnosis for relaxation were reviewed. Systematic desensitization for treatment of phobic avoidance and fear of riding elevators was continued during these sessions. She progressed through the hierarchy with imaginal exposure.

The major focus of these sessions was in vivo exposure to the use of elevators. Collaboratively Lisa and I developed an in vivo hierarchy to use the elevator at the office and began exposure during these sessions. During self-exposure she had been able to ride an elevator for one floor. The elevator at my office was identified for in vivo practice. Five floors were available for our hierarchy. An initial light relaxation exercise was conducted using previously described progressive relaxation, and Lisa's coping skills were reviewed. She was accompanied until she could ride to the fifth floor with minimal anxiety. The hierarchy was then conducted as I waiting at the designated floor for Lisa to exit the elevator. This hierarchy consisted of the following stages:

1. Walk to the elevator

2. Press call button

3. Walk into the elevator when door opens

4. Allow the door to close, press button for floor (increasing the number over time)

Lisa progressed rapidly through the in vivo hierarchy and supplemented this with her self-exposure practice. This sequence of sessions ended with a review of her coping skills. She identified these skills as self-talk, distraction, deep breathing, relaxation, imagery, and laughter. Previously established goals of treatment were reached. These included driving long distances, shopping at the mall, and riding elevators without high levels of anxiety and panic attacks. A new goal was developed collaboratively with Lisa, decreasing her anxiety around returning to work.

## Treatment Sessions 26 Through 29

These final sessions were conducted on a biweekly basis. Lisa's anxiety level increased to the moderate range while her depression level increased to the mild range. However, this increase in scores was still well below the scores obtained in the early sessions of treatment. Lisa returned to work during this time and was experiencing a great deal of anxiety on the job. However, she continued to be free of panic attacks when using elevators, driving and walking. Her use of the dysfunctional thought record focused on identifying automatic thoughts about work and modifying these thoughts.

## Follow-Up: Session 30

One month after the 29th session, we met for our 30th and last session. Lisa's temporary job had ended and she was already interviewing for a new job. Her anxiety and depression levels had decreased. No episodes of high anxiety or panic were reported. Her significant advances in coping with anxiety and panic were reviewed and reinforced. These changes were apparent in Lisa's coping with the termination of her job.

# CASE STUDY SUMMARY AND DISCUSSION

A 34-year-old single woman, Lisa, with a history of panic disorder with agoraphobia, generalized anxiety, and a phobia of elevators was treated with a combination of cognitive behavior therapy and hypnosis. The client was most interested in learning skills for control of panic as she was quite fearful of future panic attacks and avoided many of her daily activities. Therefore, the initial goal of treatment was to teach the client skills for panic control. Many of these coping skills were thought to be useful later with the treatment of generalized anxiety and phobic avoidance.

This case study illustrates the use of a comprehensive case conceptualization. This process suggested several specific treatment directions such as cognitive restructuring, relaxation training, systematic desensitization, behavioral experiments, and hypnosis. Combining hypnosis with cognitive behavioral interventions was thought to achieve several goals. It would provide a technique to combine and strengthen relaxation and imagery interventions to later employ in systematic desensitization. Hypnosis would also provide an alternative if the client experienced a paradoxical increase in anxiety during the relaxation training. A combination of cognitive behavioral homework and self-hypnosis training were considered as a method to increase the client's self-efficacy and decrease her tendency for dependency on others.

The impact of combining cognitive behavior therapy and hypnosis was clearly demonstrated in session 4. The client reported that she was contemplating stopping therapy as she was "looking for a miracle" that had not occurred in previous therapy. Two strategies were employed during this session, the introduction of hypnosis for deep relaxation and active cognitive restructuring emphasizing the client's cognitive distortions concerning therapy. It would be difficult to credit one strategy over the other for the client's continuation in therapy; however, this combination of interventions appeared to prevent the client from early termination.

Hypnosis was successful for relaxation and systematic desensitization. This success was considered when the client was introduced to hypnoanalgesia for pain control. Overall, the episodes of high anxiety or panic decreased and finally stopped at the end of treatment. The client clearly made significant strides in developing coping

skills for anxiety and panic. The client's phobic avoidance of elevators, walking in her neighborhood, and driving was also alleviated.

The case presented here illustrates the use of hypnosis for
relaxation, imagery, and pain control. These interventions closely
resemble standard cognitive interventions of progressive muscle
relaxation, imagery, and distraction. The use of nonhypnotic and
hypnotic imagery employed during systematic desensitization is illustrated by this case study. The use of hypnotic interventions appears to have increased the client's comfort level and enabled her
to effectively practice coping skills. Hypnotic imagery may be applied
in a wide variety of situations and provide practice of coping skills,
especially in situations that are dangerous or highly stressful or just
too difficult for in vivo exposure.

Hypnosis can also be integrated into cognitive behavior therapy
to achieve many other treatment goals. Hypnotic interventions may
enhance the client's ability to identify automatic thoughts and images in particular situations. Clients often describe their thoughts
as too fast to identify during stressful events. The hypnotic intervention of time expansion may increase the client's ability to identify
these thoughts and images.

Hypnosis can also aid in the identification and potential modification of underlying cognitive schemas. Schemas are usually considered to operate at a nonconscious level. These schemas are
considered to predispose and help maintain the clients' problematic
automatic thoughts, behaviors, and feelings. Hypnosis may be especially useful in the process of identifying and modifying these sche-
mata. Change at the schema level is not always possible or desirable.
However, it is thought that change at this level prevents relapse
when the client is faced with similar life situations.

The collaborative relationship is considered an essential ingre-
dient of cognitive behavior therapy. This relationship may be enhanced though the use of hypnotic interventions such as pacing and
leading. These techniques may enhance the clinicians' understanding of the client's experience and allow the client to feel better
understood. Metaphors, a common hypnotic intervention, may also
increase the client's comfort level and enable the client to view their
difficulties from an alternative perspective. Hopefully this reduces
early termination and noncompliance.

The integration of cognitive behavior therapy and hypnosis is
clearly a work in process. It is hoped that the practicing clinician

will find this case conceptualization model useful in their choice of interventions and the ongoing process of treatment. A recent seminar on integrating hypnosis into clinical practice suggested that the clinician should be guided by their "thinking as a therapist" when using hypnotic interventions (DeLaney & Voit, 2000). The use of the case conceptualization offers a framework to think from a cognitive behavior perspective when considering the integration of hypnosis and cognitive behavior therapy.

## REFERENCES

Barlow, D. H. (1993). *Clinical handbook of psychological disorders*. New York: Guilford.

Beck, A. T., & Freeman, A. (1990). *Cognitive therapy of personality disorders*. New York: Guilford.

Beck, A. T., & Steer, R. A. (1990). *Beck Anxiety Inventory*. San Antonio: The Psychological Corporation.

Beck, A. T., Steer, R. A., & Brown, G. K. (1996). *Beck Depression Inventory* (2nd ed.). San Antonio, TX: The Psychological Corporation.

Beck, J. S. (1995). *Cognitive therapy: Basics and beyond*. New York: Guilford.

Bellack, A. S., Hersen, M., & Kazdin, A. E. (Eds.). (1985). *International handbook of behavior modification and therapy*. New York: Plenum.

Brown, T. A., DiNardo, P. A., & Barlow, D. H. (1994). *Anxiety disorders interview schedule for DSM-IV, adult version*. San Antonio, TX: The Psychological Corporation.

DeLaney, M., & Voit, R. (2000, September 16 & 17) *Becoming a hypnotherapist: Integrating hypnosis into your practice*. Presented at a workshop in Danvers, Massachusetts.

Eimer, B. N., & Freeman, A. M. (1998). *Pain management, psychotherapy: A practical guide*. New York: John Wiley.

Ellis, A. (1962). *Reason and emotion in psychotherapy*. New York: Lyle Stuart.

Freeman, A. M. (1992). The development of treatment conceptualizations in cognitive therapy. In A. M. Freeman & F. M. Dattilio (Eds.), *Comprehensive casebook of cognitive therapy* (pp. 13–23). New York: Plenum.

Freeman, A., Pretzer, J., Fleming, B., & Simon, K. M. (1990). *Clinical applications of cognitive therapy*. New York: Plenum.

Golden, W. L., Dowd, E. T., & Friedberg, F. (1987). *Hypnotherapy: A modern approach*. New York: Pergamon.

Goldfried, M. R., & Davison, G. C. (1994). *Clinical behavior therapy*. New York: John Wiley.

Hammond, D. C. (1992). *Hypnotic induction and suggestion: An introductory manual*. Des Plaines, IL: The American Society of Clinical Hypnosis.

Lazarus, A. A., & Lazarus, C. N. (1991). *Multimodal life history inventory*. Champaign, IL: Research.

Persons, J. B. (1993). Case conceptualization in cognitive-behavior therapy. In
   K. T. Kuehlwein & H. Rosen (Eds.), *Cognitive therapies in action* (pp. 33–53).
   San Francisco: Jossey-Bass.
Persons, J. B. (1989). *Cognitive therapy in practice. A case formulation approach.*
   New York: W. W. Norton.
Persons, J. B., Mooney, K. A., & Padesky, C. A. (1995). Interrater reliability
   of cognitive-behavioral case formulations. *Cognitive Therapy and Research,*
   *19*, 21–34.

# Part II

# Clinical Cases Integrating CBT and Hypnosis

Chapter 5

# Hypnotherapy for Anxiety, Phobias, and Psychophysiological Disorders

William L. Golden

Anxiety, fear, worry, phobias, and stress can all be distinguished. Anxiety and fear are often used interchangeably. However, fear and worry can be considered cognitive, whereas anxiety is an emotional reaction (Beck & Emery, 1985). Worry tends to be vague, frequently in the form of "what if," whereas fears are usually specific about a perceived threat. The threat can be an external danger, or it may be internal, such as perceiving criticism, rejection, or failure as a threat to one's self-esteem. Stress is the body's response to demands made upon it. The stressor is the situation that evokes the individual's stress reaction. Stress and anxiety are not synonymous. Stress can be viewed in a positive way when an individual perceives the stressor as a challenge. When a stressful situation is perceived as threatening, and therefore involves fear or worry, the stress reaction is usually more intense. The individual usually labels their subsequent emotional reaction as anxiety. Phobias involve unrealistic fears and a habitual pattern of avoidance of the feared situations.

According to the cognitive-behavioral model, situations do not automatically cause anxiety. Anxiety-producing thoughts lead to emotional reactions such as anxiety. Visceral reactions and muscle tension are the emotional components of anxiety. Visceral reactions stem from autonomic nervous system activation, which includes increased secretion of adrenalin, hyperventilation, increased sweating, increased heart rate, vasoconstriction of the peripheral vascular system, flushing, increases (or sometimes decreases) in blood pressure, dry mouth as a result of decrease in salivation, decrease in gastric secretion, and decreased motility in the gastrointestinal tract. Increases in muscle tension also occur, and with chronic tension, the muscles can go into spasm and cause pain. Many of these changes in the sympathetic nervous system and the musculature form the basis of the symptomatic complaints of anxiety disorder patients. In susceptible individuals, chronic anxiety leads to psychophysiological symptoms such as irritable bowel syndrome (IBS), tension headaches, and migraine.

Cognitive, behavioral, and hypnotic techniques capable of modifying visceral and muscular reactions provide the treatment for the various anxiety disorders. The purpose of this chapter is to provide the reader with guidelines for using cognitive-behavior hypnotherapy (CBH) in the treatment of anxiety, phobias, and psychophysiological disorders. The chapter focuses on the treatment of three patients—a patient with a diagnosis of generalized anxiety disorder (GAD), a patient with a flying phobia, and a patient with a primary diagnosis of IBS. Their diagnoses are different, but all three patients have suffered from anxiety. As will be seen, there was a tremendous amount of overlap in the methods used to treat them.

## BEHAVIOR THERAPY AND COGNITIVE-BEHAVIOR THERAPY IN THE TREATMENT OF ANXIETY DISORDERS

Systematic desensitization (SD) is a behavior therapy technique that was developed by Wolpe (1958) for the treatment of fears and phobias. SD provides patients an opportunity to confront their fears in a gradual systematic manner, one step at a time. Usually, care is taken to make sure that a patient experiences success with one step before proceeding to a next step. Relaxation techniques, or hypnosis, are used to reduce anxiety during a patient's exposure to the feared situations. As part of the behavioral assessment, the specific stimuli or "triggers" for evoking anxiety are identified. An anxiety hierarchy is then constructed. The patient's fear or phobia is broken down to specific anxiety-producing stimuli, which are then rank ordered from the least to the most anxiety producing. SD can be done in imagination and/or in vivo (live exposure). Although Wolpe (originally used hypnosis to reduce patients' anxiety during exposure to the feared situations, he switched to Jacobson's (1929) progressive relaxation technique because many of Wolpe's patients objected to being hypnotized. Wolpe reports that he still uses hypnosis in a certain number of cases, however.

Ellis (1957) and Beck (1967) are the originators of cognitive therapy. Although there are a number of schools of cognitive psychotherapy, most of them share several significant commonalities (Golden & Dryden, 1986). Most cognitive therapists subscribe to some form of the ABC or S-O-R theoretical model. The basic concept of cognitive therapy is that it is not just the activating event or stimulus that causes emotional disturbance but that cognitions cause or contribute to maladaptive emotions. The various cognitive therapy approaches all employ some type of cognitive restructuring, where patients are taught to identify and modify maladaptive cognitions.

One approach to integrating cognitive and behavior therapy has been to add cognitive components to traditional behavior therapy techniques. Relevant to the treatment of anxiety disorders, is the modification of SD by Goldfried (Goldfried, 1971, 1973; Goldfried & Davison, 1976) and Meichenbaum (1972, 1977). Through their research, Goldfried and Meichenbaum demonstrated that applying a coping skills approach to SD improved its efficacy. In the coping skills approach, patients learn how to use relaxation techniques and coping self-statements for the purpose of reducing their anxiety during SD. Coping self-statements are constructive thoughts that patients employ during imaginal and in vivo exposures. Through these therapy techniques, patients are encouraged to mentally rehearse their coping self-statements while imagining themselves coping with stressful situations. In the original SD paradigm, the theoretical model was based on counterconditioning. Therefore, every effort was made to protect the patient from experiencing anxiety during exposure to the feared situations. Mastery imagery, where the patient imagines being free of anxiety, was used in the original SD procedure. Coping imagery has been found to be more effective than mastery imagery in the treatment of fears and phobias (Kazdin, 1974a, 1974b; Meichenbaum, 1972). A coping image is one where the patient initially experiences some anxiety but then reduces it by using coping strategies such as self-relaxation and coping self-statements.

## THE COGNITIVE-BEHAVIORAL HYPNOTHERAPY MODEL

Cognitive-behavioral hypnotherapy (CBH) involves the integration of hypnosis and cognitive behavior therapy (CBT). CBT and hypnosis share a number of commonalities that make for a natural integration of the two approaches. For example, the use of imagery and relaxation are common to both hypnosis and CBT. Furthermore, cognitive-restructuring techniques can be traced back to some of the early hypnotherapists. Bernheim (1895) and Prince and Coriat (1907) report using hypnotic suggestion to modify dysfunctional thought patterns.

CBT and CBH therapists share the same view about the cause of emotional disturbance. According to Ellis (1962) and Araoz (1981, 1985), most emotional disturbance results from a destructive type of self-hypnosis that Araoz has termed "negative self-hypnosis." Araoz explains that negative thinking and imagining are hypnotic-like when they are accepted without critical evaluation. Negative self-hypnosis is essentially the same concept described by Ellis (1962) and Beck (1967), meaning that there is a causal link between cognition and emotional reactions.

On the basis of their research, Barber and his associates have concluded that the same cognitive processes (focused thinking and imagining, expectations, and attitudes) are involved in hypnosis and CBT (Barber, 1979; Barber, Spanos, & Chaves, 1974; Spanos & Barber, 1974, 1976). Benson, Arns, and Hoffman (1981) concluded, on the basis of their research comparing self-hypnosis and relaxation techniques, that both of these techniques elicit the relaxation response. Edmonston (1981), from his review of the literature, concluded that hypnosis and relaxation are the same.

On the other hand, Kirsch, Montgomery, and Sapirstein (1995), in their meta-analysis of 18 studies in which CBT was compared to

CBH (the same CBT treatment with hypnosis added), concluded that hypnosis enhances the effectiveness of CBT. Gibbons, Kilbourne, Saunders, and Castles (1970) and Hussain (1964) report that the addition of hypnosis enhances the effectiveness of SD. However, Spanos and Barber (1976) point out that the Gibbons et al. (1970) study in particular, and studies of this type in general, confound the addition of a hypnotic induction with the addition of fear-reducing suggestions. Spanos and Barber hypothesize that it is the addition of the fear-reducing suggestions and not the hypnotic induction procedure that is responsible for the increased effectiveness of SD. According to Spanos and Barber, suggestions enhance the effectiveness of CBT techniques, such as SD because they provide the patient with a cognitive strategy. In support of the Spanos and Barber hypothesis, Woody and Shauble (1969) found that the addition of fear-reducing suggestions without a "hypnotic induction" enhanced the efficacy of traditional desensitization. The reason that fear-reducing suggestions enhance the effectiveness of SD may be the same reason that coping self-statements enhance the effectiveness of SD. Fear-reducing suggestions and coping self-statements are both cognitive strategies that patients can use for reducing anxiety. There is some evidence that adding cognitive interventions to hypnotherapy increases its effectiveness. Boutin and Tosi (1983) found that rational stage directed hypnotherapy (RSDH), which is a CBH approach that combines hypnosis and CBT strategies, was more effective than hypnosis alone in the treatment of test anxiety. Fuller (1981) found RSDH to be more effective than hypnosis alone, or cognitive restructuring alone, in treating depression in a geriatric population.

Regardless of whether hypnosis enhances CBT, or CBT enhances hypnosis, and regardless of whether the enhanced effects are attributable to hypnotic induction or cognitive strategies, from a clinical perspective, the integration of CBT and hypnosis provides a more effective treatment approach than either one alone.

## COGNITIVE-BEHAVIORAL HYPNOTHERAPY CASE CONCEPTUALIZATION

If hypnosis and CBT involve essentially the same or similar processes and techniques, then why and when would a therapist include hypnosis into the treatment plan? Even though they are quite similar procedurally, and even if they produce the same physiological state, there may still be phenomenological differences that are significant in determining how various patients respond. Barber (1978) has said that when hypnotic induction is helpful, it is not because of the powers of a hypnotic state or trance, but because of the individual's expectation or belief in the efficacy of the procedure.

Clinical experience suggests that hypnotic induction procedures are useful for patients who believe in their efficacy. Lazarus (1973) has demonstrated that treatment is more effective when the therapist matches the treatment methods to the patient's expectations and requests. Lazarus conducted a study that illustrates this point. Patients who requested hypnosis were assigned to a treatment that was labeled as either "hypnosis" or "relaxation." Although the treatments were actually identical for both groups, the patients who received "hypnosis" as they requested showed greater improvement than the group that received "relaxation." On the other hand, patients who did not state a preference for either type of therapy did equally well with the two differently labeled treatments. Within reason, the patient's expectations can be utilized not only in selecting a particular treatment, but also in designing the specific interventions. The therapist can find out from the patient what he or she expects hypnosis to be like, and tailor the induction procedure and some of the hypnotic suggestions in such a way as to match the patient's expectations and preferences. There are limits, of course, to how far a therapist should go in utilizing a patient's expectations. If a patient's expectations are unrealistic, such as expecting quick easy cures from hypnosis for difficult problems, then therapy is more likely to be effective if the therapist provides the patient with more realistic expectations.

Although there are many similarities between hypnosis and CBT, there are some differences worth noting. CBT therapists usually take a direct approach and teach coping skills to their patients. The CBH approach is also usually direct, with an emphasis on skills training. In contrast, some hypnotherapists, such as Erickson, have taken the position that direct suggestion leads to resistance. Erickson developed an approach based on indirect suggestion, which he believed bypassed the conscious resistance by the patient. Ericksonian therapists employ techniques such as paradoxical intervention, symptom prescription, and joining the resistance, which are all based on indirect suggestion (Erickson & Rossi, 1979).

Some of Erickson's techniques can be taught as self-control techniques. For example, certain patients do not respond to the usual

CBT methods for treating insomnia, such as sleep habit modification, relaxation techniques, and cognitive restructuring because they try too hard. Paradoxical intervention for such a patient might involve instructing the patient to try and stay awake instead of trying to go to sleep. Paradoxical intervention makes sense as a coping strategy when the patient is taught that the intervention is a way to overcome the vicious cycle of "the harder you try to go to sleep, the more you stay awake." The patient can be taught that the way to overcome this vicious cycle is to reverse it. The therapist can suggest, "instead of trying to go to sleep, try to stay awake and you might find that the harder you try to stay awake, the more sleepy you will become."

Some of Erickson's other techniques may also be helpful to patients who become more anxious as a result of trying too hard to follow direct suggestions. For example, one of Erickson's methods of indirect suggestion involves stating a suggestion in the form of a question. Erickson has described hypnotic induction procedures for eye fixation and hand levitation, in which every suggestion in the induction procedure is in the form of a question (Erickson & Rossi, 1979).

Erickson was probably the first to use the question form of suggestion. However, Goldfried and Davison (1976) have described a relaxation method, called the "sensory awareness" technique, in which all of the instructions are worded as questions. Goldfried and Davison credit this "sensory awareness" exercise to Weitzman.

Erickson developed a number of techniques involving indirect suggestion. However, it is beyond the scope of this chapter to describe Erickson's work, or the integration of it with CBH. The reader is referred to some of this chapter author's other writings that do cover the integration of Ericksonian hypnosis with CBT (Golden, 1986a, 1986b; Golden, Dowd, & Friedberg, 1987). Later in the chapter, the case of Jane will be presented as an example of where questions, rather than statements, were used as a hypnotic induction procedure.

## ASSESSMENT TOOLS

### S-O-R-C Assessment Model

In CBT and CBH, assessment and conceptualization are related. The CBT model provides the guidelines for conducting an assessment and provides the conceptual model for a patient's problem. Using the S-O-R-C model, "S" represents the stimuli, or antecedents for anxiety. "O" includes organism variables such as the patient's maladaptive thoughts, attitudes, beliefs, and misperceptions, as well as any physiological contributions. "R" includes the emotional, behavioral, and physiological responses of the patient. "C" in the S-O-R-C model involves reinforcing consequences that might contribute to the maintenance of the problem. Secondary gains, where the patient derives some type of "payoff" for the problem, are examples of reinforcing consequences.

As an example of assessment employing the S-O-R-C model, the case of a patient with irritable bowel syndrome (IBS) is used. The patient, Jane, to be discussed later in greater detail, worried that she would lose control of her bowels and feared disapproval and humiliation. She avoided travel and social situations. Using the S-O-R-C model, we can conceptualize her problem using the following outline:

S = Stimuli: trains, buses, cars, taxicabs, restaurants, parks, and social events
O = Organismic contributions and mediators: (a) cognitive—worries and fears such as "What if I have an accident, other people will think I'm disgusting." (b) physiological—physiological predisposition to IBS
R = Responses: (a) emotional—anxiety; (b) behavioral—phobic avoidance of trains, buses, cars, taxicabs, restaurants, parks and social events; (c) physiological—exacerbation of IBS symptoms
C = Reinforcing consequences—anxiety reduction from avoidance

In addition to this assessment, especially when dealing with psychophysiological disorders, the therapist needs to consider any possible physiological basis for the disorder and refer the patient for medical evaluation and treatment.

## Self-Monitoring

Self-monitoring is an important tool that provides the therapist and the patient with much of the information that is necessary for assessment and conceptualization of the patient's problem. Patients are educated about the rationale and purpose of self-monitoring. Typically patients are asked to record situations in which they feel anxious, as well as those they avoid. They are also taught to identify and monitor anxiety-producing thoughts. Patients are encouraged to rate their anxiety on a scale from either 1–10 or 1–100, depending on which rating system they prefer. What naturally develops, as a result of the patient and therapist reviewing the results of self-monitoring, is a shared conceptualization of the patient's problem.

## COMBINATION OF HYPNOSIS AND COGNITIVE BEHAVIOR THERAPY TECHNIQUES

This author as a therapist uses several CBT techniques in combination with hypnosis in the treatment of patients with anxiety disorders. As will be seen in the case examples, there is a great deal of overlap in the treatment strategies used across the various diagnostic categories. What follows is a description of the main CBH techniques.

### Relaxation Techniques and Hypnotic Induction Procedures

The various relaxation and hypnotic induction techniques can be combined to create a procedure that is tailored to the needs and preferences of a given patient. The patient collaborates with the therapist in the decision making about which techniques to employ. Patients are also encouraged to construct their own relaxation image as opposed to the therapist using standardized relaxation images. Getting patients involved increases the likelihood that they will follow through and use the techniques on their own as part of self-hypnosis. For detailed descriptions of various hypnotic induction procedures and deepening techniques, the reader is referred to Golden, Dowd, and Friedberg (1987).

There are physical and psychological benefits to relaxation and hypnosis alone, without the addition of any other therapeutic techniques. Nevertheless, relaxation techniques and hypnotic induction procedures, without the benefit of additional therapeutic interventions, are rarely sufficient as treatments for most anxiety disorders.

Additional therapeutic strategies are usually needed. Even in traditional hypnotherapy, other interventions are employed during hypnosis. Hypnosis is not the treatment itself; rather, hypnosis provides the context in which therapy takes place. In traditional hypnotherapy, five stages of treatment can be differentiated as follows:

1.  Orientation—history taking and assessment take place, expectations are assessed, patients are educated about hypnosis, misconceptions about hypnosis are clarified and hypnotic responsiveness is evaluated

2.  Hypnotic induction—a hypnotic induction procedure is selected and used

3.  Deepening of hypnosis—following a hypnotic induction, one or several deepening techniques are used

4.  Utilization of hypnosis—during hypnosis, therapeutic interventions are utilized

5.  Termination of hypnosis—using one of several methods, the therapist terminates the hypnosis session and the patient returns to a fully alert state

During the orientation stage, instead of testing hypnotic susceptibility, some CBH therapists, including the author, teach the patient hypnotic skills. What is done during the utilization stage depends on the theoretical orientation of the therapist as well as which techniques are part of that therapist's armamentarium. CBH therapists employ cognitive and behavioral interventions as therapy techniques during the utilization stage. After first using a hypnotic induction procedure to induce a relaxed state, the CBH therapist may use desensitization and cognitive restructuring techniques as part of the treatment.

## Hypnotic Skills Training

In traditional hypnotherapy, patients are tested for hypnotic susceptibility in order to determine whether they are good candidates for hypnotherapy. The problem with this approach is that patients can feel pressured or challenged by it. There are patients who do not test well, yet they do very well in hypnotherapy. However, the author finds that almost every patient can learn to be at least moderately responsive to hypnosis as a result of hypnotic skills training.

The concept of hypnotic skills training is based on the premise that hypnotic responsiveness is a learnable skill. Instead of testing for hypnotic susceptibility, the therapist teaches the patient how to respond to suggestion. Research has demonstrated that hypnotic responsiveness can be improved through hypnotic skills training (Diamond, 1974, 1977; Katz, 1979).

One can teach hypnotic skills by modifying the hypnotic susceptibility tests. Instead of using them as tests, the therapist can present hand heaviness, hand levitation, and arm catalepsy as exercises. In introducing hypnotic skills training, the therapist can say the following:

> In order to learn how to respond to hypnotic suggestion, first, it is important for you to learn how to respond to simple suggestions. This will be accomplished by going through a series of simple exercises. Hypnosis is not magic, nor is it something that is done to you. Hypnosis is a skill that everyone can learn, which improves with practice. One of the skills is to be able to think and imagine along with the suggestion. So if your goal is to feel relaxed, then imagining a favorite place where you have felt relaxed will help you to become relaxed. You can also relax by thinking relaxing thoughts. We can refer to these thoughts as self-suggestions; for example, as I let my arms and legs hang loose and limp, I can feel them starting to relax, my hands are open, my toes spread apart, and I feel the relaxation starting in my toes and feet, spreading to my ankles, calf muscles, knees and thighs.

Patients are also taught to block out negative thoughts (such as "this won't work"), which could interfere with their ability to respond to suggestion. The therapist can offer the following:

> If your mind wanders, refocus on the thoughts and images that are consistent with the goals of the suggestion. If needed, you can block out intrusive thoughts by using thought-stoppage. Whenever intrusive thoughts start to interfere with your concentration, you can block them out by thinking the word 'stop' and then refocus on the thoughts and images relevant to your goal.

Once the patient learns these basic concepts, they are then ready to apply them to the hand heaviness, hand levitation, and arm catalepsy exercises. Using the arm heaviness exercise as an example, the therapist can say the following:

> Now we can apply what I just taught you by using several exercises. The first one involves feelings of heaviness. Imagine holding something so heavy that, if it were real, it would make your arm feel heavy and tired and cause you to lower it. Some examples are holding a shopping bag full of groceries, a bowling ball, a huge book, or a barbell. Once you have your image, sit back and close your eyes. Hold both of your arms out, parallel, straight in front of you, palms up. Now imagine holding that heavy object in your dominant hand. Remember how your arm felt when you actually held that object. In addition to imagining it, use suggestions such as 'my arm is feeling heavy and tired, so tired that I can't keep it up, I feel the weight pulling my arm down lower and lower.' Remember to refocus if your mind wanders, and to block out any thoughts that interfere with your concentration.

If the patient has difficulty responding, the therapist uses it as a teaching opportunity. The therapist helps the patient identify what interfered, and then offers advice about how the patient could improve. For a complete transcript of a hypnotic skills training procedure, the reader is referred to Golden, Dowd, and Friedberg (1987).

## Self-Hypnosis

According to a cognitive-behavioral perspective, the same processes are involved in hetero-hypnosis and self-hypnosis. According to Barber and his associates (Barber, 1979; Barber, Spanos, & Chaves, 1974; Spanos & Barber, 1976), all hypnotic phenomena are the result of the same processes: the individual's cooperation and motivation, expectations and attitudes, and the individual's ability to become absorbed in suggestion-related thinking and imagining. According to Ellis (1962), almost all hypnosis is the result of self-talk. Ellis (1962) and Araoz (1981, 1985) have said that maladaptive emotions and self-defeating behavior are the result of an irrational negative type of self-hypnosis. Prior to therapy, most patients are unaware that they are engaging in this negative self-hypnosis. In CBH, patients learn to identify their negative self-suggestions and learn how to replace them with more constructive ones. Teaching patients to become aware of their negative self-hypnosis helps them to understand how they can control the process, and demystifies hypnosis.

Self-hypnosis provides patients with a set of coping skills. As part of their self-hypnosis training, patients are taught to use relaxation techniques, cognitive restructuring, and anxiety-reducing suggestions. The techniques that are used for inducing self-hypnosis are the same that were developed in creating their personalized hypnotic induction. The therapeutic interventions that patients employ during self-hypnosis are the same that were utilized during hetero-hypnosis. Patients are taught to apply their self-hypnosis skills on an "as needed basis." They can also prepare themselves for stressful situations. Prior to having in vivo exposure, patients can self-induce relaxation and then mentally rehearse coping with the upcoming stressful event.

## The Two-Column Method

The author has found certain cognitive restructuring techniques to be very compatible with hypnosis. Cognitive restructuring techniques can be used for formulating hypnotic suggestions for hetero-hypnosis and self-hypnosis. In particular, the two-column method is very easy for patients to learn and use on their own. The patient is instructed to divide a page in half. On one side of the page, the patient lists their anxiety-producing thoughts. On the other side of the page, the therapist lists hypnotic suggestions. The goal is to generate a set of rational thoughts that can be used as hypnotic suggestions for reducing the patient's anxiety. Here is an example of the two-column method, as it was used for generating a set of therapeutic suggestions for a patient receiving hypnotherapy for test anxiety.

| *Anxiety-producing Thoughts* | *Therapeutic Suggestions* |
|---|---|
| 1) I'll do lousy on this test. I'll never learn the material. | 1) I can do well on this test. When I've studied, I've done well on tests. I don't have to memorize everything in the book in order to do well on a test. |
| 2) I'm not as smart as everyone. | 2) I'm smart enough. I've done well on tests despite my |

> fear and now I have my
> self-hypnosis skills to help
> me. If the test is hard for
> me, it's hard for everyone
> else too.

## Desensitization

Cognitive, behavioral, and hypnotic interventions can be combined to create a CBH version of desensitization. Therapeutic suggestions, developed through cognitive restructuring techniques such as the two-column method given above, can be used during SD for the purpose of anxiety reduction. For example, for the test anxious student described above, the author suggested the following after the patient had relaxed via a hypnotic induction procedure:

> Now imagine that you are studying for your exam. And as you start to study you are thinking you can do well on this test. When you've studied, you've done well. You don't have to memorize everything in the book in order to do well on a test.

The therapist can offer similar therapeutic suggestions throughout the entire SD procedure. The SD sessions can be tape-recorded for the patient to listen to at home. In addition, patients can be encouraged to use the same therapeutic suggestions during their self-hypnosis practice at home.

## TREATMENT PLANNING

Treatment planning involves selecting techniques that are suitable for a given patient based on the patient's specific symptoms, preferences, and expectations. A patient's symptoms are an important consideration in selecting treatment techniques. Whenever dysfunctional thought patterns can be identified, some type of cognitive restructuring would be appropriate as part of the treatment program. When a patient has specific fears or phobias, desensitization would be part of the treatment package. The specific relaxation techniques to be used in a given case will depend on the preferences of the patient but also on how the patient's anxiety manifests itself.

If muscle tension were one of the patient's complaints, then some type of progressive relaxation would be part of the treatment procedure. If the patient has visceral symptoms (such as tachycardia, hyperventilation, and dizziness), then diaphragmatic breathing would be very important.

## CASE 1—MARY: TREATMENT OF GENERALIZED ANXIETY DISORDER

### Patient Background and History

Mary was 50 years old when she came to therapy for treatment of an anxiety disorder. She worked as a manager for a major corporation. Mary was new to corporate life. Previously she had been a housewife. She went back to work after her children left home, but she felt insecure because she was new to corporate life and was older than everyone else in her office. Mary felt unworthy of her job. Connie, Mary's boss, was very demanding, critical, verbally abusive, and arbitrary. She frequently yelled at Mary, sometimes even when Mary was doing exactly what she had been instructed to do. Connie would arbitrarily change her mind about what she wanted employees to do. Connie's behavior was not specific to Mary. She treated all of her subordinates the same way.

### Presenting Complaints, Assessment, and Diagnosis

Mary reported that she was unable to relax, constantly worried about making mistakes, and feared being chastised by her boss and getting fired. She complained of free-floating anxiety, her face flushing, muscle tension, heart palpitations, and waking up in the middle of the night with her heart pounding and profuse sweating. All of these symptoms began after a few episodes of Connie yelling at her at work.

Mary was referred to author/therapist by another cognitive-behavior therapist to receive hypnosis and stress management. The previous therapist mainly used cognitive interventions, which had not been effective in reducing Mary's anxiety.

In conducting an assessment on the patient, the author identified anxiety-provoking situations, maladaptive thoughts, and self-
defeating behavior. All of the anxiety-provoking situations were the
result of Mary's having direct contact with Connie, doing work that
would be supervised by Connie, or anticipating meetings with her.
When Mary woke up with anxiety symptoms in the middle of the
night, they were in response to nightmares about being abused by
her boss.

Mary's self-defeating behavior stemmed from her workaholic
behavior and her lack of assertiveness at work. On weekends, Mary
was unable to relax. She would work long hours throughout the
weekend in an attempt to try to be fully prepared for her meetings
with Connie during the week. Mary stopped socializing and had
little time for recreation. None of her workaholic behavior helped,
however, because she was anxious no matter how much she prepared. She was also unable to defend herself from the abuse she
suffered from her boss. Mary felt she deserved to be treated badly
because she believed she was incompetent and was failing at her job.

Although one might argue for a diagnosis of social phobia or
posttraumatic stress disorder in this case, the author diagnosed
Mary as having generalized anxiety disorder (GAD) because of the
pervasiveness of her anxiety and because her anxiety symptoms fit
the criteria for GAD. Although there was a phobic quality to some
of her symptoms, it was concluded that she experienced anxiety
most of the time, both in and out of the feared situations. She described her anxiety as free-floating. The author has found that what
patients refer to as free-floating anxiety can usually be connected
to fear and worry.

## Case Conceptualization

The treatment plan for Mary included cognitive, behavioral, and
hypnotic interventions. Specific treatment interventions included
a relaxation hypnotic induction technique, cognitive restructuring,
imaginal rehearsal, and assertiveness training.

Hypnotherapy was chosen for several reasons. The patient expected and wanted hypnosis. She was referred specifically for hypnosis and stress management. She had previously received a primarily
cognitive treatment without experiencing any improvement. As dis-

cussed earlier in the chapter, treatment is more effective when the therapist matches the treatment methods to the patient's expectations and requests. The other reason for selecting hypnosis was because of the patient's symptoms. The author has found hypnosis to be very effective in treating what was diagnosed as Mary's anxiety.

Assertiveness was chosen as a behavioral goal because the patient needed some skills in coping with her abusive boss. Mary was frightened that she would be fired if she stood up to her boss, which was not entirely unrealistic. So caution was taken and diplomatic assertiveness was the behavioral goal for Mary. The patient was also asked to observe how some of her peers handled Connie's abusiveness.

Cognitive therapy was included in Mary's treatment package because of the patient's numerous worries, fears, and her self-deprecation. Since the author had found certain cognitive restructuring techniques to be very compatible with hypnosis, the two-column method was the main one used with Mary for formulating therapeutic suggestions.

## Course of Treatment

Mary's therapy lasted a total of 10 sessions. The first two sessions were used for history taking, assessment, and orientation of the patient to hypnosis. During the first session, Mary's questions about hypnosis were addressed and her misconceptions about hypnosis were corrected. Hypnotic susceptibility testing was not done, because the author prefers not to challenge patients with such tests. Instead, during Mary's first session, a hypnotic skills training approach was employed. Also during the first session, various hypnotic induction procedures and deepening techniques were described to her. Mary was encouraged to collaborate in the design of her own treatment and was very enthusiastic about selecting techniques. She chose a hypnotic induction that included slow deep breathing, progressive relaxation, and a pleasant image. Her relaxation image was a beach in Maui, Hawaii. At the end of the first session, Mary was given a self-monitoring assignment. She was asked to keep a log of her thoughts and feelings throughout the week, and to list situations in which she felt anxious. She was asked to note when she was anxious and to identify any thoughts or situations that might be associated with her anxiety.

Assessment continued into the second session. A list of anxiety-producing situations was developed from Mary's self-monitoring activities. The following are the anxiety-provoking situations that were identified:

- Anticipating having a lot of work to do
- Starting a new project
- Connie telephoning to arrange a meeting
- Handing in a report to Connie
- Presenting a report to Connie without having had adequate time to prepare it
- Connie interrogating me
- Connie questioning my judgment
- Connie criticizing my work in a not very constructive manner
- Connie yelling at me

These situations were not rank ordered according to how much anxiety they provoked because Mary reported that most of them could evoke about the same amount of anxiety.

During the second session, Mary was also taught a breathing technique for producing relaxation. The breathing technique that the author typically employs is diaphragmatic breathing, at a rate of 4 seconds to inhale and 4 seconds to exhale. A patient is taught to breath in and out through the nose. Only a few minutes of slow, deep breathing are needed to produce relaxation. The author frequently teaches breathing techniques prior to an initial hypnotic induction, as it demonstrates to the patient what relaxation feels like. In this way, breathing techniques are similar to the hypnotic skills training procedure, in that both break down the process of relaxation and hypnosis into smaller more manageable steps that are easier for the patient to learn.

After giving Mary an opportunity to ask further questions about hypnosis, the author reviewed the techniques that would be employed as part of the hypnotic induction procedure. This procedure started with some slow deep breathing, followed by progressive relaxation and then the use of Mary's Maui beach image to deepen her relaxation. She was very responsive and experienced deep relaxation. A tape recording was made for Mary to use for home practice. She was given the cassette tape of her hypnotic induction and was asked to listen to it once a day. She was also encouraged to continue the self-monitoring.

At her third session, Mary reported that she had been listening to her hypnosis tape at night and was already experiencing an improvement in her sleep. The rest of the session was focused on reviewing her thought log and teaching her how to use the two-column method. She and the author collaborated in generating a list of therapeutic suggestions that would eventually be used during hypnosis. Here is an example of the two-column method that was used for developing Mary's suggestions.

| *Anxiety-Producing Thoughts* | *Therapeutic Suggestions* |
|---|---|
| 1. I won't get all the work done and Connie will get mad at me again. She'll ask me questions that I won't be able to answer and she'll yell at me. | 1. Connie puts people on the defensive by interrogating them. If I block or forget something, I can be assertive and tell her I'll get back to her with the answer. |
| 2. I don't know what I'm doing, and I'm not really that good. | 2. I do know what I'm doing. I get good feedback from Connie when she isn't under stress or in a bad mood. |
| 3. Connie realizes I'm no good and she'll fire me. | 3. Connie treats everyone that way. She needs me and even recommended me for a promotion. |
| 4. She'll find mistakes in the report I prepared for her and she'll yell at me. | 4. Everyone makes mistakes. I've gotten better at my job and when Connie is in a good mood, she gives me positive feedback. Even if I make mistakes, I don't deserve to be abused. |
| 5. It's my fault, I'm stupid, and incompetent, and deserve to be fired. | 5. I don't deserve to be treated that way. |

6. I shouldn't be so affected by Connie. It's my fault that she's getting to me.

6. She's a bully and can be quite abusive at times. Some of my fellow workers have told me how upset they get when she yells at them.

7. I'm a failure.

7. I've been successful, and have gotten consistently good written evaluations from Connie.

Mary was also given self-hypnosis training during her third session. She was instructed to go through the same steps as those on her cassette tape but told that she did not have to memorize the script on the tape. Instead, it was recommended that she use the basic principles involved in her hypnotic induction. She was instructed to practice her self-hypnosis under ideal conditions for the coming week, i.e., lights dimmed, eyes closed, telephone ringer off, lying down in bed or on a comfortable couch, or sitting in a comfortable chair. She was told that eventually she would be able to use self-hypnosis for reducing anxiety, but because hypnosis is a skill, it may take several weeks of practice before she would be successful in applying it in stressful situations. The author typically offers this advice to patients learning self-hypnosis for the first time, because many patients have the unrealistic expectation that they will be able to use hypnosis immediately and get quick results. Mary reported at her fourth session that she started applying some parts of the self-hypnosis techniques whenever she started to feel anxious and was successful in reducing her anxiety. She reported having less free-floating anxiety.

During subsequent therapy sessions, hypnosis was used to prepare Mary for the various anxiety-provoking situations that were listed earlier. Hypnosis was induced using the same procedure involving slow, deep breathing, progressive relaxation, and her Maui image. Items from her list of anxiety-producing situations were described and therapeutic suggestions were given. For example, after she had achieved a deep state of relaxation, the author suggested the following:

Now imagine that you are starting a new project this week. Imagine feeling more calm and feeling more in control than you have previously. You are thinking more rationally. You know what you are doing. There are many times when you get good feedback from Connie. You continue to get better at your job. And even if you make mistakes, you will continue to see yourself as successful and knowledgeable. Everyone makes mistakes. You will feel more confident about starting that new project. You will be calmer about it. And if you should experience some anxiety, you will be able to reduce it by using your self-hypnosis skills, breathing slow and easy, and letting go of tension with each exhalation.

In each subsequent session, several anxiety-provoking situations from Mary's list were covered in a similar manner to the one described above. In addition, Mary was given assertiveness training for dealing with her boss's abusive behavior. Mary and the therapist would brainstorm various ways to respond to Connie's abusive statements. Some of the ideas were obtained from Mary's observations of fellow workers and their sharing with her how they dealt with Connie. During therapy sessions, Mary and the author role-played how she might be assertive with Connie. Then, during hypnosis, these assertive responses were described. Mary was asked to imagine being assertive with Connie and suggestions such as the following were given:

> Connie puts people on the defensive by interrogating them. If you block, or forget something, you can be assertive and tell her you'll get back to her with the answer. Everyone gets upset when she's abusive. You can tell Connie that you feel upset when she yells. Now imagine yourself being assertive with Connie and she stops yelling. You feel proud. And you'll be able to be assertive the next time Connie is abusive.

## Outcome and Recommendations

Mary continued to show improvement throughout the treatment. She reported that her sleeping improved dramatically. Her free-floating anxiety was greatly reduced in frequency, duration, and intensity, and her fear of Connie decreased over time. There was still some residual anticipatory anxiety that Mary experienced prior to her meetings with Connie. The author explained to Mary that anticipatory anxiety sometimes remains for a while, even after a patient has been successful in handling anxiety-producing situations. Frequently, it's the last symptom to undergo extinction because one needs to have had a number of successes in handling a problematic situation before one's confidence grows. Then with increased confidence, there is usually further anxiety reduction in one's anticipatory anxiety.

Connie never stopped being abusive, but Mary was able to respond by being assertive. Connie would apologize almost every time that Mary spoke up. On one occasion, Connie explained that she was under a lot of pressure and did not mean to treat Mary that way. Connie was eventually fired, probably because of her abusive behavior, although Mary never knew the real reason. Towards the end of treatment, Mary reported that she was able to stop being a workaholic and starting to enjoy her weekends.

Mary's case illustrates several key points and applications. One important point is, that, in the author's experience, there is rarely free-floating anxiety. Thoughts often provide the bridge between a feared event and a patient's emotional reaction. This is particularly relevant in patients who would be diagnosed as having generalized anxiety disorder. Teaching patients how their thoughts generate anxiety can reduce feelings of helplessness because their emotional reactions are no longer mysterious to them. In addition, giving them the tools for cognitive change can help them to feel more in control. The advantage of a cognitive-behavioral approach to hypnotherapy is that it facilitates the development of an internal locus of control, which might be absent in traditional hypnotherapy, where the perception is that the hypnotist is in control. This case further illustrates the natural integration of hypnosis and cognitive behavior therapy.

## CASE 2—SALLY: TREATMENT OF PHOBIAS

### Patient Background and History

Sally was 45 years old when she first came to therapy for hypnosis for the treatment of her flying phobia. She came to therapy 2 weeks before she was scheduled to fly. She had postponed dealing with her fear of flying until she felt desperate and helpless. The reason that she was now going to fly after years of avoiding it was because she had promised to go with her husband to visit his family.

Sally was referred to the author for hypnotherapy, which was the treatment the patient requested. When Sally called, she reported that she had very limited time, and asked if under these conditions the author could treat her for a flying phobia. The author informed Sally that it was indeed possible and that he had helped other patients in similar situations. Sally was only able to schedule four visits prior to her flight.

Because of the limited time available for therapy, only a brief history was taken. Sally reported that flying represented independence to her. She felt guilty about independence because she felt responsible for taking care of her mother. Although Sally said her mother never said anything to make her feel guilty, Sally nevertheless felt guilty for falling in love with her husband and leaving home to get married. Sally believed she would eventually be punished. Therefore, flying represented both independence, as well as vulnerability. She believed that dying in an airplane accident would be her punishment. Sally had stopped flying after her honeymoon.

## Presenting Complaints, Assessment, and Diagnosis

Sally reported having two phobias, a fear of going to the dentist and her fear of flying. However, she only wanted to work on her fear of flying. Sally had a number of anxiety symptoms—rapid heart rate, tension, fear of dying, nightmares about airplane crashes, anxiety when she thought about flying, and a long pattern of avoidance of flying, which caused her conflict with her husband. Her fears were fairly circumscribed, so a diagnosis of a simple phobia was justified.

## Case Conceptualization

The treatment plan included cognitive, behavioral, and hypnotic interventions. Specific treatment interventions included an eye-fixation hypnotic induction technique, relaxation techniques, the use of rational statements as hypnotic suggestions, imaginal and in vivo desensitization. Desensitization via hypnosis has been found to be effective in the treatment of phobias (Marks, Gelder, & Edwards, 1968; Clarke & Jackson, 1983).

Hypnotherapy was chosen for several reasons. The author uses imaginal desensitization during hypnosis as the exposure treatment for phobic patients who request hypnosis. This patient expected and wanted hypnosis. There was limited time available for therapy, and there was not enough time to do extensive relaxation training, elaborate hierarchy construction, or a thorough desensitization. Her treatment needed to be quick and simple. Unlike the previous case, there was not enough time to teach cognitive restructuring techniques such as the two-column method, nor time for self-hypnosis training. Under these conditions, the author finds hypnosis to be valuable for several reasons. With a responsive subject, the therapist is able to rapidly induce relaxation via a hypnotic induction, without having to provide the patient with much relaxation training. It's probably not that hypnotic induction procedures produce deeper or more rapid relaxation than other relaxation techniques—Rather, the author believes that hypnotherapy can be more rapid because patients expect hypnosis to be rapid. So when a therapist proceeds rapidly in hypnotherapy, the therapist's behavior is consistent with the patient's expectations. Certainly in Sally's case she wanted and needed rapid treatment.

## Course of Treatment

Sally's therapy lasted a total of four sessions. The first session was used for taking a brief history and assessment and orienting the patient to hypnosis. The focus of the assessment was to obtain a list of anxiety-producing situations concerning flying that could be used for an anxiety hierarchy. The author and the patient were able to identify several anxiety-producing situations that were rank-ordered from least to most anxiety producing. There were few low anxiety items. Most of the items were rated as highly anxiety-producing by Sally. The items and their ratings were as follows:

1. Plane landing—40

2. Thinking about flying—45

3. Watching planes on TV—50

4. Driving to the airport—55

5. Watching planes landing and taking off—58

6. Boarding the plane—60

7. Airplane hatch closing—65

8. Plane taxiing on the runway—70

9. Plane on runway waiting to take off—75

10. Airborne—80

11. The night before the flight—85

12. Seatbelt light goes on—90

13. Plane banking—93

14. Takeoff—95

15. Turbulence—100

Sally came to therapy very receptive to using hypnosis and had very definite ideas of what she expected of it and what method should be used. She wanted an eye-fixation method of induction but otherwise wanted the author to make most of the other decisions about what was to be done in the therapy, including what suggestions were to be given. Although the author usually employs hypnotic skills training, this was not done in Sally's case because of time limitations. The author did ask her to construct a pleasant image for the purpose of relaxation. Sally selected an image of her relaxing, lying with her dog on the couch in her living room, listening to classical music. During the first session, the author proceeded with a hypnotic induction that started with eye-fixation and included several relaxation techniques. The author suggested the following to Sally:

> Pick a spot, any spot will do, and continue to stare at it, until your eyes get heavy, and tired. If your eyes should wander, just refocus on that same spot. And you may notice changes, as you continue to stare at that same spot. It may get fuzzy, or move, or change in some other way. You can just enjoy whatever you experience, and continue staring at that spot, until your eyes get heavy, and tired, and then you can let them close, so that you can start to relax.

During the eye fixation, the author typically shifts attention away from mentioning the it and proceeds to progressive relaxation. Shifting attention in this way reduces the pressure on the patient to have to respond to eye closure. The patient's relaxation image is eventually described along with suggestions of deeper relaxation some time after the patient's eyes close. Sally was very responsive to this induction.

After the hypnotic induction, the author described each item from Sally's hierarchy, proceeding in order, from the least to the most anxiety producing. While she was imagining an item, the author would provide anxiety-reducing suggestions. Although there wasn't sufficient time for the author to teach Sally self-hypnosis, he was nevertheless able to introduce elements of self-hypnosis by making suggestions such as the following to Sally:

> As you imagine being in the plane on the runway, waiting for it to take off, you can reduce any anxiety that you might feel by focusing on your breathing and purposely slowing it down, so that you are breathing slower and deeper than usual, feeling more relaxed with each exhalation, letting go of any tension with each exhalation. And imagining being in your living room, lying on your couch with Pepper (her dog) listening to classical music, seeing your French doors, the white lace curtains and the gray and black pattern of your carpet. And you can use this pleasant calming image and the slow deep breathing to keep yourself calm and in control. And if you should experience any anxiety during your flights, you will be able to calm yourself by slowing your breathing down, letting go of tension with each exhalation, and imagining your pleasant relaxing image, feeling more calm and more in control.

Despite the time limitations for this treatment, the author was still able to include a cognitive component into Sally's hypnotherapy. Based on information that he got from her, the author arrived at several rational suggestions that he thought would be effective in challenging Sally's anxiety-producing and guilt-producing thoughts. During hypnosis, the author suggested the following to her:

> It's safe to be independent. You can love both your husband and your mother. You can lead your own life and still be there for your mother. You're a good daughter. Your mother appreciates all that you have done and that you still do for her, and has told you that you are a good daughter.

The author was able to go through five items from Sally's hierarchy at each of the three desensitization sessions so that the treatment was completed by the fourth session. Sally felt more confident about flying and said she was ready to go on her airplane trip.

## Outcome and Recommendations

Sally was successful in achieving her goal of being able to take her airplane trip. She was amazed at how calm she was through most of the flight. She reported that she did experience some anxiety during a brief period of mild turbulence. But she found that the slow deep breathing and her image of her dog Pepper to be effective in reducing her anxiety.

Nine years later Sally returned to treatment. However, this time it was not for a fear of flying. She had traveled by airplane a number of times after her initial treatment and was fine, even when she experienced turbulence. This time she came to therapy to address her dental phobia, since the author had identified her dental phobia in Sally's initial session. At the time he had offered treatment for her dental fears as well, but she had declined, saying she would return at a later date. As she had done with her flying phobia, Sally avoided dealing with her dental problem until she no longer had a choice. She had avoided most dental work during those 9 years and now needed either two sets of dentures, or implants. The author used basically the same hypnotic desensitization program for treating Sally's dental fears as for treating her flying phobia. Again, Sally proved to be an excellent patient and only needed two sessions of hypnosis to become desensitized enough to be able to undergo multiple root canal procedures and have 12 teeth pulled. She opted for having partial dentures instead of implants.

This case illustrates the effectiveness of the combination of hypnosis and desensitization in treating phobic patients. Treatment tends to be straightforward and brief. Hypnosis is of great value when there is limited time for treatment.

## CASE 3—JANE: TREATMENT OF A PSYCHOPHYSIOLOGICAL DISORDER: IRRITABLE BOWEL SYNDROME

## Patient Background and History

Jane was referred to the author for treatment of anxiety, phobias, and irritable bowel syndrome (IBS). Previously, Jane had received treatment from a cognitive-behavior therapist who had initially tried various relaxation techniques with her, including breathing techniques, and imagery and progressive relaxation. Jane reported that she could not sit still during any relaxation exercise, no matter what the length, and that all of the techniques that were tried had made her more anxious. The previous therapy had evolved into talk therapy about Jane's past and her need for approval. This approach was ineffective. Jane remained symptomatic, despite also being on Imodium.

## Presenting Complaints, Assessment and Diagnosis

IBS is a disorder that includes such symptoms as diarrhea, constipation, gas, bloating, discomfort which can be sharp pain, cramps, or a continuous dull ache, a sense of urgency about having to move one's bowels, high frequency of bowel movements, and a feeling of incomplete evacuation. Many patients with IBS have anxiety about loss of control and many develop phobias about travel and social activities. Jane was scared about travel and social situations. Her symptoms included worry, tension in her jaw and lower back, irregular breathing, rapid heart rate, stomachaches, and uncontrollable diarrhea. Stress and anxiety were frequent triggers for her IBS attacks. Certain foods also seemed to be triggers. As is often the case, Jane was sensitive to fried foods, fatty foods, milk products, alcohol, caffeine, fruits and fruit juices, tomato sauce, and eating large amounts of food at any given time. Her phobia started when she was on a crowded bus and was having an IBS attack. Although she did not lose control of her bowels, she feared she was going to. Thereafter, she avoided public transportation, social situations such as social gatherings and restaurants, or any place where she feared she could be trapped and have uncontrollable diarrhea. Jane fit the criteria for DSM diagnoses of psychological factors causing a medical condition as well as agoraphobia. Based on her history, her phobia was secondary to her IBS.

## Case Conceptualization

When Jane first met with the author, she was very discouraged. She had tried traditional relaxation techniques and found they only made her feel more anxious, so she was skeptical and reluctant to try CBT again. The author explained to Jane that she needed a multifaceted treatment and suggested a treatment plan that included medical, psychiatric, nutritional, cognitive, behavioral, and hypnotic interventions. The author offered hypnosis as an alternative to traditional relaxation techniques. Given that she did poorly with direct methods of relaxation, the author thought that perhaps a hypnotic induction that involved indirect suggestion might work better.

Specific treatment interventions used in Jane's case included a hypnotic induction involving indirect suggestion, cognitive restructuring, and imaginal and in vivo desensitization. As discussed already, imaginal and in vivo desensitization is effective in the treatment of phobias. There is clinical and experimental evidence demonstrating the effectiveness of hypnosis in the treatment of IBS (Galovski & Blanchard, 1998; Gonsalkorale, Houghton, & Whorwell, 2002; Harvey, Hinton, Gunary, & Barry, 1989; Whorwell, Prior, & Faragher, 1984). CBT has also been found to be effective in the treatment of IBS (Blanchard, Greene, Scharff, & Schwarz-McMorris, 1993; Drossman, et al., 2003; Toner, Segal, Emmott, & Myran, 1999). In some of these studies, the subjects were patients who did not respond to other treatments. Probably the reason that hypnosis and relaxation techniques have such a dramatic effect on various gastrointestinal (GI) symptoms is that changes throughout the GI tract are affected by emotions, stress, and relaxation. Several studies have demonstrated physiological changes in the GI tract as a result of hypnosis (Whorwell, Houghton, Taylor, & Maxton, 1992; Klein & Spiegel, 1989). Hypnosis and relaxation techniques are of value in the treatment of IBS probably because stress is a major factor in exacerbating IBS symptoms.

The dilemma in Jane's case was that she did not respond well to relaxation techniques. Given that relaxation techniques and hypnotic induction procedures are so similar, one might assume that patients who do poorly with relaxation might be poor candidates for hypnosis as well. But in evaluating Jane's poor response to relaxation techniques, the author concluded that the reason for her difficulty with this treatment was that she was trying too hard. As discussed earlier in the chapter, Erickson's hypnotic induction procedures in which every suggestion is in the form of a question (Erickson & Rossi, 1979) can be effective with patients who become more anxious as a result of trying too hard to follow direct suggestions. Thus, Jane was receptive to the author's recommendation to try hypnosis using indirect suggestion.

## Course of Treatment

Jane was in therapy for seven months. Given the complexity of her case, this amount of time was needed to treat her for her IBS and phobias. The first two sessions were used for conducting a thorough assessment. The author obtained a complete medical and psychological history. Jane was already taking Imodium for the IBS and avoiding all of the usual "trigger" foods. However, none of these prior interventions were effective in controlling her symptoms.

Given that Jane had phobias, the assessment included obtaining a list of anxiety producing situations that could be used for an anxiety hierarchy. The items and their ratings were as follows:

1.  Entertaining at home—20

2.  Eating in a restaurant, with family, within five minutes of home—25

3.  Eating in a restaurant, with friends, within five minutes of home—30

4.  Eating in a restaurant, with family, further than a five-minute walk to home—30

5.  Eating in a restaurant, with friends, further than a five-minute walk to home—35

6.  Eating in a restaurant, with family, 20 minutes or more from home—40

7.  Eating in a restaurant, with friends, 20 minutes or more from home—45

8.  Shopping in a mall—45

9.  Subway, short distance of one or two stops—45

10.  Day of shopping outdoors—45

11.  Movie theatre, aisle seat—50

12.  Eating with fellow worker, no travel involved—50

13. Travel less than one hour after eating—55

14. Bus, no traffic—55

15. Driving in car, light traffic—55

16. Bike riding in the park—60

17. Taxicab ride, light traffic—60

18. Social event at a friend's house—65

19. Bus, light traffic—70

20. Driving in a car, alone, heavy traffic—75

21. Beach—80

22. Movie theatre, center seat—80

23. Taxicab ride, heavy traffic—85

24. Business meeting, no food—85

25. Business luncheon—90

26. Day of outdoor activities with friends—90

27. Social event like a wedding—90

28. Bus, heavy traffic—90

29. Subway, long distance between stops—95

30. Driving in a car on a highway, long distance between exits—95

31. Driving in a car with family member, heavy traffic—95

32. Subway, stuck between stops—100

33. Driving in car with friends, stuck in heavy traffic—100

The assessment revealed that Jane had numerous anxiety-producing thoughts. Jane kept self-monitoring logs throughout treatment. Starting with her third therapy session, Jane and the author started using the two-column method for formulating therapeutic suggestions. Listed below is the two-column method used for generating Jane's therapeutic suggestions. Similar anxiety-reducing suggestions were developed for each item of her anxiety hierarchy.

| *Anxiety-Producing Thoughts* | *Therapeutic Suggestions* |
|---|---|
| 1. What if I have an IBS attack out of the blue? What if that happened to me while I was in a car? | 1. If I were in a car, I'd find a bathroom. So far, I've always been able to be in control until I found a bathroom. |
| 2. What if I need to use a bathroom while I'm in a movie theatre and I don't have the aisle seat? | 2. People get out of their seats to go to the bathroom all the time. I can do the same thing. |
| 3. What if I have to go to the bathroom in the middle of a meeting or business luncheon? | 3. I can excuse myself. I'm not the first person that ever had to leave in the middle of a meeting. |
| 4. What if I have an IBS attack in front of my friends and family? | 4. They all know about it and accept me that way. |
| 5. What if I need to use a public bathroom and the ladies bathroom is occupied? | 5. I could use the men's room if I have no other choice. |
| 6. What if I have to use a public bathroom and it's really gross? | 6. I can use a "gross" bathroom if there is no choice. I may not like it, but I can do it and being able to use any bathroom gives me more control. |
| 7. What if I have an accident? Other people will think I'm disgusting. | 7. It's never happened and therefore probably won't. But I can always carry extra clothes with me whenever I have to travel. Family and friends would understand if I had an accident and I don't need the approval of strangers. |

The greatest challenge in Jane's treatment was developing a hypnotic induction procedure that was effective in helping her to achieve relaxation, since breathing techniques, imagery, and progressive relaxation had all been tried by the previous therapist without any success. During the fourth session, the author recommended using hypnosis and indirect suggestion. Jane was told that although it would include imagery, it would be different from anything she had previously tried. Each image would be presented in the form of a question. She was told that she did not have to imagine any details, nor did she have to imagine all of the various images during any given induction. She could just allow herself to respond to whichever questions she could. Jane was receptive to trying it. Some of the questions came from Weitzman's "sensory awareness" exercise that was described earlier in the chapter (see Goldfried & Davison, 1976). However, Jane was involved in the selection of the images and the wording of the questions that would be used to present each image. There were 10-second intervals between each question. The following are some of the indirect suggestions that were part of her hypnosis-relaxation induction:

Can you imagine walking outside on a beautiful day?

Can you imagine walking through a garden?

Can you imagine a flower?

If you can imagine the flower, what color is it? How many petals does it have?

Can you imagine a butterfly in flight? What does it look like?

Can you imagine walking along the beach? Can you imagine the warmth of the sun? Can you imagine the sound of the ocean as the waves break along the shore? What do they sound like? Can you imagine the sound of seagulls? Can you imagine sandpipers running in and out as the waves wash in and out?

Can you imagine a sunset? If you can imagine the sunset, what colors is it?

Can you imagine floating in warm water? Can you imagine drifting along? Can you feel light and buoyant?

Can you imagine walking in the woods during autumn? Can you imagine the different colors of the leaves?

Can you imagine the crunching sound of the leaves beneath your feet?

Jane was very responsive to this type of induction. Over the next 2 weeks, she practiced it at home by listening to a cassette tape that was recorded during her therapy session. By her fifth session, Jane's confidence about being able to relax grew. She reported that she was able to relax using the images on her own and that they no longer had to be in a question form. In contrast to her initial reaction, she now preferred that they not be worded as questions. As a result of her own experimentation, she was also able to include diaphragmatic breathing. Jane reported that she was able to induce relaxation on her own, without a cassette tape, and had been able to apply it in reducing anxiety.

Desensitization began with the seventh session and continued until the end of treatment. In each desensitization session, relaxation was induced and several of the items from Jane's anxiety hierarchy were presented. While imagining herself in each situation, the author would give Jane anxiety-reducing suggestions. Some of the suggestions were those that had been constructed in earlier sessions using the two-column method. Jane created other therapeutic suggestions on her own. Some of her own suggestions included, "I can take Imodium preventively before I go into a stressful situation, I have my self-hypnosis which keeps me calm, I'll watch what I eat and drink, I've gotten through rough situations before, there are bathrooms everywhere."

## Outcome and Recommendations

Jane chose several in vivo homework assignments each week, in which she confronted her fears and applied her techniques. She was very successful in not only reducing her anxiety but also in experiencing a dramatic reduction in her IBS symptoms. Eight months later, Jane was still in control of her anxiety and IBS symptoms. She did return to treatment. However, it was not for IBS or anxiety, but rather for counseling about making life changes. Despite going through a very stressful period, Jane remained symptom-free.

Jane's case illustrates the effectiveness of indirect suggestion as applied to an individual who previously became anxious in response to direct suggestion. In addition, this case demonstrates the dramatic effects of CBH on IBS.

# REFERENCES

Araoz, D. L. (1981). Negative self-hypnosis. *Journal of Contemporary Psychotherapy, 12*, 45–52.

Araoz, D. L. (1985). *The new hypnosis.* New York: Brunner/Mazel.

Barber, T. X. (1978). Hypnosis, suggestions and psychosomatic phenomena: A new look from the standpoint of recent experimental studies. *The American Journal of Clinical Hypnosis, 21*, 13–27.

Barber, T. X. (1979). Suggested ("hypnotic") behavior: The trance paradigm versus an alternative paradigm. In E. Fromm & R. E. Shor (Eds.), *Hypnosis: Developments in research and new perspectives* (2nd ed.). New York: Aldine.

Barber, T. X., Spanos, N. P., & Chaves, J. F. (1974). *Hypnosis, imagination and human potentialities.* Elmsford, NY: Pergamon.

Beck, A. T. (1967). *Depression: Clinical, experimental and theoretical aspects.* New York: Hoeber-Harper.

Beck, A. T., & Emery, G. (1985). *Anxiety disorders and phobias: A cognitive perspective.* New York: Basic Books.

Bernheim, H. (1895). *Suggestive therapeutics.* New York: Putnam.

Benson, H., Arns, P. A., & Hoffman, J. W. (1981). The relaxation response and hypnosis. *International Journal of Clinical and Experimental Hypnosis, 29*, 259–270.

Blanchard, E. B., Greene, B., Scharff, L., & Schwarz-McMorris, S. P. (1993). Relaxation training as a treatment for irritable bowel syndrome. *Biofeedback and Self-regulation, 3*, 125–132.

Boutin, G. E., & Tosi, D. J. (1983). Modification of irrational ideas and test anxiety through rational stage directed hypnotherapy RSDH. *Journal of Clinical Psychology, 39*(3), 382–391.

Clarke, J. C., & Jackson, J. A. (1983). *Hypnosis and behavior therapy: The treatment of anxiety and phobias.* New York: Springer Publishing.

Diamond, M. J. (1974). Modification of hypnotizability: A review. *Psychological Bulletin, 81*, 180–198.

Diamond, M. J. (1977). Hypnotizability is modifiable: An alternative approach. *International Journal of Clinical and Experimental Hypnosis, 25*, 147–166.

Drossman, D. A., Toner, B. B., Whitehead, W. E., Diamant, N. E., Dalton, C. B., Duncan, S., et al. (2003). Cognitive-behavioral therapy versus education and Desipramine versus placebo for moderate to severe functional bowel disorders. *Gastroenterology, 125*(1), 19–31.

Edmonston, W. E. (1981). *Hypnosis and relaxation: Modern verification of an old equation.* New York: John Wiley.

Ellis, A. (1957). Rational psychotherapy and individual psychology. *Journal of Individual Psychology, 13*, 38–44.

Ellis, A. (1962). *Reason and emotion in psychotherapy.* New York: Lyle Stuart.

Erickson, M. H., & Rossi, E. L. (1979). *Hypnotherapy: An exploratory casebook.* New York: Irvington.

Fuller, J. (1981). *Rational stage-directed hypnotherapy in the treatment of self-concept and depression in a geriatric nursing home population: A cognitive experimental approach.* Unpublished doctoral dissertation, Ohio State University.

Galovski, T. E., & Blanchard, E. B. (1998). The treatment of irritable bowel syndrome with hypnotherapy. *Applied Psychophysiology and Biofeedback, 23,* 219–232.

Gibbons, D., Kilbourne, L., Saunders, A., & Castles, C. (1970). The cognitive control of behavior: A comparison of systematic desensitization and hypnotically-induced "direct experience" techniques. *American Journal of Clinical Hypnosis, 12,* 141–145.

Golden, W. L. (1986a). Resistance in cognitive-behaviour therapy. *British Journal of Cognitive Psychotherapy, 1*(1), 47–56.

Golden, W. L. (1986b). An integration of Ericksonian and cognitive-behavioral hypnotherapy in the treatment of anxiety disorders. In E. T. Dowd & J. M. Healy (Eds.), *Case studies in hypnotherapy.* New York: Guilford.

Golden, W. L., Dowd, E. T., & Friedberg, F. (1987). *Hypnotherapy: A modern approach.* New York: Pergamon.

Golden, W. L., & Dryden, W. (1986). Cognitive-behavioural therapies: Commonalities, divergences and future directions. In W. Dryden & W. L. Golden (Eds.), *Cognitive-behavioural approaches to psychotherapy.* London: Harper & Row.

Goldfried, M. R. (1971). Systematic desensitization as training in self-control. *Journal of Consulting and Clinical Psychology, 34,* 228–234.

Goldfried, M. R. (1973). Reduction of generalized anxiety through a variant of systematic desensitization. In M. R. Goldfried & M. Merbaum (Eds.), *Behavior change through self-control.* New York: Holt, Rinehart, & Winston.

Goldfried, M. R., & Davison, G. C. (1976). *Clinical behavior therapy.* New York: Holt, Rinehart, & Winston.

Gonsalkorale, W. M., Houghton, L. A., & Whorwell, P. J. (2002). Hypnotherapy in irritable bowel syndrome: A large-scale audit of clinical service with examination of factors influencing responsiveness. *American Journal of Gastroenterology, 97*(4), 954–961.

Harvey, R. F., Hinton, R. A., Gunary, R. M., & Barry, R. E. (1989). Individual and group hypnotherapy in treatment of refractory irritable bowel syndrome. *Lancet, 1,* 424–425.

Hussain, A. (1964). Behavior therapy using hypnosis. In J. Wolpe, A. Salter, & L. J. Reyna (Eds.), *The conditioning therapies.* New York: Holt, Rinehart, & Winston.

Jacobson, E. (1929). *Progressive relaxation.* Chicago: University of Chicago Press.

Kazdin, A. (1974a). Covert modeling, model similarity, and reduction of avoidance behavior. *Behavior Therapy, 5,* 325–340.

Kazdin, A. (1974b). The effect of model identity and fear relevant similarity on covert modeling. *Behavior Therapy, 5,* 624–636.

Katz, N. W. (1979). Comparative efficacy of behavioral training, training plus relaxation, and sleep/trance hypnotic induction in increasing hypnotic susceptibility. *Journal of Consulting and Clinical Psychology, 47,* 119–127.

Kirsch, I., Montgomery, G., & Sapirstein, G. (1995). Hypnosis as an adjunct to cognitive-behavioral psychotherapy: A meta-analysis. *Journal of Consulting and Clinical Psychology, 63*(2), 214–220.

Klein, K. B., & Spiegel, D. (1989). Modulation of gastric acid secretion by hypnosis. *Gastroenterology, 96*, 1383–1387.

Lazarus, A. A. (1973). "Hypnosis" as a facilitator in behavior therapy. *International Journal of Clinical and Experimental Hypnosis, 6*, 83–89.

Marks, I. M., Gelder, M. G., & Edwards, G. (1968). Hypnosis and desensitization for phobias: A controlled prospective trial. *British Journal of Psychiatry, 114*, 1263–1274.

Meichenbaum, D. H. (1972). Cognitive modification of test anxious college students. *Journal of Consulting and Clinical Psychology, 39*, 370–380.

Meichenbaum, D. H. (1977). *Cognitive-behavior modification: An integrative approach*. New York: Plenum.

Prince, M., & Coriat, I. (1907). Cases illustrating the educational treatment of the psychoneuroses. *Journal of Abnormal Psychology, 2*, 166–177.

Spanos, N. P., & Barber, T. X. (1974). Toward a convergence in hypnosis research. *American Psychologist, 29*, 500–511.

Spanos, N. P., & Barber, T. X. (1976). Behavior modification and hypnosis. In M. Hersen, R. M. Eisler, & P. M. Miller (Eds.), *Progress in behavior modification*. New York: Academic.

Toner, B. B., Segal, Z. V., Emmott, S. D., & Myran, D. (1999). *Cognitive behavioral treatment of irritable bowel syndrome: The brain-gut connection*. New York: Guilford.

Whorwell, P. J., Houghton, L. A., Taylor, E. E., & Maxton, D. G. (1992). Physiological effects of emotion: Assessment via hypnosis. *Lancet, 340*, 69–72.

Whorwell, P. J., Prior, A., & Faragher, E. B. (1984). Controlled trial of hypnotherapy in the treatment of severe refractory irritable-bowel syndrome. *Lancet, 2*, 1232–1234.

Wolpe, J. (1958). *Psychotherapy by reciprocal inhibition*. Oxford: Pergamon.

Woody, R. H., & Shauble, P. J. (1969). Desensitization of fear by video tapes. *Journal of Clinical Psychology, 25*, 102–103.

Chapter 6

# Cognitive Hypnotherapy for Treating Depression

Assen Alladin

$M$ajor depressive disorder is among one of the most common psychiatric disorders treated by psychiatrists and psychotherapists. It is characterized by feelings of sadness, lack of interest in formerly enjoyable pursuits, sleep and appetite disturbance, feelings of worthlessness, and thoughts of death and dying. All depressive disorders are extremely disabling (second only to heart disease) in terms of poor quality of life and disability (Pincus & Pettit, 2001), and 15% of people with a major depressive disorder kill themselves (Satcher, 2000). Depressive disorders can usually be treated successfully with antidepressant medication and psychotherapy (Moore & Bona, 2001). However, a significant number of people with depression do not respond to either medication or an existing psychotherapy approach. Therefore, it is important for practitioners and investigators to continue to develop more effective treatments for depression. Moreover, clinical depression poses special problems to therapists, as it "takes over the whole person–emotions, bodily functions, behaviors, and thoughts" (Nolen-Hoeksema, 2004, p. 280). It is thus essential for practitioners treating depression to have a rigorous understanding and knowledge of the nature of depressive disorder. This chapter describes cognitive hypnotherapy (CH), a multimodal treatment approach to depression that may be applicable to a wide range of people who suffer from depression.

## THE PREVALENCE OF DEPRESSION

Apart from being one of the most commonly diagnosed psychological disorders, major depressive disorder is reported to be on the increase (World Health Organization, 1998). It is estimated that out of every 100 people, approximately 13 men and 21 women are likely to develop the disorder at some point in life (Kessler et al., 1994), and approximately one-third of the population may suffer from mild depression at some point in their lives (Paykel & Priest, 1992). In fact, the rate of major depression is so high that the World Health Organization's (WHO) Global Burden of Disease Study ranked it as the single most burdensome disease in the world in terms of total disability-adjusted life years among people in the middle years of life (Murray & Lopez, 1996). Moreover, major depression is a very costly disorder in terms of lost productivity at work, industrial accidents, bed occupancy in hospitals, treatment, state benefits, and personal suffering. The disorder also adversely affects interpersonal relationships with spouses and children (Gotlib & Hammen, 2002); the rate of divorce is higher among depressives than among nondepressed individuals (e.g., Wade & Cairney, 2000), and the children of depressed parents are found to be at elevated risk for psychopathology (Gotlib & Goodman, 1999). According to WHO (1998), by the year 2020 clinical depression is likely to be second only to chronic heart disease as an international health burden, as measured by cause of death, disability, incapacity to work, and medical resources used.

## DSM-IV CRITERIA FOR MAJOR
## DEPRESSIVE DISORDER

Major depressive disorder as described in this chapter was previously categorized under different labels, such as depressive disorder, affective disorders, or depressive neuroses. All these labels were grouped under the heading "mood disorders" by the DSM-III

(American Psychiatric Association, 1980) in order to emphasize the gross deviation in mood. In this chapter, the label depression is used to refer to major depressive disorder. The DSM-IV (American Psychiatric Association, 1994) formal diagnosis of major depression, also referred to as unipolar depression, requires the presence of five of the following symptoms for at least 2 weeks (either depressed mood or loss of interest and pleasure must be one of the five symptoms):

1.  Sad, depressed mood most of the day, nearly every day (or irritable mood in children or adolescents).

2.  Marked loss of interest and pleasure in all or almost all activities.

3.  Poor appetite and significant weight loss, or increased appetite and weight gain.

4.  Insomnia or hypersomnia nearly every day.

5.  Psychomotor agitation or retardation nearly every day.

6.  Fatigue or loss of energy nearly every day.

7.  Feelings of worthlessness and guilt, and negative self-concept, self-reproach, and self-blame.

8.  Diminished ability to think or concentrate, or indecisiveness.

9.  Recurrent thoughts of death or suicide.

A *major depressive episode* is the most common form of depression diagnosed in clinical practice. If two or more major depressive episodes occur, separated by a period of at least 2 months during which the individual was not depressed, *major depressive disorder, recurrence*, is diagnosed. Approximately 60% of people who have a major depressive episode will have a second episode. Among those who have experienced two episodes, 70% will have a third, and among those who have had three episodes, 90% will have a fourth (American Psychiatric Association, 2000). Recurrence is very important in predicting the future course of the disorder as well as in choosing appropriate treatments. As many as 85% of single-episode cases later experience a second episode, and the median lifetime number of major depressive episodes is four, while 25% of depressives experience six or more episodes (Angst & Preizig, 1996).

Depression is therefore considered a chronic condition that waxes and wanes over time but seldom disappears (Solomon et al., 2000). The median duration of recurrent depression is 5 months. The cognitive hypnotherapy approach to treatment described in this chapter is based on the author's experience of working with chronic depressives over the past 20 years.

In trying to define the course of major depressive disorder, researchers have come to realize that depression is a heterogeneous disorder with many possible courses. Moreover, people with the same diagnosis may vary greatly from one another. For example, some depressed patients may be diagnosed as having psychotic features such as delusions and hallucinations. Such a distinction among unipolar depressives is important as it has implications for treatment and recognizing the severity of the illness. It is well-known that depressives with delusions do not generally respond well to antidepressants, but they show better response when an anti-psychotic drug is combined with the antidepressant. It is also known that depression with psychotic features tends to be more severe than depression without delusions, and it involves more social impairment and less time between episodes (Coryell et al., 1996).

Moreover, depression co-occurs with other disorders, both medical and psychiatric. Kessler (2002), from his review of the epidemiology of depression, concludes that "comorbidity is the norm among people with depression" (p. 29). For example, the Epidemiologic Catchment Area Study (Robins & Regier, 1991) found that 75% of respondents with lifetime depressive disorder also met criteria for at least one of the other DSM-III disorders assessed in their survey. The most frequent comorbid condition with depression is anxiety. In fact, there is considerable symptom overlap in these two conditions. The presence of poor concentration, irritability, hypervigilance, fatigue, guilt, memory loss, sleep difficulties, and worry may suggest a diagnosis of either disorder. The symptoms overlap between the two conditions may be indicative of similar neurobiological correlates. At a psychological level, it seems reasonable to assume that depression can result from the demoralization caused by anxiety, for example in a case of an agoraphobic who becomes withdrawn because of the fear of going out. Conversely, a person with depression may become anxious due to worry about being unable to hold gainful employment. Although there is an apparent overlap between anxiety and depression, it is common clinical practice to focus on treating one disorder at a time. Lack of an integrated approach to treatment means that a patient may be treated only for depression while still suffering from anxiety. One of the rationales for combining hypnosis with cognitive behavior therapy, as described in this chapter, is to address symptoms of anxiety.

## TREATMENTS FOR DEPRESSION

In the past 20 years there have been significant developments and innovations in the pharmacological and psychological treatment of depression. Tricyclic antidepressant drugs for the treatment of depression have been around since the 1960s. Although these drugs reduce acute symptoms in about 60% of depressives (Nemeroff, 2000), they can take about 4–8 weeks to work (Fava & Rosenbaum, 1995), they have a number of side effects, and an overdose of a tricyclic can be fatal. Therefore, the physicians have been wary of using tricyclics with depressives, especially with patients who may have suicidal thoughts. Monoamine oxidase inhibitors (MAOIs) have also been used to treat depression, but they have not been very popular due to serious side effects and some dietary restrictions. In the past 20 years, a second generation of antidepressants, known as selective serotonin reuptake inhibitors (SSRIs), has become extremely popular in the treatment of depression. These drugs are similar in structure to the tricyclics, but they work more selectively to affect the serotonin level. Although the SSRIs do not work better than tricyclics and MAOIs, they can produce improvement within a couple of weeks and they have less severe side effects. Moreover, these drugs are not fatal in overdose and they appear to help with a range of disorders, including anxiety, binge eating, and premenstrual symptoms (Pearlstein et al., 1997). A number of other drugs such as Remeron, Serzone, Effexor, and Wellbutrin have also been introduced during the past decade. They share some similarities with SSRIs, but they can't be classified in any of the previously mentioned categories. Sometimes these drugs are used in conjunction with SSRIs. Presently there are a variety of antidepressants available, but there are no consistent rules for determining which to use first. In clinical practice, several antidepressants are used before finding one drug that works well and with tolerable side effects. Antidepressant medications have relieved severe depression and undoubtedly prevented suicide in tens of thousands of patients around the world. Although these medications are readily available, many people refuse or are not eligible to take them. Some are wary of long-term side effects. Women of childbearing age must protect themselves against the possibility of conceiving while taking antidepressants, because they can damage the fetus. In addition, 40%–50% of patients do not respond adequately to these drugs, and a substantial number of the remainder are left with residual symptoms of depression (Barlow & Durand, 2005, p. 238).

Electroconvulsive therapy (ECT) is often given to patients who don't respond to drug therapies. ECT is known to relieve depression in 50%–60% of depressives (Fink, 2001). ECT, however, remains a controversial treatment for several reasons, including causing cognitive and memory impairments, and the idea of passing electrical current through a person's brain appears primitive to some. And it is still not known how ECT works.

Although antidepressant medications and ECT work well for many depressed persons, they obviously do not alleviate the problems that may have caused the depression in the first place. Pills cannot improve the bad marriage, unhappy work situation, or family conflict that precede depression. Therefore, many depressed people benefit from psychotherapies designed to help them cope with the difficult life circumstances or personality vulnerabilities that put them at risk for depression. Psychotherapy is also sometimes the recommended treatment for people who have medical conditions (such as pregnancy and some heart problems) that preclude the use of prescribed medications.

## CBT for Treating Depression

Cognitive behavior therapy (CBT) is the most extensively tested psychosocial treatment for depression. It has been studied in over 80 controlled trials (American Psychiatric Association, 2000), it has been found to be effective in the reduction of acute distress, and it compares favorably with pharmacological treatment among all but the most severely depressed patients. Moreover, CBT reduces relapse (Hollon & Shelton, 1991) and can prevent the initial onset of first episodes or the emergence of symptoms in persons at risk who have never been depressed (Gillham, Shatte, & Freres, 2000).

Although more than 20 therapies have been called "cognitive" or "cognitive-behavioral," the cognitive approach to depression grew directly out of Beck's (Beck, 1967, 1976; Beck & Young, 1985; Young & Beitchman, 2001) observation that depressives tend to be involved in deep-seated negative thinking.

CBT is compatible with the cognitive model of depression and is drawn from several sources, including the writings of behaviorists and post-Freudian analysts (Thase & Beck, 1992). There are a number of cognitive views of depression, each of which builds on the basic observation that how people think can have profound influence on how they feel. The approach developed by Beck (1967) initially grew out of clinical observations of depressed patients and was later supported by experimental work conducted by Seligman (1975) and his colleagues. Additionally, in 1979 Beck produced a treatment manual for depression entitled *Cognitive Therapy for Depression* (Beck, Rush, Shaw, & Emery, 1979).

Beck's cognitive model of psychotherapy is based on the theory that depressives have characteristic errors in information processing. Beck (1967) argued that depressives look at the world through a negative *cognitive triad*: they have negative views of themselves, of the world, and the future. Hence, depressives have the tendency to commit many types of errors in thinking, such as jumping to negative conclusions in the absence of evidence, ignoring positive events, and magnifying negative events that support their negative cognitive triad. A wide range of studies have supported the hypothesis that depressed people show these cognitive distortions, and some longitudinal studies have demonstrated that these thinking styles predict depression over time (Abramson et al., 2002).

CBT is predicated on the notion that teaching patients to recognize and examine their negative beliefs and information-processing proclivities can produce relief from their symptoms and enable them to cope more effectively with life's challenges (Beck et al., 1979). The primary role of the therapist is to educate clients in the use of various techniques that allow them to examine their thoughts and modify maladaptive beliefs and behaviors. One of the ultimate goals of therapy is to help the client learn to use these tools independently. Such skills are not only important for symptom relief, but may also minimize the chances of future recurrence of symptoms. According to Hollon, Haman, and Brown (2002), a successful course of CBT accomplishes its goals through a structured collaborative process consisting of three interrelated components: *exploration, examination*, and *experimentation*. Each of these components is specifically designed to replace maladaptive negative thoughts with more adaptive beliefs. Exploration examines the patient's dysfunctional beliefs or personal meaning system. Examination is comprised of reviewing the evidence for and against a belief, finding an alternative explanation or interpretation, and reviewing the consequences of adopting realistic or alternative beliefs. Finally, experimentation is designed to "test" the validity of a maladaptive belief system.

## Hypnosis as a Treatment for Depression

Hypnosis has not been widely used in the management of depression, possibly due to the prevailing myth that hypnosis could exacerbate suicidal ideation in clinically depressed patients. Many writers and clinicians had the erroneous belief that failure to respond to hypnosis (in cases where depressed clients fail to respond to hypnotic induction) might cause disappointment and a sense of failure in clinically depressed clients, resulting in an increase in suicidal ideation. Recently many clinicians have argued that hypnosis, especially when it forms part of a multimodal treatment approach, is not contraindicated with depression (e.g., Yapko, 1992, 2001; Alladin & Heap, 1991). In fact, Yapko uses hypnosis to reduce symptoms of hopelessness, which is a predictor of suicidal behavior, in the early stages of his comprehensive approach to psychotherapy for depression. However, the bulk of the published literature on the application of hypnosis in the management of depression consists of case reports, and there is a great deal of variation in what therapists do with hypnosis in the management of depression (Burrows & Boughton, 2001).

## INTEGRATING HYPNOSIS AND CBT THROUGH THE CDMD

Nevertheless, several writers (e.g., Golden, Dowd, & Friedberg, 1987; Tosi & Baisden, 1984; Yapko, 2001; Zarren & Eimer, 2001) have effectively integrated cognitive therapy and hypnotherapy for treating patients with depression in their clinical practice. However, these writers have not provided a scientific rationale or a theoretical model for combining CBT with hypnosis in the management of clinical depression. Alladin (1992, 1992a, 1994; Alladin & Heap, 1991) has described a working model of nonendogenous depression referred to as the Cognitive Dissociative Model of Depression (CDMD), which provides a theoretical framework for integrating cognitive and hypnotic techniques to treat depression. The aim of this chapter is to describe this model and then to present an integrated approach to treatment, referred to as cognitive hypnotherapy (CH). CH is a structured program of therapy that utilizes hypnotherapeutic methods alongside orthodox cognitive and behavioral procedures (Alladin & Heap, 1991) in the treatment of depression.

CDMD states there are at least three pragmatic reasons for combining cognitive and hypnotic paradigms in the treatment and understanding of depression. First, since hypnosis can produce cognitive, somatic, perceptual, physiological and kinesthetic changes under controlled conditions, the combination of the cognitive and the hypnotic paradigms may provide a framework for studying the psychological processes by which cognitive distortions produce concomitant psychobiological changes underlying clinical depression. Secondly, hypnosis provides insight into the phenomenology of depression (Yapko, 1992). Like hypnosis, depression is a highly subjective experience. It allows remarkable insights into the subjective realm of human experience, thus providing a paradigm for understanding how experience, normal or abnormal, is patterned and created. Thirdly, after reviewing the strengths and limitations of CBT and hypnotherapy with depression, Alladin (1989) concluded that each treatment approach has marked limitation. For example, CBT does not allow access to unconscious cognitive restructuring, while hypnosis provides such access. On the other hand, hypnosis does not focus on systematic cognitive restructuring, whilst CBT's main focus is on cognitive restructuring via reasoning and Socratic dialogue. Alladin (1989) argued that some of the shortcomings of each treatment approach could be compensated by integrating both treatment approaches.

Furthermore, there is some empirical evidence for combining hypnosis with CBT. Recently, there has been a growing body of research evaluating the use of hypnosis with cognitive behavior techniques in the treatment of various psychological disorders. Schoenberger (2000), from her review of the empirical status of the use of hypnosis in conjunction with cognitive behavior treatment programs, concluded that the existing studies demonstrate substantial benefits from the addition of hypnosis with cognitive behavior techniques. Similarly, Kirsch, Montgomery, and Sapirstein (1995), from their meta-analysis of 18 studies comparing a cognitive behavior treatment with the same treatment supplemented by hypnosis, found that the mean effect size of the difference between hypnotic and nonhypnotic treatment was 0.87 standard deviations. Kirsch et al. concluded that hypnotherapy was significantly superior to nonhypnotic treatment. Alladin (2003) has just completed a study comparing the effects of CBT with cognitive hypnotherapy with 98 chronic depressives. The results showed an additive effect of combining hypnosis with CBT. Alladin's study also met criteria for *probably efficacious* treatment for depression as laid down by the American Psychological Association (APA) Task Force (Chambless & Hollon, 1998), and it provides empirical validation for integrating hypnosis with CBT in the management of depression. The results of Alladin's study are discussed in greater detail under the Effectiveness of Cognitive Hypnotherapy.

## The Cognitive Dissociative Model of Depression (CDMD)

The cognitive dissociative model of depression (CDMD) was conceptualized by Alladin (1994) to emphasize the biopsychosocial nature of depression and to explicate the role of multiple factors that can trigger, exacerbate, or maintain the depressive affect. The model is not a new theory of depression or an attempt to explain the causes of depression. It is an extension of Beck's (1967) circular feedback model of depression, which was further elaborated on by Schultz (1978, 1984, 2003). In combining the cognitive and hypnotic paradigms, the CDMD incorporates ideas and concepts from information processing, selective attention, brain functioning, adverse life experiences, and the neodissociation theory of hypnosis (Hilgard, 1977). It is referred to as the cognitive dissociative model of depression because it encompasses the dissociative theory of hypnosis and the cognitive theory of emotion. The model proposes nonendogenous depression to be akin to a form of dissociation produced by negative cognitive rumination, which can be regarded as a form of negative self-hypnosis.

CDMD consists of 12 interrelated components that form a circular feedback loop (see Figure 6.1). The number of components form-

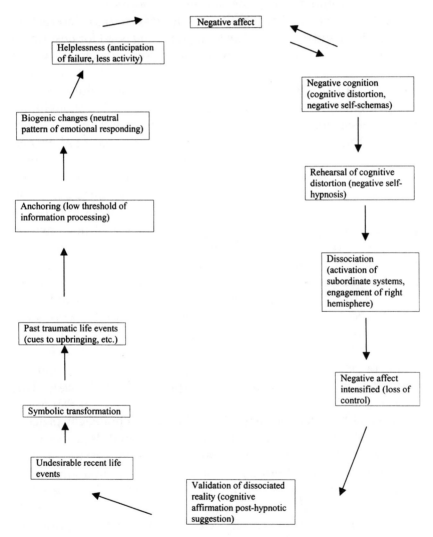

FIGURE 6.1  Cognitive Dissociative Model of Depression (CDMD) showing the constellation of 12 factors forming the depressive loop.

ing the loop and the position of each component in the loop are arbitrary. The 12 components forming the circular loop represent some of the major factors identified from the literature that may influence the course and outcome of depression. As the components are described in detail elsewhere (see Alladin, 1994), they are only briefly mentioned here in order to highlight the relationship among the 12 components forming the depressive loop.

As the model attaches significant importance to the interaction between affect and cognition, the logical starting point for describing the depressive loop is to start with affect (Negative affect), which appears at the top of the loop. The circular feedback model of depression (CFMD; Beck, 1967) maintains there is a mutually rein-forcing interaction between cognition and affect so that thought not only influences feelings, but that feelings too can influence thought content (hence the bidirectional arrows between Negative Affect and Negative cognition in Figure 6.1). Also, congruent with the concept of the "bicameral brain," proposed by Jaynes (1976), it is maintained that affect or cognition, each can independently starts the chain process of the feedback loop (Figure 1). The relationship between dysfunctional cognition and depressive affect is well documented in the literature (e.g., Haas & Fitzgibbon, 1989). An event (internal or external) can trigger a negative schema, which through cognitive rehearsal can lead to dissociation. In depression, Beck (1967, 1976) has noted the patients' constant stereotypic preoccupation with their alleged negative personal attributes. Alladin (1992a) regards such negative ruminations among some depressives to be a form of negative self-hypnosis (NSH; Araoz, 1981, 1985), which may lead to a state of partial or profound dissociation. This process can be regarded as a form of negative self-hypnosis (NSH) (Araoz, 1981, 1985).

West (1967) defines dissociation as a psychological process whereby information, incoming, ongoing or stored, is actively de-flected from integration with its usual or expected associations. Such deflection produces alteration in actions, feelings or thoughts so that for a period of time certain information is not associated or integrated with other information as it would normally or logically be. West regards such an experience to be either normal or patholog-ical. Ever since Janet (1907), the close relationship between hypnosis and dissociation was established. Janet (1889) put forward the view that systems of ideas can become split off from the main personality and exist as an unconscious subordinate personality, but capable of becoming conscious through hypnosis. The theory was applied to hypnosis and various other normal and pathological states such as automatism, amnesia, fugues and multiple personality. Hilgard (1977), by deriving concepts from cognitive psychology and information theory, reformulated the theory in contemporary terms and called it *neodissociation theory*. Like West (1967), Hilgard maintains that dissociation or *divided consciousness* is an extension of normal cognitive functioning. During ordinary consciousness, information is processed on a number of levels by a hierarchy of cognitive operations and controls. Ordinarily these operations are integrated. During hypnosis or dissociation, the integration decreases, and certain aspects of experiences are no longer available to consciousness. Dissociation or hypnotic involvement is, however, seen as a normal cognitive process on a continuum ranging from minor or limited to profound and widespread dissociation.

Although not making reference to hypnosis or dissociation, Beck et al. (1979, p. 13) state:

> In milder depressions the patient is generally able to view his negative thoughts with some objectivity. As the depression worsens, his thinking becomes increasingly dominated by negative ideas . . . and [he or she] may find it enormously difficult to concentrate on external stimuli . . . or engage in voluntary activities . . . the idiosyncratic cognitive organization has become autonomous [so] that the individual is unresponsive to changes in his immediate environment.

However, it is not suggested that hypnosis or dissociation is analogous to depression. Alladin (1992) has highlighted the similarities and differences between hypnosis and depression. He noted that the fundamental difference between the two states is terms of cognitive contents and control. The cognitive contents of hypnosis can be either negative or positive and they can be easily altered (easily controlled), while the cognitive contents of depression are invariably negative and not easily changed (not easily controlled).

According to the CDMD model, imagery is also an important aspect of cognition in determining, maintaining, and alleviating depression. Many writers (e.g., Ley & Freeman, 1984) claim that images have a greater capacity than language for attracting and retrieving emotionally laden associations. Individuals predisposed to depression tend to focus on negative thoughts and images. Schultz (1978, 1984, 2003), Starker and Singer (1975), and Traynor (1974) have provided evidence that with increasing levels of depression, depressives tend to change the contents of their imagination to negative fantasies, and consequently are unable to redirect their thinking and imagery from their current problems and negative life-concerns. Such subjectivity or emotional involvement can lead to loss of control over the intensity of emotional imagery (Horowitz, 1972) or to the dissociation of affect (Bower, 1981). In other words, the circular feedback cycle between cognition and affect repeats itself almost like a computer recycling through an infinite loop (Schultz, 1978) as the depression worsens, thus validating the depressive reality in the form of self-affirmations or posthypnotic suggestions. Neisser (1967) views such narrowing down and distortion of the environment by a few repetitive behaviors and self-attributions as characteristic of psychopathology (that is, there is an absence of reality testing).

The CDMD model also attaches importance to both conscious and nonconscious information processing. Although we are capable of rational operations, most judgments are highly influenced by what is "available"—particularly vivid information—in current memory at the time (Kahneman, Slovic, & Tversky, 1982). Since depressives are preoccupied with negative self-schemas (Dobson, 1986), their judgments are likely to be biased, leading to the maintenance of *syncretic cognition*. Syncretic cognition involves the fusion of various sources of information—visceral, postural, sensory, and mnemonic—forming an undifferentiated experiential matrix (Safer & Leventhal, 1977) that reinforces the validation of the depressive's reality both mentally and physically. Furthermore, judgements and emotions can be influenced by nonconscious cognitive processes (e.g., Williams, Watts, MacLeod, & Mathews, 1997). Shevrin and Dickman (1980), after reviewing the research evidence for nonconscious processes, concluded that no psychological model of human experience could ignore the concept of unconscious psychological processes. Work on selective attention (Posner, 1973; Sternberg, 1975) suggests that conscious psychological processes are influenced by the initial phase of cognitive activity that occurs outside of awareness. Research on subliminal perception (Shevrin, 1978) reveals that the specific emotional content of a stimulus can raise the threshold of the perception of that stimulus. These studies provide evidence that nonconscious processes may determine to a great extent what enters conscious awareness. Therefore, when a person is presented with a stimulus or situation, they may be upset not knowing why (since nonconscious thinking or evaluation may be involved). CBT, which relies on recognition and alteration of conscious cognition, may be ineffective here; however, hypnosis provides a tool for accessing nonconscious information. Integration of nonconscious information processing within the CDMD widens our understanding, assessment, and treatment of the depressive state. It was this realization that encouraged the author to combine hypnosis with cognitive therapy. Several techniques for dealing with nonconscious cognitive influence are described under the treatment section.

## Other Factors in Depression

So far the discussion has centered on information processing in depression while no mention has been made of trigger factors (internal or external), or the role of biological variables, or the influence of early experiences that contribute to the genesis and maintenance of clinical depression. The important question still remains: what are the factors that contribute to the construction or exacerbation of the "depressive reality"? Schultz (1978) has suggested that undesirable life events may further contribute to the maintenance of the depressive cycle. Klinger (1975), however, points out that it is the "symbolic transformation" of these events that is the critical factor. He suggests that undesirable life events may serve as cues to past traumatic experiences. Depressives gradually not only become more sensitive to stimuli resembling past traumatic life-events, but their reactions may also generalize to innocuous events or situations. Such selective attending or "anchoring" may explain the low threshold of information processing to emotional stimuli in depressives. Through repeated and automatic anchoring, biogenic changes may occur. Schwartz (1976, 1977, 1984) has provided evidence for the development of certain neurological pathways due to conscious cognitive focusing. It is feasible that depressives through negative cognitive focusing develop "depressive pathways." Individuals with anomalous developmental history (Guidano, 1987), and those who are biologically vulnerable (Oke, Keller, Mefford, & Adams, 1978) or genetically predisposed to depression, will be more prone to develop these depressive pathways.

People with a depressive disorder have the tendency to think more negatively (Beck et al., 1979) and hence to perceive the future as a continuous pattern of failure, relentless hardship, and inability to cope. Such catastrophic preoccupation (NSH) promotes feelings of helplessness and hopelessness about the future. These feelings are further exacerbated if the individual lacks social skills (Youngren & Lewinshon, 1980), is surrounded by adverse environmental factors (Paykel et al., 1969), or lacks social support (Brown & Harris, 1978). It is at this point in the depressive cycle that depressives are more vulnerable to suicide, or the depression can become more inflated, leading to the aggravation of vegetative symptoms. Thus, any of the 12 components in the loop can trigger depression, and the interrelationship among these factors allows the depressive loop to continue to cycle. The purpose of therapy is to break the depressive loop and to learn a variety of skills that will counter the factors that lead to the repetition of the depressive cycle.

## Multiple Interventions to Treat Depression

The use of the CDMD provides a multidimensional view of depression. The 12 factors forming the depressive loop are all interrelated, forming a constellation of emotional, cognitive, behavioral, physiological, and nonconscious processes. Focusing on any of the factors allows the client and the therapist a point of entry into the depressive loop. Once the client and the therapist gain access to this set of relationships, they can deploy various techniques (some of which are described below) as tools to unravel and reorganize this interrelated set of factors. Any one of them can be used as a target for intervention, which can simultaneously influence other processes because of their interrelated nature (Simons, Garfield, & Murphy, 1984). As depression is a complicated disorder involving multiple factors, it is unlikely that a single causative factor, either biological or psychological, will be found. Therefore, any single intervention is unlikely to be effective with every depressed patient. Although a clinical trial of CH has demonstrated that the addition of certain hypnotic techniques (hypnotic induction, relaxation, ego-strengthening, projection of problem-solving imagery, and self-hypnosis) augment the effectiveness of CBT (see Effectiveness of Cognitive Hypnotherapy), the treatment approach described below recommends multiple interventions. This is to encourage the therapist to develop a variety of techniques dealing with each factor rather than being constrained by a few strategies. This approach also reminds therapists that depression is often associated with various psychosocial difficulties and other comorbid conditions. Hence, Williams (1992), in his comprehensive review of the psychotherapies for depression, concluded that the more techniques that are used, the more effective is the treatment. Thus, cognitive hypnotherapy based on the CDMD provides a multifactorial treatment approach to depression. A therapist can easily combine the most appropriate strategies to suit a particular patient. CH normally consists of 16 weekly sessions, which can be expanded or modified according to the client's clinical needs, areas of concern, and presenting symptoms.

## THE STAGES OF COGNITIVE HYPNOTHERAPY

The stages of cognitive therapy are briefly described in this section. The sequence of these stages of treatment can be altered to suit the clinical needs of the individual client.

### Session 1: Clinical Assessments

Before initiating cognitive hypnotherapy, it is important for the therapist to take a detailed clinical history of the client and identify the essential psychological, physiological, and social aspects of their behaviors. This assessment should include functional and dysfunctional patterns of thinking, feeling, bodily responses and behaviors. In order to make a reliable diagnosis and to differentiate between subtypes of depression, the therapist is advised to use standard diagnostic criteria such as the Diagnostic and Statistical Manual of Mental Disorders (4th ed., text rev.) (DSM-IV-T-R; American Psychiatric Association, 2000), or the International Classification of Diseases (ICD-10; World Health Organization, 1992). Specific psychometric measures such as the Beck Depression Inventory–Revised (Beck,

Steer, & Brown, 1996), the Beck Anxiety Inventory (Beck & Steer, 1993), the Beck Hopelessness Scale (Beck & Steer, 1993a), the Hamilton Depression Rating Scale (HDRS, Hamilton, 1967), or the Revised Hamilton Rating Scale for Depression (RHRSD; Warren, 1994) can also be administered to determine the severity of the client's symptoms before, during, and after treatment. It is also important to assess for cognitive distortions. If a depressive client presents no significant cognitive distortions, CBT may not be appropriate, as its focus is predominantly on restructuring cognitive distortions. The abbreviated version of the Dysfunctional Attitude Scale (DAS; Weissman & Beck, 1978; Burns, 1999) can be administered to assess the level of cognitive distortions, or the client can be carefully questioned (according to the author's preference) to elicit cognitive distortions related to the cognitive triad or negative self-schemas. The following excerpt from Case 1 (Janet) represents an example of how to question the client in a structured manner to obtain the negative self-schemas.

| Therapist: | We all get involved in some sort of self-talk or inner conversation. Do you have any theme or thoughts that keep recurring in your mind, or you are preoccupied with? |
| --- | --- |
| Janet: | I'm useless, I'm lazy, I've no value, no power. |
| Therapist: | What do you think of yourself as a person? |
| Janet: | I'm worthless, I'm no good, I can't make any decision. |
| Therapist: | What do you think of yourself as a woman? |
| Janet: | Don't like being a woman. All my life I've been a servant, subservient to my mother. I hate myself, I'm stupid. |
| Therapist: | What do you think of your looks? |
| Janet: | I'm fat, unattractive, bloated, a stereotype, ugly. I don't want to be seen. |
| Therapist: | What do you think of yourself as a wife? |
| Janet: | I'm useless and lazy. |
| Therapist: | What do you think of your past? |
| Janet: | I hate the past, I hate to think of it. My mother took away my past and made me into nothing, I'm no one, nobody. |
| Therapist: | What do you think of the present? |
| Janet: | Confused, not much, devoid of interest, endless vacuum, not connected. |

| Therapist: | What do you think of the future? |
|---|---|
| Janet: | I'm scared, no future. Don't want to live like this. I'm stuck, not worth making any efforts. |
| Therapist: | Do you blame yourself for anything? |
| Janet: | It's my fault I'm like this. I must be weak. I blame myself for everything. I've been a horrible mother. |

The author also uses the Barber Suggestibility Scale (BSS; Barber & Wilson, 1978/79) to measure hypnotic suggestibility. Patients scoring low on the hypnotic suggestibility scale are not offered the hypnotic component of the treatment package; instead they are offered relaxation training as a substitute, if required.

## Session 2: First Aid for Depression

Since depressives tend to be overwhelmed by feelings of low mood, hopelessness, and pessimism, any immediate relief from these feelings provides a sense of hope and optimism. Overlade (1986) described a First Aid for Depression technique for producing immediate relief from the depressive mood. The goals of First Aid is to (a) break the depressive cycle, (b) to produce positive (nondepressive) feelings, (c) to develop antidepressive pathways, (d) to establish therapeutic alliance, and (d) to produce positive expectancy in the client. Alladin (1992, 1992a, 1994; Alladin & Heap, 1991) expanded the First Aid technique to seven stages.

1. The client is encouraged to talk about the trigger that exacerbated the depressive affect and to ventilate feelings of distress and frustration.

2. A plausible biological explanation (a "tucking reflex") of acute depression is provided in order to reduce guilt for feeling depressed.

3. The client is helped to alter the depressive posture or "tucking response."

4. The client is encouraged to make deliberate attempts to smile.

5. The client is encouraged to imagine a "funny face."

6.  The client is encouraged to "play a happy mental tape."

7.  The client is conditioned to a positive cue-word.

The First Aid for Depression can be used with or without hypnotic induction. The First Aid technique was utilized with Case 2 (Rita)
in order to help her deal with the upset caused by her husband.
Rita has a history of recurrent major depressive disorder. She was
overly preoccupied with negative self-schemas. The author therefore
decided to introduce CBT to her in the second session. She had
four sessions of CBT and was showing very good response to the
treatment. However, three days prior to her next session, Rita made
an urgent appointment to see the author as she was very upset. She
came to the session very depressed and tearful. She explained that
her husband had treated her very unfairly the previous day, which
had induced her deep depression. Her husband was leaving town
on a business trip on the previous day and asked Rita to give him
a ride to the airport. Rita indicated that she was feeling depressed
and that she did not feel confident to drive to the airport, which is
about 30 kilometers from her house. He became very angry and
accused her of being lazy and avoiding her responsibilities on the
pretense that she was depressed. The author reassured her that he
was glad that she made an appointment to see him quickly and that
he would try to help her out. After allowing her to ventilate her
distress and feelings of hurt, the author stated:

> I can understand how you feel. Reactive depression is a mammalian
> response, it is a defense mechanism. When a monkey is fighting,
> when he feels defeated, he adopts a tucking reflex, his head goes
> down, his shoulder droops and he tucks in. This tucking reflex or
> depressive posture is adopted to indicate to the dominant monkey
> that he is defeated so that the dominant monkey does not hurt
> him. We humans do the same when we are subjugated by a domi-
> nant person. By adopting the tucking reflex or depressive posture
> we are saying to the dominant person to leave us alone, we have
> had enough. But the problem with the depressive posture is that
> sometimes we find it difficult to come out of it. Reasoning does
> not help because we feel we have valid reasons to be upset. I am
> going to show you how to do something biological to get out of
> the depressive posture.
>     Would you close your eyes and imagine yourself standing in
> front of Buckingham Palace, noticing the guard on duty. Observe
> that he is standing up very straight, his head is up, his shoulders

are broad and square, and his arms are by his side. Can you imagine it? (Rita nods her head.)

Now I would like you to pretend you are the guard on duty. Sit up straight, with your head up and your arms by your side. Hold your head high, shoulders broad and square and your arms by your side, strong and straight. (Rita was no longer "tucked" in, she was holding her head up, adopting an antidepressive posture.)

Now imagine looking in a mirror and forcing yourself to smile. It is not natural to smile when you are distressed, so you have to force yourself. (Rita started to smile after a short while.)

Now I want you to remember a funny face. Remembering someone who made you laugh, something about the person's face, the way the person talks, when you imagine this person, you can't help but laugh. (After a while she started to smile more naturally and then she started to laugh.)

Now can you imagine a happy time in your life, a happy memory or a happy place? (Rita nods.) Now play this happy tape in your mind. (She progressively became more relaxed and appeared happy, and no longer looking depressed.)

From now on whenever you feel upset or depressed and do not want to feel upset or depressed, think of the word BUBBLE and you will be able to remember all the details of this exercise and you will feel much better, more optimistic.

Rita felt much better at the end of the session. The author noticed an alteration of the depressive affect in Rita, although the positive effect only lasts for about 1–4 hours in most clients who receive First Aid for Depression. The alteration of affect, although transitory, distills hope and positive expectancy, and prepares the depressive clients for the next stage of CH.

## Sessions 3–6: Cognitive Behavior Therapy (CBT)

During these four sessions, CBT is introduced to help the client identify, challenge, and eventually correct the dysfunctional beliefs that may be triggering and maintaining the depressive affect. As CBT techniques are fully described in several excellent books (e.g., Beck, 1995), they are not described in detail here. As part of the CH approach, the author uses the following sequential progression of CBT (extended over at least 4 sessions).

- Client is given an explanation of the cognitive model of depression.

- Client is advised to read the first three chapters from *Feeling Good: The New Mood Therapy* (Burns, 1999).

- Client is encouraged to identify the number of cognitive distortions (from the list of 10 described by Burns in chapter 3 of *Feeling Good*) the client ruminates with.

- Client is asked to record the ABC Form (form with three columns: A = Event; B = Automatic Thoughts; C = Emotional Responses). This homework helps the client discover the link between thoughts and feelings, rather than attributing emotional responses to events only.

- Client is introduced to disputation (D) after the client has had the opportunity to log the ABC form for a week.

- Client is introduced to the ABCDE Form. This form is an expanded version of the ABC Form, including two more columns (D = Disputation; E = Consequences of Disputation).

- Client is given a completed version (with disputation of cognitive distortions in column D and the modification of emotional and behavioral responses in column E as a consequence of cognitive disputation).

- Client is helped to differentiate between superficial ("I can't do this.") and deeper ("I'm a failure.") cognitive distortions and the focus of later sessions is on restructuring deeper self-schemas.

- Client is advised to constantly monitor and restructure their negative cognition until it becomes a habit.

The number of CBT sessions is determined by the needs of the client and the presenting symptoms.

## Sessions 7–8: Hypnosis

Hypnosis proper is introduced to the client in Sessions 7 and 8, although a brief induction procedure may be used to facilitate the First Aid technique in the second session. Hypnosis is used because it (a) induces relaxation, (b) reduces distraction, (c) maximizes concentration, (d) facilitates divergent thinking, (e) amplifies experiences, and (f) provides access to nonconscious psychological processes. However, the focus of the first two hypnotic sessions is on (a) relaxation (to prove the client can relax), (b) somatosensory changes (to reinforce the idea that the client can have different feelings and sensations), (c) demonstration of the power of the mind (via eye and body catalepsy), and (d) increasing confidence in self-hypnosis.

As this session is audiotaped, the Counting Method (see Gibbons, 1979) of induction and deepening is used. When a satisfactory deep level of "trance" is achieved, a modified version of Hartland's (1971) ego-strengthening suggestions is given. Ego-strengthening is "a way of exploiting the positive experience of hypnosis and the therapist-patient relationship in order to develop feelings of confidence and optimism and an improved self-image" (Alladin & Heap, 1991, p. 58). However, to ensure credibility and acceptance of the ego-strengthening suggestions, it is of paramount importance to first create a positive feeling and a "pleasant state of mind," and the ego-strengthening suggestions need to sound logical to the client. For example, rather than stating "every day you will feel better," it is advisable to suggest: "as a result of this treatment and as a result of you listening to your tape every day, you will begin to feel better." This set of suggestions not only sounds logical, but improvement becomes contingent on continuing with the therapy and listening to the self-hypnosis tape daily. Moreover, ego-strengthening suggestions should be seen as a component of a comprehensive approach to the treatment of depression. Alladin and Heap (1991) warn "we have here a useful procedure which may augment a carefully constructed programme of therapy, but it is not the therapy itself and if it is used as such, then disappointment and even disaster may ensue" (p. 58). After the first hypnosis session, the client is provided with an audiotape of self-hypnotic procedure for creating a good frame of mind, offering ego-strengthening suggestions, and providing posthypnotic suggestions. The homework assignment provides continuity of treatment between sessions and offers the client the opportunity to learn self-hypnosis. While in a deep hypnotic trance and in a "nice frame of mind," Bob (see Case 3 later in this chapter) was offered the following ego-strengthening suggestions.

- Day by day, as you listen to your tape, you will become more relaxed, less tense, and less depressed.

- As a result of this treatment and as a result of you listening to your tape every day, you will be able to cope better with the challenges of life every day.

- You will learn to focus more on your successes than on your failures.

- Every day you will notice feeling less depressed and more optimistic.

- You will notice feeling calmer and beginning to enjoy the struggles and challenges of life.

Before the termination of the hypnotic session, it is important to offer posthypnotic suggestions. Depressives tend to constantly focus on negative autohypnosis (NSH), especially after a negative affective experience (e.g., "I will not be able to cope."). This can be regarded as a form of posthypnotic suggestion (PHS), which can become part of the depressive cycle. The cycle is further repeated by involvement in depressive activities. In order to break the depressive cycle, it is very important to counter the NSH. Here are examples of PHS for countering NSH:

- While you focus on the situation, you will feel less depressed.

- When you plan to improve your future, you will feel more optimistic about the future.

- As you become interested in the situation, you will forget about your worries.

- As you feel involved, you will be motivated to do more things.

## Sessions 9–12: Cognitive Restructuring Under Hypnosis

Once the client becomes used to hypnosis and cognitive therapy, the next three sessions focus on (a) cognitive restructuring under hypnosis, (b) expansion of awareness and amplification of experiences, (c) reduction of guilt and self-blame, and (d) development of antidepressive pathways. These are further explained.

### (a) Cognitive Restructuring Under Hypnosis

When the client is fairly relaxed and a satisfactory level of hypnotic "trance" is achieved, suggestions are made to the client to imagine a situation that normally causes upset. Then the client is instructed to focus on the dysfunctional cognitions and associated emotional, physiological, and behavioral responses. Encouragement is given to identify or "freeze" (frame by frame, like a movie) the faulty cognitions in terms of thoughts, beliefs, images, fantasies, and daydreams. Once a particular set of faulty cognitions is frozen, the client is helped to replace it with more appropriate thinking or imagination, and then to attend to the resulting (desirable) "syncretic" response. This process is repeated until the client can confidently restructure a set of faulty cognitions related to a specific situation.

Another method of cognitive restructuring under hypnosis involves the metaphor of editing or deleting old computer files. Once in a fairly deep state of hypnotic trance, the client is encouraged to become aware of the "good feelings" (positive feelings amplified under hypnosis), and following some ego-strengthening suggestions from the therapist, the client is directed to focus on personal achievements and successes (adult ego state). Here attempts are made to get the client involved in the adult ego faculties of cognition, synthesis, integration, and reality testing and clear judgement. Once this is achieved, the client is ready to work on modification of old learning and experiences. The client is then instructed to imagine opening an old computer file that requires editing or deletion. At the outset of the session, it is usually decided which file (e.g., whenever stressed out the client revives a flurry of negative cognition) the client would like to work on. By metaphorically deleting and editing the file, the client is able to mitigate cognitive distortions, magical thinking, self-blaming, and other self-defeating mental scripts.

Hypnosis also provides a vehicle whereby cognitive distortions below the level of awareness can be explored and expanded. Very often in the course of CBT, the client reports an inability to access cognitions preceding certain negative emotions. As hypnosis provides access to unconscious cognitive distortions and negative self-schemas, unconscious unadaptive cognitions can be easily retrieved and restructured under hypnosis. This is achieved by directing the client's attention to the psychological content of an experience or situation. The client is guided to focus attention on a specific area of concern and to establish the link between cognition and affect. Once the negative cognitions are identified, the client is encouraged to restructure the maladaptive cognitions and then to attend to the resulting (desirable) responses. For example, if a person reports: "I don't know why I felt depressed at the party last week," the client is hypnotically regressed back to the party and encouraged to identify and restructure the faulty cognitions until they can think of the party without being upset. Such an approach was used with Rita (see Case 2 later in the chapter), who was unable to identify the cognition related to social and sexual withdrawal, which was interfering with her relationship with her husband, mainly through lack of communication and the tendency to overreact to him. When Rita was in a deep trance state, she was given the following suggestions:

> Therapist:    I would like you to go back in time and place in your mind to last Tuesday night when you felt upset and wanted to withdraw yourself from your husband. (pause)
>
> Take your time. Once you are able to remember the situation, let me know by nodding your chin up and down. (ideomotor signals of "chin up and down for YES" and "shaking her head side to side for NO" were set up prior to starting the regression).

After a short while, she nodded her chin.

> Become aware of the feelings, allowing all the feelings to flow through you. Become aware of your bodily reactions. Become aware of every emotion you feel.

Her breathing and heart rate increased and the muscles in her face started to contract. It became noticeable that she was feeling upset and anxious.

> How do you feel? (pause)
>
> Take your time, and you can speak up; speaking will not disturb your trance level.
>
> Rita:    I'm scared . . . it's unfair . . . no one told me he was going to be sent away. (she started to cry)

Rita recounted two traumatic incidents that occurred when she was 10 and 12 years old, respectively. When she was 10 years old, her brother Ken (2 years older than she), was sent away to live with her grand parents. Ken was supposedly a very naughty child, and the parents could not handle him, so they "got rid of him." Rita was very distressed by it because she was very close to Ken and "they never told her that Ken was going to be sent away." She cried for days, and for several nights she could not sleep. One night while she was lying in her bed at night, the thought of a dark cave came into her mind and she saw herself in that dark cave. Although it was frightening initially, later on she felt a sense of comfort; she felt closed in and she did not have to think of anything or feel anything. From this night, whenever she felt upset she would go into the cave in her mind and lock herself in. The second incident happened 2 years later. One Saturday morning the family got the news that Ken (who was still living with his grandparents) died from drowning in the local swimming pool. Immediately, it flashed into her mind that she had lost the person she loved most. She felt very upset, but only briefly, because she quickly locked herself in the "dark cave." From the regression, it became apparent that (a) Rita retreats to the dark cave whenever she feels confronted or stressed out, and (b) she is fearful of getting closer to anyone who loves her (including her husband) in case she loses that person.

| Therapist: | I want you to come back to Tuesday night when you felt upset. I want you to become aware of the thoughts and images that were going on in your mind. |
| Rita: | I can't deal with this. It's too painful. I'll lose him. I don't want to lose him. (She started to cry.) |
| Therapist: | From now on you will become completely aware of all the thoughts that go on in your mind when you are upset so that you begin to see the connection between your thinking and your feeling. |

Following this session, she was able to identify the cognition related to her upsetting feeling, and she was able to restructure her thinking and control her emotional and behavioral reaction. Two sessions focused on helping Rita to deal with the two dramatic events. Her negative experience and faulty cognitions were "reframed" by utilizing her adult ego state (she was able to reflect on the incidents utilizing her "adult ego lenses"). Following these sessions, Rita's anxiety and sexual difficulties dramatically lessened. Through her "adult ego lenses," she was able to realize that it was no longer necessary for her to retreat to the dark cave. She also realized that there is no direct relationship between loving and losing. Her relationship with her husband significantly improved.

Other hypnotic uncovering or restructuring procedures such as affect bridge, age regression, age progression, and dream induction can be used to explore and restructure negative schemas.

## (b) Expansion of Awareness and Amplification of Experiences

Hypnosis can facilitate expansion of awareness and amplification of experiences. Brown and Fromm (1990) described a technique called Enhancing Positive Affective Experience, which expands and intensifies positive feelings by (a) bringing underlying emotions into awareness, (b) creating awareness of various feelings, (c) intensifying positive affect, (d) enhancing "discovered" affect, (e) inducing positive moods, and (f) increasing motivation. Such a procedure not only disrupts the depressive cycle but also helps to develop antidepressive pathways.

## (c) Reduction of Guilt and Self-Blame

Various hypnotherapeutic techniques can also be used to reframe the client's past experiences that cause guilt or self-regret. Hammond (1990) provides several techniques for dealing with guilt and self-blame. For example, Watkins (in Hammond, p. 312) describes a technique for reducing guilt that she calls "The Door of Forgiveness," and Hammond (p. 313) and Stanton (in Hammond, 1990, p. 313) describe two techniques for "dumping the rubbish." Stanton's "The Laundry" (see Hammond, 1990, p. 313) technique helped Janet (see Case 1 later in the chapter) to deal with the guilt over her children.

## (d) Developing Antidepressive Pathways

If depressive pathways can be developed through conscious negative focusing, then it would be possible to develop antidepressive or happy pathways by focusing on positive imagery (Schwartz, 1984). During hypnosis the client is helped to focus on positive but realistic images, and is given posthypnotic suggestions about "positive focusing" or "whenever possible, imagine playing a happy tape in your mind."

## Session 9: Attention Switching and Positive Mood Induction

Depressives have the tendency to become preoccupied with catastrophic thoughts and images. Such preoccupations can easily become obsessional in nature and may impede therapeutic progress.
To break the negative ruminative cycle, depressives are trained to
switch attention away from negative cognitions and to focus more
on positive experiences. To achieve this, the client is advised to
make a list of 10 to 15 pleasant life experiences and to practice
holding each experience in their mind for about 30 seconds. The
client is encouraged to practice with the list four or five times a day
and to put negative or "undesirable" experiences (whenever the
client dwells on these) out of their mind and replace them with one
of the pleasant items from their list. This procedure provides another
technique for weakening depressive pathways and strengthening
"happy pathways." In other words, the client is learning to substitute
NSH by positive self-hypnosis. Yapko (1992) argues that since depressives utilize NSH to create the experience of the depressive
reality, they can equally learn to use positive self-hypnosis to create
an experience of antidepressive reality.

## Session 13: Active Interactive Training

This technique helps to break "dissociative" habits and encourages
"association" with the relevant environment. When interacting with
their internal or external environment, depressives tend to passively
dissociate rather than actively interact with the relevant external
information. Active interaction means being alert and "in tune" with
the incoming information (conceptual reality), whereas passive dissociation is the tendency to anchor to "inner reality" (negative schemas and associated syncretic feelings), which inhibit reality testing
or appraisal of conceptual reality.

To prevent passive dissociation, a person must (a) become
aware of such a process occurring, (b) actively attempt to inhibit
it by switching attention away from "bad anchors," and (c) actively
attend to relevant cues or conceptual reality. In other words, the
client learns to actively engage the left brain hemisphere by becoming analytical, logical, realistic, and syntactical.

Edgette and Edgette (1995, pp. 145–158) have also discussed several techniques for developing adaptive dissociation. For example, a client with habitual unadaptive dissociation can be trained to adopt adaptive dissociation, which help to

- Counter unadaptive dissociation
- Break continuous pattern
- Halt a sense of pessimism and a sense of helplessness
- Associate with success
- Integrate different parts
- Detach from toxic self-talk.

## Session 14: Social Skills Training:

Youngren and Lewinshon (1980) have provided evidence that lack of social skills may cause and maintain depression in some clients. One session (or more if required) is therefore devoted to teaching social skills, and the client is advised to read the appropriate bibliography.

## Session 15–16: Ideal Goals/Reality Training

Under hypnosis the client is encouraged to imagine ideal but realistic goals, and then to imagine planning appropriate strategies and taking necessary actions for achieving them (forward projection with behavioral rehearsal).

## BOOSTER AND FOLLOW-UP SESSIONS

Cognitive hypnotherapy as outlined above normally requires 16 weekly sessions. Some clients may, however, require fewer or more sessions. After these sessions, booster or follow-up sessions may be provided as required.

## The Effectiveness of Cognitive Hypnotherapy

Cognitive hypnotherapy (CH), based on the model described, appears to provide a pragmatic and multimodal psychological approach to the treatment of depression. The array of strategies described increases the likelihood of a therapist finding a maximally suitable treatment combination that will suit a particular client. The model also offers an innovative technique for developing antidepressive pathways. But how valuable cognitive hypnotherapy will ultimately prove to be depends on the outcome. In a preliminary uncontrolled study, Alladin (1989) compared CH with CBT (Beck's model) with 20 chronically depressed clients (10 subjects in each group). He found no significant differences between the two treatment groups in reducing depressive moods. However, the subjects in the CH group showed (1) more rapid improvement, (2) greater reduction on anxiety scores, and (3) greater increase in self-confidence. Recently, Alladin's study (2003) was expanded to empirically validate the effectiveness of CH. Specifically, the study was conducted to compare the effects of CH with the effects of a well-established treatment, CBT, in a sample of chronic depressives. The study met all the APA Task Force (Chambless & Hollon, 1998) criteria for probably efficacious treatment. Ninety-eight chronic outpatient depressives were randomly assigned to receive either CH or CBT. Eighty-four patients completed the 16-week outpatient treatment and were followed-up at 6 months (Wk 42; N = 79; 5 dropped out) and 12 months (Wk 68; N = 75; 4 dropped out). The sample included 36 men and 48 women, with a mean age of 35.46 years, and a mean duration of 6.19 years of depression; 60% of the sample was married. (See Table 6.1 for results.)

TABLE 6.1    Levels of Improvement in the CBT and CH Groups

|  | Wk 1 | Wk 4 | Wk 8 | Wk 12 | Wk 16 | Wk 42 | Wk 68 |
|---|---|---|---|---|---|---|---|
| **Depression (BDI-II)** | | | | | | | |
| CH | 39.29 | 34.69 | 28.43 | 22.57 | 16.76 | 14.65 | 12.50 |
| CBT | 39.31 | 35.17 | 30.12 | 26.14 | 21.24 | 18.44 | 15.65 |
| **Anxiety (BAI)** | | | | | | | |
| CH | 31.36 | 27.57 | 22.86 | 18.69 | 14.67 | 12.33 | 10.45 |
| CBT | 27.24 | 25.17 | 23.29 | 21.52 | 19.71 | 18.36 | 17.19 |
| **Hopelessness (BHS)** | | | | | | | |
| CH | 13.29 | 10.86 | 9.19 | 8.19 | 6.00 | 5.50 | 4.50 |
| CBT | 13.52 | 11.74 | 10.40 | 9.24 | 8.31 | 7.05 | 6.92 |

The CBT was based on the manual produced by Beck et al. (1979), and the CH was based on a paper by Alladin (1994), which was extended to become a treatment manual. In addition to CBT, the CH group had hypnotherapy consisting of (a) counting with a relaxation method of hypnotic induction and deepening of trance (adapted from Gibbons, 1979), (b) ego-strengthening suggestions (adapted from Hammond, 1990, and Hartland, 1971), (c) forward projection (image of effective coping and gradual improvement in the future), and (d) for each client, a self-hypnosis tape with ego-strengthening suggestions for home practice. The outcome measures consisted of the clients' scores on the revised Beck Depression Inventory (BDI-II), the Beck Anxiety Inventory (BAI), and the Beck Hopelessness Scale (BHS). The inclusion criteria were a DSM-IV diagnosis of recurrent major depressive disorder and a minimum objective score of 3 on the Barber Suggestibility Scale (BSS). The measures were administered in the first, fourth, eighth, twelfth, and sixteenth sessions, and at the 6-month and 12-month follow-ups. Table 6.1 shows the level of improvement in the two treatment groups.

At the end of the 16-week treatment, the majority of the patients from both groups significantly improved compared to the baseline scores. However, the CH group produced significantly larger changes in the BDI-II [$t(41) = 15.9$, $p < .001$], the BAI [$t(41) = 12.2$, $p < .001$], and the BHS [$t(41) = 12.4$, $p < .001$] scores. The improvements were maintained at 6-month and 12-month follow-up. In addition, effect size calculations indicated the CH group produced a 6.03% greater reduction in depression, a 5.08% greater reduction in anxiety, and a 8.05% greater reduction in hopelessness than the CBT group at the termination of treatment. The effect size was maintained at 6-month and 12-month follow-ups. These results indicate that the depressives from the CH group continued to improve after the termination of treatment, which can be attributed to the self-hypnosis tape. The subjects from the CH group reported that they found it very helpful to listen to their self-hypnosis tape daily after the termination of the treatment. There was also a correlation between hypnotic suggestibility and treatment outcome. Irrespective of treatment modality, the moderate to highly susceptible subjects produced significantly more improvement than the less suggestible subjects. This was more apparent at the termination of treatment (week 16) and during follow-ups (weeks 42 and 68). These results clearly demonstrate that CH is equally, or even more, effective than CBT in the management of chronic depressives. From the results of this study, one can conclude that adding hypnosis to CBT increases the effect size of the treatment. The study meets the criteria for "probably efficacious" treatment but not for "well-established treatment" since the study was conducted at a single site. Arrangements are underway to have the study replicated at two independent sites.

## CASE STUDIES

### Case 1: Janet

Janet, a 45-year-old housewife and mother of two teenage children, was referred by a psychiatrist to the author for CBT. Janet had been depressed on and off for over 12 years. She had been under the care of a psychiatrist for 4 years. She had trials of various antidepressants but showed no significant improvement. Because Janet felt "very negative about everything," her psychiatrist strongly recommended CBT.

Janet met the DSM-IV criteria for a recurrent moderate major depressive disorder and generalized social phobia. She scored in the severe range on the BDI-II and the BAI, and her score on the BHS was in the moderate range. She expressed low self-esteem and lack of confidence, and presented extensive cognitive distortions (see Session 1: Clinical Assessments). Moreover, she felt guilty for not being a good mother to her children. Her score on the BSS was in the highly susceptible range.

From the information available, it was concluded that her symptoms of depression and social anxiety were to a large extent maintained by her negative cognitions. Based on the history and assessment, the following sequential course of treatment was planned for Janet.

- Continue follow-ups with her psychiatrist as she was still on an antidepressant
- CBT for restructuring her negative cognitions
- Hypnotherapy for ego-strengthening
- Hypnotherapy for expansion of experience

- Hypnotherapy for demonstration of self-control

- Hypnotherapy for positive mood induction

- Hypnotherapy for anxiety management

- Hypnotherapy to overcome guilt

- Thought stopping and attention switching for countering negative ruminations

- Hypnotherapy for developing anti-depressive pathways

- Behavioral rehearsal under hypnosis (forward projection)

Janet had 16 sessions of cognitive hypnotherapy over a period of 6 months in the sequential stages described below. The treatment was very effective according to her psychiatrist, who decided to wean her from her medications. After the 16 sessions, the author did not follow up Janet as she was followed-up by her psychiatrist. A year after discharge, the author received a discharge letter from the psychiatrist stating that Janet was significantly improved and weaned from medication.

*Session 1: First Session Devoted to History Taking and Assessments (See Above)*

*Sessions 2–6: CBT*

It was decided to start Janet on CBT first and later introduce hypnotherapy for affect regulation and anxiety management. She had four sessions of CBT as described under Sessions 3–6: Cognitive Behavior therapy (CBT).

*Sessions 7–14: Hypnotherapy*

Janet had eight sessions of hypnotherapy spread over a period of 2 months. Although she understood the rationale for CBT and carried out her homework diligently, she still complained of symptoms of anxiety and depression, indicating that she still "felt empty inside her." The hypnotherapy sessions were therefore structured to provide as much of an experiential focus as possible (expansion and amplification of positive affect). The six reasons for using hypnosis with depression, as articulated by Yapko (1992), were fully utilized with Janet (see Hypnosis as a Treatment for Depression). The hypnotherapy sessions consisted of:

- Ego-strengthening: The ego-strengthening suggestions were tailored to counter Janet's rumination with NSH (negative self-hypnosis). The Enhancing Positive Affective Experience technique of Brown and Fromm (1990) (see Hypnotherapy for Expansion of Experience) was used to amplify and expand Janet's range of positive experiences.

- Hypnotherapy for demonstration of self-control: By amplifying and expanding positive experience and by inducing eye-and-body catalepsy, Janet was able to develop positive expectancy. She started to believe that she could produce significant emotional and behavioral changes, and was able to replace or counter anxious feelings and depressive affect.

- Hypnotherapy for positive mood induction: Following training in "thought stopping and attention switching" (see Developing Anti-depressive Pathways, and Attention Switching and Positive Mood Induction), Janet was helped to intensify positive mood under hypnosis. She was encouraged to practice positive mood induction twice a day at home.

- Hypnotherapy for her anxiety management was grounded through systematic desensitization and behavioral rehearsal.

- Hypnotherapy to help her overcome guilt: Although she was able to significantly lessen her guilt feelings through CBT, she still continued to blame herself for "neglecting" (although there was no evidence of neglect) her children. A session of hypnotherapy was therefore devoted to working with feelings of guilt and self-blame. Stanton's "laundry" technique (see Hammond, 1990, p. 313) was used to help her dump the "unwanted rubbish" (guilt and self-blame) in the "laundry." This technique involved imaging (a) a laundry, (b) filling the sink with water, (c) opening a trap door in the head, (d) pulling out the unwanted rubbish from the brain and dumping it into the water, (e) the water becoming blacker and blacker, and (f) finally, pulling the plug and letting the dirty water (guilt and self-blame) drain away.

## Session 15: Inducing Positive Moods and Developing Anti-depressive Pathways

By the end of the 14th session (after five months of therapy), Janet was feeling significantly better. Her scores on the BDI-II, the BAI, and the BHS were all in the mid-range. In the next two sessions, it was decided to consolidate the gains and start her on preventative (to reduce the chances of relapse) strategies. Guided by the work of Schwartz (1976, 1977, 1984), the author instructed Janet in how to counter NSH, induce positive moods, and develop antidepressive pathways. It was emphasized that Janet should continue with these strategies for several months even if she is discharged from the care of the author.

## Session 16: Forward Projection

In this session, Janet had a session of hypnotherapy. Under hypnosis she was instructed to rehearse effectively dealing with stressful situations in the future. The focus was particularly on countering NSH and controlling anxious and depressive feelings.

This case clearly illustrates that CBT on its own was not very helpful to Janet. However, once the hypnotic component was introduced, the treatment became more meaningful to her. Hypnosis allowed her the opportunity to experience relaxing and nondepressive feelings. The hypnotic experience therefore established positive expectancy and consolidated the therapeutic alliance. Moreover, CBT was not effective in alleviating her feelings of guilt and self-blame. The metaphorical technique used under hypnosis was very powerful. After the "laundry" session, Janet commented that she felt "lighter as if a big load" had been taken off her shoulders. On the other hand, CBT taught her to appreciate the relationship between cognition and affect, an insight that motivated her to counter NSH very actively. The treatment gain may be largely attributable to her successful countering of NSH. Janet commented that, as the treatment progressed, when faced with a stressful situation, she became more able to stand back and examine her thoughts.

As this case demonstrates, a multimodal approach to therapy for depression is highly recommended. Moreover, therapeutic flexibility should be seen as an essential component of successful treatment outcome. Furthermore, the case illustrates that both anxiety and depression can be successfully treated at the same time.

## Case 2: Rita

Rita, a 39-year-old housewife was referred to the author for psychological treatment by her family physician. Rita has been married to Paul, a 45-year-old businessman, for 16 years. They have two boys, 12 and 14 years old. Ten years ago Rita was diagnosed with a major depressive disorder by her family physician and treated pharmacologically. She showed good response to drug treatment and recovered within 6 months. However, in the past 5 years she has been having recurrent episodes of moderate depression. Recently her depression got worse and she started having suicidal thoughts. The family physician noticed that, apart from becoming more depressed recently, Rita was becoming more negative and pessimistic. He wanted to refer her to a psychiatrist, but Rita preferred to see a psychotherapist because she felt she had "lots of personal and marital issues to discuss."

When first seen by the author, Rita met the DSM-IV criteria for (a) recurrent major depressive disorder, fluctuating between moderate and severe intensity; (b) situationally predisposed panic attacks, and (c) hypoactive sexual desire disorder, lifelong type, due to psychological factors. She scored on the severe range on the BAI, the BDI-II, and the BHS, with her score on the BSS in the high susceptibility range. She was preoccupied with pervasive cognitive distortions and consistently ruminated with the belief that she is "no good," "inadequate," "a failure," and "stupid." The following treatment strategies were planned:

- CBT for restructuring her negative cognition
- CBT for reducing symptoms of depression and panic attacks
- Hypnotherapy for ego-strengthening
- Hypnotherapy for anxiety/panic management

- Hypnotherapy for positive mood induction and developing anti-depressive pathways

- Hypnotherapy for sexual dysfunction

- Social skills training for improving social interaction

As she was preoccupied and consumed with faulty cognitions, it was decided to start her on CBT. The focus of the CBT was specifically on negative themes such as her descriptors of "a sense of failure," "worthlessness," "can't cope," and "anticipatory anxiety." After four sessions of CBT, she started showing good response, as she felt less depressed and less preoccupied with suicidal ideation. Her scores on the BDI-II and BHS decreased to the moderate range, but her anxiety (BAI) score was still in the severe range. It was therefore decided to proceed with hypnotherapy for ego-strengthening and anxiety management in the next session.

Three days prior to the hypnotherapy session, she had a relapse, following an incident where she was "unfairly put down" by her husband. She was seen on the same day by the therapist as she felt severely depressed and overwhelmed. Under such crises, this therapist finds it helpful to use the First Aid for Depression. The First Aid session helped Rita get out of the crisis quickly and established her focus on the cognitive strategies she had learned.

The next four sessions focused on hypnotherapy, with particular emphasis on ego-strengthening, anxiety management, positive mood induction, and forward projection with behavioral rehearsal (using adaptive strategies for dealing with future crises). She made significant improvement in her affect and anxiety, and started to feel more confident. The next two sessions focused on assertiveness and social skills training as she tended to be "reactive," rather than "proactive" towards her husband.

By this stage of therapy, Rita had started to feel more confident and was "ready to tackle" her sexual difficulty. Rita reported having low sexual desire and little motivation to seek sexual stimulation. She had felt this way since early adolescence. Because of her difficulty, she never initiates or enjoys sex. She goes along with her husband in order to please him. However, this often causes arguments since her husband accuses her of having no interest in him. However, Rita did not want to involve her husband in the therapy; but she wanted to try hypnotherapy because she was convinced there was something wrong with her at an unconscious level that might be affecting her sexual desire and sexual activity. She also indicated that whenever her husband approaches her or shows interest in her (in nonsexual scenarios as well), she freezes and becomes withdrawn. Hypnotic regression helped to bridge the link between her affect and her cognition (see Cognitive Restructuring under Hypnosis). Reframing and utilizing the "adult ego lenses" helped her overcome her anxiety, withdrawal behaviors, and hypoactive sexual arousal difficulties.

Two further sessions with Rita were devoted to inducing positive moods in order to start her develop antidepressive pathways. Such an approach may prevent future relapse by strengthening (positive kindling) the nervous system.

Rita showed excellent response to CH and was discharged after 12 sessions, stretched over four months. She was followed up for a year, during which she had three booster sessions, mainly related to her sexual difficulties. Despite Rita's significant improvement, her family physician, as a precaution, wanted her to continue with the antidepressant for another year, before weaning her off the medication.

This case illustrates the complexity and comorbidity of major depressive disorder, which made it important to take a multimodal approach to psychological intervention. Guided by the CDMD, the therapist was able to use different points of entry into Rita's depressive loop. The case highlights the importance of dealing with issues of most concern to the client, rather than following a rigid chronology of therapy. The First Aid technique provided a concrete and rapid crisis intervention technique, which helped Rita get on her feet quickly, and it strengthened the therapeutic alliance and positive expectancy. The case also demonstrates the effectiveness of utilizing hypnotic regression to gain access to unconscious materials that may cause or maintain dysfunctional emotion and behavioral patterns. Once the cause of her lack of communication and sexual hypoarousal was unveiled, the therapist was able to utilize CBT and hypnotic techniques to alleviate Rita's difficulties. However, it is recommended that hypnotic regression is not appropriate to use in every case of sexual dysfunction. Sex therapy involving the couple should be the treatment of choice. Nevertheless, where appropriate, hypnosis can be used as an adjunct to sex therapy.

## Case 3: Bob

Bob is a 55-year-old electronics engineer. He is the codirector and cofounder of a medium-size electronics company that manufactures electronic devices for the gas and oil industries. He had a history of major depressive disorder for 6 years. He had been under the care of a psychiatrist for 4 years, mainly being treated with antidepressant medication and sleeping pills. Last year he was referred to the author by a psychiatrist because Bob was "not making significant improvement and he wanted to try an alternative to medication." Bob read an article in the paper about the cortical changes brought on by CBT and was convinced that CBT would help him; thus he requested referral to the author.

Bob met the DSM-IV criteria for (a) moderate recurrent major depressive disorder and (b) social phobia specific to his company board meetings. His BDI-II score was in the severe range and his scores on the BAI and BHS were in the moderate range. Since his anxiety is specific to board meetings, he is less anxious when not present at a meeting, or when he is not anticipating attending a meeting. He scored very high on the BSS, making him extremely susceptible to hypnosis. His cognitive distortions were mainly around themes of inferiority, lack of confidence, and sense of inadequacy.

Bob said he has always been tense and overly sensitive. Because he was slightly overweight as a teenager, he became preoccupied with his appearance and he was bullied at school. He describes his teenage years as "painful" and "scary." When he was in the eleventh grade, he was not doing very well at school. His grades dropped from 78% to 54%. He became very anxious about failing and not completing high school. Gradually he became depressed and he was prescribed antidepressant medication by his family physician. He felt better within 3 months but continued to take the medication for a year. Bob indicated that he has never recovered from this depression in the sense that he continues to be "depressed for having been depressed." Although he completed high school and went to a university and received a degree in electronic engineering, he is convinced that he is not very bright and that he is a "weak person." Although his company is successful and he is respected as the codirector of the company, he is convinced that he is not a good manager and does not provide good leadership. He believes his colleagues and workers respect him partly because he owns the company. He is scared to address or chair a meeting because he is fearful that people will find out that he is a fraud (i.e., pretending to be bright) and a "weak person, not able to make good decisions." His faulty self-schemas were also related to the fact that his father had bipolar disorder and had attempted to commit suicide on two occasions. Bob believes he is weak like his father and that he has inherited his depressive gene and therefore will never be normal. Based on Bob's history and assessment, the following course of treatment was planned.

- Continue follow-ups with his psychiatrist
- Hypnotherapy for ego-strengthening
- Hypnotherapy for demonstration of self-control
- CBT for restructuring his faulty cognitions related to anxiety and depression
- Hypnotherapy for anxiety management
- Hypnotherapy for expansion of awareness
- Thought stopping and attention switching for countering negative rumination (countering negative self-hypnosis)
- Hypnotherapy for positive mood
- Hypnotherapy for developing antidepressive pathways

Bob went through the following sequence of CH:

## Session 1: History Taking and Assessment

The first session was devoted to history taking and administration of the BDI-II, BAI, BHS, and BSS. Part of the session focused on assessing Bob's cognitive distortions (using the same format as in Case 1).

## Sessions 2–6: Hypnotherapy

Because Bob was so preoccupied with the biological cause of his anxiety and depression, it was decided to devote several sessions to hypnotherapy at the initial stage of his therapy. The sessions were devoted to ego-strengthening, positive mood induction, expansion of awareness, and demonstration of the power of his mind over his body (by producing eye and body catalepsy and challenging him to open his eyes and get out of the reclining chair). Following these sessions, Bob became fascinated with hypnosis and started reading books on it. He was intrigued that he could open his eyes or get out of the chair, which reinforced his belief that he could change and strengthen his mind and body. He started to show significant improvement and indicated to the therapist that he liked coming to therapy and looked forward to his "fascinating sessions."

## Sessions 7–12: CBT

Bob was equally intrigued with the discovery that cognition influences emotional and behavioral responses. He worked diligently on his homework and completed all the assignments. He started to modify his cognition and consequently began to feel less anxious and depressed; it became less challenging for him to chair or attend a meeting. In the 12th session he disclosed to the therapist with great excitement that "now I can decide how I want to feel, it was crazy for me to think everything was biological . . . and guess what . . . I blamed my father for my depression."

## Session 13: Thought Stopping and Attention Switching

Although Bob was less preoccupied with negative cognition, it was decided to introduce him to "thought stopping and attention switching" in order to prevent future negative ruminations.

## Sessions 13–15: Positive Mood Induction and Developing Anti-Depressive Pathways

The last session for Bob set the scene for positive mood induction under hypnosis. When in trance, Bob was led by the therapist to focus on several positive experiences from his list (compiled for the thought stopping and attention switching exercises) in order to intensify his positive experiences, and he was given posthypnotic suggestions to practice with his list every day. Since Bob might have inherited the vulnerability (diathesis) for anxiety and depression from his father, it was important to kindle the nervous system in order to prevent future relapses.

## Session 16: Discharge

Bob was doing very well and therefore he was discharged with the reassurance that he could come back to see the therapist if the need arose. Bob's psychiatrist was very pleased with Bob's progress and decided to wean him from his medication.

This case illustrates the unique potential of hypnosis to produce dramatic cognitive, emotional, and somatosensory changes. By producing significant physiological changes, the therapist was able to demonstrate to Bob that one can produce significant changes in mind and body in spite of one's genetic make-up. These new experiences fostered a sense of hope in Bob and paved the way for a strong therapeutic alliance. The sequence of approach to his therapy was dictated by Bob's concerns, and it fully utilized his belief that CBT can produce cortical changes. When dealing with a client who adopts a biological approach to his or her illness (backed by some evidence), it is recommended that the therapist utilize the client's convictions rather than try to argue with the client. Hypnosis provides a powerful vehicle for working with such clients.

## SUMMARY

By combining cognitive and hypnotic paradigms, the CDMD as a theoretical model represents how vulnerable individuals utilize NSH or cognitive distortions to create depressive reality. The CDMD model thus expands on Beck's circular model of depression and provides the basis for integrating cognitive and hypnotic strategies in the treatment of nonendogenous depression. Cognitive hypnotherapy (CH), as shown in the CDMD model, appears to provide a comprehensive and pragmatic approach to treatment of depression. It also offers an innovative technique for developing antidepressive pathways. The three cases reported here illustrate how CH can be adapted to the individual depressed client. The most recent study reported by Alladin (2003) provides empirical evidence for CH as well, but needs replication at multiple sites in order to meet APA criteria for well-established psychological treatment for depression. CH offers a variety of treatment interventions for depression, from which a therapist can choose the best strategies for a particular depressed client.

## REFERENCES

Abramson, L. Y., Alloy, L. B., Hankin, B. L., Haeffel, G. J., MacCoon, D. G., & Gibb, B. E. (2002). Cognitive-vulnerability: Stress models of depression in a self-regulatory and psychobiological context. In I. H. Gotlib & C. L. Hammen (Eds.), *Handbook of depression* (pp. 268–294). New York: Guilford.

Alladin, A. (1989). Cognitive-hypnotherapy for depression. In D. Waxman, D. Pederson, I. Wilkie, & P. Mellett (Eds.), *Hypnosis: The 4th European Congress at Oxford* (pp. 175–182). London: Whurr.

Alladin, A. (1992). Hypnosis with depression. *American Journal of Preventive Psychiatry and Neurology, 3*(3), 13–18.

Alladin, A. (1992a). Depression as a dissociative state. *Hypnos: Swedish Journal of Hypnosis in Psychotherapy and Psychosomatic Medicine, 19,* 243–253.

Alladin, A. (1994). Cognitive hypnotherapy with depression. *Journal of Cognitive Psychotherapy: An International Quarterly, 8*(4), 275–288.

Alladin, A. (2003). *Cognitive-hypnotherapy for depression: An empirical investigation.* Paper presented at the Frontiers of Hypnosis 6th National Assembly, Federation of Canadian Societies of Clinical Hypnosis, Halifax, NS, October 9–12, 2003.

Alladin, A., & Heap, M. (1991). Hypnosis and depression. In M. Heap & W. Dryden (Eds.), *Hypnotherapy: A handbook* (pp. 49–67). Berkshire, UK: Open University Press.

American Psychiatric Association. (1980). *Diagnostic and statistical manual of mental disorders* (3rd ed.). Washington, DC: Author.

American Psychiatric Association. (1994). *Diagnostic and statistical manual of mental disorders* (4th ed.). Washington, DC: Author.

American Psychiatric Association. (2000). *Diagnostic and statistical manual of mental disorders* (4th ed., text rev.). Washington, DC: Author.

Angst, J., & Preizig, M. (1996). Course of a clinical cohort of unipolar, bipolar and schizoaffective patients: Results of a prospective study from 1959 to 1985. *Schweizer Archiv fur Neurologie und Psychiatrie, 146,* 1–16.

Araoz, D. L. (1981). Negative self-hypnosis. *Journal of Contemporary Psychotherapy, 12,* 45–52.

Araoz, D. L. (1985). *The new hypnosis.* New York: Brunner/Mazel.

Barber, T. X., & Wilson, S. C. (1978/79). The Barber suggestibility scale and the creative imagination scale: Experimental and clinical applications. *American Journal of Clinical Hypnosis, 21,* 85.

Barlow, D. H., & Durand, V. M. (2005). *Abnormal psychology: An integrative approach* (4th ed.). USA: Thomson Wadsworth.

Beck, A. T. (1967). *Depression: Clinical, experimental and theoretical aspects.* New York: Hoeber.

Beck, A. T. (1976). *Cognitive therapy and emotional disorders.* New York: International University Press.

Beck, A. T., Rush, A. J., Shaw, B. F., & Emery, G. (1979). *Cognitive therapy of depression.* New York: Guilford.

Beck, A. T., & Steer, R. A. (1993). *Beck Anxiety Inventory.* San Antonio, TX: Harcourt Brace.

Beck, A. T., & Steer, R. A. (1993a). *Beck Hopelessness Scale.* San Antonio, TX: Harcourt Brace.

Beck, A. T., Steer, R. A., & Brown, K. B. (1996). *The Beck Depression Inventory-Revised.* San Antonio, TX: Harcourt Brace.

Beck, A. T., & Young, J. E. (1985). Depression. In D. H. Barlow (Ed.), *Clinical handbook of psychological disorders.* New York: Guilford.

Beck, J. (1995). *Cognitive therapy: Basics and beyond.* New York: Guilford.

Bower, G. (1981). Mood and memory. *American Psychologist, 36,* 129–148.

Brown, D. P., & Fromm, E. (1990). Enhancing affective experience and its expression. In D. C. Hammond (Ed.), *Hypnotic suggestions and metaphors* (pp. 322–324). New York: W. W. Norton.

Brown, G. W., & Harris, T. (1978). *Social origins of depression.* New York: Free Press.

Burns, D. D. (1999). *Feeling good: The new mood therapy.* New York: Avon Books.

Burrows, G. D., & Boughton, S. G. (2001). Hypnosis and depression. In G. D. Burrows, R. O. Stanley, & P. B. Bloom (Eds.), *International handbook of clinical hypnosis* (pp. 129–142). New York: John Wiley.

Chambless, D. L., & Hollon, S. D. (1998). Defining empirically-supported therapies. *Journal of Consulting and Clinical Psychology, 66,* 7–18.

Coryell, W., Leon, A., Winokur, G., Endicott, J., Keller, M., Akiskal, H. S., et al. (1996). Importance of psychotic features to long-term course in major depressive disorder. *American Journal of Psychiatry, 153,* 483–489.

Dobson, K. S. (1986). The self-schema in depression. In L. M. Hartmen & K. R. Blankstein (Eds.), *Perception of self in emotional disorder and psychotherapy* (pp. 187–217). New York: Plenum.

Edgette, J. H., & Edgette, J. S. (1995). *The handbook of hypnotic phenomena in psychotherapy.* New York: Brunner/Mazel.

Fava, M., & Rosenbaum, J. F. (1995). Pharmacotherapy and somatic therapies. In E. E. Beckham & W. R. Leber (Eds.), *Handbook of depression* (2nd ed., pp. 280–301). New York: Guilford.

Fink, M. (2001). Convulsive therapy: A review of the first 55 years. *Journal of Affective Disorders, 63,* 1–15.

Gibbons, D. E. (1979). *Applied hypnosis and hyperempiria.* New York: Plenum.

Gillham, J. E., Shatte, A. J., & Freres, D. R. (2000). Preventing depression: A review of cognitive-behavioral and family interventions. *Applied and Preventive Psychology, 9,* 63–88.

Golden, W. L., Dowd, E. T., & Friedberg, F. (1987). *Hypnotherapy: A modern approach.* New York: Pergamon.

Gotlib, I. H., & Goodman, S. H. (1999). Children of parents with depression. In W. K. Silverman & T. H. Ollendick (Eds.), *Developmental issues in the clinical treatment of children* (pp. 415–432). Boston: Allyn & Bacon.

Gotlib, I. H., & Hammen, C. L. (2002). Introduction. In I. H. Gotlib & C. L. Hammen (Eds.), *Handbook of depression* (pp. 1–20). New York: Guilford.

Guidano, V. F. (1987). *Complexity of the self: A developmental approach to psychopathology and therapy.* New York: Guilford.

Haas, G. L., & Fitzgibbon, M. L. (1989). In J. J. Mann (Ed.), *Models of depressive disorders* (pp. 9–43). New York: Plenum.

Hamilton, M. (1967). Development of a rating scale for primary depressive illness. *British Journal of Social and Clinical Psychology, 6*, 278–296.

Hammond, D. C. (Ed.). (1990). *Handbook of hypnotic suggestions and metaphors.* New York: W. W. Norton.

Hartland, J. (1971). *Medical and dental hypnosis and its clinical applications* (2nd. ed). London: Bailliere Tindall.

Hilgard, E. R. (1977). *Divided consciousness: Multiple controls in human thought and action.* New York: John Wiley.

Hollon, S. D., Haman, K. L., & Brown, L. L. (2002). Cognitive-behavioral treatment of depression. In I. H. Gotlib & C. C. Hammen (Eds.), *Handbook of depression* (pp. 383–403). New York: Guilford.

Hollon, S. D., & Shelton, M. (1991). Contributions of cognitive psychology to assessment and treatment of depression. In P. R. Martin (Ed.), *Handbook of behavior therapy and psychological science: An integrated approach* (Vol. 164, pp. 169–195). New York: Pergamon.

Horowitz, M. J. (1972). Image formation: Clinical observation and a cognitive model. In P. W. Sheehan (Ed.), *The function and nature of imagery* (pp. 282–309). New York: Academic Press.

Janet, P. (1889). *L' Automatisme psychologique.* Paris: Felix Alcan.

Janet, P. (1907). *The major symptoms of hysteria.* New York: Macmillan.

Jaynes, J. (1976). *The origin of consciousness in the breakdown of the bicameral mind.* Boston: Houghton Mifflin.

Kahneman, D., Slovic, P., & Tversky, A. (1882). *Judgment under uncertainty: Heuristics and biases.* Cambridge, UK: Cambridge University Press.

Kessler, R. C. (2002). Epidemiology of depression. In I. H. Gotlib & C. C. Hammen (Eds.), *Handbook of depression* (pp. 23–42). New York: Guilford.

Kessler, R. C., McGongale, K. A., Zhao, S., Nelson, C. B., Hughes, M., Eshleman, et al. (1994). Lifetime and 12-month prevalence of DSM-III-R psychiatric disorders in the United States: Results from the National Comorbidity Survey. *Archives of General Psychiatry, 51*, 8–19.

Kirsch, I., Montgomery, G., & Sapirstein, G. (1995). Hypnosis as an adjunct to cognitive-behavioral psychotherapy: A meta-analysis. *Journal of Consulting and Clinical Psychology, 63*, 214–220.

Klinger, E. (1975). The nature of fantasy and its clinical uses. In J. L. Klinger (Chair), *Imagery approaches to psychotherapy.* Symposium presented at the Meeting of the American Psychological Association, Chicago.

Ley, R. G., & Freeman, R. J. (1984). Imagery, cerebral laterality, and the healing process. In A. A. Sheikh (Ed.), *Imagination and healing* (pp. 51–68). New York: Baywood.

Moore, J. D., & Bona, J. R. (2001). Depression and dysthymia. *Medical Clinics of North America, 85*(3), 631–644.

Murray, C. J. L., & Lopez, A. D. (Eds.). (1996). *The global burden of disease: A comprehensive assessment of mortality and disability from diseases, injuries, and risk factors in 1990 and projected to 2020.* Cambridge, MA: Harvard University Press.

Neisser, U. (1967). *Cognitive psychology.* New York: Appleton-Century-Croft.

Nemeroff, C. B. (2000). An ever-increasing pharmacopoeia for the management of patients with bipolar disorder. *Journal of Clinical Psychiatry, 61*(Suppl. 13), 19–25.

Nolen-Hoeksema, S. (2004). *Abnormal psychology* (3rd ed.). New York: McGraw-Hill.

Oke, A., Keller, R., Mefford, I., & Adams, R. N. (1978). Lateralization of norepinephrine in human thalamus. *Science, 200,* 1411–1433.

Overlade, D. C. (1986). First aid for depression. In E. T. Dowd & J. M. Healy (Eds.), *Case studies in hypnotherapy* (pp. 23–33). New York: Guilford.

Paykel, E. S., Meyers, J. K., Dienett, M. N., Klerman, G. L., Linderthal, J. J., & Pepeper, M. P. (1969). Life events and depression: A controlled study. *Archives of General Psychiatry, 21,* 753–760.

Paykel, E. S., & Priest, R. G. (1992). Recognition and management of depression in general practice: Consensus statement. *British Medical Journal, 305,* 1198–1202.

Pearlstein, T., Stone, A., Lund, S., Scheft, H., Zlotnik, C., & Brown, W. (1997). Comparison of fluoxetine, bupropion, and placebo in the treatment of premenstrual dysphoric disorder. *Journal of Clinical Psychopharmacology, 17,* 261–266.

Pincus, H. A., & Pettit, A. R. (2001). The societal costs of chronic major depression. *Journal of Clinical Psychiatry, 62*(Suppl. 6), 5–9.

Posner, M. (1973). Coordination on internal codes. In W. Chase (Ed.), *Visual information processing.* New York: Academic.

Robins, L. N., & Regier, D. A. (Eds.). (1991). *Psychiatric disorders in America: The Epidemiologic Catchment Area Study.* New York: Free Press.

Safer, M. A., & Leventhal, H. (1977). Ear differences in evaluating emotional tone of voice and verbal content. *Journal of Experimental Psychology: Human Perception and Performance, 3,* 75–82.

Satcher, D. (2000). Mental health: A report of the Surgeon General: Executive summary. *Professional Psychology: Research and Practice, 31*(1), 5–13.

Schoenberger, N. E. (2000). Research on hypnosis as an adjunct to cognitive-behavioral psychotherapy. *International Journal of Clinical and Experimental Hypnosis, 48,* 154–169.

Schultz, K. D. (1978). Imagery and the control of depression. In J. L. Singer & K. S. Pope (Eds.), *The power of human imagination: New methods in psychotherapy* (pp. 281–307). New York: Plenum.

Schultz, K. D. (1984). The use of imagery in alleviating depression. In A. A. Sheik (Ed.), *Imagination and healing* (pp. 129–158). New York: Baywood.

Schultz, K. D. (2003). The use of imagery in alleviating depression. In A. A. Sheikh (Ed.), *Healing images: The role of imagination in health* (pp. 343–380). New York: Baywood.

Schwartz, G. (1976). Facial muscle patterning in affective imagery in depressed and non-depressed subjects. *Science, 192*, 489.

Schwartz, G. (1977). Psychosomatic disorders in biofeedback: A psychological model of disregulation. In J. D. Maser & M. E. P. Seligman (Eds.), *Psychopathology: Experimental models* (pp. 270–307). San Francisco: W. H. Freeman.

Schwartz, G. (1984). Psychophysiology of imagery and healing: A systems perspective. In A. A. Sheik (Ed.), *Imagination and healing* (pp. 35–50). New York: Baywood.

Seligman, M. E. P. (1975). *Helplessness: On depression, development of death*. San Francisco: W. H. Freeman.

Shevrin, H. (1978). Evoked potential evidence for unconscious mental process: A review of the literature. In A. S. Prangishvilli, A. E. Sherozia, & F. V. Bassin (Eds.), *The unconscious: Nature, functions, methods of study*. Tbilisi, USSR: Metsnierba.

Shevrin, H., & Dickman, S. (1980). The psychologically unconscious American. *American Psychologist, 5*, 421.

Simons, A. D., Garfield, S. L., & Murphy, G. E. (1984). The process of change in cognitive therapy and pharmacotherapy for depression. *Archives of General Psychiatry, 41*, 45–51.

Solomon, D. A., Keller, M. B., Leon, A. C., Mueller, T. I., Lavori, P. W., Shea, T., et al. (2000). Multiple recurrences of major depressive disorder. *American Journal of Psychiatry, 157*(2), 229–233.

Starker, S., & Singer, J. L. (1975). Daydreaming patterns of self-awareness in psychiatric patients. *Journal of Nervous and Mental Disease*, 313–317.

Sternberg, S. (1975). Memory scanning: New findings and current controversies. *Quarterly Journal of Experimental Psychology, 27*, 1.

Thase, M. E., & Beck, A. T. (1992). An overview of cognitive therapy. In J. H. Wright, M. E. Thase, A. T. Beck, et al., *Cognitive therapy with inpatients: Developing a cognitive milieu* (pp. 3–34). New York: Guilford.

Tosi, D. J., & Baisden, B. S. (1984). Cognitive-experiential therapy and hypnosis. In W. C. Wester & A. H. Smith (Eds.), *Clinical hypnosis: A multidisciplinary approach* (pp. 155–178). New York: J. B. Lippincott.

Traynor, J. D. (1974). *Patterns of daydreaming and their relationship to depressive affect*. Unpublished master's thesis, Miami University, Oxford, Ohio.

Wade, T. J., & Cairney, J. (2000). Major depressive disorder and marital transition among mothers: Results from a national panel study. *Journal of Nervous and Mental Disease, 188*, 741–750.

Warren, W. L. (1994). *Revised Hamilton Rating Scale for Depression (RHRSD): Manual*. Los Angeles: Western Psychological Services.

Weissman, A., & Beck, A. T. (1978). *Development and validation of the Dysfunctional Attitude Scale*. Paper presented at the Annual Meeting of the Association for Advancement of Behavior Therapy, Chicago.

West, L. J. (1967). Dissociative reaction. In A. M. Freedman & H. I. Kaplan (Eds.), *Comprehensive textbook of psychiatry*. Baltimore, MD: Williams & Wilkins.

Williams, J. M. G. (1992). *The psychological treatment of depression*. London: Routledge.

Williams, J. M. G., Watts, F. N., MacLeod, C., & Mathews, A. (1997). *Cognitive psychology and emotional disorders*. Chichester, UK: Wiley.

World Health Organization. (1992). *The ICD-10: The ICD-10 classification of mental and behavioral disorders: Clinical descriptions and diagnostic guidelines.* Geneva, Switzerland: WHO.

World Health Organization. (1998). *Well-being measures in primary healthcare/ The Depcare Project.* Copenhagen: WHO Regional Office for Europe.

Yapko, M. D. (1992). *Hypnosis and the treatment of depressions: Strategies for change.* New York: Brunner/Mazel.

Yapko, M. D. (2001). *Treating depression with hypnosis: Integrating cognitive-behavioral and strategic approaches.* Philadelphia: Brunner/Routledge.

Young, A. R., & Beitchman, J. H. (2001). Learning disorders. In G. O. Gabbard (Ed.), *Treatment of psychiatric disorders* (Vol. 1, 3rd ed., pp. 109–124). Washington, DC: American Psychiatric Association.

Youngren, M. A., & Lewinshon, P. M. (1980). The functional relation between depression and problematic interpersonal behaviour. *Journal of Abnormal Psychology, 89*, 333–341.

Zarren, J., & Eimer, B. (2001). *Brief cognitive hypnosis: Facilitating the change of dysfunctional behavior.* New York: Springer Publishing.

Chapter 7

# Cognitive Hypnotherapy and the Management of Anger

E. Thomas Dowd

In 1950, British poet W. H. Auden referred to the second half of the twentieth century as "The Age of Anxiety." However, if there is one psychological difficulty that derives from the frantic, hectic, multitasking, stress-filled, "24/7" lifestyle of the late twentieth and early twenty-first centuries, it would probably be anger. Yet, anger has curiously been an unstudied problem with relatively few thera-peutic treatments available, even though Fernandez (2002) identified it as one of the three core emotions (along with anxiety and depres-sion) of negative affect. Indeed, in some socio-cultural contexts, anger is not viewed as a problem at all; rather it is seen as an understandable, even desirable, reaction to a negative event. The term "righteous anger" describes this phenomenon, and one only need think of the reciprocal and escalating anger between members of two or more ethnic/social groups to understand anger in this context. For example, in the Hebrew Bible (or Old Testament) there are an astonishingly large number of references to anger, mostly Yahweh's anger (presumably righteous) towards the people of Israel for their sins against their God. There are also numerous references to the Israelites' anger towards Israel's enemies.

DiGiuseppe (1999) referred to anger as constructive, malevolent, or selfish, and states that few people even desire to change or control their anger. In this chapter, I describe the theory and research on the treatment of anger, the cognitive theory of anger, and how cognitive hypnotherapy might be of use in dealing with anger. I end the chapter with a sample case study. First, however, it is important to distinguish anger from related concepts such as hostility and aggression. *Webster's Third New International Dictionary* (Gove, 1981) uses "grief," "sorrow," "anguish," "strong feeling of displeasure and (usually) antagonism," and, in the medical sense, "an inflammation"—all describe anger. Synonyms include ire, rage, fury, indignation, and wrath, with anger being the most general of these terms but implicating no degree of intensity. What these descriptors suggest is an attitude (cognition) with emotional loading. Indeed, Kassinove and Sukhodolsky (1995) defined anger as a "negative, phenomenological (or internal) feeling state associated with specific cognitive and perceptual distortions and deficiencies . . . " (p. 7). Furthermore, they state that anger is associated with patterns of physical arousal and action tendencies, and usually includes a perception that another person is to blame. Edmonson and Conger (1996) defined anger as an emotion but went on to describe four components of the anger response system, i.e., the experiential, physiological, cognitive, and behavioral. This chapter will consider only the first three. DiGiuseppe, Eckhardt, Tafrate, and Robin (1994) defined anger as "an internal, mental, subjective feeling state with associated cognitions and physiological arousal patterns" (p. 232), thus incorporating all aspects but behavioral.

By contrast, aggression is an action—generally with a deliberate intent to harm a person or an object—which may or may not have an intended outcome. Aggression can be physical or verbal (Kassinove & Sukhodolsky, 1995). Hostility has been less clearly defined, sometimes being referred to as an attitude or negative evaluation (Spielberger, Reheiser, & Sydeman, 1995) and sometimes as a personality trait or style (Tsytsarev & Grodnitzky, 1995). In this sense, hostility overlaps conceptually with anger but has a more intense flavor. Neither anger nor hostility is aggression unless and until it is operationalized. Anger and hostility (expressed as frustration) often lead to aggression, however, as exemplified in various iterations of the Frustration-Aggression hypothesis (Dollard, Doob, Miller, Mowrer, & Sears, 1939).

Another related term is resentment, which *Webster's* defines as "a feeling of indignant displeasure because of something regarded as a wrong, insult, or other injury." The term "indignant displeasure" is conceptually close to, but less strong than, anger, so resentment may be seen as a low-level form of anger. Resentment that has slowly simmered for years may flare into anger under conditions of greater provocation. Thus, it may be important to treat resentment sooner in order to avoid the necessity of treating anger later.

As a result of psychology's neglect of anger disorders, the *Diagnostic and Statistical Manual of Mental Disorders–IV* does not include criteria for disorders in which anger is a primary component. Therefore, Dahlen and Deffenbacher (2001) have proposed criteria for five anger disorders: (a) adjustment disorder with angry mood, (b) situational anger disorder without aggression, (c) situational anger with aggression, (d) generalized anger disorder without aggression, and (e) generalized anger disorder with aggression. This chapter considers only (a), (b), and (d)—the rationale being that if anger is successfully treated, aggression will significantly diminish. It does not consider disorders in which anger is a secondary aspect, such as borderline personality disorder or posttraumatic stress disorder.

Most of the literature on anger and its management really concerns the treatment of violent offenders, such as domestic abusers, and other forms of conduct disorders, criminal offenses, and aggression, rather than anger *per se*. These individuals are rarely seen in a positive light. Indeed, Corvo and Johnson (2003) discuss the "vilification of the batterer" as affecting both treatment and research, which results in portraying these offenders as undeserving of therapeutic interventions. It is possible that the failure to devise treatment approaches for anger problems has occurred, at least in part, because of the undesirability of these individuals. In addition, a central characteristic of angry people is resistance to treatment (Deffenbacher, 1999; Novaco, 2002) both because anger is part of their personal identity and because it often has been useful to them. Many therapists themselves may have difficulty, because of the "benign" personality types attracted to the profession as well as their therapy training, relating to and dealing with angry clients even if the anger is not associated with aggression. Anger often evokes a therapist's counter reaction and threatens the therapeutic alliance (Ornstein, 1999).

# MODELS OF ANGER TREATMENT

DiGiuseppe (1999) describes several theoretical treatments for anger, including cognitive-behavioral, experiential, self-psychology, Buddhist, and systems approaches. In comparing these models, he notes that the cognitive-behavioral, experiential, and Buddhist approaches postulate that anger is a defense against and in reaction to low self-efficacy, feelings of helplessness, and self-denigration. Denigration by others (e.g., being "dissed") also appears to be part of this constellation. However, as DiGiuseppe points out, it is not at all clear that anger is related to low self-esteem. Despite the popularity of this idea, research has failed to substantiate it. Some theorists believe that anger (as well as narcissism) is related to *high* self-esteem that is threatened as well as the occurrence of aversive events the individual believes is neither necessary nor controllable. The cognitive-behavioral, systems, and Buddhist approaches make use of the rehearsal of new responses in anger treatment. The cognitive-behavioral and Buddhist approaches include explicit interventions to reduce physiological arousal. Because I make primary use of the cognitive-behavioral and Buddhist approaches (based in part on research findings and because the former method forms the theme of this book), I will describe these in more detail.

## The Cognitive-Behavioral Approach

*Cognitive-behavioral conceptualization.* According to Deffenbacher and colleagues (Dahlen & Deffenbacher, 2001; Deffenbacher, 1999), anger can be seen as arising from one or more of (or interactions among) three classes of variables—specific external events, internal stimuli (pre-anger state) such as thoughts and emotions, and a combination of these two. External stimuli of anger include such events as being cut off in traffic, being disrespected ("dissed") by an important person, having to wait in line, or being rejected by a significant other. Internal stimuli of anger consist of immediate cognitive states, prior anger, appraisal processes, and enduring cognitive characterstics. Immediate states include cognitive ruminations about an upcoming event, ruminations about being wronged or treated with contempt (nursing one's wrath to keep it warm), and often lead to increased feelings of anger. Expression of prior anger increases the likelihood that one will respond angrily in subsequent situations, especially if the two situations are similar. Appraisal processes include the meaning of the anger-eliciting event (primary appraisal) as well as one's perceived ability to cope with the event (secondary appraisal), whereas the cognitive basis of depression is (past) loss, the cognitive basis of anxiety is (future) danger and personal vulnerability, the cognitive basis of anger is likely personal violation, victimization, and unfairness ("How dare they treat me that way! Who do they think they are?") (Beck, 1999; Padesky & Greenberger, 1995).

Enduring cognitive characteristics, including cultural constraints and channels of the appropriate expression of anger also play a part in anger expression and in primary appraisal. Anger can be triggered by challenges to an individual's self-schemas, in such domains as violations of rules for living, moral considerations, an attack on one's personal identity, unwarranted personal frustrations, and strongly-held cultural values (Deffenbacher, 1999). For example, some individuals become angry at a relatively minor thwarting of their desires, what Albert Ellis calls "low frustration tolerance" (Ellis & Dryden, 1997). Others become angry at violations by others, of their own deeply held moral values, in such areas as abortion or pre-marital sex. Still others appear extremely sensitive to interpersonal rejection and react to it with anger, leading on occasion to spousal abuse. However, cultural values and prescriptions or proscriptions limit or channel the appropriate expression of anger. In some cultures, anger and violence are expected outcomes of certain events (e.g., stoning adulterers to death, killing of a relative) and may be described as righteous anger, whereas in other cultures, anger itself (or at least its expression) is seen as in very bad taste (e.g., Asian cultures). Furthermore, cultures often change over time, sometimes rapidly leading to inappropriate anger expressions based on past norms. Assertion training in the United States, for example, can be seen as necessitated by changing cultural norms and expectations in anger expression by certain classes of citizens. Finally, anger can arise from a confluence or interaction among all these variables.

*Cognitive behavior treatment.* CBT treatment is a multifaceted program (Dahlen & Deffenbacher, 2001; Deffenbacher, 1999). An important component, and one relatively easy to administer, is relaxation training. Because physiological arousal is such an important aspect of anger, anything that decreases that arousal is likely to reduce anger as well. Indeed, this has been shown to be the case. Relaxation alone has led to significant reductions in trait anger, the frequency and intensity of daily anger, and anger resulting from provocations. Relaxation has even been shown to be as effective as cognitive interventions as well as have a combination of cognitive and relaxation treatments, and those gains were maintained over time (Dahlen & Deffenbacher, 2001; Mayne & Ambrose, 1999). Nezu and Nezu (2003) have referred to this intervention as "quieting an angry body" and use autogenic training (a form of relaxation and self-hypnosis) to do this. They include a sample autogenic training script. Van der Kolk, McFarlane, and Weisaeth (1996) have argued that higher cerebral cognitive processing ("top down") cannot fully access or change lower nonverbal, mid-brain cognitive processing and bodily physiological states. Higher order interventions may not lead to changes in the latter areas so that direct bodily interventions ("bottom up") may be necessary. Otherwise, individuals may "understand" their problems cognitively but still encounter unexplained periodic states of angry hyperarousal.

Another class of interventions is behavioral coping, problem solving, and social skills training which target the way anger is expressed. In many instances, people behave angrily because they do not know what else to do, operating perhaps on the automatic tacit assumption that the best defense is a good offensive (and they can be quite offensive!). This lack of knowledge affects not only their motor behavior but also their verbal behavior. Problem solving training can help angry individuals to break down the often automatic and instantaneous expression of anger in problematic situations into a series of sequential and manageable steps. Social skills training can teach them to learn new, more adaptive, and effective relational skills that will help them achieve their goals in other ways. Group therapy, because of the multiple models and ideas available, as well as the instant feedback it can provide, can be especially beneficial. Structured training manuals can often be used effectively. Assertion training is one such program and, among other goals, helps individuals to distinguish anger from assertion and to display the former instead of the latter. General training in communication skills can also be effective. Behavioral coping and social skills training have been shown to be as effective as cognitive or combined cognitive-relaxation interventions in several studies (Dahlen & Deffenbacher, 2001).

A third class of treatment approaches is cognitive or cognitive restructuring interventions. These interventions focus on dysfunctional self-statements (cognitive contents) that contribute to anger responses, such as "How dare she do that to me?!" or "He has no right to be that rude!" More positive and adaptive self-statements are practiced. The interventions also target dysfunctional cognitive processes (thinking errors), such as faulty primary and secondary appraisal errors, dichotomous thinking/overgeneralization ("He always tries to hurt me on purpose!"), using imperative statements ("She should treat me better!"), or labeling ("He's a complete jerk who should be punished!"). The interventions may also address tacit cognitive schemas (cognitive structures) such as rejection or punitiveness. Deffenbacher (1999) even used humor (probably as a distancing technique) to reduce anger by providing a sense of perspective. Dahlen and Deffenbacher (2000) found that cognitive restructuring alone was as effective as full cognitive therapy (including the behavioral component) in high anger undergraduate students. However, Mayne and Ambrose (1999) reported that cognitive therapy was less effective than alternative treatments, which included various forms of cognitive behavior therapy, dynamic therapies, and relaxation treatment. They speculated that cognitive therapy was less effective because it failed to address either the physiological components of anger or the meaning systems associated with anger. Chemtob, Novaco, Hamada, and Gross (1997) found that stress inoculation (a cognitive-behavioral approach) resulted in significant gains (anger reduction) on multiple measures both after treatment and at 18-month follow-up with seriously disordered Vietnam veterans.

There has been an evolution in cognitive behavior therapy that connects directly to a Buddhist conceptualization and treatment of anger. Essentially this involves an acceptance of one's problems and negative emotions rather than rational disputation of them (Hayes & Pankey, 2003) and a *cognitive defusion* (or decentering), in which thoughts are seen as only thoughts and not necessarily as reality (Luoma & Hayes, 2003). Again, the focus is on acceptance rather than on disputation. Interestingly, there are similarities to paradoxical interventions such as symptom prescription (in which the problem is prescribed and becomes the solution) and reframing (in which a negative event is seen as positive), as described by Dowd and his colleagues (Dowd & Pace, 1989; Dowd & Trutt, 1988). From the Buddhist perspective, many practitioners (e.g., Das, 1999) now advocate combining psychotherapy with Buddha Dharma (teaching) and meditation practice.

## Buddhist Conceptualization and Treatment of Anger

I have chosen to discuss the Buddhist approach to anger treatment because of its heavy reliance on relaxation via meditation, acceptance of negative emotions, and its negation of the Self and its demands. Research has demonstrated the importance of relaxation in reducing anger. Anger often results from excessive demands for gratification and low frustration tolerance (Ellis & Dryden, 1997). Thus, treatment based on Buddhist thought and practice may be especially valuable in treating persons with excessive and inappropriate anger.

From a Buddhist viewpoint, anger is a form of suffering. All humans suffer but Buddhist practice aims to reduce or eliminate that suffering. The Four Noble Truths of Buddhism express this notion well (Das, 1997, pp. 76–77):

1.  Life is difficult.

2.  Life is difficult because of attachments and desires that are inherently unsatisfying.

3.  There is the possibility of liberation from difficulties.

4.  The way to this liberation and enlightenment is by the practice of compassion, virtue, wisdom, and meditation.

Suffering is caused by the *three poisons*: passion, aversion, and ignorance (Leifer, 1999). Passion includes desire, greed, lust, attachment, and clinging. Aversion includes hatred and aggression. These two concepts are related in that one is the polarity of the other. A central tenet of Buddhist thinking is that suffering is fundamentally caused by desire for and attachment to objects, so to the extent that we can free ourselves of desire, the less we will suffer. The 14th Dalai Lama (2000) has stated that anger comes from attachment; the more attachments we have, the more angry we get. In other words, it is important to want what you get rather than get what you want.

Aversion is a way of relating by avoiding, evading, hating, envy-ing, and destroying. Thus, the first two poisons represent a funda-mental dialectic: attraction and repulsion. Furthermore, both poles may be found in the same object, as when the desire for an identity leads to antagonism towards those with a different identity (Leifer, 1999).

The third poison, ignorance (delusion or illusion), refers to the denial or lack of awareness of the basic truths of existence. Angry clients exhibit this delusion perfectly. They are unaware of (or resist seeing) the suffering their anger causes themselves and others, and are unaware of (or refuse to face) the choice they have made to be angry.

Leifer (1999) describes three steps towards anger reduction by taking a Buddhist perspective. The first step is taking responsibility for one's anger—not an easy step because anger is generally directed towards others rather than towards one's self. Angry individuals tend to be strong externalizers and often see their anger as entirely justified. Leifer suggests educating clients about the dynamics of anger as a first step. Deffenbacher (1999) argues that these clients are usually in a precontemplative stage of change and that attention should therefore be paid to the therapeutic alliance.

Step two is in becoming aware that anger is the result of our frustrated desires and aversions. Step three is in understanding the dynamics of anger—that it reduces the sense of danger, help-lessness, and humiliation and helps establish a secure sense of iden-tity and meaning. Step four asks the individual to reflect on his or her anger as it arises. Leifer (1999) suggests asking two questions in situations arousing anger, "What did I want that I wasn't getting?" and "What was I getting that I didn't want?"

Step five is decision: the commitment not to act out anger, not to repress it, but to become aware of it and reflect on it. This is very similar to the Buddhist technique of emptying the mind. If angry thoughts arise during meditation, it is difficult, if not impossible, to repress them; it is like trying not to think of a pink elephant. Rather, it is important to be aware of them, reflect upon them, and gently turn one's mind away from them and towards emptying the mind. Or, if the object of meditation is a reflection on compassion, one can simply notice angry thoughts as they arise, reflect on them and gently turn the mind once more towards compassion. It is then possible to turn one's mind towards alternatives to anger. As with most things, this becomes easier with practice.

The Vietnamese Buddhist monk Thich Nhat Hanh (2001) goes even further. In what is essentially a symptom prescription for anger, he advocates embracing one's anger and treating it with tenderness rather than attempting to suppress it (Dowd & Trutt, 1988). Thich Nhat Hanh suggests deep relaxation (similar to that used in systematic desensitization) and mindfulness as ways of both embracing and healing anger. Mindfulness is simply being deeply aware of what is happening in the present moment. Using mindful breathing as both a recognition and a treatment of anger, Hanh (p. 164) suggests saying to one's self, "Breathing in, I know that anger has manifested in me; breathing out, I smile towards my anger." Or, "Breathing in, I know that anger is in me. Breathing out, I am taking good care of my anger" (p. 166).

Buddhism considers *right intention* to be very important. Seeing a potential Buddha in all people is a beginning. Therefore, one excellent way to reduce anger, according to the Buddhist perspective, is to practice empathy and compassion for others, especially for those with whom one is angry. Empathy enables us to understand profoundly what others are suffering (Das, 1999), to see things from the other's perspective, and to begin to understand why they do what they do—not as an excuse but as an explanation. With increased awareness of the suffering of others, and consequent empathy, we can begin to feel compassion for them. An excellent exercise, though more difficult to practice than one might imagine, is to wish strongly, while meditating, for good events to happen to one's worst enemy and for good feelings to accompany those events.

In order to help free ourselves from an undue reliance on desire and attachment and to achieve the attitude described in the statement, "Want what you get rather than get what you want," it can be helpful to practice gratitude. Too often, in our drive to achieve and to acquire things, we focus all our attention on what we don't (yet) have, rather than on what we do. The result is that we are chronically upset and dissatisfied, and often angry at those whom we see blocking our path. If we focus on gratitude for what we have (including such mundane but overlooked examples as good health or steady employment), we will likely find ourselves happier and more peaceful. Nezu and Nezu (2003) describe some ways to do this, notably it is important to be specific and to write them down.

Buddhism also considers *right action* to be very important (Das, 1997). Das (1999) discusses, as a behavioral action, the practice of warmth and kindness. Listening to others describe, even complain about, their distress can help. Finding reasons to compliment others (especially an enemy) can help. Always allowing a driver to turn in front of you (instead of speeding up to prevent it) can help. As Mark Twain once said, "Always do the right thing. It will impress some people and astonish the rest." It will encourage them to do likewise.

From the preceding description of both cognitive-behavioral and Buddhist-oriented approaches, one can see that they have much in common. Both involve relaxation training (whether it is called relaxation, meditation, or self-hypnosis) as a way of reducing the physiological arousal that is a significant aspect of the anger experience. Both involve cognitive retraining, whether it involves an analysis of negative automatic self-statements and dysfunction schemas or meditation on themes like compassion and empathy. The rationales and explanatory processes may be quite different, but the underlying techniques are much more similar.

## WHY USE HYPNOSIS?

A question which one might reasonably ask is, why use hypnosis in cognitive-behavior therapy or indeed in any kind of therapy at all? Does it add anything beyond the demonstrated efficacy of these treatments? In other words, does it possess value-added attributes?

Although it is a point of some contention, Milton Erickson thought that hypnosis was an unusually effective way to reduce or overcome resistance, especially valuable with angry clients. He used several methods to accomplish this. Foremost among them was the *utilization technique*. Essentially, it involves an acceptance of whatever the client happens to be doing or thinking right then as the best possible action or thought (Dowd, 2000). Erickson also used this technique to define anything clients did as a sign they were entering a trance. It is difficult to resist total acceptance. Erickson used the client's own associations and potential to alter "habitual attitudes and modes of functioning so that carefully formulated hypnotic suggestions can evoke and utilize other patterns of associations and potentials within the patient to implement certain therapeutic goals" (Erickson, Rossi, & Rossi, 1976, p. 20).

Erickson used the conscious-unconscious double bind as another way to bypass resistance (Erickson & Rossi, 1979). It sets up a situation whereby the client cannot resist, by dividing his/her consciousness. An example is:

> And you don't really have to pay attention to me . . . your unconscious mind will understand what I say and understand things that you can't understand. . . . (Erickson & Rossi, p. 151)

Erickson also used the negative to discharge and displace resistance in a client who expresses resistance in the form of "no." Here is an example:

> And you will make true whatever I say, will you not? (Erickson & Rossi, p. 254)

Dowd (2000) has also discussed the use of hypnosis to bypass or overcome resistance. For example, a *truism* is a statement that is so obviously true that it is difficult to disagree with it. Erickson et al. (1976) have provided several examples, such as, "You already know how to experience pleasant emotions like the warmth of the sun on your skin" or "It probably will happen as soon as you are ready." It is difficult to resist such suggestions; there is little to resist. One can also use the "yes-set," in which the client is given statements to which a "yes" answer is obvious (e.g., "You are hearing the sound of my voice, aren't you") and gradually moving to statements for which a "yes" answer might be less likely. But by then the client is in the habit of answering, "yes." This is a hypnotherapeutic example of the foot-in-the-door technique, well known in social psychology. The use of metaphors, allusions, and stories can help in presenting new and discrepant information to a client without directly appearing to be addressing the problem or concern—thus reducing potential resistance from overtly challenging the client's cognitive constructions of reality.

Dowd (2000) also describes individual differences in resistance potential (known as psychological reactance) and the use of paradoxical interventions, such as symptom prescription and reframing, to overcome resistance in clients who are especially oppositional, as angry clients are especially likely to be. The use of the Therapeutic Reactance Scale (TRS) can help identify these clients in advance (Dowd, Milne, & Wise, 1991).

There is also research evidence that hypnosis can increase the efficacy of cognitive-behavioral interventions in certain cases.

Kirsch, Montgomery, and Sapirstein (1995) examined 18 studies, from 1974 to 1993, that compared cognitive behavior treatment to CBT with hypnosis. The results indicated that clients receiving cognitive behavior hypnotherapy showed greater improvement than at least 70% of those receiving nonhypnotic CBT, by the most conservative estimate. Unfortunately, the studies they used did not assess hypnotizability, which is widely thought to influence responsiveness to hypnotherapy (Dowd, 2000). Schoenberger (2000) examined the effectiveness of hypnosis as an adjunct to cognitive behavior therapies in a narrative review. She concluded that the research demonstrated that there is a substantial benefit from the addition of hypnosis, but cautioned that the number of studies is small and many have methodological limitations. Surprisingly, the relationship between the level of hypnotizability and treatment outcome was mixed.

Thus, both clinical and experimental evidence suggest that hypnosis may add treatment efficacy to cognitive behavior therapy. The experimental evidence is particularly impressive because this is one of the relatively few occasions that comparison of one efficacious treatment to another (rather than to a control group) has produced significant differences. Therefore, the use of hypnosis with CBT appears warranted, at least with some clients.

## A CASE STUDY

I present an extended case study of anger management and treatment, using many of the ideas and techniques previously discussed. Joe (a pseudonym) came in for treatment rather unwillingly because his wife had told him she would leave him if he did not stop his explosive rages at her and their two children. Although Joe did recognize that he flew into rages easily (he called it a "quick Irish temper"), he did not consider it much of a problem because they were somewhat infrequent and he got over them quickly. However, since he did not want to break up his family, he reluctantly agreed to seek treatment. He picked a therapist (Ted) from the yellow pages because he listed a specialty in anger management.

Joe was a college graduate with a degree in business administration who worked for a local business firm in a middle management position. He was neatly dressed in a suit and tie and was verbally fluent and articulate. There was a certain guarded quality and defensiveness in his manner, however, that suggested a reluctance to examine himself closely. He reported few anger problems at work but said he did occasionally respond with "impatience," especially to those beneath him in the hierarchy. He was aware, however, that demonstrations of anger with his superiors or customers (which whom he occasionally came in contact) might cost him his job, so he was more discreet and circumspect with them. When Ted asked him what he did at work to restrain his anger, he only replied that he "stifled it." After further conversation, it appeared that Joe managed to suppress a verbal outburst but would privately fume about the incident for some time.

## Assessment

Ted administered the Therapeutic Reactance Scale (Dowd et al., 1991), the State-Trait Anger Expression Inventory–2 (Spielberger, 1999), and the State-Trait Anxiety Inventory (Spielberger, Gorusch, & Lushene, 1970). The score on the TRS showed that Joe was above the 75th percentile on reactance, suggesting that he resisted directions from others, was relatively autonomous, strove for dominance, was not particularly tolerant, and lacked self-control. The score was not high enough to suggest severe problems, however. Scores on the STAXI–2 showed a moderately high score on *trait anger/temperament* and an even higher score on *trait anger reaction*, suggesting that Joe tended to be quick-tempered and impulsive in general but was even more likely to become angry in response to provocations. *State anger* scores were not high, suggesting that Joe was not angry in the testing situation. Joe scored high on both *anger expression/out* and *anger expression/in*, suggesting that he both expressed anger overtly at times and suppressed it at other times. Joe was lower than average on *anger control/out* and *anger control/in*, suggesting that he did not work to prevent or control his anger. Surprisingly, the *STAI trait anxiety* score was also high, suggesting that Joe was an anxious person.

## Treatment

Joe underwent treatment for anger management in nine sessions, including cognitive hypnotherapy.

### First Session

Because Joe was not really self-referred, denied the seriousness of his problem, and appeared to be both potentially oppositional and anxious, Ted moved slowly in the first session. Most of the time was devoted to building the therapeutic alliance and reinforcing Joe's initial steps for treatment. Ted did not challenge any of Joe's statements or interpretation of his anger, only clarifying, asking for more information, and attempting to reduce Joe's anxiety by presenting himself (Ted) as a nonthreatening figure who would not automatically side with his wife. At the end of the session, Ted asked Joe to keep a log of the times he became angry during the next week, the situation that seemed to trigger it, and what he was thinking at the time.

### Second Session

Joe came in, reporting two angry incidents, both at home. He had flown into a rage when one of his children had come home with a lower than expected grade report from school. He had berated his son, telling him he would never make anything of himself if he kept that up! His wife had then entered the fray, siding with the child, with the result that Joe felt they had allied against him. This only made him angrier. The other incident concerned his younger son, who had come home in tears after being bullied at school. Joe berated him for not standing up for himself, and his wife again intervened with the same result. Joe was unable, however, to identify what he thought at the time and became visibly anxious even by the question.

Accordingly, Ted asked Joe if he would like to try a little experiment, to which Joe suspiciously agreed. Ted asked Joe to sit back in his (comfortable) chair and relax to the best of his ability. He told Joe that whatever would happen in the relaxation would be good because it happened (a statement difficult to resist). Relaxation is a nonthreatening experience and pleasant for most people (unless they try too hard) so Ted used a standard relaxation induction, progressive muscle relaxation. At the end of the session, Ted asked Joe to once again record angry incidents before the next session.

## Third Session

Joe reported feeling more relaxed during the week, much to his surprise. There was one angry incident, much like the two the week before, but he still could not identify what he was thinking at the time.

Ted then asked Joe if he would like to undergo hypnosis to help him reduce his anger. Joe was initially resistant, but a discussion of the myths about hypnosis (Dowd, 2000) indicated that he was primarily concerned with the illusion that he would be under Ted's control. Ted assured him that the experience was much like the relaxation he had experienced the week before and that he would always remain in control [all hypnosis is self-hypnosis] and could terminate the trance anytime he wished.

Ted used a variant of the progressive muscle relaxation he had used with Joe the week before, with the addition of a deepening technique as follows [truncated for space]:

> And now I'd like you to imagine yourself at the seashore, watching the waves come in—and go out . . . in and out, in and out. And every time you see the waves come in, take a breath; when they go out—breathe out. And every time you breathe out, you can, if you wish, go deeper into a trance—just as deep as you want to go—but no further. Don't go any further into a trance than you can—and want to [a truism].

Previous discussion had shown that Joe found using the wave motion at the seashore extremely relaxing. In fact, Joe found the trance experience quite pleasant and was eager to try it again. His reactions during this initial trance induction (e.g., deep breathing) led Ted to believe that Joe was a good hypnotic subject, important in using hypnotherapy effectively (Dowd, 2000). Ted asked him once again to monitor his angry episodes during the next week.

## Fourth Session

Somewhat to his surprise, Joe reported no angry episodes during the previous week. It is not uncommon for self-monitoring to reduce symptoms, at least temporarily, but he still could not identify what he thought just prior to an angry episode.

Accordingly, Ted asked Joe to enter a hypnotic trance (which was by now beginning to feel comfortable) and assisted him in doing so. Ted then asked him to allow his mind to let go of all previous thoughts by the following suggestion:

> And now, Joe, as I continue to talk, I'd like you to gradually let all thoughts and sensations fade from your mind—not pushing, not forcing, but gradually allowing it to happen . . . it's a good feeling, isn't it, and perhaps a new one . . . to just allow things to happen. [Based in part on his TRS score, Ted suspected Joe had an early maladaptive schema of *entitlement/grandiosity* and *insufficient self-control/self-discipline* (Young, Klosko, & Weishaar, 2003).] You don't have to do anything, you don't have to be anything; just relax and allow what will happen to happen—and feel comfortable in that, very comfortable. And the more you do this, the more relaxed you can become—and the more relaxed you become, the more you can do this [an adaptive spiral].

This theme was repeated with variations for several minutes. When Joe emerged from the trance, he said he could not remember ever feeling so relaxed and comfortable. Ted discussed the implications of this new experience with Joe for the remainder of the session.

## Fifth Session

Joe came into this session in great excitement. An incident had occurred in which Joe's wife had done something of which Joe did not approve—and his first inclination had been to get angry. But the statement from the last session, "You don't have to do anything . . . ," had popped into his mind and, although he did feel anger, he suddenly decided that he didn't really have to feel angry, and that the anger was not as intense. Joe experienced this as a tremendous relief but could not explain why.

Accordingly, Ted asked Joe to enter a trance and let his "mind lay flat" (Dowd, 2000), i.e., relax and empty his mind, and think of the questions, "What did I want that I was not getting? What was I getting that I did not want?" Ted then asked him to meditate on them until an answer came. After several minutes, Joe suddenly said, "RESPECT!! I want respect—and I'm not getting it!" Ted gradually and gently helped him come out of the trance, and they spent the rest on the session discussing what happened.

Two cognitive themes emerged from this discussion. First, Joe thought/felt that he was not respected by his wife and children, nor by his coworkers, although this feeling was especially strong with his family. Several of Joe's automatic thoughts were identified, including, "I deserve more respect than I'm getting! Not getting what I want makes me angry! I don't know what to do about it." Ted identified two cognitive distortions in Joe's thinking processes (Beck, 1995): *using imperative statements* (having a fixed and unreasonable idea of how others should behave) and *catastrophizing* (predicting the future entirely negatively). The former tended to lead to anger while the latter tended to lead to anxiety. Furthermore, Joe gradually became aware that the relief he felt when he knew he did not have to become angry was due to feeling more in control of himself and therefore more powerful.

## Sixth Session

Ted further probed into Joe's early life. He came from a family with a remote, sometimes absent father, who had a hearing impairment and (Joe thought) used that to his advantage when he wanted to opt out of a discussion. His mother was excitable and irritable, with six children closely spaced. Joe reported that he never knew what would irritate her or when, and consequently he kept a low profile in the family. He rarely received much positive direction or comment from his parents, only criticism from his mother for what he did wrong. He appeared to have modeled his own family interpersonal behavior on that of his mother, both because it was all he knew and because it was often effective for her in getting what she wanted. In addition to the early maladaptive schemas identified earlier, Ted also identified *emotional deprivation* (the expectation that one will not receive emotional support from others).

## Seventh Session

At this session, Joe reported that his angry outbursts had subsided considerably, both in frequency and intensity, but that now he was aware of feeling anxious in situations that resulted in anger. He was not initially able to label the new feeling as anxiety, as it took time for Ted to help him realize what the feeling really was. Ted connected this feeling to the previously identified self-statement, "I don't know what to do . . . " and began to suspect a partial early maladaptive schema of *failure* (feeling one has failed, is defective, less successful). However, this schema seemed largely confined to Joe's interpersonal relations at home. He was especially afraid that his two sons would not achieve well in life so that the times they brought home mediocre grades or showed problems with social skills reinforced Joe's fears. He felt ultimately responsible for their success; that he had failed if they did not succeed. Joe seemed to feel and be competent at work, although even in that setting thoughts of failure would occasionally emerge, especially when he was criticized by a superior.

## *Eighth Session*

In this session, Ted developed the following hypnotic routine to help Joe overcome his cognitive distortions and early maladaptive schemas. By now Joe was comfortable with trance and looked forward to the relaxation and sense of comfort it provided.

> Joe, you have learned many things in the last few weeks, haven't you? ["Yes set"]. You know that you want respect, don't you? You know that you should have it, don't you? But how do you get it? Why should you get it? You don't quite know, do you? But you are beginning to know how to get it and why are you? [Cascading "Yes set"]. Perhaps more than you think. You've learned perhaps you can control more than you think, more than you know. [Addresses insufficient self-control]. How do you do this? And, you're afraid, aren't you, that you might fail! [Addresses failure.] Not controlling makes you afraid, doesn't it? But perhaps you've already learned one very important thing—the tremendous control power of holding back . . . not doing, not trying. You don't really have to control everything . . . and you can't . . . but perhaps you don't need to, do you? Perhaps you've discovered the greater control in giving UP control . . . that only those people truly in control can afford to relax their control, even a little [a paradoxical suggestion.] Not doing . . . it's quite powerful, isn't it? And you can find increasing comfort in slowing down, letting go, backing off . . . letting other people find their own way, feeling comfortable in their ability to do so . . . allowing them to become them . . . feeling comfort in knowing that they can do it [Addresses failure] . . .

After the hypnotherapeutic routine was completed, Ted asked Joe to imagine the waves at the seashore coming in and going out the next time he felt anger arising, and to relax.

*Ninth Session*

Joe found the ocean wave image quite helpful in reducing his anger and was able to restrain himself from intervening angrily during an altercation between his sons during the week. He was surprised at how comfortable he felt not trying to control events. He was even more surprised when his wife to some extent took his place as the control agent, attempting to separate the boys. Accordingly, Ted used the following hypnotic routine to help Joe consolidate his gains:

> You have learned many things recently, haven't you, Joe? You've learned how to relax and not control—feeling more comfortable by doing so. You have begun to find increasing comfort in not doing, not acting—the tremendous power in holding back (a para-doxical suggestion)—letting things happen, feeling comfortable they will. But perhaps the most important learning is that events can take an unexpected turn, can't they? And you can be pleasantly surprised by that—knowing that things may work out well—not because you controlled them but because you let them happen, allowed them to occur, feeling good about holding back, relaxing, allowing things to develop, to happen in their own way, at their own speed, feeling good about this and about many things you will learn in the future, about yourself, about others . . . " (Opening to the future).

*Future Sessions*

Over the next few weeks, Ted worked with Joe, in trance and outside it, in helping him to identify and change these life themes. He also referred Joe to a social skills training group where he could learn how to behave assertively without anger and to proactively direct and guide his sons, rather than punish them. He learned to use more positive interactional behavior rather than predominantly negative behavior. His relationships steadily improved. He still described himself as having an "Irish temper" (of which he was a little proud) but accepted it with grace and humor as well as emotional distance.

In this chapter, I have described a cognitive hypnotherapy approach to anger management. I want to caution the reader, however, that anger is a difficult problem to overcome and that anger therapy often takes two steps forward and one step backward; or sometimes even one step forward and two steps backward. A relaxed, "go slow" attitude on the part of the therapist, as well as a sense of humor and the ironic, can also go a long way towards overcoming this difficult psychological problem.

## REFERENCES

Beck, A. T. (1999). *Prisoners of hate.* New York: HarperCollins.
Beck, J. S. (1995). *Cognitive therapy: Basics and beyond.* New York: Guilford.
Chemtob, C. M., Novaco, R. W., Hamada, R., & Gross, D. (1997). Cognitive-behavioral treatment for severe anger in posttraumatic stress disorder. *Journal of Consulting and Clinical Psychology, 65,* 184–189.
Corvo, K., & Johnson, P. J. (2003). Vilification of the "batterer": How blame shapes domestic violence policy and interventions. *Aggression and Violent Behavior, 8,* 259–282.
Dahlen, E. R., & Deffenbacher, J. L. (2000). A partial component analysis of Beck's cognitive therapy for the treatment of general anger. *Journal of Cognitive Psychotherapy: An International Quarterly, 14,* 77–95.
Dahlen, E. R., & Deffenbacher, J. L. (2001). Anger management. In W. J. Lyddon & J. V. Jones (Eds.), *Empirically supported cognitive therapies: Current and future applications* (pp. 163–181). New York: Springer Publishing.
Dalai Lama. (2000). *Transforming the mind.* London: Thorsons.
Das, Lama Surya. (1997). *Awakening the Buddha within.* New York: Bantam Doubleday Dell.
Das, Lama Surya. (1999). *Awakening the sacred: Creating a spiritual life from scratch.* New York: Random House.
Deffenbacher, J. L. (1999). Cognitive behavioral conceptualization and treatment of anger. *JCLP/In Session: Psychotherapy in Practice, 55,* 295–309.
DiGiuseppe, R. (1999). End piece: Reflections on the treatment of anger. *JCLP/In Session: Psychotherapy in Practice, 55,* 365–379.
DiGiuseppe, R., Eckhardt, C., Tafrate, R., & Robin, M. (1994). The diagnosis and treatment of anger in a cross-cultural context. *Journal of Social Distress and the Homeless, 3,* 229–261.
Dollard, J., Doob, L. W., Miller, N. E., Mowrer, O. H., & Sears, R. R. (1939). *Frustration and aggression.* New Haven, CT: Yale University Press.
Dowd, E. T. (2000). *Cognitive hypnotherapy.* Lanham, MD: Rowman & Littlefield.
Dowd, E. T., Milne, C. R., & Wise, S. L. (1991). The Therapeutic Reactance Scale: A measure of psychological reactance. *Journal of Counseling and Development, 69,* 541–545.
Dowd, E. T., & Pace, T. M. (1989). The relativity of reality: Second-order change in psychotherapy. In A. Freeman, K. M. Simon, L. E. Beutler, & H. Arkowitz (Eds.), *Comprehensive handbook of cognitive therapy* (pp. 213–226). New York: Plenum.
Dowd, E. T., & Trutt, S. (1988). Paradoxical interventions in behavior modification. In M. Hersen, R. M. Eisler, & P. E. Miller (Eds.), *Progress in behavior modification* (Vol. 23, pp. 96–130). Thousand Oaks, CA: Sage.

Edmonson, C. B., & Conger, J. C. (1996). A review of treatment efficacy for individuals with anger problems: Conceptual, assessment, and methodological issues. *Clinical Psychology Review, 16,* 251–275.

Ellis, A., & Dryden, W. (1997). *The practice of rational-emotive-behavior therapy.* New York: Springer Publishing.

Erickson, M. H., & Rossi, E. L. (1979). *Hypnotherapy: An exploratory casebook.* New York: Irvington.

Erickson, M. H., Rossi, E. L., & Rossi, S. I. (1976). *Hypnotic realities.* New York: Irvington.

Fernandez, E. (2002). *Anxiety, depression, and anger in pain: Research findings and clinical options.* Dallas, TX: Advanced Psychological Resources.

Gove, P. B. (Editor-in-Chief). (1981). *Webster's Third New International Dictionary of the English Language* (Unabridged). Springfield, MA: Merriam-Webster.

Hanh, Thich Nhat. (2001). *Anger: Wisdom for cooling the flames.* New York: Riverhead.

Hayes, S. C., & Pankey, J. (2003). Acceptance. In W. O'Donohue, J. E. Fisher, & S. C. Hayes (Eds.), *Cognitive behavior therapy: Applying empirically supported techniques to your practice* (pp. 4–9). New York: Wiley.

Kassinove, H., & Sukhodolsky, D. G. (1995). Anger disorders: Basic science and practice issues. In H. Kassinove (Ed.), *Anger disorders: Assessment, diagnosis and treatment* (pp. 1–26). Washington, DC: Taylor & Francis.

Kirsch, I., Montgomery, G., & Saperstein, G. (1995). Hypnosis as an adjunct to cognitive-behavioral psychotherapy: A meta-analysis. *Journal of Consulting and Clinical Psychology, 63,* 214–220.

Leifer, R. (1999). Buddhist conceptualization and treatment of anger. *JCLP/In Session:Psychotherapy in Practice, 55,* 339–351.

Luoma, J. B., & Hayes, S. C. (2003). Cognitive defusion. In W. O'Donohue, J. E. Fisher, & S. C. Hayes (Eds.), *Cognitive behavior therapy: Applying empirically supported techniques to your practice* (pp. 4–9). New York: Wiley.

Mayne, T. J., & Ambrose, T. K. (1999). Research review on anger in psychotherapy. *JCLP/In Session: Psychotherapy in Practice, 55,* 353–363.

Nezu, C. M., & Nezu, A. M. (2003). *Awakening self-esteem: Spiritual and psychological techniques to enhance your well-being.* Oakland, CA: New Harbinger.

Novaco, R. W. (2002). Anger control therapy. In M. Hersen & W. Sledge (Eds.), *Encyclopedia of psychotherapy* (pp. 41–48). Amsterdam: Academic.

Ornstein, P. H. (1999). Conceptualization and treatment of rage in self-psychology. *JCLP/In Session: Psychotherapy in Practice, 55,* 283–293.

Padeskey, C. A., & Greenberger, D. (1995). *Clinician's guide to mind over mood.* New York: Guilford.

Schoenberger, N. E. (2000). Research on hypnosis as an adjunct to cognitive-behavioral psychotherapy. *International Journal of Clinical and Experimental Hypnosis, 48,* 154–169.

Spielberger, C. D. (1999). *Manual for the State-Trait Anger Expression Inventory–2.* Odessa, FL: Psychological Assessment Resources.

Spielberger, C. D., Gorsuch, R. L., & Lushene, R. D. (1970). *Manual for the State-trait Anxiety Inventory (STAI).* Palo Alto, CA: Consulting Psychologists.

Spielberger, C. D., Reheiser, E. C., & Sydeman, S. J. (1995). In H. Kassinove (Ed.), *Anger disorders: Assessment, diagnosis and treatment* (pp. 49–68). Washington, DC: Taylor & Francis.

Tsytsarev, S. V., & Grodnitzky, G. R. (1995). Anger and criminality. In H. Kassinove (Ed.), *Anger disorders: Assessment, diagnosis and treatment* (pp. 91–108). Washington, DC: Taylor & Francis.

Van der Kolk, B. A., McFarlane, A. C., & Weisaeth, L. (1996). *Traumatic stress: The effects of overwhelming experience on mind, body, and society.* New York: Guilford.

Young, J. E., Klosko, J. S., & Weishaar, M. E. (2003). *Schema therapy: A practitioner's guide.* New York: Guilford.

Chapter 8

# Treating Treatment Failures: Hypnotic Treatment of Posttraumatic Stress Disorder*

Marc I. Oster

*Scenario 1:* The hospital's heliport is located near the adult psychiatric unit. During group therapy, the members hear the increasing noise from the helicopter's engine and the sound of the propeller blades cutting the air. Suddenly one group member dives for cover under a table in the room.

*Scenario 2:* A young man is brought in for psychiatric evaluation some weeks following an explosion and fire at his workplace. Besides an array of anxiety and depressive symptoms, he is guilt ridden because he had warned the employer of the safety hazards at his plant. But an explosion occurred and the young man's hands were severely burned as he tried to rescue his friend, only to watch him burn to death in what should have been a preventable accident.

*Scenario 3:* Jane looks terrified; she can't speak much, her eyes are bulging from their sockets. She is shaking and perspiring as she curls up in the office chair. She recounts having been abducted, held hostage, been drugged, and raped repeatedly over the course of a weekend. She

---

says she escaped only when she befriended one of her guards, who forgot to give her another tranquilizer, and she had killed him to escape.

*Scenario 4:* Joseph's alcohol problem worsens every December. He withdraws. He has more nightmares than usual and relives having his Army buddy die in his arms in a ditch in Vietnam just before Christmas 1965.

These case descriptions reveal symptoms that arose from these individuals' exposure to overwhelming or traumatic life events. Over time these people would chronically experience such symptoms as impaired affect modulation; self-destructive and impulsive behavior; dissociative symptoms; somatic complaints; feelings of ineffectiveness, shame, despair, or hopelessness; a shattering of their previously held assumptions about their safety and security; social withdrawal; feeling constantly threatened; and having impaired relationships with others.

## MISDIAGNOSIS OF PTSD

Proper diagnosis plays an important role in the proper treatment of posttraumatic stress disorder or PTSD. A unique feature of PTSD, compared to other mental disorders, is that it, almost by definition, is comprised of an unusual array of symptoms. Some of these symptoms might resemble another independent disorder. Oftentimes, as described in the case in this chapter, the clinician making the initial assessment notes the obvious symptoms of another disorder, then stops their investigation, and erroneously concludes that the patient is suffering from that particular disorder; hence, making a misdiagnosis. For example, the initially obvious symptoms might include those of phobic anxiety or depression. The investigation terminates and a misdiagnosis of anxiety disorder or mood disorder is made without further consideration of alternative explanations for those symptoms. In some instances, the clinician may suffer from a confirmatory bias. In this case, the clinician sees only the symptoms that fit a disorder of their interest or of the focus of their clinic—again overlooking other possible diagnoses.

Of course, the problem with misdiagnosis is that the treatment does not fit the problem or the disorder. Some of the patient's symptoms may improve to some degree, but the underlying disorder

remains untreated, and the patient remains symptomatic and untreated. Alternatively, as in the case presented later on, the patient
may be further misdiagnosed with another complex disorder, such
as a dissociative disorder, or may be labeled a treatment failure.
Once the patient was determined a treatment failure, the main focus
of attention was on getting her out of the current treatment setting.

This chapter addresses the application of cognitive behavior
therapy using hypnosis as the medium of delivery, with an individual
suffering from an undiagnosed or misdiagnosed posttraumatic stress
disorder. Alternative diagnoses for this patient had included multiple
personality disorder, borderline personality disorder, and recurrent
depression. First, however, a summary of the diagnostic criteria for
posttraumatic disorder is presented as background.

## PTSD DIAGNOSTIC CRITERIA

The diagnostic criteria and clinical features of posttraumatic stress
disorder are discussed at length elsewhere (DSM-IV, APA, 1994). For
our purposes, those criteria will be summarized here. For the reader
not familiar with PTSD or the DSM criteria, it is recommended they
refer to the DSM-IV.

The diagnostic criteria and features of posttraumatic stress disorder (PTSD) has at its foundation a traumatic event(s) to which
a person was somehow exposed. The seriousness of the event is
determined by the probability of actual or threatened death or serious injury, a threat to the physical integrity of the person in question,
or to other people, and the person's response or reaction has to
have included an intense fear or an intense feeling of helplessness.

Secondly, the person must repeatedly reexperience the event.
This is not simply a "mental" recollection of the event, but much
more like a reliving of the event(s).

The third aspect of PTSD is a persistent avoidance of anything
associated with the traumatic event(s) along with an emotional
numbing (not present before the trauma).

The characteristics reported above are experienced as more
than simply not feeling oneself, having a bad day or even a bad
week, or having had the experience described once or twice in the
past. These symptoms are pervasive, extreme, all encompassing of

the person's life every day or most every day. They are not an indication of a self-limiting phase or experience.

Persistent symptoms of increased arousal (not present before the trauma) are the fourth feature of PTSD and include sleep difficulties, irritability or outbursts of anger, difficulty concentrating, hypervigilance, and an exaggerated startle response.

Finally, the disturbance must cause clinically significant distress or impairment in social, occupational, or some other important area of functioning.

## A BRIEF REVIEW OF TREATMENT
## APPROACHES FOR PTSD

Rothbaum, Meadows, Resnick and Foy (2000) reviewed the literature on CBT treatments for PTSD to determine which approaches have been effective, based on empirical studies. The authors identified eight CBT treatments for PTSD: exposure therapy, systematic desensitization, stress inoculation training, cognitive processing therapy, cognitive therapy, assertiveness training, biofeedback, relaxation training, and three different combined treatment conditions. Rothbaum et al. found that across all studies reviewed, and for a wide variety of traumas, the most supported choice of treatment from their list of eight was exposure therapy. Clients receiving exposure therapy are asked to confront their fears until their anxiety reduces. The second best supported treatment was stress inoculation training, but only for female sexual assault survivors.

Meichenbaum (1994) utilizes a constructive narrative perspective or CNP in which he focuses on the stories or the accounts people tell themselves following traumatic experiences, as well as from other events in their lives. The stories entail both behavioral responses and affective responses that are brought together to bring coherence and meaning to the person's experience. The case below demonstrates how the patients' stories, which they have told themselves, can evolve into stories encompassing skills and meaning that are more resilient, future, and recovery oriented.

Dowd (2000), including the work of Beck (1995), described a number of ways in which the use of imagery in cognitive behavior therapy resembles hypnotic techniques, and can be used with clients with PTSD. These are delineated below.

**Identifying images:** A patient tries to elicit a spontaneous image. However, either the patient does not recognize any images of a distressing situation or is reluctant to describe the images they do have. Rather than using standard cognitive techniques, such as asking what thoughts might be going through their mind at a given time, an imagery identifying technique might be helpful. I have found that in hypnosis this approach can be both very dramatic and very productive in very short order. For example, in hypnosis, the patient is asked to respond using an ideomotor signal (i.e., a raised finger) when an image, idea, or thought of some importance comes to mind. With each signaling sequence, I ask the patient to describe what they are experiencing at that time. Then I suggest they go back and permit more information (thoughts, ideas, or images) to come to the surface, again signaling when they have the experience. Often, the patient will begin producing useful pieces of information that are then brought together concerning some significant experience. Briefly, ideomotor signals are thought to be nonverbal representations of cognitive activity, particularly unconscious activity. Cheek (1993) suggested that these nonverbal replies to the clinician's questioning represented a more accurate response than one elicited verbally and suggested a direct communication pathway to the unconscious mind.

**Following images to completion:** The therapist encourages the patient to imagine the remainder of the scenario, or the rest of the story, rather than stop at a distressing scene or point in time. Here, using this technique, I am trying to bridge the distressing event so the patient can continue moving forward.

**Coping in the image:** The patient is asked to imagine herself coping better in the image they have just experienced. This is much like role-playing in imagery, a rehearsal in imagery, of a successful outcome to a certain situation.

**Changing the image:** A therapist may ask what one would rather have happened in a situation rather than work at having the patient imagine alternative scenarios. For example, a patient who is anxious and worrisome about a medical procedure reported they had a frightening one done as a child, and saw fear and worry on the face of the adults around her. In hypnosis, the patient was asked what they would have liked the adult to have said or done, to which she replied, "To say, 'everything will be alright.' "

**Jumping ahead in time:** This is similar to hypnotic age progression (Hammond, 1998). It involves asking the patient to imagine herself in the future, perhaps at the completion of a long and difficult project. For example, when doing childbirth preparation with a mother-to-be, I will ask her to imagine her baby's face when it is put on her chest. Focusing on the baby's face takes her away from the often arduous experience of labor and alters her sense of time for the labor process.

**Repeating the image:** Repetition of a new behavior is an effective way to facilitate change. When new behaviors are repeated during hypnosis, they are done so with mastery so that the experience of the new behavior is a positive one. This process can be much like a hypnotic systematic desensitization, which is similar to the concept of dilution or titration of the intensity of an event or memory.

**Substitution:** The substituting of one image with a less distressing one.

**Distancing:** Spatial distancing involves the client's imagining the problems moving farther and farther away, receding into the distance. With temporal distancing, the patient imagines the problem being removed by time or date.

When these cognitive behavior techniques are administered with hypnosis, the patient's experience of the technique can be much more powerful. Because of the relationship-enhancing effect of hypnosis, the patient can manage more distressing material or images in hypnosis than without, as they experience their relationship with the clinician more intensely. This may speed up the therapeutic process.

## THE BENEFIT OF HYPNOSIS IN THE TREATMENT OF PTSD

In cognitive behavior therapy, hypnosis can be used to enhance relaxation, generate imagery, and heighten expectations of success, change self-defeating thoughts, and initiate new behaviors. Hypnosis facilitates reinforcement of future orientation in time—experiencing the reinforcement following the success experienced in hypnosis, and in desensitization. Imagery is a common aspect of hypnotically informed psychotherapy. It enables the patient to experience a thought and to assess their reaction and perception. Some perceptual phenomena reported by hypnotized patients include hallucinations, visual illusions, enhancing visual and auditory acuity. Patients with the capacity to experience such phenomena can make use of this ability in psychotherapeutic treatment. This is similar to the Gestalt empty chair technique done in hypnosis. The empty chair technique is usually a role playing exercise that allows the client to increase their awareness of problems.

Hypnotic techniques can be useful in crisis management to help patients stop flashbacks and reorient themselves to external reality when these altered states occur. Hypnotic techniques are useful in ego strengthening and for supporting patients during crises. Access to self-statements or beliefs about oneself is often gained in hypnosis and aids the patient to properly incorporate understandings.

In summary, hypnosis combined with cognitive behavior strategies, can be helpful in treating PTSD, by teaching the patient relaxation, self-regulation or control techniques, rapid interruption of crisis situations, to reduce or eliminate symptoms, process memories, modify thoughts or self-statements concerning the trauma and one's response to the trauma, to enhance one's understanding of their experiences, and to integrate the experiences in order to return to a more effective level of functioning.

## CASE PRESENTATION

The application of hypnotically enhanced cognitive behavior therapy for treating posttraumatic stress disorder is presented, making use of a case description that highlights the various features of hypnotic CBT.

### Client Background

My work with Sharon, the case presented in this chapter, may appear a bit unusual. As indicated below, Sharon was referred by psychologist Dr. Wilson. Sharon's case was presented to me as a treatment failure. Upon inquiry, Dr. Wilson explained that Sharon was a long-term patient in the HMO's system. She had a debilitating condition that was chronic. The HMO's goal was to stabilize or improve Sharon's condition so that she might either benefit from the kind of therapy provided by the HMO or be transferred to another source for continued treatment.

For similar referrals from Dr. Wilson's HMO, I usually spend about 10 hours reviewing records, conducting an evaluation, discussing my findings with the patient, presenting my treatment recommendations and plan, and then initiating that plan, if appropriate. Of the 10 hours, approximately 6 are spent in direct contact with the patient. The treatment component of our work together is videotaped. A written report and the videotape were sent to Dr. Wilson. The report outlined my findings and recommendations, much like the presentation that follows. The videotape provided him with a visual demonstration of how he might continue Sharon's therapy, much like a reference tool.

## General Information

Sharon was a 32-year-old, white, married female with an associate's degree in computer science. She was a homemaker. She stood 5'4" and weighed 127 pounds.

Sharon's HMO employed Dr. Wilson, a psychologist, who referred Sharon to me. He met with Sharon for four sessions, an intake and three follow-up sessions. At the third follow-up session, he recommended that she see me, which she did approximately 1 month later.

In discussing the referral with Dr. Wilson, he informed me that Sharon had recently been discharged from the hospital. This was her second hospitalization for emotional problems, the first being for substance abuse treatment. Sharon had no treatment between her substance abuse treatment and her posthospital intake with Dr. Wilson.

**Client's Presenting Complaint:** "Manic-depressive illness and many chronic health problems make it hard to cope some days. I have a lot of blank spaces in my past that it may or may not benefit me to remember. Lots of sexual abuse, verbal abuse from my first husband; memories of traumatic past experiences haunt me unmercifully."

**History of Present Illness:** Sharon reports her problems are made worse by depression, ill health, arguments with her husband, bad dreams, flashbacks, triggering of bad memories, and bad weather. In the past, she resorted to alcohol and drug use/abuse in order to cope. She reports, and her records support, that she has been drug and alcohol free since 1990. She now finds relaxation therapy, travel, gardening, time spent with friends in recovery, and therapy to be helpful. However, in the month preceding our consultation, Sharon reported being very dissatisfied with her life and very tense.

**Social and Work History:** Sharon was 32 years old. She sells her own artwork in a number of local retail stores. These are usually craft works. She has worked clerical and other jobs, but her poor physical condition has made much of that too difficult. She is married for the second time. The first marriage, ending in divorce, was a violent and abusive relationship.

**Medical History:** Sharon's recent hospitalization yielded the following diagnoses: bipolar disorder, history of poly substance abuse in remission, irritable bowel syndrome, migraine headaches, history of endometriosis and hysterectomy, and a recent rib fracture. Current medications include: Depakote, Zoloft, Premarin, Donnatol, Zantac, Lodine, vitamins, and Fibercon. She reported craving chocolate. She provided me a five-page, single-spaced, typed list annotating her medication history. Sharon was seen four times by her primary therapist following her recent hospitalization.

**Family History:** There is a long history of mental illness in Sharon's family, including alcoholism and depression in her mother and sister; schizophrenia and depression in her father; and bipolar disorder, attention deficit disorder, mental retardation, and psychosis in her brother.

**Recent Stressors:** In early summer 1994 Sharon's father died. In spring 1994 her brother was committed to a state mental health facility for his deteriorating condition. Her mother was drinking more and experiencing changes that Sharon recognized as advanced alcoholism. Sharon had been unemployed since the last of 1994.

## DSM-IV Diagnosis

Axis I:        Posttraumatic Stress Disorder (309.81)
               Bipolar I Disorder, Mixed, Severe Without Psychotic
               Symptoms (296.63; based on previous therapist's con-
               clusions)
               Poly substance abuse, in remission (supported by
               medical history)

Axis II:       None

Axis III:      IBS, complications from scarring from multiple surger-
               ies, migraines, fractured right rib, hysterectomy, reha-
               bilitation of right knee (10% disability)

Axis IV:       *Problems with primary support group:* mentally ill sib-
               ling for whom patient is guardian; discord with an-
               other sibling
               *Occupational problems:* unemployment, underemploy-
               ment, discord with coworkers, job dissatisfaction
               *Problems with access to healthcare services:* inade-
               quate health care services and insurance.

Axis V:        GAF = 45 (at intake)

## Assessment Methods

To assess PTSD, Meichenbaum (1994) suggests beginning with an
open-ended interview, progressing through more semi-structured
and structured interviews, and assessing possible comorbid conditions. This approach helps to reduce the risk of missing alternative
diagnoses as discussed above or missing complicating comorbid
conditions.

The methodology I used with Sharon involved a two-pronged
approach. The first addressed the diagnostic considerations. The
second addressed the patient's hypnotic capacity and experience.
Sharon came to me with several complex diagnoses—none of which
was PTSD—and she had been labeled a treatment failure. My first
focus of attention was the differential diagnosis question. Besides
using the procedures described below, I approached my information
gathering as Meichenbaum described. I began with having Sharon
provide me a free narrative of her history and symptoms. By this I
mean I asked her to tell me her story while I listened with minimal
interruptions. Although I had read much of her history in advance,

telling her story in person added valuable flavor to both our experiences. After her free narrative, we went through the details again with my asking her questions for clarification. Then she completed questionnaires in which she described her symptoms. This was followed with general psychological testing (e.g., an MMPI or other standardized assessments). These instruments ask about specific symptoms but not in an organized manner, for example, not all the PTSD symptoms are clustered together. Semi and structured interviews (e.g., the DES [Carlson & Putnam, 1993] and the Dissociative Disorders Interview Schedule, DDIS [Ross & Haber, 1989]) asked about more specific symptoms. I ended this process by reviewing with Sharon and asking her directly about the DSM PTSD criteria. I used this approach not only to address the differential diagnostic issues, but also to ensure that my early questioning would not cue or lead Sharon to present symptoms she might think I was looking for, rather than tell her actual experiences.

## Procedures

*Review of Previous Records:* Because of the travel distance between myself and Sharon and her referring clinician, I asked that they forward to me, or that Sharon bring with her, any previous psychological testing, progress notes, or other records. This material was needed, in part, to save time and to avoid replicating the history-taking and testing that we had recently completed. Second, such records, especially the hospital or progress notes, often reveal information that is overlooked or forgotten when the patient is questioned. In Sharon's case, these records included her MMPI-2 profile from Dr. Wilson, notes from her recent hospitalization, and Dr. Wilson's notes on her progress.

*Multimodal Life History Inventory* (Lazarus & Lazarus, 1991): I have found this instrument useful for several reasons. First, as intended by its authors, it provides a comprehensive, multidimensional collection of data about a patient in seven areas of their life: behavior, affects, sensations, images, cognitions, interpersonal, and biological. These areas well represent the bio-psycho-social formulation. Inquiry into these areas is useful and important. Second, I use this structured format because it ensures that little, if any, potentially useful information will be overlooked, either by the patient or myself.

Third, since I have the patient complete the inventory at home, it affords them the opportunity to think in depth about these various areas before we begin our work together. For example, patients have remarked that they found the assignment useful and are sometimes able to see patterns in some aspect of their life that they had overlooked.

*Dissociative Experiences Scale* (DES, Carlson & Putnam, 1993): The DES is a brief, self-report measure to help identify persons *with* dissociative pathology. This measure was chosen because (a) the series of patients referred by Dr. Wilson all carried a question about the presence or extent of dissociative pathology, including Multiple Personality Disorder (now known as Dissociative Identity Disorder or DID) and (b) Sharon also presented with dissociative-like symptoms that were a concern to both Dr. Wilson and the HMO clinic staff. These symptoms included reports of "zoning out" and "cloudy confusion." In Sharon's case, her history, as revealed in the Life History Inventory, DDIS, past medical records, and the records provided by Dr. Wilson, was more consistent with the experience of posttraumatic stress disorder than with MPD/DID.

On the DES, Sharon's score was a 40. While this score is above the cutoff score of 30 for dissociative psychopathology, Carlson and Putnam point out that 61% and as many as 83% of those who score high on the DES do not have MPD, and are likely to have posttraumatic stress disorder or some non-MPD dissociative disorder. In reviewing the interpretive tables provided by Carlson and Putnam, I found that Sharon's score of 40 was consistent with PTSD.

*Gudjonsson Suggestibility Scale* (GSS, Gudjonsson, 1984): The GSS was used with Sharon because of its utility in assessing suggestibility. This was of significance in this case for several reasons. First, contained in Dr. Wilson's referral was the hope that I would use hypnosis for the purpose of exploration pertaining to Sharon's past trauma, and for resources that might help her experience better success in therapy. As to Sharon's exploring the trauma, one might conclude that there was little to explore. She possessed a rather detailed knowledge of those events, and has since their inception. However, were this not the case and exploration was indicated, understanding Sharon's degree of suggestibility would be important because it provides information as to the potential for developing her pseudo-memories or further distortion of her existing memories. Third, the degree of Sharon's suggestibility might determine if her experience of hypnosis is better accessed from a more directive or nondirective approach. Sharon's score in the GSS indicated she was very highly suggestible, in the 98th percentile. Given this result, I felt she would be a high risk for suggested memories, and that she might be responsive to more direct suggestion.

*Hypnotic Induction Profile* (HIP, Spiegel & Spiegel, 2004): The HIP was used as a general measure of hypnotizability. It was chosen for its brevity, especially since it was used in conjunction with a larger battery of measures, and for its ease of administration. Following its administration, I explained the results to Sharon. I found that the positive results on this measure of her hypnotizability created positive expectancy for the upcoming, more detailed hypnotic work. The HIP also indicated other areas that Sharon might have some difficulty with clinically. For example, she had difficulty with the amnesia aspect of the HIP, and the hand/hand levitation suggestion. The difficulty with the suggested levitation might indicate her limited responsivity to ideomotor communication. Thus, for example, if there was a need for ideomotor communication, it might require more training time. While there is controversy, particularly around the relationship between the eye-roll sign and conclusions about hypnotizability, Frischholz et al. (1992) indicated that the HIP eye-roll sign combined with the induction score yields a correlation with the Stanford Form C of .70. In that report, they also indicated that the relationship between the subject's self-rating and the Stanford Form C was 65.

*Attitudes Towards Hypnosis* (ATH, Spanos, Brett, Menary, & Cross, 1987): I use the ATH in an attempt to assess the patient's positive and negative attitudes towards hypnosis. Specifically, I look for areas that will require more attention during the patient education portion of my work as I attempt to reduce the negative expectancy resulting from the patient's misconceptions about hypnosis. These beliefs, conceptions, or attitudes fall into the general areas of positive beliefs, mental stability, and fearlessness.

*Archaic Involvement Measure* (AIM, Nash & Spinler, 1989): This measure was used to assess the degree of relational involvement experienced by Sharon. The utility of such a measure, specific to hypnosis-mediated therapy, is that the therapeutic alliance correlates significantly with outcome. Such a measure might offer some predictive power pertaining to outcome, or offer some direction for future alliance enhancement prior to further intervention, thus making for a greater likelihood of success in subsequent session interventions.

*Field Inventory* (FI, Field, 1966): The FI was used as a subjective measure of Sharon's experience. The findings can be compared to objective measures, such as the HIP, and to the AIM. If there were a clear distinction between the objective experience and Sharon's subjective experience, as indicated on the FI, one might examine her subjective experiences in more detail to better understand her hypnotic experience, or lack of hypnotic experience.

As a prelude to intervention, I conducted an assessment of Sharon's hypnotic capacity, first by assessing her general attitude towards hypnosis (ATH). Her attitude and expectations were hopeful and reasonable. The GSS indicated her total suggestibility score at the 98th percentile, or very highly suggestible. The HIP yielded a score of 9, in the moderate to high range. She appeared to lack ability in the amnesia and ideomotor skills areas. Using less structured suggestion, she reported rich visual, auditory, and kinesthetic hallucinations. Thus, I felt she would be a good candidate for hypnosis. Following the hypnotic intervention, the AIM and the FI measured the extent of her relational involvement and the depth of her involvement, respectively, in the experience. Both scores were average. Thus, Sharon's subjective report of her experience was consistent with the prehypnosis assessment of her potential. Sharon was average in her potential, but highly suggestible.

## COGNITIVE BEHAVIORAL CASE CONCEPTUALIZATION AND TREATMENT PLANNING

Case conceptualization and treatment planning are discussed in the context of the summary of Sharon's assessment and in terms of her treatment goals and rationale for those goals.

## Assessment Findings

Sharon was a very cooperative and engaging patient. She put forth an honest effort and was very patient and tolerant of the many requests I made of her. I trust that the conclusions based on this consultation are valid and reliable.

Sharon's mental status was essentially within normal limits. There was no suicidal plan or intent reported. There were no signs of psychotic experiences or dissociative episodes.

Generally speaking, I found a remarkable and encouraging degree of continuity across all the various measures and instruments. When discussing this with Sharon and her husband, I referred to this feature as a common denominator. In this regard, I was looking for the feature or diagnostic area that tied together the symptoms she was endorsing.

Actually, the first common denominator was the array of symptoms Sharon had endorsed. At first glance, one might conclude that there was a validity problem because of the multidimensional nature of her symptoms. In fact, there are several conditions that produce such clusters, such as manic-depressive illness, borderline personality, posttraumatic stress disorder, and multiple personality disorder. While there were some borderline features noted (i.e., impulsivity and rapid mood shifts), the full diagnostic picture was not present. Additionally, the DES and Sharon's history made MPD/DID an unlikely conclusion. Thus, I felt the common features that coordinated Sharon's "other symptoms" complaint was bipolar and posttraumatic stress disorder.

The second common feature was her depression. Depression was significant on the MMPI-2 and within the various records provided, such as the Multimodal Life History Inventory.

The third common feature was her concern about her health. Again, this presented as a vast array of symptoms, which would be hard to explain as a single condition. However, her history indicates that she had suffered from an array of medical problems.

The fourth feature was substance abuse. Although not currently an active problem (based on her report, her husband's report, and medical records from recent hospitalization), the condition emerges in her honest response to historical questions.

The fifth and final feature was posttraumatic stress. When I reviewed the 21 diagnostic criteria, Sharon endorsed 19 of the 21. The MMPI-2 and the DES supported this finding.

In discussing the goals of this intervention, I view Sharon's presentation in terms of (a) the place of this intervention on a continuum of Sharon's whole treatment process and (b) the place of this intervention on a continuum of the diagnostic issues affecting Sharon. The goals then would be short term in nature.

In determining what those goals might be, a number of factors were considered (Hammond, 1989). First is the complexity of Sharon's symptoms or problems. They are long-standing and historical in nature. The symptoms are multiple and complex (e.g., PTSD). Some symptoms are biologically mediated. Second, Sharon tends to be internally focused and is resistant to external influence. However, she has developed a powerful and healthy relationship with Dr. Wilson and, based on that relationship, with me as well. Third, Sharon's expectations are realistic and oriented toward her active participation in the process. Fourth, even though Sharon had been in treatment (e.g., at Hazelden and a recent hospital stay) and had recently initiated treatment with Dr. Wilson, I would consider her to be in the very initial stages of treatment. Her present motivation is high and that is consistent with historical reports—she doesn't give up. Fifth, diagnostically, Sharon's presentation is complex (PTSD, history of substance abuse, physical and sexual trauma, severe mental illness in her family). Sixth, Sharon's hypnotic capacity is in the upper moderate to high range and she is highly suggestible.

In summary then, Sharon's symptoms are complex; she has been resistant to external influence; her expectations for our work are realistic and she's willing to work at it; has had previous treatment, including hospitalizations; her presentation is complex with a family history of mental illness; and she is hypnotically responsive and suggestible.

## Treatment Goals

### Goal 1

Define, encourage, and support the collaborative nature of our work together; Sharon's work with Dr. Wilson, and how all three of us, along with her husband, are a team.

a.  Use the quality and strength of Sharon's relationship with Dr. Wilson and his relationship with me (Diamond, 1984; Levitt & Baker, 1983).
b.  Use ongoing feedback between Sharon and myself; between Sharon, her husband, and myself, and between myself and Dr. Wilson (Cochrane, 1991; Oster, 1994).

## Rationale

Those cited above have demonstrated the utility and power of the relationship as a factor in the therapeutic process. Meichenbaum and Turk (1987) have shown that when patients do not have an active part in their treatment and a collaborative role, they are less likely to follow their doctor's prescriptions. I have described (Oster, 1995) the benefit and importance of individualizing or tailoring the intervention. Diamond (1984) has shown that the alignment, or convergence, of therapist and patient goals serves to make the therapy work. Meichenbaum and Turk (1987), in their review of the literature on treatment adherence, found that approximately 45% of the variance resides in the patient-clinician relationship. Like others, Norcross (2002) reported as much as 65% of the outcome variance can be attributed to relationship-related factors.

## Goal 2

Stabilization of symptoms; establishment of an atmosphere of safety, security, trust, and confidence in our work together.

a.  Use or address the therapy and therapist expectations that Sharon identified as being important in her Multimodal Life History Inventory.
b.  Within the hypnotic session itself, use her own needs, perceptions, words and images to create an environment of comfort, safety and security (Meichenbaum & Turk, 1987; i.e., the chair holding her, "feeling tightly wrapped").
c.  Later in the hypnotic session have her practice the therapeutic task and, when appropriate, let me do some of those tasks for her (i.e., our airplane ride).

## Rationale

Contemporary treatment stresses the establishment of a foundation of safety, security, and stability before any further trauma work can proceed (Brown, 1995; Brown & Fromm, 1986; Phillips & Frederick, 1995; Meichenbaum, 1994). The importance of the patient being heard by the clinician and the clinician's utilizing and respecting the patient's words and stories is demonstrated by Meichenbaum (1994); Oster (1995); and Meichenbaum and Turk (1987).

## Goal 3

Use techniques for symptom reduction and coping with symptoms (Brown & Fromm, 1986; Lazarus, 1989).

a.   Intervene in her understanding of her symptoms, for example "cloudy confusion."
b.   Use methods of perceptual change or alteration (e.g., Hammond, 1988; reframing, creating new understandings or endings, dissociation).
c.   Use methods for alteration and/or reduction of affect (e.g., Hammond, 1988; reframing or affect tolerance).
d.   Enhancement of insight and/or unconscious exploration (i.e., hypnotic dreaming).

## Rationale

In spite of this patient's previous therapy, I see her as being at the very early stages (Brown & Fromm, 1986; Phillips & Frederick, 1995) of treatment. Here the focus is on foundational work and stability. Without these resources, nothing else will progress successfully.

## Goal 4

Demonstrate alternative ways of understanding her past (Deyoub & Epstein, 1977).

a.   Enhancement of insight (i.e., guided imagery).
b.   Demonstrating perceptual changes (i.e., the case of Robert and Shirley and the "Box of Memories").

c.   Behavioral control or self-regulation (e.g., Hammond, 1988; Meichenbaum, 1985; modeling and rehearsal, posthypnotic suggestion, time projection, end result imagery).

## Rationale

Meichenbaum's (1994) constructive narrative perspective addresses the patient's need to find a new meaning for their life, thus putting the traumatic past in a new perspective. This session differs slightly in that I offer possibilities as to how that new meaning can be created. Without the acquisition of new skills and perspectives that can be internalized, Sharon is at greater risk for relapse.

## Goal 5

Relapse prevention.

a.   Identify and prepare for high-risk situations.
b.   Make lifestyle and perceptual modifications as appropriate.

## Rationale

If the work only focuses on change or change in the present, when the patient faces future external challenges, she will be caught unaware and ill prepared (Meichenbaum, 1994; Oster, 1995). We attempt to address what some of those factors are and plan for them accordingly (Wilson, 1992).

## Session Sequence

The session described below represents the fifth of the 6 hours I spent with Sharon. During that time I also met with Sharon and her husband. I had subsequent phone contact with Sharon and with Dr. Wilson, her psychologist.

## Treatment Plan/Outline

1. **Induction:**
   *Rain forest and lagoon imagery:* This imagery was developed

by Sharon during the hypnotic assessment and is used to reinduce hypnosis. The induction took 2 minutes.

2.  **Deepening:** Deepening or intensifying one's involvement in the experience using the methods below. Use of multiple methods, called fractionation, enhances the intensity and effectiveness of the process. The deepening phase took 3 minutes.

    *   dissociation

    *   catalepsy

    *   arm drop

    *   confusion[1]

3.  **Containment, creating structure, and security:** took 4 minutes.

    *   Chair wrapping around her (security and safety: When sitting in the chair, she sinks into it and experiences the large chair wrapping itself around her).

    *   Safely and tightly wrapped: Using her words in creating imagery.

    *   Back brace, support metaphor: To create the feeling of being tightly wrapped, I described the experience of wearing a back brace following back surgery. At the time of our session, Sharon was recovering from a fractured rib, so the imagery was very relevant to her situation.

4.  **Intervention I: Coping Skills:** took 27 minutes.
    The coping skills interventions were focused on three main themes. The first was to create a sense of safety and structure in both in our therapeutic alliance and within herself. Second was to help Sharon develop coping skills to help her manage daily stressors and anxieties. Finally, the third theme was focused on the initial work in reconciling her trauma.

    *   *"Zoning Out"*

        *   control panel: stress inoculation

- turning down the dials on the panel
- reframe it as a symptom

- *"Other Symptoms"*

  - turn down dial
  - in session testing, inquiry, and practice
  - recall good feelings
  - further testing
  - posthypnotic suggestion and integration

- *"Cloudy Confusion"*

  - airplane ride (see Appendix A)
  - lift-off = arm levitation: Using this hypnotic phenomenon, Sharon has a sense of control of her experiences. Each time the arm levitates and drops, it heightens the hypnotic experience and serves to reinforce the suggestions.
  - time distortion
  - use perspective (looking down) vs. standing on the road
  - encourage trust, collaboration
  - hypnotic dream: Understand something important for self, clouds to go away
  - re-establish self control—arm levitation
  - suggesting the clouds are gone
  - ideomotor signal—arm drop
  - systems check: turn down the dials; in-session state rating
  - symptom reframing: symptoms are signals for her to attend to her internal experiences rather than the symptoms viewed as a disorder in themselves.

- what purpose do symptoms serve, what is my body telling me?

- posthypnotic suggestion for self-hypnosis & subsequent inductions in therapy.

5. **Intervention II: Meaning and Dealing With the Past:** took 13 minutes and set the stage for addressing the trauma and beginning to change her narrative.

- deepening

- case of Robert[2] (PTSD): similar symptoms, alcohol abuse, trauma, anniversary reactions, coping with the past

- respecting the past and able to move forward

- the Box of Memories[3]

- Shirley:[4] similar symptoms—depression, losses

- challenge for insight, finding meaning for herself from the stories of Robert and Shirley and acquiring coping skill from the Box of Memories.

6. **Closing Phase:** took 2 minutes.

- time distortion

- recall what's important to recall now and not recall what is not important to recall at this time. (This is both a coping technique and a means to help her avoid analyzing and taking apart what we've done.)

- as time passes, you'll have a "sense of impending meaning" coming to you. Sometimes the changes are not always behavioral but perceptual or attitudinal.

- reinforce her efforts and ability as a subject: actually telling her about her ability and efforts to further enhance her esteem and belief that what was done will work.

- suggestions for future success

7. **Termination:** phase took about 1 minute.

- permissive with suggestions for renewal, integration, & reorientation

## Additional Sessions and Discussion of Outcome

As we had hoped, Sharon was able to continue for a period of time with Dr. Wilson, the HMO psychologist. She later returned to see me for additional follow-up because Dr. Wilson became less available due to illness.

Sharon's case had some positive, but unexpected, outcomes outside of what the plan hoped to accomplish. In the session, she used the image of a lagoon as a safe place. In subsequent sessions with Dr. Wilson, she decided to modify that image and included in her safe place a white tiger and a panther. Further, she purchased figurines of a white tiger and panther, which she brings to sessions with her. She also modified the image of the box that gets put on the shelf. She made a brocade covering for a real box. The box contains, she says, "junk thoughts." When she feels stronger or weaker, she places the figurines either directly on top of the box, or off to one side. When she feels the need to adjust the dials on the control panel, she imagines the animals sitting next to her, looking over her. The animals help to control the dials.

About 6 months later Sharon had some problems with her medication, specifically the Depakote, which managed her mood swings. Not being able to take the medicine led to severe highs and lows. Sharon reported she was able, via hypnosis and self-hypnosis, to eliminate the severe highs. But this led to more severe lows. However, her use of the control panel imagery and the animal figurines managed to balance out both extremes of her mood.

I had 4 additional hours with Sharon. The first was the hour immediately following the reported session. During this hour I conducted an exit interview with Sharon and her husband to review my findings and recommendations again. Specifically, at that time, I saw no need to use hypnosis, or any other method, to explore her past. I felt she was too tenuous in her stability for that type of work at that time. I felt the focus of subsequent efforts should be on maintaining and enhancing stability and creating both internal structure and external structure—her therapy. Once the foundation is solidly in place, she and Dr. Wilson can assess if such past exploration becomes necessary. During the additional 3 hours, over subsequent visits, we continued to use hypnosis approximately one-third of the time. This time was used to fine tune and reinforce our previous work. I used the other two-thirds of the time to support Sharon and her husband. It appeared that Dr. Wilson would soon become unavailable as predicted. Those hours were also used to discuss Dr. Wilson's unavailability and how I could help to coordinate further outpatient care. Sharon's husband accompanied her and participated in those sessions.

Sharon continued to exercise her hypnosis skills and use of the related imagery. Additionally, she continued her medication. She reported her mood as being more balanced and even, with more normal highs and lows. Further, she found the imagery of the box into which she puts her "junk thoughts" to be very helpful.

Sharon did not express a need to explore the memories of her abusive past. Again, these were memories that were always known to her. Sharon was content to focus on, and strengthen, her stability. Her next step, she reported, was to return to regular employment; she had been working part-time. She realized that when her work hours begin to climb toward 45 per week, it was a warning sign, a symptom that she needed to explore. This tended to mean that she was becoming manic or over committing herself, a situation she wants to remain alert to and stop before she suffers a more serious mood swing.

## RECOMMENDATIONS TO CLINICIANS

Clinicians planning to integrate hypnosis into their CBT treatments should attend to some, perhaps obvious, caveats. These guidelines are consistent with good ethical practice and are, in fact, spelled out in the Code of Conduct of the American Society of Clinical Hypnosis (ASCH, 2003). In brief, these include practicing within one's discipline or license, practicing within the bounds of one's competence and experience, and not treating conditions with hypnosis that the clinician is not capable of treating. For example, before using hypnosis to treat PTSD, one might first gain a degree of mastery with lesser complex anxiety disorders. Further, when integrating this new tool into one's practice, regular consultation and/or supervision are important.

A major element of treating patients with PTSD involves addressing their memories. The issue of hypnosis and memory, especially traumatic memory, is a long and complex one, one beyond the scope of this chapter. However, the clinician should be aware of certain cautions when using hypnosis with traumatized patients and their memories. For a current and in-depth discussion of these issues, the reader is referred to Brown, Scheflin, and Hammond (1998) and Yapko (2003). The ASCH has published guidelines for such work (Hammond et al., 1995).

From my experience of training clinicians to use hypnosis, I found that the frustrations they often encounter are with how to put into practice what they've learned, or how to integrate hypnosis with what they already do clinically—and how to do so ethically. My experiences illustrate this challenge. I had just finished lecturing at a workshop. A dentist approached me and asked how he should respond to a request from a relative to use hypnosis to help the relative stop smoking. Was this appropriate for him to do? The issue was about working on the relative and not about the smoking cessation. It *is* appropriate for a dentist to use this kind of treatment. In a similar situation, a male obstetrician asked, if when using hypnosis during an examination or treatment of a patient, he should have a nurse in the room with him. The answer for both doctors was the same, "What would you typically do if you had the same situation presented to you and you did not use hypnosis?" The answer is, you would do what you typically do.

Adding hypnosis to one's repertoire doesn't require changing one's discipline or ethics. The clinician who is informed about hypnosis is adding to, or enhancing what they already do. In terms of thoughtful, ethical practice, the psychologist, dentist, or physician who now incorporates hypnosis into their work is still a psychologist, dentist, or physician and should do what they usually do when working with a patient. That includes careful and proper evaluation of the patient and their complaints, determination of the best and alternate forms of treatment, a determination if hypnosis can be useful and is appropriate to use with the situation, and procurement of informed consent as appropriate. The ethical and thoughtful practitioner would do with hypnosis nothing differently than what they would do without hypnosis. We are health care professionals who use hypnosis in our work; we are not just hypnotists.

# NOTES

1. Deepening via confusion:
   And I'd like the unconscious mind to know that it's this hand that's floating there, we'd like some of the air in the hot air balloon to go away, and as the air in the hot air balloon dissipates, the hand begins to drop; float downward towards the arm of the chair, slowly and steadily, floating gently downward a little at a time, and soon it will come to rest on the arm of the chair. And when it does, I don't know at first if Sharon will feel her fingertips touching the arm of the chair, followed by her fingers and her thumb and then the palm of her hand. I don't know if the palm of the hand and the thumb will touch first, by the fingertips and then the fingers and then the front of her hand (hand begins downward movement). That's right. As that hand lowers down deeper and deeper and down further, when that hand does come to rest completely and fully on the arm of the chair. . . .

2. Robert, referred to in the opening paragraphs as well as the treatment outline, was able to alter the ways in which he viewed and reacted to his memories of traumatic events. A version of his experience was offered to Sharon as an example of another person with similar experiences and how he overcame his obstacles.

3. Box of Memories was imagery I shared with Sharon as a method of coping with her past. She would put all her bad memories into a box, which was then sealed and placed in a safe place. Should she need to, she can later open the box and address the memories.

4. Shirley's story about her experiences of having found new ways of coping with her trauma was used as an example for Sharon as a woman who was successful at overcoming her trauma.

## APPENDIX A: AIRPLANE RIDE METAPHOR

Sharon came to see me with an array of strange symptoms, including posttraumatic stress disorder. She harbored a lot of distrust, especially of men, who had been her abusers. One area of Sharon's treatment was her symptom of "cloudy confusion."

In the intake interview, I had asked her what she is like as an employee. Her reply came with a slight smile and the comment, "Let's just say I like to fly my own plane." During the hypnosis session, I asked Sharon if she'd like to go on a plane ride with me. She agreed, and I asked if she'd like to fly the plane, which of course she did. I then offered a rather detailed description of our plane taking off and flying around the countryside. I described for her, still in hypnosis, a device on the plane that permitted us to view the scenery beneath the plane—a bombardier's scope. I reminded her that when we stood on the ground below, say out in farm country, all we could see is what's in front of our face. But when we looked through this scope, first we noticed that the clouds parted and the sky became clear. As we looked down at the ground, we saw the road we had stood on. Now we see how that road moves across the countryside and connects to other roads and how the roads divide the farm fields. We see the hills and valleys moving across the area, flowing into one another, and so forth. Upon seeing this, we say to our selves, "Oh, now I get it!" We see how all the different parts of the countryside are connected to the others, how from this new perspective, it all makes sense. I then ask her if I might fly the plane—a challenge for her to trust me. She agrees, tells me to take the controls, and she pushes back in the seat to take a nap and ponder the perspective below. After a few minutes, she retakes the controls and soon lands the plane. Sharon comes to recognize her "cloudy confusion" as her body's signal to her that she needs to step back and take a closer look at what is happening in her life at that time.

## REFERENCES

American Psychiatric Association. (1994). *Diagnostic and statistical manual* (4th ed., DSM-IV). Washington, DC: American Psychiatric Press.

American Society of Clinical Hypnosis. (2003). *Code of conduct.* Bloomingdale, IL: Author.

Beck, J. S. (1995). *Cognitive therapy: Basics and beyond.* New York: Guilford.

Brown, D. P. (1995). Pseudomemories: The standard of science and the standard of care in trauma treatment. *American Journal of Clinical Hypnosis, 37,* 1–24.

Brown, D. P., & Fromm, E. (1986). *Hypnotherapy and hypnoanalysis.* Hillsdale, NJ: Erlbaum.

Brown, D. P., Scheflin, A. W., & Hammond, D. C. (1998). *Memory, trauma, treatment, and the law.* New York: W. W. Norton.

Carlson, E. B., & Putnam, F. W. (1993). An update of the Dissociative Experiences Scale. *Dissociation, 6,* 16–27.

Cheek, D. B. (1993). *Hypnosis: The application of ideomotor techniques.* New York: Prentice Hall.

Cochrane, G. J. (1991). Client-therapist collaboration in the preparation of hypnotic interventions: Case illustrations. *American Journal of Clinical Hypnosis, 33,* 254–262.

Deyoub, P. L., & Epstein, S. J. (1977). Short-term hypnotherapy for the treatment of flight phobia: A case report. *American Journal of Clinical Hypnosis, 19,* 251–254.

Diamond, M. J. (1984). It takes two to tango: Some thoughts on the neglected importance of the hypnotist in an interactive hypnotherapeutic relationship. *American Journal of Clinical Hypnosis, 27,* 3–13.

Dowd, E. T. (2000). *Cognitive hypnotherapy.* Northvale, NJ: Jason Aronson.

Field, P. B. (1966). An inventory scale of hypnotic depth. *International Journal of Clinical and Experimental Hypnosis, 13,* 238–249.

Frischholz, E. J., Braun, B. G., Sachs, R. G., & Schwartz, D. R. (1992). Construct validity of the Dissociative Experiences Scale: II: Its relationship to hypnotizability. *American Journal of Clinical Hypnosis, 35,* 145–152.

Gudjonsson, G. H. (1984). A new scale of interrogative suggestibility. *Personality and Individual Differences, 5,* 303–315.

Hammond, D. C. (1988). *The integrative hypnotherapy model.* Unpublished manuscript, University of Utah School of Medicine, Salt Lake City, UT.

Hammond, D. C. (1989). *Integrative hypnotherapy: Factors in decision making.* Unpublished manuscript, University of Utah School of Medicine, Salt Lake City, UT.

Hammond, D. C. (1998). *Hypnotic induction and suggestion: An introductory manual.* Bloomingdale, IL: American Society of Clinical Hypnosis.

Hammond, D. C., Garver, R. B., Mutter, C. B., Crasilneck, H. B., Frischholz, E., Gravitz, M. A., et al. (1995). *Clinical hypnosis and memory: Guidelines for clinicians and for forensic hypnosis.* Bloomingdale, IL: ASCH.

Lazarus, A. A. (1989). *The practice of multimodal therapy.* Baltimore, MD: Johns Hopkins University Press.

Lazarus, A. A., & Lazarus, C. N. (1991). *Multimodal Life History Inventory.* Champaign, IL: Research Press.

Levitt, E. E., & Baker, E. L. (1983). The hypnotic relationship: Another look at coercion, compliance and resistance: A brief communication. *International Journal of Clinical and Experimental Hypnosis, 31,* 125–131.

Meichenbaum, D. (1985). *Stress inoculation training.* New York: Pergamon.

Meichenbaum, D. (1994). *A clinical handbook/practical therapist manual for assessing and treating adults with post-traumatic stress disorder (PTSD).* Ontario, Canada: Institute Press.

Meichenbaum, D., & Turk, D. (1987). *Facilitating treatment adherence: A practitioner's guidebook*. New York: Plenum.

Nash, M. R., & Spinler, D. (1989). Hypnosis and transference: A measure of archaic involvement. *International Journal of Clinical and Experimental Hypnosis, 37*, 129–144.

Norcross, J. C. (2002). Empirically supported (therapy) relationships. In J. C. Norcross (Ed.), *Psychotherapy relationships that work: Therapist contributions and responsiveness to patients*. New York: Oxford University Press.

Oster, M. I. (1994). Psychological preparation for labor and delivery using hypnosis. *American Journal of Clinical Hypnosis, 37*, 12–21.

Oster, M. I. (1995). *Brief (hypno) therapy: The non-traditional use of hypnosis in a traditional setting*. Paper presented at the 38th Annual Scientific Meeting of the American Society of Clinical Hypnosis, San Diego, CA.

Phillips, M., & Frederick, C. (1995). *Healing the divided self: Clinical and Ericksonian hypnotherapy for post-traumatic and dissociative conditions*. New York: Norton.

Ross, C. A., & Heber, S. (1989). Dissociative disorders interview schedule. In C. A. Ross (Ed.), *Multiple personality disorder: Diagnosis, clinical features, and treatment* (Appendix A, pp. 313–334). New York: Wiley.

Rothbaum, B. O., Meadows, E. A., Resnick, P., & Foy, D. W. (2000). Cognitive-behavioral therapy. In E. B. Foa, T. M. Keane, & M. J. Friedman (Eds.), *Effective treatments for PTSD: Practice guidelines from the International Society for Traumatic Stress Studies*. New York: Guilford.

Spanos, N. P., Brett, P., Menary, E. P., & Cross, W. P. (1987). A measure of attitudes towards hypnosis: Relationship with absorption and hypnotic susceptibility. *American Journal of Clinical Hypnosis, 30*, 139–150.

Spiegel, H., & Spiegel, D. (2004). *Trance and treatment: The clinical use of hypnosis* (2nd ed.). Washington, DC: American Psychiatric Press.

Wilson, P. H. (1992). Depression. In P. H. Wilson (Ed.), *Principles and practice of relapse prevention*. New York: Guilford.

Yapko, M. D. (2003). *Trancework: An introduction to the practice of clinical hypnosis* (3rd ed.). New York: Brunner-Routledge.

Chapter 9

# The Strategic Integration of Hypnosis and CBT for the Treatment of Mind/Body Conditions[*]

Carol Ginandes

$T$he ability of the mind to evoke physiological changes in the body is now well documented by burgeoning research, primarily in the fields of psychoneuroimmunology, behavioral medicine, and increasingly, hypnosis (Ader, Felton, & Cohen, 1991; Astin, Shapiro, Eisenberg, & Forys, 2003; Kiecolt-Glaser, McGuire, Robles, & Glaser, 2002). Contemporary hypnosis has been shown to be useful in many psychological, behavioral, and medical applications (Brown & Fromm, 1987; Covino & Frankel, 1993; Fredericks, 2001; Lynn, Kirsch, Barabasz, Cardena, & Patterson, 2000). Throughout the centuries, however, hypnotic techniques and trance rituals have been utilized to alter sensory perception, influence physiological functioning, and mediate the course of physical healing. Ancient Babylonian and Egyptian physicians used such rituals to invoke the healing powers of the gods; subsequently, Greek and Roman physicians sent their patients to convalesce in dedicated temples where they were enjoined to conjure "visions" of improvement. Eastern cultures have always cultivated mind/body practices, including yoga and tai chi, as well as many forms of meditation. Other traditional practices combine an admixture of chanting, dancing, drumming, and shamanic "journeying" to achieve altered states, not only for access to the transcendent, but also for the stimulation of healing (Arambula, Peper, Kawakami, & Gibney, 2001; Holroyd, 2003; Venkatesh, Raju, Shivani, Tompkins, & Meti, 1997).

## ORIGINS OF MEDICAL HYPNOSIS

The birth of Western medical hypnosis occurred in the eighteenth century with Franz Anton Mesmer's manipulation of what he called the forces of "animal magnetism." He believed these were influenced by planetary gravitation and the interconnecting "fluidium." Using his "mesmeric passes," he laid claim to remarkable healing cures of conditions that would today be considered functional and psychosomatic. His rate of cure was so impressive that it led to a damning investigation by the French Royal Commission of 1784. The committee pronounced Mesmer a fraud and declared, ironically, that his results were due "merely to the results of the imagination" (Leskowitz, 1999).

This discrediting of Mesmer's theories and techniques apparently set the course of medical hypnosis back several decades. Yet it resumed significantly in the work of British surgeon James Esdaile who practiced in India in the 1840s. Prior to the introduction of chemical anesthesia, Esdaile documented hundreds of surgical procedures that he performed in the field at a time that also predated antibiotics and antiseptic sterilization. His contribution also anticipated by some 150 years, the current research focus on the medical and psychobiological potential of adjunctive hypnotic interventions. Esdaile's integration of hypnotic techniques in the 1840s (in which he induced profound states of pre and intra-operative catatonia) resulted in his prescient observations: The utilization of adjunctive medical hypnosis resulted in comparatively lower rates of mortality, postsurgical infection, and complications. Patients also apparently experienced significantly less pain through the use of these hypnotic techniques. Unfortunately, with the advent of chemical anesthesia later in the nineteenth century, the use of adjunctive surgical hypnosis was abandoned for a century.

Only in the last 25 years have those historical threads been picked up through advances in behavioral medicine, psychoneuroimmunology, and integrative medicine. Hypnosis has increasingly been rediscovered as an adjunctive treatment modality (Benson, Arns, & Hoffman, 1981; Miller & Cohen, 2001; Zachariae et al., 1990).

## CONTEMPORARY APPLICATIONS OF HYPNOSIS

Contemporary applications of clinical hypnosis include four categories: psychological, behavioral, medical, and self-development. In the area of contemporary medical applications, there are a wide variety of surgical, medical, and dental uses of hypnosis that can reliably affect both the behavioral and somatic aspects of illness.

To date, most medical applications of hypnosis have been functional, adjunctive ones used in a remarkably wide range of nonpsychiatric applications; hypnosis can be used to moderate the behavioral, functional aspect of medical conditions with an eye toward symptom improvement and enhanced tolerance of uncomfortable and/or anxiety producing procedures. Such applications, for example, include lowering patient anxiety in medical procedures (such as claustrophobia in brain imaging scan patients), creating analgesia, diminishing blood flow to a surgical site, and controlling anticipatory emesis associated with chemotherapy (Blankfield, 1991; Hilgard & Hilgard, 1994; Lang, Benotsch, Fick, Lutgendorf, Berbaum, & Berbaum, 2000; Redd, Andresen, & Minagawa, 1982; Montgomery, DuHamel, & Redd, 2000). Medical hypnosis has also been documented to be useful in many stress-mediated conditions, including allergy, asthma, psychogenic cardiovascular disorders, insomnia, gastrointestinal problems, headaches, and dermatological conditions (Palsson, Turner, Johnson, Burnelt, & Whitehead, 2002; Patterson, Goldberg, & Ehde, 1996; Shenefelt, 2000).

Although rigorous, randomized controlled trials are few, Pinnell and Covino's meta-analysis (2000) of medical applications of hypnosis highlights particularly persuasive evidence of efficacy in the areas of preoperative surgical preparation, asthma, dermatological disorders, obstetrics, gastrointestinal conditions, hemophilia, and adjunctive treatment for postchemotherapy emesis. Unfortunately at the present time, such well-documented adjunctive hypnosis treatments continue to be almost entirely absent from the menu of treatment options offered by insurers and health care providers in medical settings.

## POTENTIAL STRUCTURAL HEALING WITH HYPNOSIS

The capacity of the hypnotic state to alter autonomic, brain wave, and immune functioning (Benson, 1975; Crawford, Gur, Skolnick, Gur, & Benson, 1993; Graffin, Ray, & Lundy, 1995; Madrid & Barnes, 1991) suggests its capacity to effect structural tissue change and anatomical healing as well as functional improvement. Somatic medical applications of hypnosis include the cutting-edge area of what could be called "structural healing"; this is the use of hypnosis to influence the course and speed of physical healing itself on the tissue level. Despite the numerous functional, adjunctive medical applications that have been documented, only a few randomized clinical trials have explored the potential use of hypnosis to stimulate the acceleration of actual structural or tissue change. There have, however, been numerous clinical case reports, such as those documenting the removal of warts and other psychocutaneous skin diseases (Ewin, 1992; Shenefelt, 2000) and the healing of burns. When they used hypnotic interventions within the first few hours of a severe burn, Ewin (1983) and Patterson et al. (1996) documented both blocking of the inflammatory reaction as well as actual modification of the size of the structural lesion in third degree burns.

But such uses of hypnosis, which include the accelerated healing of wounds and the amelioration of systemic disorders, have been tested infrequently and are not yet recognized as part of mainstream medicine or even of the hypnotic armamentarium. However, recent pilot trials indicate that somatic healing is a fertile area for clinical and research explorations of this modality.

### Studies Showing Accelerated Healing

The author's collaborative research focus has been in this area. We have documented the use of a paced, multisession hypnotic intervention to accelerate the healing of nondisplaced ankle fractures in a sample of twelve otherwise healthy young adult patients who presented for treatment at the orthopedic emergency service of Massachusetts General Hospital in Boston, MA during the study period. At 6 weeks after the fractures, the group receiving the adjunctive hypnotic intervention demonstrated radiographic evidence of bone healing typical of $8^1/2$ weeks as opposed to the controls (Ginandes & Rosenthal, 1999). A more recent study showed the acceleration of early postsurgical wound resolution in a group of 18 otherwise healthy women undergoing reduction mammaplasty. At both 1 and 7 weeks after surgery, the hypnotically-treated group evidenced significantly faster healing of surgical incisions than either the attentional or "usual care only" controls, p = .001 (Ginandes, Brooks, Sando, Jones, & Aker, 2003).

## Physiological Correlates of Hypnotic States

The mechanism by which hypnotic instructions are actually translated into cellular activity by the body has not been fully deciphered (Rossi, 1993). Despite the plethora of clinical applications, the underlying psycho-physiology through which hypnosis creates physical changes and/or healing has yet to be fully researched or conclusively understood (Crawford, 2001; DePascalis, 1999). But recent brain studies utilizing new imaging technologies have shown changes in cerebral blood flow patterns as well as activation of different cortical areas and brain wave patterns on EEG (Rainville, Hofbauer, Bushnell, Duncan, & Price, 2002). Additionally Rossi (2003) has posited the possible hypnotic activation of gene manifestations and the stimulation of neurogenesis. Such work is beginning to confirm what hypnosis practitioners have clinically documented over the last two centuries—that the hypnotic state, coupled with suggestions, may affect autonomic, immune and endocrine system processes that have been thought to elude voluntary alteration. These include such functions as heart rate, blood pressure, breathing, blood glucose levels, calcium metabolism, oxygen saturation, gastric secretions, muscular relaxation, electro-dermal activity, circulatory changes, and basal metabolism. Such capacities make hypnosis a viable, if not the premier, choice in the clinical mediation of stress-related disorders.

From the literature on rehabilitation and sports medicine come reports of hypnosis used to enhance performance and stimulate functional improvements. These include decreased spasticity and increased range of motion in neuromuscular disorders such as multiple sclerosis, cerebral palsy, and Parkinson's disease (Mauersberger, Artz, & Gurgevich, 2000; Medd, 1992; Wain, Amen, & Jabbari, 1990). It has also been used to increase self-esteem, lower depression, and attenuate adjustment reactions to handicaps (Appel, 1990). From the literature of sports psychology come reports of enhanced physical performance with a combination of hypnotic muscular relaxation and imaginative practice that facilitates neuromuscular reeducation (Warner & MacNeil, 1988).

## THE USE OF HYPNOSIS TO ENHANCE CBT IN MIND/BODY TREATMENT

The larger question then is not whether medical hypnosis can be used to provide functional and structural healing benefits, but how to develop effective clinical methodologies for doing so. Within the space constraints of this chapter, it is not possible to do justice to the host of applications of hypnosis to specific illness conditions. Traditionally, hypnosis texts have included scripted suggestions targeting various, specific medical complaints (Hammond, 1990). Alternatively, Ericksonian hypnosis practitioners have worked with an unscripted, utilization approach to each patient (Gilligan, 1987; Lankton & Lankton, 1983; Erickson, 1977).

The author's clinical specialty in behavioral medicine has led her to believe that it is most effective to use a multimodal, integrative hypnotic treatment model (Ginandes, 2002). This enables the clinician to address each patient individually but also includes an eclectic armamentarium of techniques that can be flexibly adapted. The combination of this eclectic hypnosis toolkit with a cognitive behavioral (CBT) approach may well be much more effective than either hypnosis or CBT alone (Clarke & Jackson, 1983; Kirsch, Montgomary, & Sapirstein, 1995). This integrative model can provide the skilled practitioner with a fully outfitted "doctor's bag" that can be adapted for the adjunctive hypnotic treatment of almost any mind/body condition. A schematic overview of some of these advantages is conceptualized as follows:

# Hypnosis Techniques in the "Doctor's Bag"

## 1. Amplification of Behavioral Rehearsal Imagery

The targeting of outcome behaviors and goal setting, which are hallmark CBT strategies, can be significantly enhanced by utilizing the intensification of multisensory evocation and the increased vividness of imagined outcomes implicit in the hypnotic state.

Thus, in addition to the corrective cognitive self-statements used in CBT, the evocation of desired behaviors in trance allows for a bihemispheric access to mental rehearsal. This enables the patient to engage not only verbal, left hemispheric brain functions but also the kinesthetic, synesthetic, emotional, visual, and lower brain stem functions in the service of heightened evocations of the desired outcome scenario. The following case illustrates this:

> **MS patient achieving perambulation.** A middle-aged woman suffering from advanced multiple sclerosis at the outset of clinical treatment was not ambulatory, but she very much wanted to be able to walk again, even for a short distance. She began by using a self-hypnotic suggestion ("I will walk again") repeatedly. In addition, I taught her to enter a hypnotic state and to mentally rehearse, in a vivid fashion, the kinesthetic motor integration necessary for standing and walking. She practiced consistently on a daily basis. At the end of 6 weeks; she was able to walk an entire city block using just a cane (Ginandes, 2004, p. 5).

## 2. The Psychophysiology of Hypnosis to Stimulate Organic Healing

As previously mentioned, cutting-edge research on burns, fracture, and wound healing is beginning to confirm what has long been clinically observed—that accessing the psychophysiology of the trance state stimulates structural as well as functional healing. Although CBT strategies often use basic relaxation techniques to countercondition stress/anxiety reactions (Barlow & Cerney, 1988; Beck & Emery, 1990), hypnotic evocations of profoundly deep and prolonged states of physiological relaxation in trance may take the patient to a deeper state of physical renewal. De facto, hypnotic practice can be utilized as behavioral entrainment and rehearsal of

the psychophysiology needed for reestablishing mind/body homeostasis as well as mental equilibrium. The insertion of relevant hypnotic suggestions while the patient is in such deep level of trance can
potentiate activation of unconscious resources that complement the
cognitive intentionality of CBT.

Site-specific "targeted suggestions" designed to foster specified
healing outcomes, such as accelerated incision healing, have been
shown to manifest in objectively observed effects (Ginandes, Brooks,
Sando, Jones, & Aker, 2003). In addition, states of trance can be
kinesthetically or verbally "anchored" with physical or verbal associ-
ational cues (Gilligan, 1987) so that such states of physiological
downshifting can be reaccessed almost instantly. If indeed, the
trance state is the portal to the body's own self-reparative "software,"
then regular access to the physiology of the trance state can actually
foster physiological recovery far more effectively *with* hypnosis than
with CBT alone (Rossi & Cheek, 1988).

## 3.   *Working Through Unconscious Impasses*

The access to the patient's inner life and to the unconscious psychological realms that are made so available through hypnosis afford
additional advantages over CBT techniques alone. Hypnotic explorations enable the therapist to identify and access the underlying
dynamic material and resistance to therapeutic improvement
(Edelstein, 1982) and to work through the abundant psychological
and emotional sequelae of illness.

Hypnotic explorations using hypnoprojective techniques, ideomotor questioning, and ego state therapy (Brown & Fromm, 1986;
Cheek, 1994; Frederick & McNeal, 1999) readily allow for consultation
with the patient's unconscious to access images, memories, feelings,
and associations that lie below the conscious waterline. Such material can be used to identify unconscious psychodynamic issues,
as well as conflicts and secondary gain motivations that may be
perpetuating symptoms or blocking recovery. A case example
follows.

**A case of genital warts.** A 23-year-old woman, who had been
diagnosed with genital warts, entered treatment with me at the
suggestion of her mother who had heard that it was possible
to cure warts with hypnosis. The young woman, who had been

undergoing a variety of medical treatments including freezing and injections of interferon in her genital area, was eager to try a less invasive approach.

The history of her problem emerged as follows: she had been sexually assaulted in her college dorm room by one of several young men who slept over in the girls' living room after a party. The man, whom she had never dated, entered her room in the night. She did not disclose the incident for almost a year, at which time the warts had emerged. She then told her parents, went for rape counseling, and initiated medical treatment, but she did not pursue tracking down the young man or pressing charges.

Knowing the possibility of alleviating the warts with hypnosis in a fairly straightforward way, I wanted first to make sure that there were no mitigating psychological issues that would make the treatment fail. Sure enough, in trance, she revealed that she felt that the warts were her just punishment for a sexual relationship that she had had the year prior to the rape. She felt certain that her parents had assumed she was a virgin prior to the rape. She described her parents as good and loving, but she was angry that sexuality had never been acknowledged while she was growing up. She felt guilty about her sexual feelings, and some part of her felt she needed to continue to punish herself.

In trance, after establishing ideomotor signals, I asked her whether she would be willing to strike a bargain with the punishing part of herself in order to find a better solution. She spontaneously came up with the idea of a "homework assignment" of doing sit-ups each day. Although she disliked doing them, she felt she could accept her own suggestion that every time she felt the needed to punish herself, she could do a few sit-ups. She was delighted with the bargain with herself and emerged from trance saying "that way I will be able to have a flatter belly too." Further hypnotic work with her focused on working through the trauma of the rape, fortifying her self-esteem, and giving herself permission to reown her sexuality in a more positive way. We then focused on using more directive hypnotic imagery to alleviate the warts. By the third week of treatment, the warts were in remission (Ginandes, 2004, p. 35).

## 4.   Tailoring Hypnotic Imagery/Suggestions

Such unconscious access provided by hypnotic uncovering work reveals the patient's own unique representational system (Gilligan,

1987) and native sensory dominance. This enables the therapist to personalize suggestions for a specific patient by eliciting images from that patient's psyche itself. The therapist is then enabled to speak the patient's own "inner language" and to customize hypnotic suggestions that will resonate the most effectively with the patient's particular psychology. Using hypnotic dialogue, the therapist can elicit the patient's own healing images rather than simply impose stock ones or ones generated by the therapist's psyche.

> **Healing from abdominal surgery.** A 28-year old woman had recently undergone abdominal surgery and wanted to heal quickly. In hypnotic dialogue, I invited her inner self to conjure up an image that would accelerate the healing of her surgical incision. She started to laugh suddenly. When I inquired about what she had imagined, she said that she had spontaneously seen a group of gray haired "grannies" with knitting needles. They were all sitting in a row of rocking chairs essentially knitting up her incision. It subsequently healed beautifully (Ginandes, 2004, p. 49).

This particular image was poignant for its psychological as well as its physical impact, especially as the patient's mother, whom the patient had wished to have at her side for the surgery, had been unable to come. So the maternal comfort provided by the patient's own unconscious imagery provided some much-needed ego strengthening. Probably no therapist of any persuasion could have devised a suggestion as well tailored to this patient's psychological and medical needs as this one generated by her own unconscious. Therefore, the most direct way to elicit this healing image was through hypnotic inquiry.

In addition, hypnotic language can be used to target specific healing outcomes by breaking down the components of a course of recovery into clearly described steps made vivid through visualization in trance. This case illustrates this point.

> **Stroke patient regaining movement.** I treated a stroke patient who was a musician wishing to regain movement in his left arm. He was given descriptive suggestions enumerating specific micro-movements leading toward the gross extension of his arm so that he could draw the bow across the strings of his violin.

Subsequent suggestions were than targeted to regaining finer motor positioning and coordination in the fingers themselves in successive approximations. His range of motion began to improve after this work in conjunction with his regular physical therapy (Ginandes, 2004, p. 62).

## 5.  Moderation of Physical Discomfort and Pain Control

The alteration of physical sensations through hypnotic phenomena can afford well-documented pain relief (Hilgard & Hilgard, 1994), comfort, and distraction from unpleasant medical surroundings. "Hypnotic phenomena," which are intrinsic to the hypnotic state, and built into standard induction techniques, are capable of evoking the subjective experience of perceptual shifts, dissociation, changes in weight (heaviness, lightness, arm levitation), temperature, (warmth, coolness), degree of sensation (numbness, analgesia, anesthesia), blood circulation toward and away from a site, and a changed experience of body boundaries. These kinds of shifts in perceptions make hypnosis an ideal technology for addressing aspects of patients' chronic or acute physical distress.

The hypnotic phenomenon of time distortion, which is readily accessible in trance, is one in which the subjective perception of the passage of time is spontaneously or purposely altered. This intrinsic hypnotic capacity can be utilized for myriad therapeutic benefits including the subjective shortening of periods of pain and the lengthening of intervals of perceived comfort. Posthypnotic suggestions are used to anchor the patient's capacity to retrieve time distorted (expanded) periods of comfort outside of the session whenever it would be beneficial. Patient mastery of such hypnotic techniques can increase the range and, perhaps, the effectiveness of behavioral medicine interventions. The following case is one such example.

**Cancer patient receiving relief.** A young woman being treated for colon cancer had a bad reaction to her chemotherapy medication. The mucosa of her mouth became inflamed and filled with ulcers. She was in such physical discomfort that she could not eat anything, not even the protein shakes offered to her. For particular medical reasons, insertion of a feeding tube was not a viable option at that time. In addition, she had become agitated and depressed, lying alone in her hospital bed, unable to sleep. Working at her bedside, I was able to elicit a deep state of hypnotic trance relaxation; I then suggested that the time she was spending in the hospital could fly by in an instant while she was absorbed in the beautiful Hawaiian beach scene she had conjured up. I suggested that while in this imagined tropical setting, she could sip a most wonderful "cooling and soothing" tropical beverage that would instantly heal, coat, and protect her mouth and throat as she drank it. And then she could find herself drifting off into a deep, replenishing sleep. Further suggestions targeted subsequent deeper and more rapid access to trance and relaxation. I suggested that she could use this imagery to relieve a variety of her symptoms. Her agitated depression, anorexia, insomnia, and mouth ulcerations all began to clear up after this intervention (Ginandes, 2004, p. 78).

## 6.  Alleviate Illness—Generated Emotional Distress

What amount to negative hypnotic suggestions are often given unwittingly by medical staff to patients in distress. For example, a young woman patient with interstitial cystitis reported being told by her well-respected urologist, "It will only get worse in time," and was encouraged to have bladder bypass surgery at the age of 18. Positive hypnotic suggestions can be formulated to relieve the emotional distress and constellation of feelings triggered by illness, such as anxiety, anger, depression, hopelessness, loneliness, and guilt (Goodnick, 1997). Ego-strengthening techniques (Frederick & McNeal, 1999; Phillips, 1996) can be used to enhance self-esteem in the face of illness-generated vulnerability. Hypnotic strategies of anticipating positive outcomes, retrieving old resource states, "changing personal history" (Yapko, 2003, pp. 423–425), and creating powerful hypnotic suggestions, all work well to counteract the erosion of self-confidence and extreme sense of vulnerability that accompany medical illness and treatment.

Additionally, the nurturant aspects of the hypnotic relationship can be used to create a healing therapeutic vessel to support the process of recovery (Diamond, 1987). When people are ill, they need to be nurtured and taken care of both literally (physically) and figuratively (psychologically). The hypnotic relationship provides such an opportunity. Patients regularly report feeling very "given to" just by being verbally guided into trance. The addition of personalized suggestions can exponentially enhance this sense of receiving care.

Medical patients also need to be empowered to be proactive in participating in their own treatment and recovery. Although CBT approaches emphasize self-efficacy (Bandura, 2004; Wiedenfeld et al., 1990), hypnosis can amplify a felt sense of mastery that can replace a global sense of illness-generated helplessness. Just learning to practice self-hypnosis can provide a shift to an internal locus of control with a strong practice effect, as the following case exemplifies.

**Self-hypnosis to cope with radiation treatment.** A young woman who had undergone surgery to remove a metastatic tumor from her breast was heading into a course of radiation therapy. She related her grief and hopelessness about enduring her upcoming month of daily radiation treatments, not to mention the possibility that she might not recover. She found the radiation treatment itself terrifying: mounting the cold radiation table, having to raise her arms up over her head with her pelvis and legs tilted upwards, being told to hold still for 15 minutes while the machine irradiated her chest. She related feeling as though she were impaled on a medieval torture rack. She would become utterly frantic and unable to quiet her racing thoughts. This in turn made the 15 minutes seem like an even longer ordeal.

It soon became clear that she was gifted with a rich and vivid ability to conjure scenes and events in her mind and that we could tap this resource to help alleviate her agony. Inviting her to settle onto the couch and to get completely comfortable at her own pace, I suggested that she let herself drift off to a place in her memory, a natural setting where she had experienced a sense of beauty and emotional sanctuary. She almost immediately let me know that she had located such a place, one she had visited on a vacation in Mexico some time before. She had spent time at a wonderful health spa in the mountains where the morning ritual was for the group to arise before sunrise, and walk up a mountain path in a landscape of wild sage and scrub, to arrive at a plateau lookout where they would await the sunrise. There she would sit on a mountaintop rock and feel the sun warming her face and body as she looked out on the stunning valley below. We developed this scene in some detail, as she heightened her perceptions of the quality of the morning air and light, the fragrances, the sounds, the textures, the colors, and the temperature. I suggested that she could encode this sense of peacefulness and perspective for future reference and that it was a resource that would serve her in good stead in her upcoming treatment.

A few days later I received an excited message from the patient who was attending her daily radiation treatment. She related the following story:

> I don't know how this happened, but when I found myself on the radiation table, suddenly I closed my eyes and found myself back on that mountaintop in Mexico. The radiation table had turned into the big rock on the mountain top, and the radiation itself was like the sun warming me. The sound of the radiation machine was very loud and buzzing, so I turned it into a swarm of friendly insects. The radiation technicians turned into the other hikers. And my radiologist (about whom she had very positive feelings) suddenly appeared, a little late as usual, at the top of the mountain with me! We stood up and held hands together, looking out over the valley and then toasted into the air: 'To the cure!' The 15 minutes on the table which had seemed absolutely endless before was over in an instant.

I had not given her explicit suggestions of how to integrate the elements of the Mexican mountain scene so elegantly into her own healing solution, but I had conveyed to her that her own unconscious mind would find a way to use these inner resources not only to help her tolerate the treatment but also to help her transform the misery of her radiation regimen. As her treatment went on, she developed an array of trance skills to help her manage her discomfort, and to feel more at peace with herself. Her doctors noted how much better she looked a week into the treatment and were surprised (Ginandes, 2004, p. 84).

For someone heading into the physical distress of radiation and chemotherapy and the concomitant feelings of fear and despair they evoke, the prospect of being able to transform the experience into one of comfort and well-being may be utterly inconceivable. Yet, for this patient, learning how to do this for herself in the office and then on the radiation treatment table was a life-changing event. Her new ability to access her own self-healing resources for comfort and for a sense of mastery changed her identity from that of a victimized cancer patient to an empowered, skillful partner in her own healing.

## PERSONALIZATION AND THE CREATION OF A PHASE-ORIENTED PROTOCOL

As a clinical practitioner, my perspective is not that *everything* can be "cured," but that almost every mind/body condition can be positively affected through a hypnotic intervention in concert with the CBT approaches of relaxation, goal setting, and the cognitive restructuring of negative thought patterns. The hypnotic work can range from a single but well-targeted hypnotic suggestion to an extensive, phase oriented, multisession hypnotic protocol. The use of such strategies can reduce anxiety, enhance comfort, alleviate depression, and/or speed the healing of the condition itself. The two overarching components of this use of hypnosis are: the personalization of treatment and the creation of a phase-oriented treatment protocol.

### Advantages of Consulting the Unconscious

The working assumption in treatment with hypnosis is that the practitioner's job is to help the patient tap into inner healing resources, images, metaphors and healing solutions (Yapko, 2003). The personalization of treatment requires the therapist to be versed in various hypnoanalytic strategies such as ideomotor questioning (Cheek, 1994), Ego State Therapy (Watkins & Watkins, 1997) and hypnoprojective techniques (Brown & Fromm, 1986). Such strategies enable the therapist to elicit the patient's unconscious imagery and to work with it to move the treatment forward. An example of this would be the creation of a self-regulating rheostat, an imaginary "comfort meter," to be used to maintain equilibrium during times of escalating distress during medical treatment. This type of imagery is sometimes utilized as a familiar behavioral technique for the modulation of anxiety and mood regulation. However, eliciting personal imagery generated from the patient's access to it in trance can further enhance such a strategy. The next case illustrates:

**Reducing the anxiety of prostate cancer surgery.** A man with prostate cancer was referred to me 2 weeks prior to his surgery. His understandable anticipatory anxiety had risen to such a pitch that he was on the verge of psychosis. It seems that instead of focusing his attention on his understandable fears of possibly dying during the surgery or from the cancer, he had developed a very circumscribed obsessive thought. He was convinced that he would not be able to regulate his body temperature in the hospital room, and that he would either be too warm or too cold. He feared that he would catch pneumonia and die, not from the cancer, but from lack of a proper blanket. He had become exceedingly agitated at this obsessive thought, which he could not control. A psychiatrist had begun a trial of medication to which the patient responded by becoming even more agitated and despondent. Since there was no time to do a significant piece of therapeutic work prior to the surgery, I was called upon to work creatively and quickly to try to obtain some modulation of the patient's anxiety before it blossomed into a full-scale psychosis. First, I worked with him on developing hypnotic skills of deep psychophysiological relaxation and then mentally retiring to a special inner healing sanctuary. There he could anticipate spending his time during the procedure and for the duration of his hospital convalescence. In his "sanctuary," I invited him to create a custom designed high-tech garment; this would be part bathrobe, part baby's bunting, and part blanket, and it would have its own magical thermostat. The thermostat would enable the blanket to automatically adapt to his needs for warmth and/or ventilation at every moment. With this imagery, which he developed in the office and practiced at home, the patient was able to proceed with the surgery successfully. He experienced a level of comfort he had never anticipated and, indeed, avoided catching pneumonia which he had dreaded. Subsequently, of course, he had to reconfront his obsessive-compulsive illness that had surfaced prior to surgery (Ginandes, 2004, p. 97).

## Creating a Phase-Oriented Protocol

Often, behavioral directives or even hypnotic preoperative suggestions for enhanced tolerance of a surgical procedure are proffered at a certain point during a medical intervention. For these applications, a single exposure to suggestions may be quite adequate and effective, as was true in the following case.

**Claustrophobic MRI experience.** A young woman with a knee injury required an MRI, which she had put off because of her claustrophobia. She was an avid golfer. After some preparatory self-hypnosis training in my office, she decided to use her skills for the duration of the scan. After a half hour, the technician informed her that the procedure was over and that he was bringing her out of the machine. She called back, "Oh no, not yet, I can't come out yet!" When the technician asked her why, she replied, "I'm only on the twelfth hole." She had become so completely absorbed in her trance in which she imagined herself playing golf that she was impervious to her prior fears of claustrophobia during the diagnostic procedure (Ginandes, 2004, p. 31).

Although such a straightforward approach may be of significant benefit, both my experience and clinical research suggest that it may often be useful to create a hypnotic intervention that addresses the patient's emotional and physical healing needs as they change and vary throughout the different stages of illness and recovery. For example, with a phase-oriented protocol administered over several sessions, the practitioner can target preoperative anticipatory anxiety prior to a surgical procedure, then present a new set of suggestions to elicit the speedy return of the client's postoperative bodily functioning. These may be followed by yet another set of suggestions devoted to fostering tissue healing, followed in turn by suggestions for mental rehearsal of rehabilitation in the weeks after surgery. Such a protocol, whether scripted, as it would need to be for standardized research, or more personalized, as it would be for individual treatment, "paces" the stages of a normative course of recovery. It may also be used to encourage an accelerated and/or smoother course of surgery and recovery. This concept guided the creation of the multi-session accelerated healing protocols developed for our bone healing (Ginandes & Rosenthal, 1999) and surgical wound healing research (Ginandes, Brooks, et al., 2003). An example of such a protocol design template from the research follows.

## Multi-Session Hypnotic Healing Protocol

Those patients randomized to the hypnosis group received 8 half hour weekly sessions with the study clinician commencing 2 weeks prior to surgery and continuing through 6 postoperative weeks.

... In a method similar to that utilized in the prior pilot study on hypnotically augmented fracture healing (Ginandes & Rosenthal, 1999), each of the weekly hypnotic segments paced the normative phase-oriented tasks of wound healing but also introduced suggestions emphasizing accelerated recovery. Overall, the suggestions targeted decreased inflammation, visible soft tissue wound repair, and accelerated tissue remodeling. The protocol included the phrasing of hypnotic suggestions in both direct and indirect formats, including both structured and open-ended content to promote personalization. . . . The preoperative sessions were designed to stimulate positive expectancy of comfortable and speedy recovery and to provide trance instruction. Postoperative interventions were structured to address pain, accelerate incision healing, return to normal activity and adjust to change in body image.

The two preoperative sessions established rapport, dispelled common hypnosis misconceptions, tested hypnotizability and provided induction practice with suggestions for a smooth surgery experience, diminished bleeding at the surgical site, diminution of painful sensations, and expectancy for rapidly paced healing. Imagery included the creation and kinesthetic anchoring of a personal "healing sanctuary" and mental practice of appropriate regulation of blood flow to and from the site pre and post operatively. To practice pain management, skills for glove anesthesia and transfer were taught. Pain sensations were reframed as "sensations of healing." In the subsequent postoperative sessions suggestions emphasized rapid, healthy passage through wound healing phases: inflammation, tissue formation, re-epitheliazation, angiogenesis, collagen remodeling, wound contraction etc. . . . For example, the phase of tissue formation and remodeling included suggestions such as "your skin is knitting together rapidly becoming strong, smooth and elastic." Additional suggestions invited participants to use "a special, healing lotion or cream or maybe even a healing light to massage your incisions in a way that feels comforting and smoothing" to prevent scar tissue from forming.

Psychological suggestions targeted continued comfort, a return of energy, and a sense of well-being. The second, third and fourth postoperative intervention scripts, in addition to reinforcing accelerated healing, flagged a rapid return of energy using time distortion and future pacing to that time when "now that the surgery seems so long ago." A subsequent session added the suggestion for adjustment to positive change in body image ("seeing such a healthy and well proportioned image in the mirror, appreciating this positive change in a whole, healthier you"). Such suggestions for positive adjustment to change in body image were made as the literature suggests that breast surgery can significantly affect body image. Although reduction/reconstruction surgeries are positive in outcome, there can be an initial sense of loss pursuant to radical alteration of a body part . . . (Ginandes, Brooks, et al., 2002, pp. 5–6).

## INTEGRATING CBT AND HYPNOSIS: "THE EXTENDED STRATEGIC TREATMENT MODEL"

An important consideration then becomes, in what order and in what way does the use of a hypnotic intervention best complement a CBT approach for mind/body conditions? What is an adaptable schematic approach for the practitioner wishing to be equipped for almost any patient presenting with medical issues? Several clinicians have highlighted the usefulness of stage oriented treatment (Brown & Fromm, 1987; Covino & Bottari, 2001; Ginandes, 2003; Herman, 1992; Phillips & Frederick, 1995; Prochaska & Velicer, 1997). To this end, I have conceptualized the components and sequence of interventions that I have found useful for a multitude of complaints as an "Extended Strategic Treatment Model for Recalcitrant Mind/Body Healing" (Ginandes, 2002). This approach enables the practitioner to address not only straightforward behavioral or medical complaints (such as preparation for surgery or procedural phobias) but also to be able to tackle cases in which complex mind/body conditions have proven impervious to medical treatment and/or straightforward medical hypnosis. I have previously illustrated the model in detail using a composite case described as a male patient presenting with incapacitating paruresis ("shy bladder syndrome"). This young man made considerable progress through a first approach using hypnotically facilitated desensitization and relaxation as applied to his personal anxiety hierarchy; mental rehearsal practice was followed by subsequent in vivo exposure trials.

However, at a certain point in the anxiety hierarchy, his pace of progress began to stall and then to halt. At that juncture, I shifted into a hypnoanalytic approach. This enabled us to access the deeper levels of conflict and resistance that were perpetuating his symptoms. Such a complicated case can require a course of long-term, multimodal, integrative therapy in which the practitioner, from my perspective, does well to include: (a) the sequential utilization of hypno-behavioral and hypnoanalytic approaches; (b) the uncovering and integrative developmental work with the "somatic ego states" associated with the illness condition (Frederick, 1996; Frederick & Phillips, 1995; Ginandes, 2004); and (c) the extended treatment time frame required for significant psychodynamic and psychophysiological change to occur (Ginandes, 2002).

These elements of the model may be usefully applied to all mind/body casework. The specifics of the myriad hypnotic techniques that can be utilized in the service of this kind of comprehensive treatment are best learned in an extended training workshop. Although a full description of this approach exceeds the limits of this chapter, an outline of the suggested components and phases of such integrative treatment follows:

1. *Assessment:* Perform a complete psychological, developmental history and assessment even with medical patients if possible. Although the dictates of managed care incite the practitioner to premature interventions, it is very important to know a patient well before broaching hypnotic work. This is necessary to avoid potential emotional minefields that can become retraumatizing with the revivification implicit in trance. It is also important to educate patients who may be harboring "hypnophobic" myths and fears based on prior exposure to hypnosis in the public domain.

2. *Develop a Hypno-Behavioral Intervention* strategy adapted to the patient's presenting problem. This first involves determining the patient's representational system either through careful observation afforded by active listening or imagery elicitation techniques. Then teach the patient to utilize a battery of hypno-behavioral techniques (Ginandes, 2001). As a first step, training in a variety of relaxation techniques (augmented by hypnotic deepening) can be adapted in a personalized course of hypnotic desensitization for myriad phobias and anxiety symptoms. After using relaxation training for the alleviation of anxiety, the creation of personalized imagery that targets

"site-specific healing" (Ginandes et al., 2003; Ginandes & Rosenthal, 1999) and the hypnotic future pacing of mental rehearsal for rehabilitation are the next steps.

3. *Create a Self-Hypnosis Practice Module:* Train the patient to do self-hypnosis, and practice it in the session. Teach the patient how to utilize key self-suggestions that are created in the course of treatment sessions. Utilize many repetitions of these suggestions for reinforcement between sessions. Encourage patients to develop a routine for self-hypnotic practice to ratify a sense of mastery with a hypnotic skill set. Create a personalized module with a practice log.

4. *Assess Treatment Results:* After following these hypno-behavioral steps, many patients will have made significant progress and/or will have accomplished a satisfactory treatment response. However, if the practitioner determines that progress has been inadequate, the next phase of treatment is needed to delve more deeply into possible psychological issues that may be forestalling treatment gains.

5. *Use Hypnoanalytic Uncovering to Access Unconscious Material:* If there appear to be blockages in healing progress, an assessment is made to discover if there are unresolved emotional conflicts, trauma, and/or secondary gain issues at play beneath the level of conscious awareness. Assess whether the symptom or condition has been attempting to express feelings or to serve another psychological function. At this stage, the therapist does well to consider the presence of fears of letting go of the illness or pain, fears of change, fears of new challenges, and the fear of losing helping supports. The hypnotic armamentarium is ideally equipped with strategies to move the treatment beyond the hypno-behavioral phase. An advanced hypnosis practitioner can fruitfully utilize a multitude of methods at this phase of treatment, including techniques to foster ideodynamic communication, hypnoprojective techniques, and ego state therapy to dialogue with the unconscious (Frederick & Phillips, 1995).

Retrieving and anchoring resource states and memory material and communicating with any "somatic ego states" associated with the illness condition can foster the working through of conflicts (Ginandes, 2004). Then the therapist can proceed with utilization, reframing, and integration strategies; it is also important to ascertain whether the patient can obtain inner "permission to heal" (Ginandes, 2000) and thereby allow the course of recovery to proceed.

6. *Extended Treatment Time Frame:* The healing of mind/body complaints that have been somatically entrenched for a long time will often require extended treatment time to change the associated behavioral, psychological, and biological dysfunctions. Therapists who choose to treat complex conditions do well to plan to be available for the long haul, to ratify small gains and stepwise progress, as well as to anticipate setbacks and resistance. This mind-set is more in line with the tradition of hypnoanalytic treatment than behaviorally focused, short-term therapy. The use of a "biologically paced" (Ginandes & Rosenthal, 1999) protocol in the phase-oriented treatment of mind/body conditions strengthens such an extended treatment plan by addressing what is paramount at each phase of recovery.

7. *Stages of Countertransference:* By definition, work with difficult mind/body cases will evoke countertransference feelings in the therapist. In phase-oriented work, it is common for the therapist to move through stages of countertransference, which may include a sense of urgency, exuberant optimism, frustration, and discouragement (Meier, Back, & Morrison, 2001). The therapist's self-awareness will hopefully offset the naturally occurring tendency to distance oneself psychologically from an ill patient when extended treatment gets bogged down. The therapeutic challenge is to transform this tendency to withdraw into a greater determination to go the distance needed for full recovery.

To illustrate how the course of this integrative, extended, phase oriented treatment model may be more helpful than either CBT or hypnosis alone, I offer some simplified case vignettes that may be helpful. The first case illustrates how a straightforward behavioral treatment for a habit disorder was enhanced by the integrative model.

**Smoking cessation.** A woman who had begun to smoke as a teen and had continued for 25 years had been in treatment with me for some time when her husband died of lung cancer. Her grown daughter was pressuring her to stop smoking, and she herself worked as a health counselor in the public schools. She wanted to stop but had found it virtually impossible. We began with a behavioral approach using relaxation training focused around slowing and deepening her breathing so as to gain control of her generalized anxiety and to be able to delay smoking impulses. She complied and dutifully charted her cigarette consumption, attendant feelings, and breathing relaxation practice segments. After a couple of weeks, she succeeded in feeling much more in control of her impulses to smoke but continued to be unable to cut back. At this point I invited her to join me in a hypnotic effort to assess whether there might be any (undermining) psychological issues in addition to the evident physiological addiction to prevent her from stopping smoking. She was skilled in trance work from our previous treatment work together and was readily responsive to utilization of an affect bridge technique (Watkins, 1971) over a couple of sessions to discover the source of her impasse. In trance, she wept as she remembered that as a child of seven, when her mother had died and her father had gone off into the Armed Services, she had been passed around to the homes of various relatives. She had deeply resented this, and, feeling like an outsider, she often felt very angry with the adults who took care of her. However, she was careful to be on her best behavior so as not to offend them and be abandoned again. She became convinced early on that expressing any anger was unacceptable. She then began to piece together that as a young teenager she had begun to smoke because it was "safer to put a cigarette in (my) mouth" than to allow angry words to come out of it. We then did some ego state therapy work to see if a child part of her would be willing to allow the adult part of her self to start expressing her feelings verbally and to relinquish the smoking as a substitute. She assented to this and, after working this through in trance, was subsequently able to use her behavioral relaxation and pattern interruption strategies again to great advantage. She subsequently and successfully stopped smoking (Ginandes, 2004, p. 158).

Another case illustrates how hypnosis can facilitate the amelioration of medical conditions presenting with unclear etiology:

**A swollen tongue.** A patient in treatment for low self-esteem came into my office for her regular session. On this particular day, when she tried to speak, her words were garbled and indistinct as though she were speaking through a large cotton wad. She did her best to convey that her tongue had swollen up so that she could barely speak. She indicated that she had seen her internist for a full examination that morning but that he had been puzzled by her condition and offered no treatment suggestions other than watchful waiting.

Since we had used trance work before, I asked if she wanted to further explore her predicament. When she had settled into trance, I wondered out loud whether her tongue, the presenting "somatic ego state," might have something to communicate. Her distinct nod encouraged me to proceed. Would it be all right for her tongue to begin to tell us what was on its mind? I asked. With little hesitation, she related that her tongue needed "to speak" to her boyfriend with whom she had had a stormy battle the day before. Knowing this patient's history and her fear of expressing anger (due to a long struggle with parental disapproval), I suggested that it might be helpful to express whatever she needed to say to her boyfriend in the safety of our session. I invited her to visualize him seated across from her and to allow her tongue to say whatever was going to be most helpful for her to resolve her physical problem. With barely a pause, she began to speak to, or rather to lambaste, him in a full emotional account of how angry she was and of how he had hurt her feelings in a recent incident. She went on at some length, and, when she stopped, I asked whether her tongue had expressed what it needed to for it to begin to return to its normal size. When she replied affirmatively, I suggested that she reorient herself to the office, and we continued the session in a normal mode of dialogue. She was surprised at how angry she really was and how clearly she had been able to express her feelings in her altered state. It was time to finish up the session, so we agreed to continue to work with these feelings in the next meeting, and she departed. The next day she called me to report that her tongue had begun to shrink dramatically back to its normal size, and that she was having a much easier time talking (Ginandes, 2004, p. 17).

Sometimes, the material that emerges with hypnoanalytic uncovering work is so idiosyncratic that even the most seasoned therapist would not be able to predict the possible influence of deep psychodynamic influences on the workings of the body.

**Fibroids.** A 27-year-old woman came to me with a concern about multiple uterine fibroids that were threatening to impede her ability to get pregnant. She requested hypnosis to work on eliminating these benign tumors. She appeared to be a very pleasant, somewhat shy, noticeably soft-spoken and docile young woman. I assumed that a permissive, directive approach would be reasonable.

After a standard relaxation and breath-focused induction, she indicated that she did want to address the matter of the fibroids. All of a sudden, a rather imperious, loud and unmistakably angry voice tone alerted me to the presence of an unexpected ego state. This persona, who sounded much older than my patient, was clearly annoyed at my assumption that she wished to eliminate the fibroids! She assured me that, in fact, she had no wish to get rid of them. Rather, she had very protective maternal feelings toward them. She was concerned that the fibroids might feel neglected and jealous when the fetus arrived in utero as they had been there first. It is interesting to note that this young woman was herself an older sibling. At this point, I was rather surprised and somewhat stymied by the situation. How could we accomplish the consciously stated goal of eliminating the fibroids so that she could get pregnant while taking into account the formidable mother bear persona that had just emerged? Not knowing how to solve this conundrum, I decided the only thing I could do would be to have her consult her own unconscious for the solution. So I asked the maternal ego state how she could both accomplish her goal of getting pregnant and making sure that the fibroids did not feel neglected in the process? There was silence for a couple of minutes and then a big smile came across her face as the solution emerged. Her own creative solution was to give all the fibroids very attractive but tight fitting little jackets. In addition to feeling stylish, warm, and well taken care of, she noted that the cinched waist jackets would serve to inhibit any further expansion of their girth! Soon after this session, the patient became pregnant, carried the baby to term and never, to my knowledge, had surgery for the fibroids (Ginandes, 2004, p. 187).

Of course, I would have never been able to arrive at the extraordinary solution that the patient's own unconscious had produced. This kind of dialogue, at times with the ego states, and at other times with the greater unconscious, can be important even in seemingly straightforward cases of medical hypnosis.

Two other cases presented here illustrate how this integrative model can facilitate the mind/body healing of medical conditions found to be intractable through medical approaches alone. Although these cases do not constitute irrefutable scientific evidence of such effects, they do appear to suggest that clinical outcome may be improved with the use of these strategies.

> **Prostatitis.** A man in treatment was approaching his 50th birthday. He was distressed, feeling that he had not accomplished anything in his life. We worked cognitively to identify his negative core beliefs about himself and to explore alternative self-statements. His bitterness persisted, however. He was in the final stages of divorce proceedings initiated by his wife. Two weeks before the court hearing, he came down with a case of prostatitis. After an intensive course of antibiotics, he had not improved significantly. Familiar with the mind/body construct, he announced that he had decided that the condition was due to "stress." He was unable to be any more specific on the conscious level, but he was willing to explore the symptom hypnotically. In trance, I invited that part of him that was responsible for maintaining the prostatitis to come forward. The patient immediately became visibly flushed and angry. Then he proclaimed in a vehement tone that he was totally "pissed off" at his wife for leaving him. When I asked that part what else it was feeling, he revealed that he felt that he had "pissed his life away." Furthermore, he was angry that he was facing the prospect of having to look for new women to date, and he realized that his prostatitis would protect him from having to test his fears of sexual performance. We then had an entree into addressing these various issues. After the patient worked through these feelings and concerns, the prostatitis subsided (Ginandes, 2004, p. 189).

The following is a case example that further highlights the complexities of such work with intractable conditions. In this case, although straightforward medical hypnosis and CBT relaxation strategies were helpful for some degree of relief in the initial stages of treatment, without the use of subsequent uncovering and integration, a greater degree of symptom relief would likely not have been available.

This case illustrates that it may be more important to respect the patient's unconscious need to retain some degree of symptomatic suffering to maintain psychological homeostasis despite the therapist's countertransference pull to "cure" the symptoms. Even though the cure may be incomplete, it is apparent that much more healing progress can sometimes be made with the integrative hypnotic CBT model than with CBT alone.

> **Hyperemesis.** I was working with a 31-year old teacher who came into treatment early on in her second pregnancy. She had been plagued by severe nausea throughout her first pregnancy but had delivered a healthy first baby. She feared that she would suffer hyperemesis throughout the second pregnancy. She had to excuse herself at work every 15 minutes because of the nausea. She had been fully worked up medically, and no physical cause for her debilitating emesis had been found. We did a course of relaxation training to help her calm down and distract herself in an effort to moderate her symptoms. However, through my history taking, it became apparent that this symptom might have had its roots in issues from her childhood. Her parents had been concentration camp survivors, and she herself experienced survivor guilt. In addition, her mother had been treated for cancer right after the client's first pregnancy and had developed nausea with chemotherapy. Further history revealed her memories of significant trauma. When she was five, she had found a book of photographs of concentration camp survivors on a table at home.
>
> At this point in treatment, she was willing to utilize hypnotic exploration. I invited the "somatic ego state" that had perpetuated the nausea in the first pregnancy to come forward. What emerged was a child ego state that had decided early on that she would never bring a child into the world to suffer. The trance dialogue with the ego state of the symptom revealed that it was, in fact, attempting to serve a purpose. Because of what had happened to her parents, the patient was convinced that the world was a very unsafe place and that she needed to be hypervigilant. If she were the least bit off guard, perhaps something terrible might happen. Her unconscious had apparently developed the nausea as a way of keeping her sufficiently uncomfortable all the time. This continual discomfort, like a sentinel standing guard, would keep her vigilant all of the time. Thus, she would protect the fetus from harm. With this unfolding saga, it became clear that the therapeutic task was to focus on developing other strategies for being protective and for hon-

oring her family history. We were able to address some of this in trance. However, the trauma work from early childhood would clearly have involved weeks or months of integrative therapy that were not available to her with the exigencies of her current pregnancy. After doing what we could with the ego state that was perpetrating the nausea, I began to inquire during her trance as to her willingness to alleviate the emesis.

What emerged by way of a reply was that she could allow herself to reduce the nausea—but only by 50%. Although, of course, I wished that she could eliminate it entirely, this was all she could give herself permission to do at that time. She came into the next session reporting that the intervals between vomiting episodes were significantly longer, about 50% to be exact, and that this was giving her considerable relief in her job environment. With more work with the nauseated ego state, we were able to negotiate for more percentage reductions, but the bargaining held to 30% retention of the symptom. And this was only when she was clear that she could still be attentive to the fetus and be a little more comfortable at the same time. I hid my countertransferential disappointment that we had not had a complete remission of the symptom. My patient, on the other hand, was thrilled with the outcome, as she felt significantly better and was able to continue working throughout her pregnancy. She subsequently delivered a healthy baby, and we were then able to continue our treatment work (Ginandes, 2004, p. 234).

## CONCLUSION

In conclusion, it seems clear that the treatment of mind/body problems requires a flexible and comprehensive armamentarium of intervention strategies. Some patients may benefit greatly from cognitive restructuring or from goal setting as applied to treatment regimens. Others may benefit from relaxation methods that tone down the alarm system of an overreactive sympathetic nervous system that is causing stress-induced conditions. However, it is my observation as a clinician that the vast majority of patients will benefit even more from the phase-oriented interweaving of CBT and various hypnobehavioral and hypnoanalytic treatment interventions that are carefully paced and integrated into an extensive fabric of treatment that will, over time, support recovery.

## REFERENCES

Ader, R., Felton, D., & Cohen, N. (Eds.). (1991). *Psychoneuroimmunology* (2nd ed.). New York: Academic.

Appel, P. R. (1990). Clinical applications of hypnosis in the physical medicine and rehabilitation setting: Three case reports. *American Journal of Clinical Hypnosis, 33*, 85–93.

Arambula, P., Peper, E., Kawakami, M., & Gibney, K. H. (2001). The physiological correlates of Kundalini yoga meditation: A study of a yoga master. *Applied Physiology and Biofeedback, 2*, 147–153.

Astin, J., Shapiro, S., Eisenberg, D., & Forys, K. (2003). Mind-body medicine: State of the science, implications for practice. *The Journal of the American Board of Family Practice, 16*, 131–147.

Bandura, A. (2004). Health promotion by social cognitive means. *Health Education and Behavior, 2*, 143–164.

Barlow, D. H., & Cerny, J. A. (1988). *Psychological treatment of panic.* New York: Guilford.

Beck, A. G., & Emery, G. (1990). *Anxiety disorders and phobias: A cognitive perspective* (Reprinted ed.). New York: Basic.

Benson, H. (1975). *The relaxation response.* New York: Avon.

Benson, H., Arns, P., & Hoffman, J. W. (1981). The relaxation response and hypnosis. *International Journal of Clinical and Experimental Hypnosis, 29*, 259–270.

Blankfield, R. P. (1991). Suggestion, relaxation, and hypnosis as adjuncts in the care of surgery patients: A review of the literature. *American Journal of Clinical Hypnosis, 33*, 172–186.

Brown, D., & Fromm, E. (1986). *Hypnotherapy and hypnoanalysis.* Hillsdale, NJ: Erlbaum.

Brown, D., & Fromm, E. (1987). *Hypnosis and behavioral medicine.* Mahwah, NJ: Lawrence Erlbaum.

Cheek, D. B. (1994). *Hypnosis: The application of ideomotor techniques.* Needham Heights, MA: Allyn & Bacon.

Clarke, J. C., & Jackson, A. (1983). *Hypnosis and behavior therapy: The treatment of anxiety and phobias.* New York: Springer Publishing.

Covino, N. A., & Frankel, F. H. (1993). Hypnosis and relaxation in the medically ill. *Psychotherapy and Psychsomatics, 60*, 75–90.

Covino, N. A., & Bottari, M. (2001). Behavioral theory and smoking cessation. *Journal of Dental Education, 65*(4), 340–347.

Crawford, H. J., Gur, R. C., Skolnick, B., Gur, R. E., & Benson, D. M. (1993). Effects of hypnosis on regional cerebral blood flow during ischemic pain with and without suggested hypnotic analgesia. *International Journal of Psychophysiology, 15*, 181–195.

Crawford, H. J. (2001). Neuropsychophysiology of hypnosis: Towards an understanding of how hypnotic interventions work. In G. D. Burrows, R. O. Stanley, & P. B. Bloom (Eds.), *International handbook of clinical hypnosis* (pp. 61–84). New York: John Wiley.

De Pascalis, V. (1999). Psychophysiological correlates of hypnosis and hypnotic susceptibility. *International Journal of Clinical and Experimental Hypnosis, 47*, 117–143.

Diamond, M. J. (1987). The interactional basis of the hypnotic experience: On the relational dimensions of hypnosis. *International Journal of Clinical and Experimental Hypnosis, 35*, 95–115.

Edelstein, M. G. (1982). Ego state therapy in the management of resistance. *American Journal of Clinical Hypnosis, 25*, 15–20.

Erickson, M. H. (1977). Hypnotic approaches to therapy. *American Journal of Clinical Hypnosis, 20*, 20–35.

Ewin, D. M. (1983). Emergency room hypnosis for the burned patient. *American Journal of Clinical Hypnosis, 26*, 5–8.

Ewin, D. M. (1992). Hypnotherapy for warts (verruca vulgaris): 41 consecutive cases with 33 cures. *American Journal of Clinical Hypnosis, 35*, 1–10.

Frederick, C. (1996). Functionaries, janissaries, and daemons: A differential approach to the management of malevolent ego states. *Hypnos, 23*, 37–47.

Frederick, C., & McNeal, S. (1999). *Inner strengths: Contemporary psychotherapy and hypnosis for ego-strengthening.* Mahwah, NJ: Lawrence Erlbaum.

Frederick, C., & Phillips, M. (1995). Decoding mystifying signals: Translating symbolic communications of elusive ego states. *American Journal of Clinical Hypnosis, 38*, 87–96.

Fredericks, L. E. (2001). *The use of hypnosis in surgery and anesthesiology.* Springfield, IL: Charles C. Thomas.

Gilligan, S. G. (1987). *Therapeutic trances: The cooperation principle in Ericksonian hypnotherapy.* New York: Brunner/Mazel.

Ginandes, C. (2000). *Accessing "permission to heal" in hypnotic dialogues with medically ill patients.* Presented at the 42nd Annual Scientific Meeting the American Society of Clinical Hypnosis, Baltimore, Maryland.

Ginandes, C. (2001). *Component strategies for targeted hypnotic healing.* Unpublished workshop handout.

Ginandes, C. (2002). Extended strategic therapy for recalcitrant mind/body healing: An integrative model. *American Journal of Clinical Hypnosis, 45*, 91–102.

Ginandes, C. (2004). *Extended strategic therapy to accelerate mind/body healing.* Unpublished manuscript.

Ginandes, C. (2004, November). *Six players on the inner stage: Using ego state therapy with the medically ill.* Paper presented at the annual meeting of the Society for Clinical and Experimental Hypnosis, Santa Fe, NM.

Ginandes, C., Brooks, P., Sando, W., Jones, C., & Aker, J. (2003). Can medical hypnosis accelerate post-surgical wound healing? Results of a clinical trial. *American Journal of Clinical Hypnosis, 45*, 333–351.

Ginandes, C., & Rosenthal, D. (1999). Using hypnosis to accelerate the healing of bone fractures: A randomized controlled pilot study. *Alternative Therapies in Health and Medicine, 5*, 67–75.

Goodnick, P. J. (1997). Medical illness and depression. *Psychiatric Annals, 27*, 339–340.

Graffin, N. F., Ray, W. J., & Lundy, R. (1995). EEG concomitants of hypnosis and hypnotic susceptibility. *Journal of Abnormal Psychology, 104*, 123–131.

Hammond, D. C. (Ed.). (1990). *Handbook of therapeutic suggestions and metaphors.* New York: W. W. Norton.

Herman, J. L. (1992). *Trauma and recovery.* New York City: Basic Books.

Hilgard, E. R., & Hilgard, J. R. (1994). *Hypnosis in the relief of pain* (Rev. ed.). New York: Brunner-Routledge.

Holroyd, J. (2003). The science of meditation and the state of hypnosis. *American Journal of Clinical Hypnosis, 46,* 109–128.

Kiecolt-Glaser, J. K., McGuire, L., Robles, T. F., & Glaser, R. (2002). Emotions, morbidity, and mortality: New perspectives from psychoneuroimmunology. *Annual Review of Psychology, 53,* 83–107.

Kirsch, I., Montgomery, G., & Sapirstein, G. (1995). Hypnosis as an adjunct to cognitive-behavioral psychotherapy: A meta-analysis. *Journal of Counseling and Clinical Psychology, 63,* 214–220.

Lang, E. V., Benotsch, E. G., Fick, L. J., Lutgendorf, S., Berbaum, M. L., Berbaum, K. S., et al. (2000). Adjunctive non-pharmacological analgesia for invasive medical procedures: A randomised trial. *Lancet, 355,* 1486–1490.

Lankton, S., & Lankton, C. (1983). *The answer within: A clinical framework of Ericksonian hypnotherapy.* New York: Brunner/Mazel.

Leskowitz, E. (1999). Mesmerism, hypnosis and the human energy field. In E. Leskowitz (Ed.), *Transpersonal hypnosis* (pp. 13–25). Boca Raton, FL: CRC Press.

Lynn, S. J., Kirsch, I., Barabasz, A., Cardena, E., & Patterson, D. (2000). Hypnosis as an empirically supported clinical intervention: The state of the evidence and a look to the future. *The International Journal of Clinical and Experimental Hypnosis, 48,* 239–259.

Madrid, A. D., & Barnes, S.H. (1991). A hypnotic protocol for eliciting physical changes through suggestions of biochemical responses. *American Journal of Clinical Hypnosis, 34,* 122–128.

Mauersberger, K., Artz, K., Duncan, B., & Gurgevich, S. (2000). Can children with spastic cerebral palsy use self-hypnosis to reduce muscle tone? A preliminary study. *Integrative Medicine, 2,* 93–96.

Meier, D., Back, A., & Morrison, R. (2001). The inner life of physicians and care of the seriously ill. *Journal of the American Medical Association, 286,* 3007–3014.

Medd, D. (1992). The use of hypnosis in multiple sclerosis: Four case studies. *Contemporary Hypnosis, 9,* 62–65.

Miller, G. E., & Cohen, S. (2001). Psychological interventions and the immune system: A meta-analytic review and critique. *Health Psychology, 20,* 47–63.

Montgomery, G., DuHamel, K., & Redd, W. H. (2000). A meta-analysis of hypnotically induced analgesia. *International Journal of Clinical and Experimental Hypnosis, 48,* 138–153.

Palsson, O. S, Turner, M. J., Johnson, D. A., Burnelt, C. K., & Whitehead, W. E. (2002). Hypnosis treatment for severe irritable bowel syndrome: Investigation of mechanism and effects on symptoms. *Digestive Diseases and Sciences, 47,* 2605–2614.

Patterson, D. R., Goldberg, M. L., & Ehde, D. M. (1996). Hypnosis in the treatment of patients with severe burns. *American Journal of Clinical Hypnosis, 38,* 200–212.

Phillips, M. (1996). Our bodies, ourselves: Treating the somatic manifestations of trauma with ego-state therapy. *American Journal of Clinical Hypnosis, 38*(2), 37–49.

Phillips, M., & Frederick, C. (1995). *Healing the divided self: Clinical and Ericksonian hypnotherapy for dissociative and post-traumatic conditions.* New York: W. W. Norton.

Pinnell, C. M., & Covino, N. A. (2000). Empirical findings on the use of hypnosis in medicine: A critical review. *The International Journal of Clinical and Experimental Hypnosis, 48*(2), 170–194.

Prochaska, J. O., & Velicer, W. F. (1997). The transtheoretical model of health behavior change. *American Journal of Health Promotion, 12*(1), 38–48.

Rainville, P., Hofbauer, R. K., Bushnell, M. C., Duncan, G. H., & Price, D. D. (2002). Hypnosis modulates activity in brain structures involved in the regulation of consciousness. *The Journal of Cognitive Neuroscience, 14*, 887–901.

Redd, H., Andresen, G. V., & Minagawa, R. Y. (1982). Hypnotic control of anticipatory emesis in patients receiving cancer chemotherapy. *Journal of Consulting and Clinical Psychology, 50*, 14–19.

Rossi, E. (1993). *The psychobiology of mind-body healing: New concepts of therapeutic hypnosis* (2nd ed.). New York: W. W. Norton.

Rossi, E. (2003). Gene expression, neurogenesis, and healing: Psychosocial genomics of therapeutic hypnosis. *American Journal of Clinical Hypnosis, 45*, 197–216.

Rossi, E. L., & Cheek, D. B. (1988). *Mind-body therapy: Ideodynamic healing in hypnosis.* New York: W. W. Norton.

Shenefelt, P. D. (2000). Hypnosis in dermatology. *Archives of Dermatology, 136*, 393–399.

Venkatesh, S., Raju, T. R., Shivani, Y., Tompkins, G., & Meti, B. L. (1997). A study of the structure of the phenomenology of consciousness in meditative and non-meditative states. *Indian Journal of Physiology and Pharmacology, 41*, 149–153.

Wain, H., Amen, D., & Jabbari, B. (1990). The effects of hypnosis on a Parkinsonian tremor: A case report with polygraph/EEG recordings. *American Journal of Clinical Hypnosis, 33*, 94–98.

Warner, L., & McNeil, M. (1988). Mental imagery and its potential for physical therapy. *Physical Therapy, 68*, 516–521.

Watkins, J. G., (1971). The affect bridge: A hypnoanalytic technique. *The International Journal of Clinical and Experimental Hypnosis, 19*, 21–27.

Watkins, J., & Watkins, H. (1997). *Ego states: Theory and therapy.* New York: W. W. Norton.

Wiedenfeld, S. A., O'Leary, A., Bandura, A., Brown, S., Levine, S., & Raska, K. (1990). Related impact of perceived self-efficacy in coping with stressors on components of the immune system. *Journal of Personality and Social Psychology, 59*, 1082–1094.

Yapko, M. (2003). *Trancework* (3rd ed.). New York: Brunner-Routledge.

Zachariae, R., Kristensen, J. S., Hokland, P., Ellegaard, J., Metzem, E., & Hokland, M. (1990). Effect of psychological intervention in the form of relaxation and guided imagery on cellular immune function in normal healthy subjects: An overview. *Psychotherapy and Psychosomatics, 54*, 32–39.

Chapter 10

# Hypnotherapy and Cognitive Behavior Therapy for Pain and Distress Management in Cancer Patients

Gary R. Elkins and Joel D. Marcus

Pain is a serious problem that many cancer patients face. Cognitive behavior therapy and hypnotic interventions can be an effective combination to help control this pain. Seventy-five percent of patients with advanced cancer suffer pain, and, of those, 40%–50% report it as moderate to severe and 20%–30% report it as very severe (Bonica, 1990). Distress is the term used to characterize the psychological components of cancer care. This term can allow the patients to define their subjective level of discomfort surrounding the nature and treatment sequela to the disease. As further defined:

> Distress is a multifactorial unpleasant emotional experience of a psychological (cognitive, behavioral, emotional), social, and/or spiritual nature that may interfere with the ability to cope effectively with cancer, its physical symptoms and its treatment. Distress extends along a continuum, ranging from common normal feelings of vulnerability, sadness, and fears to problems that can

become disabling, such as depression, anxiety, panic, social isolation, and existential and spiritual crisis. (Holland, 1999)

As many as 20%–40% of cancer patients demonstrate a significant level of distress (Roth, Kornblith, Batel-Colel, et al., 1998; Zabora, Brintzendhof, Curbow, Hooker, & Piantadosi, 2001). The levels of distress correlate with the cancer site and type, as well as with age and other variables. Undertreated cancer pain negatively affects sleep, energy, and normal activity. Further, chronic cancer pain can lead to anxiety, depression, and can negatively affect quality of life (Montour & Chapman, 1991) that in turn further exacerbates the patient's distress.

## PHARMACOLOGICAL MANAGEMENT OF PAIN

Opiate analgesics are recognized as the mainstay in the usual medical treatment for severe pain among cancer patients with bone metastasis (Jacox, Carr, Payne, et al., 1994). However, cancer patients frequently experience severe pain that is not fully relieved by standard pharmacological treatment. Thus, it is important for hypnotherapists to be familiar with medications used for pain. The World Health Organization (WHO, 1990) devised a three-step analgesic ladder outlining the use of nonopiate analgesics, opiate analgesics, and adjuvant medications for progressively severe pain. According to this schema, a nonopioid analgesic, with or without an adjuvant agent, should be tried first. If pain persists or increases on this regimen, the patient should be switched to a weak opiate plus a nonopioid agent, with or without an adjuvant medication. If pain continues or intensifies despite this change in therapy, a strong opiate analgesic is usually prescribed, with or without a nonopioid and/or an adjuvant agent. The use of opiates is usually reserved for patients with moderate or severe pain. Unlike the nonsteroidal anti-inflammatory agents and other adjunctive therapies, the pure opiates do not have a maximum dose, so the patient can potentially receive an effective regimen without excessive toxicities (Jacox et al., 1994).

There are several medications available that can be administered orally once or twice daily, or a transdermal patch can be applied every 3 days. Morphine and oxycodone are available as long-acting opiates. Morphine products are available, MS Contin and Oramorph SR, which are normally administered twice daily, and Kadian, which can be given once daily. Oxycodone is available as OxyContin, which can be administered orally twice daily. Fentanyl is available as a transdermal preparation known as Duragesic. This patch can be applied to the skin and changed every 72 hours. In addition to the long-acting products, the patient will need additional medications for breakthrough pain.

## HYPNOTHERAPY FOR PAIN MANAGEMENT

It is recognized that nonpharmacologic pain relief methods should be integrated within treatment programs (Jacox, Carr, et al., 1994). This is consistent with the consensus statement from the National Cancer Institute Workshop on cancer pain that "Under treatment of pain and other symptoms of cancer is a serious and neglected public health problem" and that " . . . every patient with cancer should have the expectation of pain control as an integral aspect of his/her care throughout the course of the disease" (National Cancer Institute, 1990).

Hypnotic relaxation is a frequently cited form of nonpharmaco-logic cognitive pain control. Hypnotic relaxation may be defined as a deeply relaxed state involving mental imagery (Woody, Bowers, Oakman, 1992; Elkins, 1997; Hammond & Elkins, 1994).

In the use of hypnotic relaxation for pain management, the focus is on instructing the patient in relaxation and mental imagery. The patient learns a cognitive method of pain management that is utilized at the discretion of the patient and within the patient's own control. The successful effect is to introduce a nonpharmacologic method of pain control that may decrease unnecessary dependency on anal-gesics for pain. Hypnotic relaxation is a safe method, which, when properly used, has no harmful side effects. The patient, with the support of the physician, utilizes it so that there is a partnership between doctor and patient in the patient's care.

The use of instruction in hypnotic relaxation for pain relief has been demonstrated in a number of studies (Hilgard & LeBaron, 1982; Stern, Brown, Ulett, & Sletten, 1977). For example, instruction in hypnotic relaxation is of benefit for pain control in patients with burns (Patterson, Questad, & Boltwood, 1987). Also, the amount of pain reduction in experimental settings produced by psychological interventions is correlated with measures of hypnotizability whether or not hypnotic induction is completed (Spanos, Kennedy, & Gwynn, 1984; Spinhoven, 1988; Tenenbaum, Kurtz, & Bienias, 1990).

Spiegel and Bloom (1983) demonstrated a combined treatment of group psychotherapy and hypnosis with women with metastatic breast cancer. Participants in the treatment group were involved in support groups that included hypnotic relaxation exercises as one component. Those who received the support group and hypnotic relaxation exercises demonstrated significantly better ability to control pain compared with the cancer patients who received group support without hypnosis or who were in the control group. At their one-year follow-up, the women who received treatment reported half the amount of pain compared with those in the control group.

Also, Syrjala, Donaldson, Davis, Krippes, and Carr (1995) conducted a randomized clinical trial comparing oral mucositis pain levels in four groups of cancer patients receiving bone marrow transplants. These included: (a) traditional treatment control, (b) therapist support, (c) hypnotic relaxation training, and (d) a training package of cognitive-behavioral coping skills, which included hypnotic relaxation. Treatment groups received two training sessions prior to treatment and twice weekly "booster" sessions for 5 weeks. Results indicated that patients who received hypnotic relaxation or in combination with a package of cognitive-behavioral coping skills demonstrated less pain in comparison to the two other groups.

Hypnotic relaxation has been found to be of significant benefit in reducing anxiety (Elkins, 1986; Wadden & Anderton, 1982). Furthermore, patients who develop anxiety disorders may be more hypnotizable than others (Frankel, 1974). Cancer patients frequently experience anxiety due to anticipation of the illness or anticipation of entering the final stages of life.

Cancer patients also frequently experience anxiety due to anticipation of potential treatments leading to significant side effects such as nausea and vomiting (Roberts, Piper, Denny & Cuddeback, 1997). Hypnotic relaxation in the treatment of cancer patients involves the use of relaxation and mental imagery to induce relaxation, reduce anxiety and distress, and help patients detach themselves from obsessional thoughts (Araoz, 1983). Several studies have suggested that hypnotic relaxation is of benefit to cancer patients for managing anxiety. For example, Kraft (1990) completed a preliminary study of the possible value of hypnotic relaxation in the management of 12 terminally ill patients with cancer. The case illustrations suggested a reduction in anxiety and depression. Our experience has indicated that hypnotherapy is well accepted by cancer patients and is a powerful adjunct to the standard oncology care.

## ASSESSMENT CONSIDERATIONS AND TECHNIQUES WITH CANCER PATIENTS

Working with cancer survivors requires the clinician to see the patient and their symptoms on multiple levels. The National Comprehensive Cancer Network (NCCN) screening assessment tool (Holland, 1999) can provide the clinician a valuable resource for conceptualizing the patient's issues on a variety of levels. To conceptualize the patient, their disease, distress and pain, the clinician must see the patient in their totality. A cognitive behavioral assessment lends itself to the development of specific hypnotic interventions that can address the entirety of the patient.

Anxiety may be assumed to be present whenever the patient presents for therapy with the diagnosis of a possibly life-threatening disease. On occasion, overt symptoms of anxiety may not be evident. Further probing may reveal a more typical constellation of symptoms of chronic anxiety such as sweating, sleeplessness, muscle tension, rapid heart beat, and so on. These symptoms are all very amenable to hypnotic intervention. Constant repeated exposure of the body to these anxiety symptoms will produce a stress reaction within the patient that can further debilitate their physical condition, frequently manifesting itself in greater fatigue. This, in turn, further aggravates the anxiety, leading to more stress. This self-perpetuating cycle feeds on itself.

The functional assessment integrates the bio-psycho-social factors in case formulations. The functional analysis can be defined as an "assessment-derived integration of all of the important functional relationships among variables" using a problem-solving model. What are the functional variables that interact to create distress in the patient? A "functional relationship" basically addresses the question of which variable results in (e.g., functions) to initiate the onset or maintain the problem or pain and distress. The most simplistic view of a functional relationship is to ask "How does the patient maintain the problem? And "What is the 'function' of the response to the pain or distress?" Once this function can be perceived, a healthier method of coping and responding may be offered. Examples of this can be what is the relationship between the patient's self-perception and the result of a surgery or treatment? What do they believe will happen? How will this benefit, or change them? Do they have previous experiences with someone that has had similar treatments and expressed a great deal of suffering or perhaps even death? How does their response recreate or perpetuate that pattern or response?

In planning hypnotherapy, the focus is on symptoms and problems. It is critical that the patient has a realistic understanding of what the pain actually "means" in the disease process. Are there underlying beliefs/schemas that guide cognitive processing? The assessment must define and measure core problems in concrete, behavioral terms. This can be best standardized by the use of a 0–10 visual analog scale. This scale is used to assess the patient's pain pre and posthypnosis intervention; weekly average of, and worst pain experienced during the week. These items are rated on a 10 cm numeric pain intensity scale, the answers ranging from zero (0) "no pain at all" to ten (10) "as much pain as I could stand." Previous research has validated the use of this scale as an accurate representation of a patient's perception of pain (Houde, 1982; Syrjala & Chapman, 1984; Montgomery & Kirsch, 1997). Having multiple points of assessment allows the patient and clinician to draw concrete definitive correlations between the use of hypnosis, and the level of pain and distress. This is also extremely useful in defining the benefits of frequency in the use of self-hypnosis. On a cognitive level the use of the 0-10 visual analog scale is beneficial in encouraging the patient to see the self-efficacy of the intervention. Having the patient define the problem can often lead to the descriptor of the solution. The problem statement should be simple, descriptive, comprehensive, and behavioral. It may even be what the client might not consider a problem. When developing information about the problem, a brief description of it, followed by associated cognitions, emotions, and behaviors is appropriate. However, it may be more critical to find the exceptions to the problem such as discovering when and where the pain and distress do not happen.

It is also recommended that an assessment of hypnotizability be included in the cognitive behavioral assessment for use of hypnotherapy in the management of pain and distress in cancer patients. This will provide the clinician and patient a road map for the directions of the intervention. It has been recognized that individuals vary in their ability to respond to hypnotherapy for pain control (Bates, 1993). It has been suggested that highly hypnotizable individuals are likely to be able to benefit from hypnotherapy (Hilgard & Hilgard, 1975; Patterson & Ptacek, 1997). This fact makes the measurement of hypnotizability an important factor in clinical work and experiments that utilize hypnosis for pain and distress. In order to measure hypnotizability, it is necessary to complete a hypnotic induction and then determine the individual's response to specific hypnotic suggestions of increasing difficulty. There are a number of scales that have been developed for this purpose such as the Hypnotic Induction Profile (Spiegel & Spiegel, 1978) and the Stanford Clinical Scale of Hypnotic Susceptibility (Morgan & Hilgard, 1978–1979). However, in clinical work the assessment of hypnotizability may be estimated by the patient's response to suggestions for hypnotic phenomena such as relaxation, involuntary response to suggestions, dissociation, and imagery.

Also specific arenas or domains of hypnotic phenomenon may be identified so that these talents can be used as therapeutic tools to achieve the desired results. Examples of these domains include the ability to change somatasenory information, the ability to have a nonvolitional or automatic response to hypnotic suggestions, the ability to dissociate to a different time, place or situation and the ability to use amnesic talents. Amnesic talents can be the ability to respond to a posthypnotic suggestion for amnesia. Anticipation of pain or distress surrounding a treatment or procedure can lead to considerable anxiety. It may be helpful for patients to have less intense awareness/immediate memory of pain or distress experienced in the past. Suggestions can include "remembering to forget and forgetting to remember." These are just some of the "tools" or hypnotic talents that the patient may have at their disposal that a clinician must be aware of to fully maximize the patients healing ability.

# THE "CRISIS MATRIX" MODEL
# OF HYPNOTHERAPY INTERVENTION

There is a need for a broad and inclusive model of integration of mind-body interventions for cancer care. This is supported by the observation that symptoms relating to psychological distress and existential concerns are even more prevalent than pain and other physical symptoms, especially among those with life-limiting conditions. Therefore, the purpose of the hypnotic model presented here is to help improve the patient's total psychological, social, and spiritual well-being. This model of interventions is offered to assist the clinician in developing and implementing appropriate hypnotherapeutic treatment for patients with cancer. The focus of the hypnotherapy is to ameliorate the effects of pain and distress in an effort to restore a level of psychological and physical well-being. Within the context of this model of therapy for patients with cancer, the goals of the hypnotic intervention are to provide relief from emotional and physical distress. Other areas of focus include assisting the patient with the psychological adjustment to their disease status and treatment process.

Studies show that patients with life-threatening illnesses and their families will experience multiple symptoms and have ongoing needs for psychological, social, spiritual, and practical support throughout their illness. One of the primary issues of palliative care for patients with advanced cancer is symptom control and maintaining a quality of life (Breitbart, Jaramillo, & Chochinov, 1998). As with pain, dyspnea impacts the psychological, physical, and emotional well-being of individuals. Dyspnea is defined as shortness of breath or difficulty in breathing. Hypnotic relaxation is used to alleviate the disease processes of pain and dyspnea. As patients learn to control their pain and dyspnea, their level of distress and anxiety may diminish and their quality of life improve. Langendijk et al. (2000) reported a significant association between improvement of dyspnea and changes in global quality of life measures in patients with inoperable non-small cell lung cancer. The following model combines naturalistic solution-oriented hypnosis within the framework of a situational crisis matrix. Hypnotic interventions are tailored to each stage in the crisis matrix.

Oncologists and palliative pain care specialists are skilled in the management of physical symptoms. However, the management of complex psychological, psychiatric, and psychosocial issues facing patients with terminal illnesses is frequently beyond the clinical expertise of most medically oriented clinicians. The assessment and treatment of the sequela of terminal illness and the application of health and behavioral intervention procedures require a professional skilled not only in the preservation of physical health but also in the maintenance of mental and spiritual health. In this context, health behavioral intervention procedures are used to modify the psychological, behavioral, and emotional factors identified as important to or directly affecting the patient's health.

This model of hypnotic intervention for cancer care is offered so that the clinician, through the use of hypnosis, can help meet the needs of the patient and their family on many levels. Hypnosis is offered to patients in conjunction with traditional cancer care. Issues of overall quality of life; pain management; and family well-being and functioning are regularly evaluated.

This model of hypnotic intervention to be used with cancer patients may be conceptualized as a "crisis matrix." Here crisis is defined as a response to hazardous events and is experienced as a painful state (Kaplan & Sadock, 1991). A crisis state tends to mobilize powerful reactions to help the person alleviate their discomfort and return to a state of emotional equilibrium (Aguilera, 1998) similar to what existed prior to the advent of the crisis. However, if the individual is unable to resolve the crisis and uses maladaptive reactions, the painful state will intensify, the crises deepen, and the condition exacerbates itself. Emotional distress, depression, and anxiety are all significantly associated with pain and may be a primary or secondary focus of treatment.

The hypnotic intervention develops naturalistically and developmentally from the first stage of the crisis matrix. From the pronouncement of the fact that the disease is in evidence and the advent of curative measures until the patient's final breath, this model uses the patient's own talents, abilities, and history to ease their suffering and improve their quality of life.

## Stages of the Crisis Matrix Model

The crisis matrix model follows four stages as described below.

### Stage 1 The Initial Crisis

The initial crisis stage is generally preceded with the confirmation of the patient's disease. This phase is typically characterized by the patient's shock and denial, and a disruptive impact on their supportive relationships as well as the patient's disorientation.

Hypnotic interventions are aimed at helping the patient reframe their diagnosis as an opportunity to enjoy and appreciate the quality and quantity of life that is still available to them. A review of the efficacy of the intervention is done at each session to allow for refinement of the imagery. Cognitive reframing is used to allow the patient to process images of change that are developed in the hypnotic context. Frequently the issue of pain is the precipitating event that leads a patient to seek assistance from a health care professional. Intensive training in the use of hypnosis begins at this time. The patient is exposed to a variety of hypnotic phenomena that may be useful, such as time distortion, dissociative phenomena, and other self-soothing hypnotic strategies. Intensive training in self-hypnosis is initiated at this stage.

## Stage 2 Transition

The transitional stage occurs after the denial of the initial stage has dissipated. Strong emotional reactions are common. These behaviors are similar to traditional grief and loss reactions. Of particular concern during this phase is the meaning that the patient may ascribe to their pain. Attempts to deal with pain from a pharmacological standpoint can be injurious in that they may convey to the patient a feeling of helplessness as the oncology team attempts to find the best pharmacological intervention. The patient's feelings of desperation, isolation, and hopelessness can come to the fore as their denial of the initial stage fades.

Treatment goals for this phase aim to maximize the patient's psychosocial function through hypnotic support of adaptation and exploration of feelings. There are significant behavioral goals to be met as well. Some of these goals include stress reduction and an active investment in a personal wellness regime.

Hypnotic interventions at this stage frequently involve helping the patient create a metaphorical journey. A metaphor that is often helpful to a terminally ill patient is, for example, the transformation of a chrysalis into a butterfly.

## Stage 3 Acceptance

Patients are not as likely to initially present for therapy in the crisis matrix at this juncture. Acceptance of one's health status is not a one-time event but a process. For patients who do achieve a measure of acceptance, the focus of the intervention shifts to "living" and maintaining gains in the face of repeated challenges on all fronts: physical, psychological, and spiritual. This is done with the awareness that there will be further physical setbacks. As the disease process continues, it is probable that the pain will become more and more an integral part of their lives. The pain and distress may be seen as taking on a life or identity of their own. The approach of this phase is to implement a philosophy of supported empowerment, allowing the patient to direct the treatment process to the management of the pain and attendant symptoms secondary to the treatment process. They are encouraged to find the way, through the implementation of a hypnotic intervention, to best meet the needs of their pain and distress management.

Hypnotic interventions focus on the use of self-hypnosis for the management of and possible enhancement of the body's immune functioning. Constant reiteration of the nurturing effects of stress reduction are provided in the hypnotic context and if at all possible, a notation of the generalizing effect in other areas of the patients' life can assist them to see that hypnosis is an effective tool with a wide range of uses, i.e., cognitively, behaviorally and psychologically. This is encouraged through the process of inviting the patient to hypnotically listen and respond to the body's wisdom and become cognizant of the other changes that may be occurring in various parts of their lives. Once again, the use of visual analog scaling is a very powerful tool to bring about an awareness of the change the patient is undergoing that may otherwise go unnoticed and unappreciated. Another hypnotic focus of the interventions may include the use of hypermenisa to a time and place prior to the advent of the pain and distress—preferably before the diagnosis of the cancer.

## Stage 4 Preparation for Death

In this stage of the crisis matrix, the focus of the intervention completely changes. In the previous three stages, the emphasis has been on the patient's appreciation of living. The prospect of death has always been in evidence, but at this stage it comes to the forefront of the therapeutic intervention.

Visualization and hypnosis can assist the patient through their death and dying process. Pain management becomes a primary issue. Hypnotically assisted dissociation from the pain is a crucial element. Inviting the patient to hypnotically project him/herself to the future and to visualize family members coping satisfactorily with their demise can help the patient to feel more at ease with their pending death, consequently reducing their stress and vulnerability to hastening the disease process.

In this stage of the crisis matrix, the clinician should be fully cognizant of the various cognitive and emotional states already in evidence and utilize them to achieve a positive therapeutic aim. This is different from traditional methods of therapy in which what the patient presents with (fear, anger, confusion) is being altered to fit the therapist's model of what they believe should be occurring.

## USING HYPNOTHERAPY
## FOR PALLIATIVE CANCER CARE

Helping to provide palliative care for patients with cancer is a daunting task for any clinician. The case reported below demonstrates the theoretical basis and practical implementation of hypnosis and cognitive behavioral interventions as a primary modality in the care of an end-stage cancer patient. The integration of data collected from the assessment of clinical hypnotizability is cited as a primary component in the development of a treatment strategy. Patients at highest risk for depression are those with advanced stages of cancer and (Massie & Holland, 1990) poorly controlled pain. In order to treat the patient from a holistic perspective, the inclusion of the family as an integral portion of treatment is also discussed.

The following case demonstrates the use of the crisis matrix model of hypnotherapy with palliative care cancer patients and demonstrates the implementation of a brief measure of clinical hypnotizability. Although no formal scale was attempted with this patient, a brief measure of hypnotizability was utilized. Items or domains of hypnotic phenomenon demonstrated to be useful in the development of a viable hypnotherapeutic treatment plan were identified, assessed, and incorporated into the hypnotherapeutic treatment plan. These domains included the patient's ability to achieve a state of dissociation, experience a nonvolitional or involuntary response to hypnotic suggestions, and change a somatasensory appreciation of a physical state.

# The Case of Mrs. D

Mrs. D was a 69-year-old woman with a refractory ovarian carcinoma. She had also been diagnosed with deep vein thrombosis. She had been experiencing difficulty with Coumadin due to her ongoing chemotherapy. Approximately 1 year prior to her referral to a therapist, her primary physician took the opportunity to address end-of-life issues with her. At that time she was having a difficult time tolerating what was fifth-line chemotherapy. When she came in for therapy, she acknowledged the possibility that she had fewer than 6 months to live and appeared to be leaning toward stopping all therapy. Mrs. D and her PCP had also discussed the benefits of hospice at that time.

Mrs. D was initially uncertain about the use of hypnosis for management of her pain for her ovarian cancer. I described hypnosis to Mrs. D as a state of focused attention with relaxation during which suggestions for being pain free could be instituted. I then assessed Mrs. D for hypnotizability with an abbreviated scale of hypnotizability due to her compromised physical status. She was in the middle range of hypnotizability, endorsing four of six possible items. She was positive for arm heaviness and a very high positive for dissociation and imaginary involvement. She was negative on the amnesia item.

The dissociation item involves suggestions for the patient to imagine, for example, being in a garden and experiencing many wonderful phenomena and sensations. Mrs. D noted that she felt that she was actually in a rose garden rather than just visualizing it, and was able to describe the surroundings with exquisite detail, finding herself very lost in it. She described in great detail a stream and a fountain in the garden.

Her subjective level of pain and distress was endorsed at a level of 6 pre-session on the 0–10 visual analog scale. At a posthypnotic intervention or susceptibility level, it was reassessed on the same scale at a level of 3. She did note that before cogitating on her level of pain, that she had "totally forgotten the pain" for a brief time and that it was essentially nonexistent for a while. We explored this in great detail. She noted that this was the first time she had essentially been pain free in her recent memory. I incorporated these images and verbalizations into future hypnotic interventions. She recounted that she did feel more comfortable after the hypnosis session as verified by a pre and postsession evaluation with the 0–10 visual analog scale.

Future sessions with Mrs. D followed a predictable pattern of a hypnotic relaxation induction followed by deepening and dissociation, with the patient using a visualization of going into the garden and traveling down a path. She achieved comfort in her visualization of a garden, of being able to appreciate the sight, smells, and sounds. This imagery was incorporated into future interventions with some success.

I offered additional interventions to Mrs. D, generally using her preference to dissociate. This generally consisted of her finding a fountain in the garden, putting her hand in the fountain, developing numbness and tingling, and finding an anesthetized glove and placing it on her abdomen, the site of her ovarian cancer. She felt that this was a significant improvement in the intervention, finding that she had no pain left after the "glove" intervention. Her ability to dissociate was determined by the hypnotizability scale. Mrs. D was also very comfortable using the glove intervention. She used placed it either physically on her body or visualized it on the parts of her body parts that were most prone to discomfort because of her ovarian cancer.

Mrs. D was developing skills with hypnosis and utilizing hypnotic interventions effectively for management of her pain. She seemed delighted with the interventions, showing some degree of ability to utilize them to manage her pain and discomfort. She later informed me by telephone that she had gotten home from our session and slept once again for 6 solid hours, and that she had experienced a great deal of rest and comfort from this. "I've been in incredible amounts of pain. I used self-hypnosis yesterday and was able to sleep for an hour." She was quite distressed about recurrent insomnia and was able to implement self-hypnosis to both decrease her pain and distress and subsequently to increase her ability to sleep.

As her condition progressed, Mrs. D began to experience distress due to nausea as well as pain. To intervene, I provided a hypnotic intervention with a traditional relaxation, followed immediately by deepening and dissociation. The general metaphor was altered, focusing more on somatic issues of dissociation, e.g., Mrs. D leaving her body in the chair and developing great comfort, as well as "blanketing her body in warm layers of comfort." I changed the metaphor somewhat so that it included more dissociative aspects, e.g., being able to leave her body in the chair and being able to appreciate her "garden of comfort." Several images regarding the slowing of the motility of the stream going through her garden were offered as a metaphor for her alimentary process. This was an effort to help her to allow her body to relax and the muscles in her stomach to slow down their motility. Other images of the slow-moving stream in her garden were incorporated into the intervention. What follows are the hypnotic suggestions I used to help Mrs. D alleviate her pain and distress.

## Mental Imagery for Comfort

"Now in a moment I am going to ask you to notice some images in your mind . . . you can hear my voice with one part of your mind and with another part of your mind going to a pleasant, peaceful garden of comfort where you notice and experience everything there, every sound, every sight, every sensation of comfort . . . each and every image and scene bringing you more and more comfort . . . more comfort and control. . . . Now allow yourself a special door that will lead you to experience more comfort. . . . Going into the garden where you find the comfort that you need . . . and here finding comfort. Now walking to that door and perhaps going through the door to a place where it is so comfortable, quiet and calm. . . . "

## Deepening and Dissociation

"As you enter an even deeper level of hypnosis, you may notice a floating sensation, less aware of your body, just floating in space. Leaving your body here as you sit in your garden, enjoying the cool comfortable stream that flows normally and naturally through the garden, cooling and comforting. . . . Your body floating in a feeling of comfort and your mind, just so aware of being in that pleasant garden. As your body floats, find even more comfort. Your mind blocks from conscious awareness any excessive discomfort, and it is possible that you can feel more and more relaxed."

## Posthypnotic Suggestions

" . . . and as you become more comfortable and more in control you will find that, more and more, you are able to sleep very well and fully, your feeling of well-being will improve, and your quality of life will improve. You will not be bothered by any excessive anxiety, and any distress will become less frequent and less severe. *Farther and farther away . . . just not that important, smaller and smaller . . . so much so . . . that it just won't seem that important. . . . "*

The actual process of the beginning of Mrs. D's grieving as well as the process of saying "good-bye" was initiated. It was reframed with the family members that saying "good-bye" did not mean giving up hope; saying "good-bye" was framed as a way of saying thanks and expressing love. Mrs. D and her family made great inroads in conquering denial and accepting the reality of her disease as well as initiating the process of grieving.

At our final meeting, Mrs. D complained of acute pain. I immediately performed a hypnotic intervention focusing on feelings of great comfort. This was a rapid induction, followed immediately by deepening and disassociation. We utilized her previous images of a garden with the images of nature providing her relief and comfort. Her breathing was noted to be deepening during the intervention, as well as her facial muscles to be relaxing and flattening with an overall decrease in her level of distress. The intervention followed immediately with more disassociation and with suggestions for comfort, as well as for utilizing the metaphor of nature to symbolize the cycle of life. She was having some pain, but managed it with self-hypnosis and opiates. The family and attending physician later reported that Mrs. D died peacefully at home in the company of her family as she had hoped.

## CONCLUSION

Hypnotherapy for management of pain and distress in cancer patients is a daunting but exciting prospect. The patient can utilize cognitive and behavioral strategies that originate in the hypnotic context to decrease their pain and distress in a conscious waking state. As the patient becomes more and more cognizant of the cognitive and behavioral changes that occur in the conscious waking state, they may become more and more amenable to integrating hypnotherapeutic techniques into their daily treatment regimen. We have found a "crisis matrix" model to be useful in planning and implementing hypnotherapeutic interventions in the context of cancer care, using the four stages of initial crisis, transition, acceptance, and preparation for death. The case of Mrs. D has illustrated the value of using hypnotherapy for the management of pain and distress that accompany advanced cases of cancer.

## REFERENCES

Aguilera, A. C. (1998). *Crisis intervention theory and methodology* (8th ed.). St. Louis, MO: Mosby.

Araoz, D. L. (1983). Use of hypnotic techniques with oncology patients. *Journal of Psychosocial Oncology, 1*(4), 47–54.

Bates, B. L. (1993). Individual differences in response to hypnosis. In J. W. Rhue, S. J. Lynn, & I. Kirsch (Eds.), *Handbook of clinical hypnosis* (pp. 23–54). Washington, DC: American Psychological Association.

Bonica, J. J. (1990). Cancer pain. In J. J. Bonica (Ed.), *The management of pain* (2nd ed., Vol. 1, pp. 400–460). Philadelphia: Lea & Febiger.

Breitbart, W., Jaramillo, J. R., & Chochinov, H. M. (1998). Palliative and terminal care. In J. C. Holland (Ed.), *Psycho-oncology* (pp. 437–449). New York: Oxford University Press.

Elkins, G. R. (1986). Hypnotic treatment of anxiety. In W. C. Wester (Ed.), *Clinical hypnosis: A case management approach* (pp.142–157). Cincinnati, OH: C. J. Krebbiel.

Elkins, G. R. (1997). *My doctor does hypnosis.* Chicago: ASCH Press.

Frankel, F. H. (1974). Trance capacity and the genesis of phobic behavior. *Archives of General Psychiatry, 31,* 261–263.

Hammond, D. C., & Elkins, G. R. (1994). *Standards of training in clinical hypnosis.* Chicago: ASCH Press

Hilgard, J. R., & LeBaron, S. (1982). Relief of anxiety and pain in children and adolescents with cancer: Quantitative measures and clinical observations. *International Journal of Clinical and Experimental Hypnosis, 30,* 417–442.

Hilgard, E. R., & Hilgard, J. R. (1975). *Hypnosis in the relief of pain.* Los Altos, CA: William Kaufmann.

Holland, J. (1999). NCCN practice guidelines for the management of psychosocial distress. National Comprehensive Cancer Network. *Oncology, 13*(5a), 113–147.

Houde, R. W. (1982). Methods for measuring clinical pain in humans. *Acta Anaesthesiol Scand., 74* (Suppl.), 25–29.

Jacox, A., Carr, D. B., Payne, R., et al. (1994). *Management of cancer pain: Clinical practice guideline, No. 9* (AHCPR Publication 94–0592). Rockville, MD: U.S. Public Health Service, Agency for Health Care Policy and Research.

Kaplan, H. I., & Sadock, B. J. (1991). *Synopsis of psychiatry: Behavioral science clinical psychiatry* (6th ed.). Baltimore: Williams & Wilkins.

Kraft, T. (1990). Use of hypnotherapy in anxiety management in the terminally ill: A preliminary study. *British Journal of Experimental and Clinical Hypnosis, 7*(1), 27–33.

Langendijk, J. A., Aaronson, N. K., ten Velde, G. P., de Jong, J. M., Muller, M. J., & Wouters, E. F. (2000). Pretreatment quality of life of inoperable non-small cell lung cancer patients referred for primary radiotherapy. *Acta Oncology, 39*(8), 949–958.

Massie, M. J., & Holland, J. C. (1990). Depression and the cancer patient. *Journal of Clinical Psychiatry, 51*(Suppl.), 12–17, discussion 18–19.

Montour, C. M., & Chapman, C. R. (1991). Pain management and quality of life in cancer patients. In R. K. A. Lehmann & D. Zech (Eds.), *Transdermal fentanyl: A new approach to prolonged pain control* (pp. 42–63). Berlin: Springer-Verlag.

Montgomery, G. H., & Kirsch, I. (1997). Classical conditioning and the placebo effect. *Pain, 72*, 107–113.

Morgan, A. H., & Hilgard, J. R. (1978–1979). The Stanford Hypnotic Clinical Scale for Adults. *American Journal of Clinical Hypnosis, 21*, 134–147.

National Cancer Institute. (1990). *NCI workshop on cancer pain.* September 14–15, 1990, Bethesda, Maryland.

Patterson, D. R., & Ptacek, J. T. (1997). Baseline pain as a moderator of hypnotic analgesia for burn injury treatment. *Journal of Consulting and Clinical Psychology, 65*, 60–67.

Patterson, D. R., Questad, K. A., & Boltwood, M. D. (1987). Hypnotherapy as a treatment for pain in patients with burns: Research and clinical considerations. *Journal of Burn Care and Rehabilitation, 8*, 263–268.

Roberts, C. S., Piper, L., Denny, J., & Cuddeback, G. (1997). A support group intervention to facilitate young adults' adjustment to cancer. *Health and Social Work, 22*(2), 133–41.

Roth, A. J., Kornblith, A., & Batel-Copel, L. (1998). Rapid screening for psychologic distress in men with prostrate carcinoma: A pilot study. *Cancer, 82*, 1904–1908.

Spanos, N. P., Kennedy, S. K., & Gwynn, M. I. (1984). Moderating effects of contextual variables on the relationship between hypnotic susceptibility and suggested analgesia. *Journal of Abnormal Psychology, 93*, 285–294.

Spiegel, D., & Bloom, J. R. (1983). Group therapy and hypnosis reduce metastatic breast carcinoma pain. *Psychosomatic Medicine, 45*(4), 333–339.

Speigel, H., & Spiegel, D. (1978). *Trance and treatment: Clinical uses of hypnosis.* New York: Basic Books.

Spinhoven, P. (1988). Similarities and dissimilarities in hypnotic and nonhypnotic procedures for headache control: A review. *American Journal of Clinical Hypnosis, 30*, 183–194.

Stern, J. A., Brown, M., Ulett, G. A., & Sletten, I. (1977). A comparison of hypnosis, acupuncture, morphine, valium, aspirin, and placebo in the management of experimentally induced pain. *Annals of the New York Academy of Sciences, 296*, 175–193.

Syrjala, K. A., Donaldson, G. W., Davis, M. W., Kippes, M. E., & Carr, J. E. (1995). Relaxation and imagery and cognitive-behavioral training reduce pain during cancer treatment: A controlled clinical trial. *Pain, 63*(2), 189–98.

Syrjala, K. A., & Chapman, C. R. (1984). Measurement of clinical pain: A review and integration of research findings. *Advances in Pain Research, 7*, 71–101.

Tenenbaum, S. J., Kurtz, R. M., & Bienias, J. L. (1990). Hypnotic susceptibility and experimental pain reduction. *American Journal of Clinical Hypnosis, 33*, 40–49.

Wadden, T. A., & Anderton, C. H. (1982). The clinical use of hypnosis. *Psychological Bulletin, 91*, 215–243.

Woody, E. Z., Bowers, K. S., & Oakman, J. M. (1992). A conceptual analysis of hypnotic responsiveness: Experience individual differences and context. In E. Fromm & M. R. Nash (Eds.), *Contemporary hypnosis research*. New York: Guilford.

World Health Organization. (1990). *Cancer pain relief*. Geneva, Switzerland: WHO.

Zabora, J., Brintzendhof, S. K., Curbow, B., Hooker, C., & Piantadosi, S. (2001). The prevalence of psychological distress by cancer site. *Psycho-Oncology, 10*, 19–28.

Chapter 11

# Treating Sleep Disorders Using Cognitive Behavior Therapy and Hypnosis

Gina Graci and Kathy Sexton-Radek

O sleep, O gentle sleep
Nature's soft nurse, how have I frightened thee,
That thou no more wilt weight my eyelids down
And sleep my senses, in forgetfulness?
(William Shakespeare, King Henry IV, 3.1)

Sleep is a phenomenon common to all human beings, who spend one-third of their lives asleep. Sleep has been defined as an altered state of consciousness with reduced responsiveness to external stimuli (Fordam, 1988; Hodgson 1991). The true purpose of sleep remains unknown, but hypotheses abound (Benington, 2000). Sleep has been postulated to facilitate learning and memory consolidation (Sejnowski & Destexhe, 2000; Blissitt, 2001), maintenance of synaptic efficacy (Krueger & Obal, 1993), immunologic restoration (Born, Lange, Hansen, Molle, & Fehm, 1997), and overall homeostasis (Benington, 2000). Yet recent reviews have found inconclusive results for these claims (Maquet, 2001; Siegel, 2001). Nevertheless, it appears that sleep serves an important restorative function and is composed of many complex behavioral and physiological processes.

The sleep-wake cycle is controlled through a complex regulatory process that involves a 24-hour pattern of biological functions, including sleep, cortisol levels, reproductive hormones, thermoregulation, and melatonin and growth hormone production which collectively play an important role in the regulation of sleep-wake cycles and their disorders. Traditionally control of the sleep-wake cycle was thought to rest primarily within the suprachiasmic nucleus (SCN), a brain structure that is located near the hypothalamus. If any part of this mechanism is disturbed, sleep disorders typically result.

Many individuals erroneously believe that patients are sleeping when in a hypnotic trance. Sleep and hypnosis are distinctly different from each other, even though they may appear similar. A hypnotic trance can be viewed as a more highly suggestible state of relaxation and a trance doesn't necessarily lead to sleep, whereas in sleep there is a perceptional disengagement and unresponsiveness to the environment (Kryger, Roth, & Dement, 2001). Electrical recordings of brain waves called electroencephalographic (EEG) studies show that hypnosis is characterized by waking EEG patterns and not those of sleep (Evans, 1999). Hypnosis promotes relaxation facilitating sleep in anxious or tense individuals.

To date, there is a paucity of empirical research pertaining to the use of combining CBT and hypnosis to treat sleep disturbance. However, there is a plethora of research suggesting that CBT and hypnosis is therapeutic for a variety of psychological, behavioral, and medical disorders. While relaxation therapies and self-hypnotic strategies have been investigated in the treatment of sleep disorders as single treatment modalities, more emphasis must be placed on establishing the efficacy of combined CBT and hypnotic treatment. This gap in the literature is primarily due to clinicians who are trained in hypnotherapy who generally do not have the appropriate training to treat sleep disorders and vice versa.

The goal of this chapter is to educate clinicians regarding how to incorporate the use of cognitive behavior treatment (CBT) with hypnosis in the treatment of sleep disorders. A summary of the basic science of sleep medicine as applied to CBT is provided. This summary includes an explanation of the sleep-wake cycle, sleep stages, review of the most common categories of sleep disorders, and a discussion of the general and specific cognitive behavioral approaches to insomnia treatment and case examples of treating sleep disturbance using CBT with hypnosis methodology.

Behavioral sleep medicine is a subspecialty of behavioral medicine. The cognitive-behavioral approach to case formulation, assessment, treatment, and research design is a central unifying factor of the field. With hypnotic medications being so frequently prescribed and increasing incidence of sleep disturbances reported, the field has burgeoned. Health professionals quickly prescribe hypnotic agents for sleep; however, the majority of sleep complaints can be alleviated with behavioral techniques. The key element to behavioral approaches for treatment of sleep disorders is that an experienced sleep disorder clinician conducts a sleep disorder evaluation. Results of the evaluation will determine what treatment(s) will be provided. The most common treatment generally includes education and behavioral modification. The key element in providing treatment for sleep disorders using this combined therapeutic approach is that the clinician must have experience or knowledge of sleep disorder treatments.

Much emphasis has been placed on the assessment and treatment of insomnia, the most common sleep disorder. However, the sleep medicine field has expanded to include additional empirically-based treatments of several sleep disorders including pediatric sleep disorders, circadian rhythm disorders, parasomnias and patients receiving continuous positive airway pressure (CPAP) (Kies & Kushidu, 2003; Stepanski, 2003; Stepanski & Perlis, 2003). Both individual and group administered cognitive-behavioral treatments have been utilized with these populations. Intervention programs have centered on areas of sleep hygiene and adjustment of sleep schedules. Future areas include the development and refinement of scripted and structured approaches to treatment efficacy, and the application to individuals across the life span (Spielman & Anderson, 1999; Reite, Ruddy, & Nagel, 2002).

## A REVIEW OF THE SLEEP STAGES

Sleep architecture refers to the various stages in the sleep-wake cycle, typically defined by an (EEG) recording. In healthy individuals without sleep problems, these stages occur in a regular pattern throughout a 24-hour period. Sleep is of two types, dream or rapid eye movement (REM) sleep that occurs every 1.5 hours throughout the sleep interval, or 18%–25% of the sleep period. REM periods vary from a number of minutes to an hour or more. REM sleep has a characteristic physiological pattern distinguished by the lateral saccadic rhythm of the eyes, absence of muscle movement (atonia), and heightened cardiovascular arousal. Studies of the REM period by self-report have revealed the changing themes from everyday events to surreal wish fantasies toward the end of the sleep period.

In contrast, non-REM (nREM) sleep occupies a greater portion of the sleep period. nREM is further subdivided into stages 1, 2, 3, and 4 with corresponding physiological activity to each. Stage 1 is considered light sleep and is estimated to be approximately 5% of the sleep period. Stage 2 sleep is about 60% of the sleep interval and is considered to be formally "sleep." Stages 3 and 4 sleep are often collapsed together and are classified as deep sleep, a physiological event characterized by slow brain wave patterns and increased immune system activity. Non-REM comprises approximately 10%–15% of the sleep period.

A night of sleep is characterized as a predicted pattern beginning with the initiation of sleep onset (Stage 1) and progression to Stages 2, 3, and 4. Within 90 minutes after sleep onset, the first REM episode (generally four to five REM episodes per night) occurs. Following this sleep period, the cycle repeats itself with at least four cycles of sleep per night. An excess or deficit in the amount of a type of sleep (e.g., no REM), a misordering of the timing of sleep (e.g., sleep begins with REM) or an intrusion from sleep represent conditions for further study to determine if a sleep disorder exists.

## SLEEP DISORDERS

Several different types of sleep disorders have been successfully treated with a combined approach of using CBT and hypnosis. A review of these sleep disorders will be provided.

### Insomnia Disorders

Insomnia is a complex, multifaceted complaint that may involve difficulties falling asleep, staying asleep, early morning awakenings (with an inability to return to sleep), and/or a complaint of nonre-freshing sleep that produces significant impairment (Savard & Morin, 2001; Edinger, Bonne, et al., 2004). The International Classification System of Sleep Disorders (ICSD Association, 1997) and the Diagnostic Statistical Manual, Version IV (DSMI-IV) (1994) are the two classification systems currently used for diagnosing insomnia.

Insomnia have been commonly classified by its duration: transient defined as less than 2 weeks; short-term lasting between 2 and 4 weeks, and chronic defined as lasting more than 4 weeks (Maczaj, 1993). Timing of the sleep disturbance is important for classifying insomnia into three types: delayed sleep onset (difficulty falling asleep), impaired sleep continuity (difficulty staying asleep), and early-morning awakening (Aldrich, 2000; Edinger, Bonnet, Bootzin, Doghramji, Dorsey, Espie, Jamieson, McCall, Morin, & Stepanski, 2004). In each of these types of insomnia complaints, the key feature is that the individual has difficulty initiating and/or returning to sleep. It is essential that clinicians differentiate between patients who are naturally short sleepers (i.e., less than 6 hours) from those whose sleep has been shortened and fragmented from psychological, medical, pharmaceutical, environmental, and/or behavioral factors. The complaint of impaired functioning assists the clinician from distinguishing short-sleepers from truly disturbed sleepers.

The description of the insomnia complaint (duration, timing, severity, etc.) may help determine its cause. The key element in any form of insomnia involves some type of increased arousal state. The two common types of insomnia disorders (not including insomnia associated with a medical disorder) are adjustment and psychophysiological sleep disorders. Adjustment sleep disorder is a condition in which an individual has experienced a significant life stressor(s), (such as death of a loved one or receiving a life threatening illness), which interferences with sleep. This type of sleep disorder is more commonly associated with a transient sleep disturbance and generally abates within 1 month. However, when this type of transient insomnia does not attenuate over time, it can progress to chronic insomnia, often accompanied by depression. In comparison, psychophysiological insomnia is a sleep disorder that results from the presence of heightened arousal in which somatized tension and learned sleep preventing associations (e.g., nervousness, anxiety, ruminative thoughts) interfere with nocturnal sleep.

The most prominent feature of insomnia remains the complaint of poor sleep, either in inadequate duration or quality, which impacts quality of life, mood, energy, and daytime functioning (Morin, 2000a). In both laboratory and natural settings, sleep deprivation following insomnia has been associated with a decline in cognitive function, inability to engage in work or recreational activities, loss of hedonic capacity, a sharp decline in quality of life, as well as alterations to immune and neuroendocrine function (Savard, Miller, Mills, O'Leary, Harding, Douglas, Mangan, Belch, & Winokur, 1999; Ehrenberg, 2000; Lamberg, 2000).

Chronic insomnia needs to be recognized and addressed by clinicians because it is a major risk factor for clinical depression (Sateia, Doghramji, Hauri, & Morin, 2000), as well as influencing other morbidities. Clinicians must take into account a detailed history of the nature, duration, severity, and course of the insomnia complaint, and investigate the contribution of psychological, medical, behavioral, and environmental factors (Morin, 2000b; Mills & Graci, 2004). There are several risk factors for insomnia that need to be addressed. Insomnia is more common among females, older individuals, and the depressed or anxious (Morin & Ware, 1996; Aldrich, 2000; Savard, Simard, Blanchet, Ivers, & Morin, 2001). Additionally, low socioeconomic status, chronic physical illness, pain syndromes, limited education, recent life stressors, certain medications, and the use of alcohol are also associated with complaints of insomnia.

Spielman and Glovinsky (1991) developed a conceptual model of insomnia (see Figure 11.1) that is prominent in assessments and treatment. Predisposing conditions such as health concerns may lower the threshold for insomnia symptoms. Precipitating factors are events that surround the onset of insomnia, while perpetuating factors account for the maintenance of the condition over time. These are represented in Figure 11.1. Accordingly, assessment approaches are directed at the identification of each arousal area. The work of Morin (1996) is a complete resource on the conceptualization, assessment, and treatment of insomnia.

A significant factor in continuing sleep problems are patients' faulty beliefs and attitudes about sleep and sleep disturbance (Savard & Morin, 2001). Many patients believe that 8 hours of continuous sleep each night is necessary to maintain daily functioning. However, there is wide variability in nightly sleep patterns. When able to sleep *ad libitum*, the normal range of sleep time among healthy individuals ranges from 6–10 hours or more (Lee, 1997). Further,

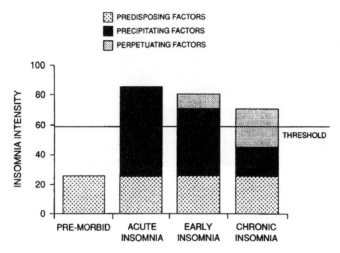

FIGURE 11.1    The natural history of insomnia.

there appears to be no evidence that occasional loss of sleep has any lasting effect. Nevertheless, sleep disturbance often elicits anxiety about continued sleep disturbance, leaving patients lying in bed worrying about whether they will get to sleep or get enough sleep in the coming night. This kind of worry and anxiety further contributes to sleep disturbances.

Once a pattern of sleep disturbance has been set, several factors serve to maintain that disturbance. Of course, the continuing use of maladaptive sleep behaviors, including an excessive amount of time in bed, napping, and an irregular sleep-wake cycle, will both maintain and possibly worsen sleep disturbances (Morin, 1993).

## Excessive Sleepiness Disorders

Hypersomnia and excessive daytime sleepiness diagnoses apply when individuals complain of a constant need for sleep. When an individual falls asleep as a manifestation of hypersomnia, it is usually in inappropriate places and circumstances. These symptoms may indicate the disorders of sleep apnea, where breathing stops during sleep, causing the individual to have light fragmented sleep at night; or narcolepsy, where the sleep pattern is completely disordered with the onset of a REM period (instead of nREM) beginning the night of sleep. In both conditions, excessive daytime sleepiness is prominent. Pathology in the sleep pattern, general medical disorders, psychiatric factors, neurological causes, medications, toxins, and neurodegenerative disorders are all possible causes of excessive sleepiness and somnolence. The clinician must rule out these causal factors of disturbed sleep before implementation of therapeutic techniques. Patients experiencing disorders of excessive daytime sleepiness that have these causal factors will not respond to psychotherapeutic techniques because their sleepiness is not attributable to psychological or behavioral factors.

## Circadian Rhythm Disorders

Circadian rhythm disorders are characterized by delayed or advanced onset of sleep. Individuals with these conditions may have experienced extremely long schedules of wakefulness and, in effect, moved through their typical sleep period. Jet lag, shift work schedules, and prolonged wakefulness secondary to medication and pain/discomfort may trigger these schedule changes. Some individuals begin a sleep period before the actual time they feel sleepy. This advancement in their sleep period often leads to frustration due to the early morning wake time (e.g., bedtime at 8 p.m. and wake time at 3 a.m.). Furthermore, others may experience a delay in their sleep period that also can lead to frustration because the onset of sleep occurs when most individuals are waking up in the early morning. Psychotherapeutic techniques may be appropriately applied when a patient is experiencing either an advancement or delay in sleep that is attributable to behavioral (and not biological) factors. Treatment approaches are focused on changing patients' sleep schedule (Chesson, Littner, Davila, Anderson, Grigg-Danberger, Hartse, Johnson, & Wise, 1999; Kunz & Hermann, 2000; Ancoli-Israel, 2003; Doghramji, 2003). For example, a college student who stays up late voluntarily and as a result goes to bed late in the morning. This voluntary behavior can shift the onset of the sleep period to late morning that can mimic a delayed sleep disorder.

## Parasomnia Sleep Disorders

Parasomnias are disorders of arousal that occur during the night. An individual may engage in abnormal movement or behaviors that interrupt the sleep cycle. Somnambulism (sleep walking), sleep terrors, nightmares, nocturnal eating, REM behavior disorder, bruxism, and rhythmic movement disorder are common parasomnias. A routine all-night polysomnogram (nocturnal sleep study) may be required before a diagnosis can be given (e.g., REM behavior disorder). Patients are treated individually with educative approaches, stress management, and in some cases, medication.

## ASSESSMENT OF SLEEP

### Patient Self-Report

Structured sleep interviews are useful in obtaining information on the nature, history, and severity of sleep disturbances (Bastien, 2001) and practitioners are strongly encouraged to utilize them. An empirically validated measure, the Pittsburgh Sleep Questionnaire, is the standard in the field (Buysse, Reynolds, Monk, Berman, & Kupfer, 1989). Stepanski (2003) also developed a basic interview questionnaire to evaluate for sleep disorders that may be easily administered by health care professionals (Stepanski, Rybarczyk, Lopez, & Stevens, 2003). The Epworth Sleepiness Scale is a commonly used questionnaire of self-reported sleepiness; it does not provide diagnostic information. The patient is asked to indicate how sleepy they feel in eight common conditions (e.g., watching television, sitting and reading, etc.).

In the absence of detailed assessment, patients should be asked about the onset, timing, quantity, and quality of their sleep (e.g., "When did you first notice difficulties sleeping?" "How have you been sleeping lately?" or "On a scale of one to ten, with one being the worst sleep you can imagine and ten being the most restful and refreshing, how would you rate your sleep on average over the past week?"), and their level of fatigue (e.g., "How tired have you been during the day?"). If either or both of these questions are answered in the affirmative, then further investigation is warranted.

Additional inquiries into sleep functioning should include investigation into the timing of patients' sleep disturbance "Do you have difficulty falling asleep, staying asleep, or both?" Patients identified with a sleep problem should be asked to monitor their sleep in the form of a sleep diary. The standard in the field is for clinicians to require patients keep at least 2 weeks of sleep logs. Weekly review of sleep logs is essential for monitoring progress. Appendix A contains an example of a sleep diary, which requires the participant to directly and quickly respond to a variety of sleep areas in a checklist fashion. Commonly, the participant records bedtime, wake-up time, number of awakenings, and the occurrence of behaviors known to affect sleep such as stress, caffeine consumption, nicotine, alcohol, and medication use. However, sleep diaries are subject to error because they are subjective ratings of sleep. It is sometimes beneficial to obtain corroborative information about sleep functioning from patients' bed-partners. Lastly, assessing the use of alcohol, caffeine, nicotine, and daytime napping are essential in determining if behavior is the primary determinant of sleep disturbance.

# THERAPEUTIC APPROACHES FOR MANAGEMENT OF SLEEP DISORDERS

## Cognitive Behavioral Treatment of Sleep Disorders

Treatment of sleep disorders using cognitive behavioral treatment involves the same principles used in cognitive therapy, except therapy is directed towards altering dysfunctional beliefs and attitudes about sleep (Lichstein & Morin, 2000). Any treatment strategy should begin with patient education. Patients need to learn how to recognize sleep problems, as well as how they and their provider team can help them. Appendix A provides an example of an 8-week script of materials for the treatment of insomnia (Espie, Inglis, Tessier, & Harvey, 2001; Morin, 1996) that may be altered to treat other sleep disorders.

The clinician is also encouraged to use a "multicomponent" approach to treatment of sleep disorders. The multicomponent approach includes three general approaches to behavioral treatment of sleep disorders: education (e.g., sleep hygiene behaviors), stimulus control, and sleep restriction therapies (Manber & Kuo, 2002). After a brief educational session, the patient initiates the behaviors at home. During subsequent clinic visits, a follow-up inquiry of the success of these behaviors is warranted, as is a discussion of specific barriers to achieving the goals of treatment. All three require that patients monitor their sleep patterns as they initiate these changes while monitoring their sleep/rest/wake times using a sleep self-monitoring form (e.g., sleep diary) or other assessment instrument.

## Behavioral Factors

### Patient Contributors to Sleep Disturbance

Patients may also contribute to the initiation and maintenance of sleep disturbance. For instance, patients often lack knowledge about foods, drinks, medications, and physical activities with psychostimulant properties that can interfere with sleep. Further, patients may know little about stress reduction or relaxation techniques that may promote sleep onset. Patients may also overuse "over-the-counter" or "herbal remedies" that were designed for short-term use only. These are examples of maladaptive behaviors that interfere with nocturnal sleep and are termed poor sleep hygiene behaviors (Hauri, 1989; Hauri, 2001). Sleep hygiene refers to the organization of activities (e.g., presleep behaviors) that promote sleep and minimize sleep disturbance. Typically, it incorporates the following behaviors:

- Reduce the intake of nicotine, caffeine, and other stimulants

- If stimulants must be taken, avoid them in the afternoon or evening

- Avoid alcohol near bedtime

- Keep a regular daytime schedule for work, rest, meals, treatment, exercise, and other daily activities

- When doing strenuous exercises, perform them in the earlier part of the day rather than in the late afternoon or evening

Insomnia complaints can often be corrected by implementing these "proper" sleep hygiene behaviors. For instance, some patients are reluctant to avoid napping during the day, or patients unintentionally fall asleep during the day. This unintentional sleep is often a major contributor to the onset and maintenance of insomnia. An analogy this author commonly uses is that the body is similar to a battery. It is assumed that by bedtime, a person's "battery" is at zero or near a zero cell charge. It is during the nocturnal sleep period that the "battery" recharges itself so that by the time the "body" awakens, the "battery" should be close to a 100% cell charge. As the day progresses, the "battery" expands energy thereby decreasing the cell charge so that by the end of the day, the "battery" is near a zero charge. If an individual naps during the day, the battery recharges itself so that by bedtime, the "battery" is not depleted of energy and the individual is alert and awake. This scenario assists in explaining the onset and maintenance of insomnia. First, because the "battery" still has a charge to it, falling asleep may be delayed for hours until the "battery" depletes its energy. Secondly, an individual may be able to fall asleep but awakens earlier than usual because the battery recharged itself during sleep and will remain awake for the remainder of the nocturnal sleep period.

*Stimulus Control.* The overall goal of stimulus control is to train the patient, through a learning paradigm, to associate the bed with sleeping and sleeping with the bed. In addition, the patient learns to "set" their sleep/wake cycle. A general guideline is to educate patients about the bedroom environment. The bedroom is for sleep and intimate activities. It should be considered a safe haven and an environment that is conducive to sleep. To achieve these goals, the following behaviors are suggested:

- Go to bed only when sleepy

- No activity should be pursued in bed other than sleep (sexual activity is an exception); in other words, reading, eating, watching television, or completing homework are not to be done in bed, but in another area of the home

- If sleep does not come within 15 or 20 minutes of retiring at night, get out of bed and engage in relaxing behavior, returning to bed only when sleepy (this may be repeated as often as needed throughout the night)

- Wake at the same time every day, regardless of the amount of sleep achieved during the night

- Avoid daytime naps

*Sleep Restriction.* A sleep diary is used to determine baseline sleep onset times and to calculate sleep efficiency. In other words, if the patient spends 8 hours in bed, but only achieves 5 hours of sleep, on average, their sleep efficiency is 5/8 or 63%. The patient is then directed to spend only 5 hours in bed each night (but never restrict patients to less than 5 hours). The patient continues this sleep instruction until a sleep efficiency rating of 90% or more (3.6 hours) is achieved. Then $1/2$ hour is added to the patient's allotted time in bed, and this schedule is maintained until a sleep efficiency of 90% is achieved. This pattern is followed until the patient reaches a target sleep time.

In addition to these three specific strategies, a more general cognitive behavioral approach is implemented. For example, many patients who have difficulty sleeping begin to worry about their lack of sleep and the nightly struggle to achieve restful sleep. They may ruminate more about their sleep patterns than the current psychosocial stressors they are experiencing. They begin to develop cognitions that only amplify the problem. Sleep difficulties may be seen as a potential contributor to ongoing problems. They may become concerned, as one recent patient did, that lack of sleep will result in poor job performance, which will result inevitably in termination from employment and loss of the family's resources that will preclude his children (ages 5 and 12) from going to college and achieving successful careers. Patients may be challenged on the veracity of these statements, and encouraged to produce alternative thoughts. They can then be encouraged to compare the veracity of the worried cognitions with the alternatives.

## Additional Techniques

Patients are also likely to benefit from the understanding and use of a variety of relaxation techniques. These range from relatively simple techniques that require 3–5 minutes of teaching to much more complex shifts in the patient's view of life, which requires 2 months or more of teaching. Some of these techniques are as follows:

- *Progressive muscle relaxation.* In this technique, the patient learns to stretch and relax successive areas of the body in an effort to "teach" the body what relaxation feels like. For example, a patient is told to squint her eyes as tightly as she can, hold them for a count of 5, and then relax them completely. She repeats this 2 to 3 times, and then moves to her mouth. She holds her mouth open and stretched as tightly as possible for a count of 5, and then releases the muscles, allowing her mouth to relax. She repeats this 2 to 3 times, and then moves to her neck, repeating this procedure in multiple areas, all the way down to her toes.

- *Biofeedback.* Biofeedback allows the patient to control body temperature and tension using an electronic feedback system. This technique requires both equipment and training, and is not likely to be of benefit to patients who have multiple medical problems to address.

- *Guided imagery.* Here, a patient is directed to sit or lie comfortably and take two or three deep breaths, closing their eyes. He is directed or guided by a health care professional to either a peaceful scene of his own making or one that the health care professional provides. He is "dropped into" the scene with progressively broader awareness. First, he is instructed to see all that is around him (e.g., for a beach scene, he'll see sand, sky, clouds, ocean, waves, birds, cliffs or dunes, etc.). He is then directed to open up his auditory sense, hearing the scene as well as seeing it (e.g., the crash of the waves, the call of the birds, etc.). Following that, he is directed to open his olfactory sense, to smell his surroundings (the salt of the sea, etc.). He then opens up to the tactile sense of the scene (his toes in the warm sand, the coolness of the breeze, the warmth of the sun, the feel of the sand and the water against his fingers). Finally, he is asked to imagine what it feels like to be in the scene. He is encouraged to feel peaceful, relaxed, calm, satisfied, and without pain. After the patient is lead through this process once or twice, a tape of one of the sessions is provided for the patient to use at home before retiring for the evening.

## A Review of the Hypnosis Literature

Hypnosis has been used successfully to alleviate insomnia (Borkovec & Fowles, 1973; Bauer & McCanne, 1980; Hammond, 1990; Spiegel & Spiegel, 1990; Stanton, 1990; Hauri, 1993; Hadley, 1996; Weaver & Becker, 1996; Stanton, 1999; Dement & Vaughan, 2000; Hauri, 2000; Kryger, 2004); nightmares, night terrors, and sleepwalking (Gerard, 2002). Cognitive-behavior therapy has successfully been used primarily to treat insomnia (Morin, 1991; Edinger, Hoelscher, Marsh, Lipper, & Ionescu-Pioggia, 1992; Morin, 1993; Morin, 1996; Morin, 1999b; Lichstein, Wilson, Johnson, 2000; Edinger, Wohlgemuth, Radtke, Marsh, & Quilliam, 2001; Espie, Inglis, Tessier, & Harvey, 2001; Morin, 2001; Nowell & Buysse, 2001; Perlis, Sharpe, Smith, Greenblatt, & Giles. 2001; Harvey, Inglis, & Espie, 2002; Manber & Kuo, 2002; Edinger, 2003; Morin, 2003; Morin, Bastien, & Savard, 2003; Roth, 2004), and hypnotic strategies have been used to treat arousal disorders. With treating arousal disorders, generally 1 to 2 sessions of hypnotherapy have been used focusing on relaxation and self-hypnosis at bedtime.

## Hypnosis in the Treatment of Insomnia

Clinical hypnosis is a safe and effective method of treating insomnia because it allows the clinician to gain access to the underlying problem (Modlin, 2002). Self-hypnosis is considered a voluntary relaxation technique (Dement & Vaughan, 2000) that is similar to meditation because it can ease the body and mind, preparing the body for sleep (Kryger, 2004). Hypnosis and self-hypnosis offer rapid methods to manage anxiety and worry, facilitating deep relaxation, and controlling mental over-activity and decreasing physiological arousal, which are cardinal symptoms of insomnia (Bauer & McCanne, 1980; Hammond, 1990).

There are somatically based insomnias, but these have been found to be unamenable to hypnotic interventions (Weitzenhoffer, 2000). Some of the psychological insomnias (i.e., individuals becoming upset either prior to sleep onset or waking up after sleep onset and experiencing difficulty returning to sleep because they become anxious about not sleeping or losing sleep) are very amenable to hypnosis.

## Relevance of Treating Sleep Disorders Using Hypnosis and CBT

The most common sleep disorder that has combined CBT with hypnosis has been the insomnia disorders. It is widely agreed that effective treatment of insomnia must assume a multidisciplinary approach in which physiological, psychological, behavioral, and environmental interventions receive equal emphasis. Approximately 70%–80% of patients treated with nonpharmacological interventions benefit from treatment (Morin & Azrin, 1987; Morin & Azrin, 1988; Morin, 1999b; Morin, 2003; Morin, Bastien, & Savard, 2003; Morin, 2004). For patients with chronic primary insomnia, nonpharmacological treatments are likely to reduce sleep onset and/or wake after sleep onset to below 30 minutes with sleep quality and satisfaction scores significantly increasing (Morin, 1999a; Morin, 1999b). Three treatments meet the American Psychological Association (APA) criteria for empirically supported behavioral treatments for insomnia: stimulus control therapy, progressive muscle relaxation, and paradoxical intention, and three other treatments meet APA criteria for probably efficacious treatments: sleep restriction, biofeedback, and multifaceted cognitive-behavior therapy. Cognitive behavior therapy has been found to show significantly more long-lasting improvements following treatment to pharmacological agents in treating chronic primary insomnias (Edinger, Wohlgemuth, Radtke, Marsh, & Quilliam, 2001a) because CBT is able to target the underlying problem, whereas termination of pharmacological agents can cause a rebound of the initial sleep difficulties.

## IMPLEMENTATION OF CBT WITH HYPNOSIS

A comprehensive review of CBT implementation with sleep disorders is contained in the work of Morin (1996). It is essential that the extent of the sleep disturbance be determined. Keeping a sleep diary (see Appendix A) for a minimum of 2 weeks is the standard practice in the sleep medicine field. The sleep diary provides documentation through a time sampling of the patient's sleep pattern. The bedtimes, minutes to fall asleep, number of wake-ups, and ratings of alertness/ sleepiness provide the clinician with an understanding of the patient's sleep pattern. Additional assessment with specific measures of personality and sleep disturbance perception may also be necessary.

    The following two cases represent an amalgamation of cases and groups that we have treated using the concepts, assessments, and CBT treatments for sleep. The individuals described in these two cases participated in the 8-week sleep class detailed in Appendix B, originally developed by Morin.

## Case 1: Sleep Managed by Lifestyle Changes

Mr. Marks is a 23-year-old African-American male referred for behavioral counseling. His presenting problem was inability to fall asleep at night. This problem was reported to occur since "high school" (i.e., approximately 8 years ago). He stated that 30-minute to one-hour sleep onsets occurred three to four times per week. The sleep onset difficulty has worsened in the last 8 months with three or more nights per week experienced as difficult sleep onset of 2 hours or more.

Mr. Marks has worked for a shipping company for the last 4 years. He was promoted to a shift supervisor 1 year ago. He has always worked the 3 p.m. to 11 p.m. shift in the shipping company facility. Mr. Marks' medical history is unremarkable. He related his sleep onset difficulty with appropriate frustration. He denied depression and anxiety symptoms and use of drugs. He reported himself to be a social drinker of 3 to 4 drinks per month. He is of average build and normal weight. Mr. Marks reported his work week bedtimes ranging from midnight to 12:30 a.m. and weekend bedtimes set at 2:30 a.m. (on average). He reported waking up between 9:30-to-0 a.m. daily. He denied napping.

Mr. Marks lives alone in an apartment, owns his car, and indicated basketball, cards, and music listening as his hobbies. He lives within a 2-mile radius of more than 15 family and extended family members, of which he reported a "good" relationship.

Mr. Marks was familiar with relaxation techniques as he reported on several self-help music/scripted tapes that he had purchased over the years. He indicated receptivity to learning hypnosis and to the logging of his sleep.

### Summary

Mr. Marks' participation vacillated in the 8-week CBT program. In the initial introductory session and until week one, he indicated his willingness to "learn new things," which reflected his view of the hypnosis component. He complied with daily sleep log recordings and initial questionnaires for the program. Mr.

Marks attended each class and was early despite a 45-minute
public transportation commute. Within each session time, Mr.
Marks was quietly attentive. He watched class members and
myself as we spoke. He acknowledged conversation points with
a nod but never spoke spontaneously. During each session, a
rotation to each class member reporting how their sleep that
past week was and any outstanding experiences related to their
sleep were queried. Mr. Marks' report was similar each week.
He involved himself in Internet card games on a daily basis for
3–5 hours at a time. Mr. Marks reported stress with this activity
when the game doesn't "go his way," which he indicated was
highly unpredictable.

Mr. Marks implemented a mild sleep restriction schedule
and reported reluctance with the aspect of maintaining a regular
wake-up time (He stated, "You mean even on my day off?"). His
sleep diaries by weeks four and five indicated an average of 20
minutes daily variation around the assigned wake up time. What
was more difficult for Mr. Marks, it seemed, was the cessation
of invigorating music (i.e., rap, recordings of def poetry) that
he had typically listened to on nights when he returned from
work. This stimulating material seemed to have an alerting effect
on him rather than the "wind down" effect he thought. After the
hypnosis instruction during class, Mr. Marks reported feeling
very relaxed and stated when asked that he thought it would
be helpful to "wind down" with such taped instruction. However,
it seemed, based on the beginning session rotations that Mr.
Marks didn't identify himself as that person who could "wind
down" with the taped instruction. Despite this restriction, his
adherence to the sleep restriction and absence of other remarkable sleep disturbing hygiene practices allowed him to progress
from initial 72% sleep efficiency to 85% by week four. After
the presentation of sleep hygiene and the appearance of mild
weather in late spring in Chicago (not always common), Mr.
Marks learned the value of light exercise and purchased a bi-
cycle. His cycling 2 to 3 times a week in the morning, together
with the natural bright light and sun exposure in the morning,
contributed the progression of his sleep efficiency to 87%, and
ultimately, at the last reporting, to 93%.

Mr. Marks participated in an 8-week CBT Sleep Class using
hypnosis. He reported satisfaction at the mid-point and upon
completing the class. Mr. Marks' initial sleep efficiency of 72%
changed over the course of his participation to a final value of

93%. Mr. Marks attributed his success in feeling "rested" and sleeping well to sleep restriction techniques of reduced time in bed and the implementation of sleep hygiene principles of exercising in the morning, reducing alcohol intake overall, and a regular wake-up time. Mr. Marks reported feeling relaxed during the group-led hypnosis sessions but found his home practice felt "awkward."

## Case 2: Slight Success

A 54-year-old female presenting with difficulty initiating sleep for at least 3 of 7 nights per week this last month and a lifelong pattern of sleep disturbance at least one night per week. Ms. Jared has been divorced for 17 years with one disabled adult child in her home and another living independently nearby. She reported a history of thyroid problems, depressed mood, tinnitus, lower back pain, migraines, flu episodes three times a year, and repeated dental procedures (i.e., root canal, crown) this last year. She works as a high school language teacher. She denied falling asleep at work, when driving, and when conversing. She indicated excessive sleepiness in the mid-afternoon and falling asleep while grading papers.

A standard sleep interview ruled out a sleep disorder. She was referred to the 8 week CBT group. Her initial sleep efficiency was 81% and her final was 86%. Ms. Jared reported relief at the 4-week mark when her sleep restriction plan seemed less intrusive and disturbing. She glibly commented in class about her defiance of the sleep hygiene practices and continued to read and watch T.V. in bed in the early evening. Ms. Jared reported using the hypnosis tape on a daily basis every evening before starting dinner and evening activities. She explained that it gave her a "jump start" to "unwinding" from her day. Ms. Jared missed the last session of the group.

In Case 1, the patient transformed his sleep quality using lifestyle changes. The impetus, however, came after weeks four and five of the 8-week sleep program. This indicates a likely impact from the sleep restriction procedure (see Appendix B). Chronicity of the sleep disturbance, psychopathology such as depression and anxiety disorders, and medically sensitive sleep disorders such as sleep apnea, restless leg syndrome, and narcolepsy can be determined in this manner. However, assessment should be ongoing with the clinician utilizing self-diaries and self-report throughout the treatment process (Morin, 1996).

In Case 2, the patient seemed to have experienced success from the sleep restriction and hypnosis components, but not the sleep hygiene. Adherence to the sleep hygiene practices (which were mentally stimulating for her) would have further increased her sleep efficiency ratings. Her practical implementation of the home practice hypnosis tape likely deactivated her cumulative arousal pattern from the emotional and physical demands of her day. She would have benefited from a review of the science of sleep medicine that occurs in Session 8, as it would give her a better understanding of the reasoning for the behavior she was asked to implement.

## Intervention

Appendix B contains a topical outline of the eight-session CBT intervention with hypnosis that was used with clients whose cases were just described. This protocol involves four phases. Following the formal assessment, an introduction to the protocol should include an explanation of each approach and a brief rationale. The first session is spent as an overview of the program and a presentation of basic sleep facts.

The treatment is cognitive-behavioral. A conveyance of thought-directing behavior needs to be clearly stated as a premise. The focus of treatment is on current behaviors and dysfunctional thoughts. The CBT protocol consists of four phases: behavioral, cognitive, hypnosis training, and educative. The ordering of the first two phases is essential and is substantiated by empirical studies (Morin, 1996). The hypnosis training is added to this programming rather than the traditional progressive muscle training in an attempt to deliver a potent induction of relaxation using hypnosis.

In the first behavioral component, the patient, in the course of three sessions, is given a detailed explanation of behavioral approaches (e.g., sleep restriction and stimulus control). Spielman and Glovinsky (1991) developed sleep restriction as a method to stimulate the homeostatic sleep drive. Restricting the amount and setting the timing of sleep in this procedure heightens sleep propensity. Patients are motivated to try this intervention; however, after

2–3 days on the regimen, encouragement and repeated explanation of the rationale are necessary to increase treatment compliance. The sleep diary responses are used to compute a sleep efficiency ratio (total sleep time divided by total time in bed multiplied by 100). It is convention to use an 85% sleep efficiency as a marker for acceptable quality sleep and justification to decrease the sleep restriction (i.e., increase time spent in bed) by an increment of 30 minutes. A minimum of 5 hours restricted is used in the field.

The cognitive component takes place during weeks five and six. Beck, Rush, Shaw, and Emery (1979) have provided a cognitive restructuring perspective to sleep disturbance. Unrealistic expectations and dysfunctional cognitions are adjusted using an educative approach based on a review of the basic sleep facts presented during week one. Attention to patient's reluctance and distortions by the clinician is essential. Morin (1996) advises the use of a three-step process: first, identify patient-specific dysfunctional cognitions; second, confront and challenge their validity, and third, replace them with more adaptive and rational substitutes. The cognitive phase during weeks four and five helps to alleviate excessive worry about sleep and in turn, reduce daytime worries that are accumulated and lead to heightened cognitive activity (i.e., worry).

The hypnotic module is introduced at weeks 6 and 7; however, some clinicians integrate hypnosis techniques at the beginning of the treatment intervention. A quick assessment of hypnotizability may be conducted during this period or at the beginning of the intervention. In either case, basic and more advanced induction methods are employed and hypnotic suggestions consisting of increasing both quality and quantity of sleep are recommended.

The education phase is last in the protocol because it has the least amount of empirical support. Diet, exercise, environmental factors such as light, noise, and temperature are presented. While knowledge of sleep hygiene factors may be moderate or high, individuals usually persist in their usage (Sexton-Radek, 2003).

The implementation of scripted CBT sleep interventions may help to educate and alleviate the sleep disturbance symptomology. Initially, the practitioner designs a pilot treatment and after repeated usage compares outcome of patients in order to identify areas of change and improvement. CBT sleep interventions are not only useful for individual therapy cases but also can be applied to group settings.

## Conclusions

Inquiry into sleep functioning has definitely been neglected by most health care professionals. Patients are generally reluctant to raise the question of sleep with their physician or health care provider (Engstrom, Strohl, Rose, Lewandowski, & Stefanek, 1999). The attention during patient-provider encounters often focuses on treatment, test results, and medical decision making. In addition, patients rarely consider sleep difficulty to be a significant problem that can be appropriately addressed by their provider. Therefore, unless the clinician directly inquires about sleep disturbance, the issue is likely to remain unaddressed.

Behavioral treatment approaches are initially more time-consuming and more expensive than hypnotic medications. However, over the life span of total physician visits and prescriptions, it may be more cost effective for patients to engage in behavioral treatments. Current research findings support the use of behavioral approaches for treating sleep disorders such as insomnia because these approaches resolve the underlying problem associated with the sleep disturbance, whereas pharmaceutical agents are a band-aid approach to treatment. Emphasis must be placed on establishing the combined CBT and hypnotherapy approach to treating sleep disorders. In the meantime, it may be beneficial for hypnotherapists to gain specialty training in the treatment of sleep disorders.

## REFERENCES

Aldrich, M. (2000). Cardinal manifestations of sleep disorders. In M. H. Kryger, T. Roth, & W. C. Dement (Eds.), *Principles and practice of sleep medicine* (3rd ed., pp. 526–528). Philadelphia: W. B. Saunders.

American Psychiatric Association. (1994). *Diagnostic and statistical manual of mental disorders DSM-IV (4th ed.).* Washington, DC: American Psychiatric Association.

Ancoli-Israel, S. (2003). The role of actigraphy in the study of sleep and circadian rhythms. *Sleep: Journal of Sleep and Sleep Disorders Research, 26*(3), 342–392.

Bastien, C., Vallieres, A., & Morin, C. M. (2001). Validation of the Insomnia Severity Index as an outcome measure for insomnia research. *Sleep Medicine, 2*, 297–307.

Bauer, K. E., & McCanne, T. R. (1980). An hypnotic technique for treating insomnia. *International Journal of Clinical and Experimental Hypnosis, 28*(1), 1–5.

Beck, A. T., Rush, A. J., Shaw, B. F., & Emery, G. (1979). *Cognitive therapy of depression*. New York: Guilford.

Benington, J. H. (2000). Sleep homeostasis and the function of sleep [see comment]. *Sleep, 23*(7), 959–966.

Blissitt, P. A. (2001). Sleep, memory, and learning. *Journal of Neuroscience Nursing, 33*(4), 208–215.

Borkovec, T. D., & Fowles, D. C. (1973). Controlled investigation of the effects of progressive and hypnotic relaxation on insomnia. *Journal of Abnormal Psychology, 82*(1), 153–158.

Born, J., Lange, T., Hansen, K., Molle, M., & Fehm, H. L. (1997). Effects of sleep and circadian rhythm on human circulating immune cells. *Journal of Immunology, 158*(9), 4454–4464.

Buysse, D. J., Reynolds, C. F., III, Monk, T. H., Berman, S. R., & Kupfer, D. J. (1989). The Pittsburgh Sleep Quality Index: A new instrument for psychiatric practice and research. *Psychiatry Research, 28*(2), 193–213.

Chesson, A. L., Littner, M., Davila, D., Anderson, W. M., Grigg-Danberger, M., Hartse, K., et al. (1999). Practice parameters for the use of light therapy in treatment of sleep disorders. *Sleep: Journal of Sleep Research and Sleep Medicine, 22*(5), 641–660.

Dement, W., & Vaughan, C. (2000). *The promise of sleep*. New York: Random House.

Doghramji, K. (2003). Treatment strategics for sleep disturbance in patients with depression. *Journal of Clinical Psychiatry, 64*(Suppl 14), 24–29.

Edinger, J. D. (2003). Cognitive and behavioral anomalies among insomnia patients with mixed restless legs and periodic limb movement disorder. *Behavioral Sleep Medicine, 1*(1), 37–53.

Edinger, J. D., Bonnet, M. H., Bootzin, R., Doghramji, K., Dorsey, C. M., Espie, C. A., et al. (2004). Derivation of research diagnostic criteria for insomnia: Report of an American Academy of Sleep Medicine Work Group. *Sleep 27*(8), 1567–1596.

Edinger, J. D., Hoelscher, T. J., Marsh, G. R., Lipper, S., & Ionescu-Pioggia, M. (1992). A cognitive-behavioral therapy for sleep-maintenance insomnia in older adults. *Psychology and Aging, 7*(2), 282–289.

Edinger, J. D., Wohlgemuth, W. K., Radtke, R. A., Marsh, G. R., & Quillian, R. E. (2001a). Cognitive behavioral therapy for treatment of chronic primary insomnia: A randomized controlled trial. *JAMA: Journal of the American Medical Association, 285*(14), 1856–1864.

Edinger, J. D., Wohlgemuth, W. K., Radtke, R. A., Marsh, G. R., & Quillian, R. E. (2001b). Does cognitive-behavioral insomnia therapy alter dysfunctional beliefs about sleep? *Sleep: Journal of Sleep and Sleep Disorders Research, 24*(5), 591–599.

Ehrenberg, B. (2000). Importance of sleep restoration in co-morbid disease: Effect of anticonvulsants. *Neurology, 54*(5 Suppl 1), S33–37.

Engstrom, C. A., Strohl, R. A., Rose, L., Lewandowski, L., & Stefanek, M. E. (1999). Sleep alterations in cancer patients. *Cancer Nursing, 22*(2), 143–148.

Espie, C. A., Inglis, S. J., Tessier, S., & Harvey, L. (2001). The clinical effectiveness of cognitive behaviour therapy for chronic insomnia: Implementation and evaluation of a sleep clinic in general medical practice. *Behaviour Research and Therapy, 39*(1), 45–60.

Evans, F. J. (1999). Hypnosis and sleep: The control of altered states of awareness. *Sleep and Hypnosis, 1*(4), 232–237.

Fordam, M. (1988). Patient problems: A research base for nursing care. In L. Wilson-Barnett & J. Bateup (Eds.) (pp. 148–181). London: Scutari.

Gerard, K. (2002). A review of hypnosis in the treatment of parasomnias: Nightmare, sleepwalking, and sleep terror disorders. *Australian Journal of Clinical and Experimental Hypnosis, 30*(2), 99–155.

Hadley, J. (1996). Sleep. In J. Hadley & C. Staudacher (Eds.), *Hypnosis for change* (pp. 203–210). New York: MJF Books.

Hammond, D. (1990). Sleep disorders. In D. Hammond (Ed.), *Handbook of hypnotic suggestions and metaphors* (pp. 220–221). New York: W. W. Norton.

Harvey, L., Inglis, S. J., & Espie, C. A. (2002). Insomniacs' reported use of CBT components and relationship to long-term clinical outcome. *Behaviour Research and Therapy, 40*(1), 75–83.

Hauri, P. (1989). The cognitive-behavioral treatment of insomnia. Eating, sleeping, and sex. In A. J. Stunkard & A. Baum (Eds.), *Perspectives in behavioral medicine* (pp. 181–194). Hillsdale, NJ: England, Lawrence Erlbaum Associates, Inc.

Hauri, P. J. (1993). Consulting about insomnia: A method and some preliminary data. *Sleep: Journal of Sleep Research and Sleep Medicine, 16*(4), 344–350.

Hauri, P. J. (2000). The many faces of insomnia. [References]. In D. I. Mostofsky & D. H. Barlow (Eds.), *The management of stress and anxiety in medical disorders* (pp. 143–159). Needham Heights, MA: Allyn & Bacon.

Hauri, P. J. (2001). *Insomnia*. National Sleep Medicine Course, Leesburg, Virginia, American Academy of Sleep Medicine.

Hodgson, L. A. (1991). Why do we need sleep? Relating theory to nursing practice. *Journal of Advanced Nursing, 16*(12), 1503–1510.

*International classification of sleep disorders revised: Diagnostic and coding manual.* (2001). Rochester: American Academy of Sleep Medicine.

Johns, M. W. (1991). A new method for measuring daytime sleepiness: The Epworth Sleepiness Scale. *Sleep, 14*, 540–545.

Kies, T. F., & Kushidu, C. A. (2003). Treatment efficacy of behavioral interventions for obstructive sleep apnea, restless legs syndrome, periodic leg movement disorder and narcolepsy. In M. L. Perlis & K. L. Lichstein (Eds.), *Treating sleep disorders: Principles and practice of behavioral sleep medicine* (pp. 136–165). New York: John Wiley.

Krueger, J., & Obal, F. (1993). A neuronal group theory of sleep function. *Journal of Sleep Research, 2*(2), 63–69.

Kryger, M. (2004). *A woman's guide to sleep disorders* (1st ed.). New York: McGraw-Hill.

Kryger, M. H., Roth, T., & Dement, W. C. (2001). Principles and practice of sleep medicine. *Depression and Anxiety, 13*(3), 157.

Kunz, D., & Hermann, W. M. (2000). Sleep-wake cycle, sleep-related disturbances, and sleep disorders: A chronobiological approach. *Comprehensive Psychiatry, 41*(2) (Suppl. 1), 194–115.

Lamberg, L. (2000). Sleep disorders, often unrecognized, complicate many physical illnesses. *Journal of the American Medical Association, 284*(17), 2173–2175.

Lee, K. A. (1997). An overview of sleep and common sleep problems. *ANNA Journal, 24*, 614–623.

Lichstein, K. L., Wilson, N. M., & Johnson, C. T. (2000). Psychological treatment of secondary insomnia. *Psychology and Aging, 15*(2), 232–240.

Lichstein, K. L., & Morin, C. M. (Eds.). (2000). *Treatment of late-life insomnia.* Thousand Oaks, CA: Sage Publications, Inc.

Manber, R., & Kuo, T. (2002). Cognitive-behavioral therapies for insomnia. In T. L. Lee-Chiong, M. J. Satela, M. A. Carskadon, & M. A. Carskadon (Eds.), *Sleep medicine* (pp. 177–185). Philadelphia: Hanley & Belfus.

Maquet, P. (2001). The role of sleep in learning and memory. *Science, 294*(5544), 1048–1052.

Mills, M., & Graci, G. (2004). Sleep disturbances. In C. Yarbro, M. Goodman, & M. Frogge (Eds.), *Cancer symptom management* (3rd ed., pp. 111–134). Sudbury, UK: Jones & Bartlett.

Modlin, T. (2002). Sleep disorders and hypnosis: To cope or cure? *Sleep and Hypnosis, 4*(1), 39–46.

Morin, C. (1991). Cognitive and behavioral perspectives in the treatment of chronic insomnia. *Science et Comportement, 21*(4), 273–290.

Morin, C. (2001). *Combined treatments of insomnia.* Washington, DC: American Psychological Association.

Morin, C. M. (1993). *Insomnia: Psychological assessment and management.* New York: Guilford.

Morin, C. M. (1996). *Insomnia: Psychological assessment and management.* New York: Guilford.

Morin, C. M. (1999a). Behavioral and pharmacological treatment for insomnia: Reply. *Journal of the American Medical Association, 282*(12), 1130–1131.

Morin, C. M. (1999b). Empirically supported psychological treatments: A natural extension of the scientist-practitioner paradigm. *Canadian Psychology, 40*(4), 312–315.

Morin, C. M. (2000a). The nature of insomnia and the need to refine our diagnostic criteria. *Psychosomatic Medicine, 62*(4), 483–485.

Morin, C. M. (2000b). The nature of insomnia and the need to refine our diagnostic criteria [comment]. *Psychosomatic Medicine, 62*(4), 483–485.

Morin, C. M. (2003). Measuring outcomes in randomized clinical trials of insomnia treatments [see comment]. *Sleep Medicine Reviews, 7*(3), 263–279.

Morin, C. M. (2004). Insomnia treatment: Taking a broader perspective on efficacy and cost-effectiveness issues. *Sleep Medicine Reviews, 8*(1), 3–6.

Morin, C. M., & Azrin, N. H. (1987). Stimulus control and imagery training in treating sleep-maintenance insomnia. *Journal of Consulting and Clinical Psychology, 55*(2), 260–262.

Morin, C. M., & Azrin, N. H. (1988). Behavioral and cognitive treatments of geriatric insomnia. *Journal of Consulting and Clinical Psychology, 56*(5), 748–753.

Morin, C. M., Bastien, C., & Savard, J. (2003). Current status of cognitive-behavior therapy for insomnia: Evidence for treatment effectiveness and feasibility.

[References]. In M. L. Perlis & K. L. Lichstein (Eds.), *Treating sleep disorders: Principles and practice of behavioral sleep medicine* (pp. 262–285). New York: John Wiley.

Morin, C. M., & Ware, J. (1996). Sleep and psychopathology. *Applied and Preventive Psychology, 5*(4), 211–224.

Nowell, P. D., & Buysse, D. J. (2001). Treatment of insomnia in patients with mood disorders. *Depression & Anxiety, 14*(1), 7–18.

Perlis, M. L., Sharpe, M., Smith, M. T., Greenblatt, D., & Giles, D. (2001). Behavioral treatment of insomnia: Treatment outcome and the relevance of medical and psychiatric morbidity. *Journal of Behavioral Medicine, 24*(3), 281–296.

Reite, M., Ruddy, J., & Nagel, K. (2002). *Concise guide to evaluation and management of sleep disorders* (3rd ed.). Washington, DC: American Psychiatric Association.

Roth, T. (2004). Measuring treatment efficacy in insomnia. *Journal of Clinical Psychiatry, 65*(Suppl 8), 8–12.

Sateia, M. J., Doghramji, K., Hauri, P. J., & Morin, C. M. (2000). Evaluation of chronic insomnia. An American Academy of Sleep Medicine review. *Sleep, 23*(2), 243–308.

Savard, J., Miller, S. M., Mills, M., O'Leary, A., Harding, H., Douglas, S. D., Magan, C. E., Belch, R., & Winokur, A. (1999). Association between subjective sleep quality and depression on immunocompetence in low-income women at risk for cervical cancer. *Psychosomatic Medicine, 61*(4), 496–507.

Savard, J., & Morin, C. M. (2001). Insomnia in the context of cancer: A review of a neglected problem. *Journal of Clinical Oncology, 19*(3), 895–908.

Savard, J., Simard, S., Blanchet, J., Ivers, H., & Morin, C. M. (2001). Prevalence, clinical characteristics, and risk factors for insomnia in the context of breast cancer. *Sleep, 24*(5), 583–590.

Sejnowski, T. J., & Destexhe, A. (2000). Why do we sleep? *Brain Research, 886*(1–2), 208–223.

Sexton-Radek, K. (2003). *Sleep quality in young adults*. Lewiston, NY: Edwin Mellen.

Siegel, J. M. (2001). The REM sleep-memory consolidation hypothesis. *Science, 294*(5544), 1058–1063.

Spiegel, D., & Spiegel, H. (1990). Hypnosis techniques with insomnia. In D. Hammond (Ed.), *Handbook of hypnotic suggestions and metaphors* (p. 255). New York: W. W. Norton.

Spielman, A. J., & Anderson, W. M. (1999). The clinical interview and treatment planning as a guide to understanding the nature of insomnia: The CCNY insomnia interview. In S. Chokroverty (Ed.), *Sleep disorders medicine: Basic science, technical considerations, and clinical aspects* (2nd ed., pp. 385–426). Boston: Butterworth Heinemann.

Stanton, H. (1990). Visualization for treating insomnia. In D. Hammond (Ed.), *Handbook of hypnotic suggestions and metaphors* (pp. 254–255). New York: W. W. Norton.

Stanton, H. E. (1999). Hypnotic relaxation and insomnia: A simple solution? *Sleep and Hypnosis, 1*(1), 64–67.

Stepanski, E. (2003). Behavioral sleep medicine: A historical perspective. *Behavioral Sleep Medicine, 1*(1), 4–21.

Stepanski, E., Rybarczyk, B., Lopez, M., & Stevens, S. (2003). Assessment and treatment of sleep disorders in older adults: A review for rehabilitation psychologists. *Rehabilitation Psychology, 48*(1), 23–36.

Stepanski, E. J., & Perlis, M. L. (2003). A historical perspective and commentary on practice issues. In M. L. Perlis & K. L. Lichstein (Eds.), *Treating sleep disorders: Principles and practice of behavioral sleep medicine* (pp. 3–26). New York: John Wiley.

Weaver, D. B., & Becker, P. M. (1996). *Treatment of insomnia with audiotaped hypnosis.* Paper presented at the 38th Annual Scientific Meeting and Workshops on Clinical Hypnosis, Orlando, Florida.

Weitzenhoffer, A. (2000). The induction of hypnosis. In A. M. Weitzenhoffer (Ed.), *The practice of hypnotism* (pp. 135–220). New York: John Wiley.

## APPENDIX A: SLEEP DIARY EXAMPLE

# Daily Sleep Diary

Date: _____

Please place an "X" through every hour (square) that you were able to sleep. If you slept only $1/2$ hour during that period, please fill the square with a single diagonal line.

| a.m. | | | | | | | | | | | | p.m. | | | | | | | | | | | |
|---|---|---|---|---|---|---|---|---|---|---|---|---|---|---|---|---|---|---|---|---|---|---|---|
| 12–1 | 1–2 | 2–3 | 3–4 | 4–5 | 5–6 | 6–7 | 7–8 | 8–9 | 9–10 | 10–11 | 11–12 | 12–1 | 1–2 | 2–3 | 3–4 | 4–5 | 5–6 | 6–7 | 7–8 | 8–9 | 9–10 | 10–11 | 11–12 |

What time did you get up out of bed in the morning? _____

What time did you get into bed in the evening? _____

Was there anything in particular that woke you this morning (for example, alarm clock, outside noise, light in window)?
_____

During the day, did you exercise vigorously? _____ Yes   _____ No
  If yes, what time of day did you exercise?
  _____ Morning   _____ Afternoon   _____ Evening
  How long was your exercise session? _____ minutes
  What kind of exercise do you do?

Did you drink any beverages or eat any foods that contained caffeine during the 24-hour period? _____ Yes   _____ No
  (these would include coffee, tea (hot or iced), soda pop, chocolate)
  If yes, what time of day did you consume these?
  _____ Morning   _____ Afternoon   _____ Evening
  How many 8-oz. cups or glasses of caffeinated drinks did you consume? _____
  What kind and how much of caffeinated food products did you consume?

Did you use nicotine-containing products (cigarettes, snuff, cigars, patch, inhaler, gum) during this period? _____ Yes   _____ No

If yes, what time of day did you use them?

\_\_\_\_ Morning  \_\_\_\_ Afternoon  \_\_\_\_ Evening

How much nicotine did you use (e.g., # cigarettes or cigars, dosage of patch, etc.)?

---

Did you drink alcohol during this period?

If yes, what time of day did you drink?

\_\_\_\_ Morning  \_\_\_\_ Afternoon  \_\_\_\_ Evening

What kind of alcohol do you drink (check all that apply)?

\_\_\_\_ Beer  \_\_\_\_ Wine  \_\_\_\_ Mixed drinks  \_\_\_\_ Liquor

How much did you drink (e.g., # beers, # 6-oz. glasses of wine, # 2-oz. drinks containing liquor)

---

Please list all of the medicines (prescribed, over-the-counter) and other drugs (e.g., cocaine, marijuana) you took in this period:

| Medicine or drug | Amount taken | Time of day |
|---|---|---|
|  |  |  |
|  |  |  |
|  |  |  |
|  |  |  |

# APPENDIX B: SLEEP CLASS FOR PATIENTS

[Modified with permission from Morin (1993)]

*Session 1*

1. Baseline Procedures
   a. Review procedure for sleep diary
   b. Reinforce patient for recording

2. Overview of Program
   a. Approach is cognitive, behavioral and educative, medical aspects as they relate
   b. Behavioral change of sleep entails change in each area

3. Agenda of Sessions 1–8

4. Self-management Approach Guided by Structure of Class
   a. Development of self-control and problem-solving skills related to sleep issues
   b. Distinguish this approach from sleep hygiene strategies and discussion of medications
   c. Explain the active/collaborative role of patient in treatment process
   d. Focused, one topic per session approach recording homework

5. Cognitive-Behavioral Explanation of Insomnia Sleep Disturbance
   a. Identification of trigger factors that predispose, precipitate and perpetuate poor sleep
   b. Conceptual model of insomnia is presented
   c. Allow questions related to trigger factors and model of insomnia

6. Basic Sleep Facts Presented
   a. Types of sleep, characteristics, and patterning of sleep
   b. Prevalence and consequences of insomnia
   c. Life span changes to sleep quality
   d. Medical factors (i.e., pain, fatigue from treatment, medication)

7.  Set Goals and Control for Remaining Sessions
    Materials needed:   Sleep Diary

*Session 2*

1.  Baseline Procedures
    a.  Review procedure for sleep diary
    b.  Reinforce patient for recording

2.  Presentation of Elements of Sleep Restriction and Stimulus Control Procedure
    a.  Review use of sleep log to determine sleep efficiency score
    b.  Restrict time in bed
    c.  Reduce/eliminate napping
    d.  Go to bed only when sleepy
    e.  Maintain a regular wake-up time
    f.  Sleep environment becomes conditioned to wakefulness through stimulus control

3.  Link of Sleep Restriction and Stimulus Control to Basic Sleep Facts from Session 1

    Materials:   Sleep Diary
                 Cognitive Behavioral Measures

*Session 3*

1.  Baseline Procedures
    a.  Review procedure for sleep diary
    b.  Reinforce patient for recording

2.  Cognitive Behavioral Procedures
    a.  Review use of sleep log to determine sleep efficiency score
    b.  Restrict time in bed
    c.  Reduce/eliminate napping
    d.  Go to bed only when sleepy
    e.  Maintain a regular wake up time
    f.  Sleep environment becomes conditioned to wakefulness through stimulus control

3.  Home Practice
    Any problems integrating new practices?

4. Facilitation of Adherence to Sleep Restriction
   a. Identification of activities to do when unable to sleep and out of bed
   b. Identification of cues to sleepiness
   c. Determining "light" activities to combat urge to sleep
   d. Public commitment to program to family/friends to elicit support
   e. Discussion of need to rearrange activities

5. Review Assignment of Sleep Restriction, Activities to Maintain Assignment(s), Sleep Diary

   Materials Needed: Sleep Diary

*Session 4*

1. Baseline Procedures
   a. Review procedure for sleep diary
   b. Reinforce patient for recording

2. Cognitive Behavioral Procedures
   a. Review use of sleep log to determine sleep efficiency score
   b. Restrict time in bed
   c. Reduce/eliminate napping
   d. Go to bed only when sleepy
   e. Maintain a regular wake-up time
   f. Sleep environment becomes conditioned to wakefulness through stimulus control

3. Facilitation of Adherence to Sleep Restriction
   a. Identification of activities to do when unable to sleep and out of bed
   b. Identification of cues to sleepiness
   c. Determining "light" activities to combat urge to sleep
   d. Public commitment to program to family/friends to elicit support
   e. Discussion of need to rearrange activities

4. Cognitive Therapy Introduction
   a. Introduction of cognitive therapy principles and rationale

   b. Integrate model of insomnia explanation to cognitive therapy

   c. Review application of cognitive therapy with vignettes

      i. Identify concepts of misperceptions about insomnia

      ii. Discuss dysfunctional beliefs and evidence from basic sleep facts presentation

      iii. Alter unrealistic sleep expectation

   d. General discussion of specific vignettes/statements that apply to patients' situation

   Materials:   Sleep Diary
                 Modified Beliefs and Attitude about Sleep Scale

## Session 5

1. Baseline Procedures
   a. Review procedure for sleep diary
   b. Reinforce patient for recording

2. Cognitive Behavioral Procedures
   a. Review use of sleep log to determine sleep efficiency score
   b. Restrict time in bed
   c. Reduce/eliminate napping
   d. Go to bed only when sleepy
   e. Maintain a regular wake-up time
   f. Sleep environment becomes conditioned to wakefulness through stimulus control

3. Cognitive Therapy Review
   a. Introduction of cognitive therapy principles and rationale
   b. Integrate model of insomnia explanation to cognitive therapy
   c. Review application of cognitive therapy with vignettes
      i. Identify concepts of misperceptions about insomnia
      ii. Discuss dysfunctional beliefs and evidence from basic sleep facts presentation
      iii. Alter unrealistic sleep expectation
   d. General discussion of specific vignettes/statements that apply to patients' situation

4. General Review

5.  Presentation of Sleep Hygiene
    Discussion of medications and other factors and their measured effects on sleep

    Materials:   Sleep Diary
                 Summary Sheet

*Session 6*

1.  Baseline Procedures
    a.  Review procedure for sleep diary
    b.  Reinforce patient for recording

2.  Cognitive Behavioral Procedures
    a.  Review use of sleep log to determine sleep efficiency score
    b.  Restrict time in bed
    c.  Reduce/eliminate napping
    d.  Go to bed only when sleepy
    e.  Maintain a regular wake-up time
    f.  Sleep environment becomes conditioned to wakefulness through stimulus control

3.  Cognitive Therapy Review
    a.  Introduction of cognitive therapy principles and rationale
    b.  Integrate model of insomnia explanation to cognitive therapy
    c.  Review application of cognitive therapy with vignettes
        i.   Identify concepts of misperceptions about insomnia
        ii.  Discuss dysfunctional beliefs and evidence from basic sleep facts presentation
        iii. Alter unrealistic sleep expectation
    d.  General discussion of specific vignettes/statements that apply to patients' situation

4.  Hypnosis
    a.  Rationale explained
    b.  Description of varied approaches and theoretical/orientation
    c.  Therapist-patient relationship
    d.  Relaxation induction
    e.  Cognitive therapy–imagery hypnosis
    f.  10–15 minute example

5. Discussion of application of hypnosis for home practice

    Materials:   Sleep Diary
                 Hypnosis Summary Sheet
                 CD/Cassette tape of hypnosis

*Session 7*

1. Baseline Procedures
   a. Review procedure for sleep diary
   b. Reinforce patient for recording

2. Cognitive Behavioral Procedures
   a. Review use of sleep log to determine sleep efficiency score
   b. Restrict time in bed
   c. Reduce/eliminate napping
   d. Go to bed only when sleepy
   e. Maintain a regular wake-up time
   f. Sleep environment becomes conditioned to wakefulness through stimulus control

3. Cognitive Therapy Review
   a. Introduction of cognitive therapy principles and rationale
   b. Integrate model of insomnia explanation to cognitive therapy
   c. Review application of cognitive therapy with vignettes
      i. Identify concepts of misperceptions about insomnia
      ii. Discuss dysfunctional beliefs and evidence from basic sleep facts presentation
      iii. Alter unrealistic sleep expectation
   d. General discussion of specific vignettes/statements that apply to patients' situation

4. Hypnosis
   a. Rationale explained
   b. Description of varied approaches and theoretical
   c. Therapist-patient relationship
   d. Relaxation induction
   e. Cognitive therapy—imagery hypnosis
   f. 10–15 minute example

5. Practice of Hypnosis 10–15 minutes

6.  Discussion

    Materials:   Sleep Diary
                 Hypnosis Summary Sheet
                 CD/Cassette tape of hypnosis

*Session 8*

1.  Baseline Procedures
    a.  Review procedure for sleep diary
    b.  Reinforce patient for recording

2.  Cognitive Behavioral Procedures
    a.  Review use of sleep log to determine sleep efficiency score
    b.  Restrict time in bed
    c.  Reduce/eliminate napping
    d.  Go to bed only when sleepy
    e.  Maintain a regular wake-up time
    f.  Sleep environment becomes conditioned to wakefulness through stimulus control

3.  Cognitive Therapy Review
    a.  Introduction of cognitive therapy principles and rationale
    b.  Integrate model of insomnia explanation to Cognitive Therapy
    c.  Review application of cognitive therapy with vignettes
        i.    Identify concepts of misperceptions about insomnia
        ii.   Discuss dysfunctional beliefs and evidence from basic sleep facts presentation
        iii.  Alter unrealistic sleep expectation
    d.  General discussion of specific vignettes/statements that apply to patients' situation

4.  Sleep Hygiene Overview

5.  Relapse Prevention Strategies Presentation
    a.  Discuss lapse, relapse
    b.  Reiterate gains made, discuss patients' coping
    c.  Identify high-risk situation and tasks to engage in

6.  General review, statement of progress

    Materials: Sleep Diary

Chapter 12

# Becoming a Practitioner of Cognitive Behavior Therapy and Hypnosis

Robin A. Chapman

This final chapter was inspired by several sources, including Michael Mahoney's (1995) book chapter "The Psychological Demands of Being a Constructive Psychotherapist" and DeLaney and Voit's (September 16 & 17, 2000) workshop on integrating hypnosis into clinical practice. These writers, who have struggled with the integration of these concepts, have addressed elements of psychotherapy practice and suggested future directions for practice and integration.

This chapter addresses these suggestions through the lens of my experience of becoming a practitioner who combines cognitive behavior therapy and hypnosis. This view is consistent with the central purpose of this book, which is to provide the practitioner a practical guide to integrating cognitive behavior therapy and hypnosis. This final chapter guides the practitioner through a series of questions intended to help clarify their individual approach to integration.

This book grew out of my personal experience with integrating cognitive behavior therapy and hypnosis. I was teaching a graduate class in cognitive behavior therapy and presenting clinical cases from my practice that utilized hypnosis. The students questioned the use of hypnosis because they understood that cognitive behaviorists are supposed be "scientific" and reject the old psychodynamic construct of the unconscious. Many fellow professionals also had difficulty accepting the idea of integrating these two approaches. I remember being met with a roll of the eyes and an exasperated voice: "You do that with your patients? There's no evidence that it works." The issue of integrating cognitive behavior therapy and hypnosis also arose during my American Society of Clinical Hypnosis (ASCH) clinical hypnosis certification process. My supervisor for this certification suggested that I study the integration of CBT and hypnosis and present the results to his clinical hypnosis class. My review of the literature at that time produced few resources to guide the practitioner's clinical thought process in using hypnosis and cognitive behavior therapy.

A plethora of clinical casebooks is available to practitioners on a wide range of theories and therapies. Practitioners often find these casebooks helpful in informing and guiding their work. In fact, several very good clinical hypnosis casebooks are available (Rhue, Lynn, & Kirsch, 1993; Golden, Dowd, & Friedberg, 1987) and similarly for a variety of psychotherapies (Freeman, Pretzer, Fleming, & Simon, 2004). The clinical hypnosis casebooks usually include several chapters on the use of cognitive behavior therapy and hypnosis. Books describing a single author's perspective of integrating cognitive behavior therapy and hypnosis are also available (Zarren & Eimer, 2002; Dowd, 2000). As discussed earlier in this book, one can find several excellent volumes discussing theory and research from social learning perspectives (Spanos & Chaves, 1989; Kirsch, Capafons, Cardena-Buelna, & Amigo, 1999). It was not the aim of this book, however, to replicate these offerings, rather to offer a practical guide for the practicing professional interested in using cognitive behavior therapy and hypnosis together.

A practitioner can find training for a variety of cognitive behavioral approaches and can earn credentials and a diplomate (board certification) demonstrating advanced competency. Clinical hypnosis also provides a similar path for obtaining training and experience leading to certification and eventually a diplomate. However, the practitioner must develop their own expertise and knowledge for integration of cognitive behavior therapy and hypnosis. This is reflected in the variety of approaches to the integration of CBT and hypnosis discussed in this book.

The preceding chapters represent an array of clinical approaches to the integration of cognitive behavior therapy and clinical hypnosis. The current clinical approaches for their integration follow a theoretical and clinical practice continuum. This continuum ranges from social learning models on one end to eclectic models on the other.

Regardless of the clinical approach, the practitioner interested in the use and integration of cognitive behavior therapy and hypnosis must consider several practical questions before proceeding.

## WHAT THEORETICAL ORIENTATION WILL I USE?

The individual practitioner must decide whether the use of hypnosis fits into their theoretical perspective since theory guides research and clinical practice. The practitioner is faced with multiple models of cognitive behavior theory and therapy. Clinical hypnosis also presents the practitioner with multiple models of hypnosis. Cognitive behavior practitioners and theorists have tended to associate hypnosis with psychodynamic theory and therapy. This may well be due to the traditional relationship between the theories of the unconscious and psychodynamic therapy and hypnosis. However, there is a clinical precedence for the combination of cognitive behavior therapy and clinical hypnosis. Joseph Wolpe (1990) used hypnosis in his early development of systematic desensitization. Meichenbaum and Gilmore (1984) developed a perspective that includes a cognitive view of the unconscious. Additionally, Alford and Beck's (1997) formulation provides a role for nonconscious processing. It is clear that within the cognitive behavior model there is a rapidly evolving trend toward integration with other schools of therapy and models of human behavior (Craighead, Craighead, Kazdin, & Mahoney, 1994).

The preceding chapters demonstrate that practitioners may adhere to current cognitive models, extend the cognitive model, or utilize broader eclectic models. Clearly, practitioners are not of a single mind regarding cognitive behavior theory. Golden describes a model in chapter five that incorporates both behavioral and cognitive elements. In chapter 4, I describe a model that integrates cognitive behavior therapy and hypnosis based on Beck's cognitive model (Alford & Beck, 1997). Finally, Ginandes in her chapter on the treatment of mind/body conditions, blends cognitive and psychodynamic models.

The practitioner in the early stages of integrating cognitive behavior therapy and hypnosis may consider using the theoretical approach that most closely resembles their current clinical understanding. This model, in turn, may be used to generate a case conceptualization that guides the choice of treatment strategies, including the use of hypnosis.

## WHAT IS HYPNOSIS GOOD FOR?

The practitioner of cognitive behavior therapy has developed a theoretical understanding and must now consider whether hypnosis would be useful to add to their therapeutic armamentarium. Many of the aims of hypnosis can be achieved using other techniques such as relaxation training or mindfulness training. Self-regulation therapy offers a cognitive behavior model that uses suggestion without specifically using hypnosis (Kirsch et al., 1999). The practitioner must also consider their client population. Clients with clinical problems such as psychosis, cognitive disabilities, or attentional problems are considered problematic for the use of hypnosis.

In reviewing the literature on effectiveness, Marcus and Reinecke in chapter 2 stress that additional, well-controlled outcome studies are needed to establish whether hypnosis is an efficacious treatment in its own right, and whether it is a clinically useful adjunct to other forms of psychotherapy, such as CBT. Additionally, Marcus and Reinecke suggest that practitioners should not anticipate that hypnosis would be an effective intervention for all problems or for all individuals.

This book describes clinical cases using cognitive behavior therapy with hypnosis in the treatment of clinical problems, including cancer-related pain, depression, mind/body conditions, posttraumatic stress disorder, anger management, anxiety, phobias, psychophysiological problems, and sleep disorders. Oster in chapter 3 describes additional needs for treatment, such as preparation for childbirth, resolving psychological problems, skin disorders, intestinal problems, stress management, performance enhancement, and fear of flying. Clearly, one of the significant strengths of hypnosis is its adaptability to multiple clinical areas and theoretical approaches. Oster poses the following response when asked what hypnosis is good for, "That depends. What is it you are looking to accomplish?" This question is probably relevant for the use of cognitive behavior strategies. Oster concludes that hypnosis can be used to reduce or eliminate symptoms, to explore or understand one's history or dynamics, to teach self-control or self-regulation, and to enhance or strengthen one's sense of confidence.

## WHAT LEVEL OF COGNITIVE BEHAVIOR TRAINING AND HYPNOSIS TRAINING WILL I NEED?

Once the practitioner has developed a theoretical base and has determined that the addition of hypnosis will be an aid in accomplishing his or her clinical ends, obtaining appropriate clinical training is the next challenge in developing this integrated use of cognitive behavior therapy and hypnosis. This preparation is critical for developing a professional and ethical level of competence.

Associations for practicing professionals, such as the American Psychological Association and the National Association for Social Work, address the importance of acquiring competency in the services that individual practitioners provide. Practitioners are generally expected to acquire competency through education, training, supervised experience, and consultation.

Many practitioner training programs offer academic training in cognitive behavior therapy and some offer clinical hypnosis as an elective. Practitioners have several options for acquiring competency in cognitive behavior therapy—through workshops, professional schools and universities, and training programs. A practitioner can earn recognition of their training, including certificates and board certification. The American Board of Professional Psychology offers board certification in behavioral therapy, which includes applied behavioral analysis, cognitive behavior therapy, and cognitive therapy.

338    INTEGRATING CBT AND HYPNOSIS

Additional education and training for using hypnosis are provided by the International Society of Hypnosis and the Society for Clinical and Experimental Hypnosis. The American Society of Clinical Hypnosis (ASCH) and its component associations provide training and certification in hypnosis. This training is offered to physicians, psychologists, social workers, master's degreed nurses, family therapists, dentists, podiatrists, chiropractors, mental health counselors, and speech pathologists.

Psychologists can receive education and training through the American Psychological Association's Division 30, the Society for Psychological Hypnosis. Additionally, the American Boards of Clinical Hypnosis oversee board certification in hypnosis for psychologists, social workers, dentists, and physicians.

## RECOMMENDATIONS FOR INTEGRATING COGNITIVE BEHAVIOR THERAPY AND HYPNOSIS INTO CURRENT PRACTICE

A blueprint for developing a professional identity and competence for the integration of CBT and hypnosis may include the following steps. Many cognitive behavioral practitioners may hold negative thoughts and images concerning the use of hypnosis. Thus, before the practitioner begins this process, he or she must consider their level of experience, interest, and comfort in using hypnotic strategies. They must ask themselves if hypnosis fits into their model of cognitive behavior therapy. The practitioner can then begin their training in clinical hypnosis. I recommend participation in training programs similar to ASCH, which grants a certificate after a course of training and consultation with a practicing professional. Clinical hypnosis consists of a wide variety of techniques and approaches. Ongoing training and consultation with others can enhance one's practice of hypnotic strategies as well.

Finally, once trained, the practitioner must determine the appropriateness of using hypnosis with cognitive behavior therapy according to each individual client. I recommend Person's case conceptualization approach, which I described in chapter 4 (Persons, 1989). Case conceptualization routinely guides the choice of various cognitive behavioral strategies for the client. These strategies could easily include the use of hypnosis.

# FUTURE DIRECTIONS

As future cognitive behavioral practitioners develop their case conceptualization and potential treatment alternatives, hypnosis may become just one of the standard treatments along with systematic desensitization, cognitive restructuring, and behavior rehearsal. An alternative direction may be the eclectic approach, where the practitioner combines treatments from several psychotherapy models to best suit their case conceptualization and treatment decisions.

This book does not offer a single model for the clinical practitioner, but offers multiple approaches to the integration of CBT and hypnosis. It is important, however, to develop a uniform model that can be empirically tested. This is clearly one of the major attributes of cognitive behavior therapy, as it allows a systematic application which can be evaluated. Single clinical case studies provide a rich resource for qualitative analysis and eventual controlled research. The efforts of these practitioners may offer potential models for study and result in more effective treatment.

Eventually, a model may emerge that will be appropriate for controlled studies. This cognitive behavior/hypnosis approach may meet the criteria developed by the Division of Clinical Psychology (Division 12) of the American Psychological Association (Chambless & Hollon, 1998). Initial efforts in this direction can be seen in Aladdin's chapter in this volume on cognitive behavior and hypnotic treatment of depression and Ginandes' chapter on mind/body treatment.

It is my hope that hypnosis will be embraced by cognitive behavioral practitioners as they embrace other strategies. In the future, hypnosis may simply be viewed as just another strategy to use in cognitive behavior therapy. Eclectic therapists may find even more comprehensive approaches for integrating cognitive behavior therapy and hypnosis in their work with clients.

## REFERENCES

Alford, B. A., & Beck, A. T. (1997). *The integrative power of cognitive therapy.* New York: Guilford.
Chambless, D. L., & Hollon, S. D. (1998). Defining empirically supported therapies. *Journal of Consulting and Clinical Psychology, 66,* 7–18.

Craighead, L. W., Craighead, W. E., Kazdin, A. E., & Mahoney, M. J. (1994). *Cognitive and behavioral interventions: An empirical approach to mental health problems*. Boston: Allyn & Bacon.

DeLaney, M., & Voit, R. (2000, September 16 & 17) *Becoming a hypnotherapist: Integrating hypnosis into your practice*. Presented at a workshop in Danvers, Massachusetts.

Dowd, E. T. (2000). *Cognitive hypnotherapy*. Livingston, NJ: Jason Aronson.

Freeman, A., Pretzer, J., Fleming, B., & Simon, K. M. (2004). *Clinical applications of cognitive therapy* (2nd ed.). New York: Springer Publishing.

Golden, W. L., Dowd, E. T., & Friedberg, F. (1987). *Hypnotherapy: A modern approach*. New York: Pergamon.

Kirsch, I., Capafons, A., Cardena-Buelna, E., & Amigo, S. (1999). *Clinical hypnosis and self-regulation, cognitive-behavioral perspectives*. Washington, DC: American Psychological Association.

Kirsch, I., & Lynn, S. J. (1995). The altered state of hypnosis. *American Psychologist, 50*, 846–858.

Mahoney, M. J. (1995). The psychological demands of being a constructive psychotherapist. In R. A. Neimeyer & M. J. Mahoney (Eds.), *Constructivism in psychotherapy* (pp. 385–400). Washington, DC: American Psychological Association.

Meichenbaum, D., & Gilmore, J. B. (1984). The nature of unconscious processes: A cognitive-behavioral perspective. In D. Meichenbaum & K. S. Bowers (Eds.), *The unconscious reconsidered* (pp. 273–298). New York: John Wiley.

Persons, J. B. (1989). *Cognitive therapy in practice: A case formulation approach*. New York: W. W. Norton.

Spanos, N. P., & Chaves, J. F. (1989). *Hypnosis: The cognitive behavioral perspective*. Buffalo, NY: Prometheus.

Rhue, J. W., Lynn, S. J., & Kirsch, I. (1993). *Handbook of clinical hypnosis*. Washington, DC: American Psychological Association.

Wolpe, J. (1990). *The practice of behavior therapy* (4th ed.). New York: Pergamon.

Zarren, J. I., & Eimer, B. N. (2002). *Brief cognitive hypnosis: Facilitating the change of dysfunctional behavior*. New York: Springer Publishing.

# Index